# RESEARCH METHODS AND STATISTICS IN PSYCHOLOGY

## Hugh Coolican

## Hodder & Stoughton

LONDON  SYDNEY  AUCKLAND  TORONTO

*To Rama, for space, love and support, and to our first child, for whom we've got some surprises.*

## Acknowledgements

*Professor D. B. Bromley, University of Liverpool and Sue Wilkinson, Coventry Polytechnic, for information supplied; Dave Barratt, Epping Forest College, for the original version of the report-writing checklist; Richard Gross for reviewing draft work and much helpful advice; both my Social Care students at Ware College and Rama for allowing me to pilot materials on them and giving me their reactions.*

*British Library Cataloguing in Publication Data*
Coolican, Hugh
    Research methods and statistics in psychology.
    1. Psychology. Research. Methodology
    I. Title
    150.72

    ISBN 0 340 52404 9

First published 1990

Typeset by Apek Typesetters, Nailsea, Bristol
Printed in Great Britain for the educational publishing division of Hodder and Stoughton Ltd, Mill Road, Dunton Green, Sevenoaks, Kent by Richard Clay Ltd, Bungay, Suffolk.

# CONTENTS

# Preface

After the domination of behaviourism in Anglo-American psychology during the middle of the century, the impression has been left, reflected in the many texts on research design, that the experimental method is the central tool of psychological research. In fact, a glance through journals will illuminate a wide array of data-gathering instruments in use outside the experimental laboratory and beyond the field experiment. This book takes the reader through details of the experimental method, but also examines the many criticisms of it, in particular the argument that its use, as a paradigm, has led to some fairly arid and unrealistic psychological models, as has the empirical insistence on quantification. The reader is also introduced to non-experimental method in some depth, where current A-level texts tend to be rather superficial. But, further, it takes the reader somewhat beyond current A-level minimum requirements and into the world of qualitative approaches.

Having said that, it is written at a level which should feel 'friendly' and comfortable to the person just starting their study of psychology. The beginner will find it useful to read part one first, since this section introduces fundamental issues of scientific method and techniques of measuring or gathering data about people. Thereafter, any reader can and should use it as a manual to be dipped into at the appropriate place for the current research project or problem, though the early chapters of the statistics section will need to be consulted in order to understand the rationale and procedure of the tests of significance.

I have tried to write the statistical sections as I teach them, with the mathematically nervous student very much in mind. Very often, though, people who think they are poor at mathematical thinking find statistics far less difficult than they had feared, and the tests in this book which match current A-level requirements involve the use of very few mathematical operations. Except for a few illuminative examples, the statistical concepts are all introduced via realistic psychological data, some emanating from actual studies performed by students.

This book will provide the A-level, A/S-level or International Baccalaureate student with all that is necessary, not only for selecting methods and statistical treatments for practical work and for structured questions on research examples, but also for dealing with general issues of scientific and research methods. Higher education students, too, wary of statistics as vast numbers of psychology beginners often are, should also find this book an accessible route into the area. Questions throughout are intended to engage the reader in active thinking about the current topic, often by stimulating the prediction of problems before they are presented. The final structured questions imitate those found in the papers of several Examination Boards.

I hope, through using this book, the reader will be encouraged to *enjoy* research; not to see it as an intimidating add-on, but, in fact, as the engine of theory without which we would be left with a broad array of truly fascinating ideas about human experience and behaviour with no means of telling which are sheer fantasy and which might lead us to models of the human condition grounded in reality.

If there are points in this book which you wish to question, please get in touch via the publisher.

Hugh Coolican

# PART I

# INTRODUCTION

## Psychology and Research

Student: I'd like to enrol for psychology please.
Lecturer: You do realise that it includes quite a bit of statistics, and you'll have to do some experimental work and write up practical reports?
Student: Oh . . .

When enrolling for a course in psychology, the prospective student is very often taken aback by the discovery that the syllabus includes a fair-sized dollop of statistics and that practical research, experiments and report-writing are all involved. My experience as a tutor has commonly been that psychology students are either 'escaping' from school into further education or tentatively returning after years away from academic study. Both sorts of student are frequently dismayed to find that this new and exciting subject is going to thrust them back into two of the areas they most disliked in school. One is maths – but rest assured! Statistics, in fact, will involve you in little of the maths on a traditional syllabus and will be performed on real data most of which you have gathered yourself. Calculators and computers do the 'number crunching' these days. The other area is science.

It is strange that of all the sciences – natural and social – the one which directly concerns ourselves as individuals in society is the least likely to be found in schools, where teachers are preparing the young for social life! It is also strange that a student can study all the 'hard' natural sciences – physics, chemistry, biology – yet never be asked to consider what a science *is* until they study psychology or sociology.

These are generalisations of course. Some schools teach psychology. Others nowadays teach the underlying principles of scientific research. Some of us actually enjoyed science and maths at school. If you did, you'll find some parts of this book fairly easy going. But can I state one of my most cherished beliefs right now, for the sake of those who hate numbers and think this is all going to be a struggle, or, worse still, boring? Many of the ideas and concepts introduced in this book will already be in your head in an informal way, even 'hard' topics like probability. My job is partly to give names to some concepts you will easily think of for yourself. At other times it will be to formalise and tighten up ideas that you

1

have gathered through experience. For instance, you already have a fairly good idea of how many cats out of ten ought to choose 'Poshpaws' cat food in preference to another brand, in order for us to be convinced that this is a real difference and not a fluke. You can probably start discussing quite competently what would count as a representative sample of people for a particular survey.

Returning to the prospective student then, he or she usually has little clue about what sort of research psychologists do. The notion of 'experiments' sometimes produces anxiety. 'Will we be conditioned or brainwashed?'

If we ignore images from the black-and-white film industry, and think carefully about what psychological researchers might do, we might conjure up an image of the street survey. Think again, and we might suggest that psychologists watch people's behaviour. I agree with Gross (1987) who says that, at a party, if one admits to teaching, or even studying, psychology, an initial reaction is likely to be 'Oh, I'd better be careful what I say from now on'. Another strong contender is 'I suppose you'll be analysing my behaviour' (said as the speaker takes one hesitant step backwards) in the mistaken assumption that psychologists go around making deep, mysterious interpretations of human actions as they occur. (If you meet someone who does do this, ask them something about the evidence they use, after you've finished with this book!) The notion of such analysis is loosely connected to Freud who, though popularly portrayed as a psychiatric Sherlock Holmes, used very few of the sorts of research outlined in this book – though he did use unstructured interviews and the case study method (Chapter 8).

## So what is the nature of psychological research?

Although there are endless and furious debates about what a science is and what sort of science, if any, psychology should be, a majority of psychologists would agree that research should be scientific in some respects, the main ones being that it should be objective, controlled and checkable. There are very many definitions of science but, for present purposes, Allport's (1947) is useful. Science, he claims, has the aims of:

> '. . . understanding, prediction and control above the levels achieved by unaided common sense.'

What does Allport, or anyone, mean by 'common sense'? Aren't some things blindingly obvious? Isn't it indisputable that babies are born with different personalities, for instance? Let's have a look at some other popular 'common-sense' claims.

> *Before* reading my comments on the right-hand side of Box 1, have a think about any challenge you might wish to make to the claims made. What evidence would you want to consider?

I have used these statements, including the controversial ones, because they are just the sort of thing people claim confidently, yet with no hard evidence. They are 'hunches' masquerading as fact. I call them 'armchair certainties (or theories)' because this is where they are often claimed from.

*Box 1 'Commonsense' claims*

| | |
|---|---|
| 1 Women obviously have a maternal instinct – look how strongly they want to stay with their child and protect it | Have we checked how men would feel after several months alone with a baby? Why does child abuse occur then? |
| 2 Michelle is so good at predicting people's star sign – there must be something in astrology | Have we checked that Michelle gets a lot more signs correct than anyone would by just guessing? Have we counted the times when she's wrong? |
| 3 So many batsmen get out on 98 or 99 – it must be the psychological pressure | Have we compared with the numbers of batsmen who get out on all other totals? |
| 4 Women are less logical, more suggestible and make worse drivers than men | Women score the same as men on logical tests in general. They are equally "suggestible," though boys are more likely to agree with views they don't hold but which are held by their peer group. Women are more likely to obey traffic rules and have less expensive accidents. Why else would 'one lady owner' be a selling point? |
| 5 I wouldn't obey someone who told me to seriously hurt another person if I could possibly avoid it | About 70% of people who could have walked free from an experiment, continued to obey an experimenter who asked them to give electric shocks to a 'learner' who had fallen silent after screaming horribly. |

I hope you see why we need evidence from research. One role for a scientific study is to dispel 'common-sense' myths by checking the facts. Another is to produce 'counter-intuitive' results like those in item five. Let me say a little more about what scientific research is by dispelling a few myths about it.

## Myth No. 1: 'Scientific research is the collection of facts'

All research is about the collection of data but this is not the sole aim. First of all, facts are not data. Facts do not speak for themselves. When people say they do they are omitting to mention essential background theory or assumptions they are making.

> A sudden crash brings us running to the kitchen. The accused is crouched in front of us, eyes wide and fearful. Her hands are red and sticky. A knife lies on the floor. So does a jam jar and its spilled contents. The accused was about to lick her tiny fingers.

I hope you made some false assumptions at the start of that description. But, as it is, do the facts alone tell us that Jenny was stealing jam? Perhaps the cat knocked the jam over and Jenny was trying to pick it up. We constantly assume a lot beyond the present data in order to explain it. Facts are DATA interpreted through

THEORY. DATA are what we get through EMPIRICAL observation, where 'empirical' refers to information obtained through our senses. It is difficult to get raw data. We almost always interpret it immediately. The time you took to run 100 metres (or, at least, the position of the hands) is raw data. My saying you're 'quick' is interpretation. If we lie on the beach looking at the night sky and see a 'star' moving steadily we 'know' it's a satellite, but only because we have a lot of received astronomical knowledge, from our culture, in our heads.

**The empirical method**    The original empirical method had two stages:

1. Gathering of data, directly, through our external senses, with no preconceptions as to how it is ordered or what explains it.

2. INDUCTION of patterns and relationships within the data.

*Induction* means to move from individual observations to statements of general patterns (sometimes called 'laws').

If the proverbial Martian made empirical observations on Earth it (Martians have one sex) might focus its attention on the various tubes which hurtle around, some in the air, some on the ground, some under it, and stop every so often to take on little bugs and to shed others.

The Martian might then conclude that the little bugs taken on were food . . . and the ones discharged . . .?

Now we have gone beyond the original empirical method. The Martian is constructing *theory*. This is an attempt to explain *why* the patterns are produced, what forces or processes underly them.

It is inevitable that human thinking will go beyond the patterns and combinations discovered in data analysis to ask, 'But why?'. It is also naïve to assume we could ever gather data without some background theory in our heads, as I tried to demonstrate above. Medawar (1963) has argued this point forcefully, as has Bruner who points out that, when we perceive the world, we always and inevitably 'go beyond the information given'.

**Testing theories – the hypothetico-deductive method**    This Martian's theory, that the bugs are food for the tubes, can be tested. If the tubes get no bugs for a long time, they should die. This prediction is a HYPOTHESIS. A hypothesis is a statement of what should be the case *if* a certain theory is true. Testing the hypothesis shows that the tubes can last indefinitely without bugs. Hence the hypothesis is disproved and the theory requires alteration or dismissal. This manner of thinking is common in our everyday lives. If the dustbin is still full then the dustmen haven't been. Here's another example:

> Tragedy strikes! The television goes off in the middle of the big film. Wendy's theory is that the fuse has gone. John says 'Nah! That telly's been on the blink for months.' Interesting. We have two competing theories. Time for an experiment. Wendy replaces the fuse with one that was definitely working in the iron. If the television now works it was probably the fuse. If it doesn't, it can't have been the fuse.

Wendy's hypothesis is 'The television will work when we put in a good fuse.' This will happen if Wendy's theory, that the fuse has blown, is true.

Notice that if we confirm the hypothesis we don't confirm the theory. Other explanations are still possible. If the television *does* work this could be because there had been a temporary cut in transmission, though you'd probably have eliminated this hypothesis by checking other channels.

It may even be that, where you think A causes B to happen, the relationship is, in fact, the other way around. The theory that mothers talk more to young daughters (than young sons) because girls are naturally more talkative, and the opposite theory, that girls are more talkative because their mothers talk more to them are both supported by the evidence that mothers do talk more to their daughters. Evidence is more useful when it supports one theory and *not* its rival.

The stand-up comic Ben Elton (1989) is onto this when he says:

> Lots of Aboriginals end up as piss–heads, causing people to say 'no wonder they're so poor, half of them are piss-heads'. It would, of course, make much more sense to say 'no wonder half of them are piss-heads, they're so poor'.

**Deductive logic**    Theory-testing relies on the logical arguments we were using above. These are examples of DEDUCTION. Stripped to their bare skeleton they are:

|  | *Applied to theory-testing* | *Applied to the TV problem* |
|---|---|---|
| 1 If X is true then Y must be true | 1 If theory A is true, hypothesis 1 is true | 1 If the fuse has blown, the TV will work with a new one |
| 2 Y isn't true | 2 Hypothesis 1 is disconfirmed | 2 The TV doesn't work with a new fuse |
| 3 Therefore X can't be true | 3 Therefore, theory A is wrong | 3 It's not a blown fuse |
| or | or | or |
| 2 Y is true | 2 Hypothesis 1 is confirmed | 2 The TV now works |
| 3 X could still be true | 3 Theory A could still be true | 3 It could have been the fuse |

It is often not a lot of use getting more and more of the same support for your theory. If I claim that all swans are white because the sun bleaches their feathers, it gets a bit tedious if I keep pointing to each new white one saying 'I told you so'. All we need is one black swan to blow my theory wide apart.

If your hypothesis is disconfirmed, it is not always necessary to abandon the theory which predicted it, in the way that my simple swan theory must go. Very often you would have to adjust your theory to take account of new data. For instance, if the TV works when Wendy replaces the fuse, John can claim that the fault in the TV is intermittent and has cured itself during the fuse change. But if he clung to this view when the same events occurred two years later we might suspect his adherence was emotional rather than rational.

Theories are not usually proven finally true. They get supported by evidence which doesn't contradict them and which would be predicted from them. But for every piece of evidence there is often an alternative explanation, outside the theory. For instance, it might be claimed that similarity between parent and child in intelligence is good evidence for the view that intelligence is genetically transmitted. The similarity also supports, however, the view that children learn from their parents and share similar environments.

Putting together the empirical method of induction, and the hypothetico-deductive method, we get what is traditionally taken to be the 'scientific method', accepted by many psychological researchers as the way to follow in the footsteps of the successful natural sciences. The steps in the method are shown in box 2.

*Box 2   Traditional scientific method*

> - Observation and gathering of data
> - Induction of generalisations, laws
> - Development of explanatory theories
> - Deduction of hypotheses to test theories
> - Testing of the hypotheses
> - Support or adjustment of theory

Scientific research projects, then, may be concentrating on the early or later stages of this process. They may be exploratory studies, looking for data from which to create theories, or they may be hypothesis-testing studies, aiming to support or challenge a theory.

There are many doubts about, and criticisms of, this model of scientific research, too detailed to go into here. The reader might like to consult Gross (1987) or a number of more specialised texts.

### Myth No. 2: 'Scientific research involves dramatic discoveries and breakthroughs'

If only research was as simple as the TV fuse problem was. Life would produce dramatic breakthroughs every day. Unfortunately, the classic discoveries are all the lay person hears about. In fact, research plods along all the time, largely according to figure 1. Although, from reading about research, it is easy to think about a single project beginning and ending at specific points of time, there is, in the research world, a constant cycle occurring.

A project is developed from a combination of the current trends in research thinking (theory) and methods, other challenging past theories and, within psychology at least, from important events in the everyday social world. The investigator might wish to replicate (repeat) a study by someone else in order to verify it. Or they might wish to extend it to other areas, or to modify it because it has weaknesses. Every now and again an investigation breaks completely new ground but the vast majority develop out of the current state of play.

Politics and economics enter at the stage of funding. Research staff, in universities, colleges or hospitals, have to justify their salaries and the expense of the project. Funds will come from one of the following: university, college or hospital research funds; central or local government; private companies; charitable institutions; and the odd private benefactor. These, and the investigator's direct employers, will need to be satisfied that the research is worthwhile to them, to society or to the general pool of scientific knowledge.

The actual testing or 'running' of the project may take very little time compared with all the planning and preparation along with the analysis of results and report-writing. Some procedures, such as an experiment or questionnaire, may be tried out on a small sample of people in order to highlight snags or ambiguities for which adjustments can be made before the actual data gathering

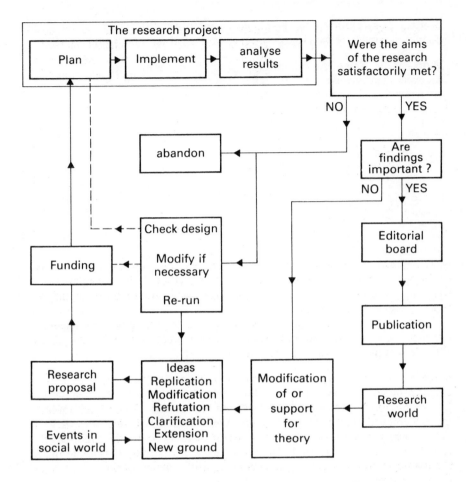

*Figure 1  The research cycle*

process is begun. This is known as PILOTING. The researcher would run PILOT TRIALS of an experiment or would PILOT a questionnaire.

The report will be published in a research journal if successful. This term 'successful' is difficult to define here. It doesn't always mean that original aims have been entirely met. Surprises occurring during the research may well make it important, though usually such surprises would lead the investigator to re-think, re-plan and run again on the basis of the new insights. As we saw above, failure to confirm one's hypothesis can be an important source of information. What matters overall, is that the research results are an important or useful contribution to current knowledge and theory development. This importance will be decided by the editorial board of an academic journal (such as the British Journal of Psychology) who will have the report reviewed, usually by experts 'blind' as to the identity of the investigator.

Theory will then be adjusted in the light of this research result. Some academics may argue that the design was so different from previous research that its challenge to their theory can be ignored. Others will wish to query the results and may ask the investigator to provide 'raw data' – the whole of the originally recorded data, unprocessed. Some will want to replicate the study, some to modify . . . and here we are, back where we started on the research cycle.

### Myth No. 3: 'Scientific research is all about experiments'

An experiment involves the researcher's control and manipulation of conditions or 'variables', as we shall see in chapter 5.

Astronomy, one of the oldest sciences, could not use very many experiments until relatively recently when technological advances have permitted direct tests of conditions in space. It has mainly relied upon *observation* to test its theories of planetary motion and stellar organisation.

It is perfectly possible to test hypotheses without an experiment. Much psychological testing is conducted by observing what children do, asking what people think and so on. The evidence about male and female drivers, for instance, was obtained by observation of actual behaviour and insurance company statistics.

### Myth No. 4: 'Scientists have to be unbiased'

It is true that investigators try to remove bias from the way a project is run and from the way data is gathered and analysed. But they are biased about theory. They interpret ambiguous data to fit their particular theory as best they can. This happens whenever we're in a heated argument and say things like 'Ah, but that could be because . . .'. Investigators *believe* in their theory and attempt to produce evidence to support it. Mitroff (1974) interviewed a group of scientists and all agreed that the notion of the purely objective, uncommitted scientist was naïve. They argued that:

> . . . in order to be a good scientist, one had to have biases. The best scientist, they said, not only has points of view but also defends them with gusto. Their concept of a scientist did not imply that he would cheat by making up experimental data or falsifying it; rather he does everything in his power to defend his pet hypotheses against early and perhaps unwarranted death caused by the introduction of fluke data.

# Do we get on to psychological research now?

Yes. We needed to cut some paths through the language and logic of scientific research, since most, but not all, psychological investigators would claim to follow a scientific model. With a few basic concepts under our belts then, let's answer some 'wh' questions about the practicalities of psychological research.

### What is the subject matter for psychological research?

The easy answer is 'humans'. The more controversial answer is 'human behaviour' since psychology is literally (in Greek) the study of mind. This isn't a book which will take you into the great debate on the relationship between mind and body or whether the study of mind is at all possible. This is available in other general textbooks (e.g. Gross 1987).

Whatever type of psychology you are studying you should be introduced to the various major 'schools' of psychology (Psycho-analytic, Behaviourist, Cognitive Humanist, . . .) It is important to point out here, however, that each school would see the focus for its subject matter differently – behaviour, the conscious mind, even the unconscious mind. Therefore, different investigatory methods have been developed by different schools.

Nevertheless, the initial raw data which psychologists gather from humans can *only* be observed behaviour or language (verbal report). There are approaches which gather data from animals too, though usually in the hope of shedding more light on the nature of humans in the long run.

## Why do psychologists do research?

Well, I've answered this in general terms already. All research has the overall aim of collecting data. To be specific, research will usually have one of two major aims: To gather purely descriptive data or to test hypotheses.

**Descriptive research**    A piece of research may establish the ages at which a large sample of children reach certain language development milestones or it may be a survey (Chapter 8) of current adult attitudes to the use of nuclear weapons. If the results from this are in numerical form then the data are known as QUANTITATIVE and we would make use of DESCRIPTIVE STATISTICS (chapter 13) to present a summary of findings. If the research presents a report of the contents of interviews or case studies (chapter 8), or of detailed observations (chapter 7), then the data may be largely QUALITATIVE (chapter 4), though parts may well become quantified.

The descriptive data may well be analysed in order to generate hypotheses, models, theories or further research directions and ideas.

**Hypothesis testing**    A large amount of research sets out to test one RESEARCH HYPOTHESIS or more by showing that differences or relationships between people already exist, or that they can be created through experimental manipulation. In an experiment the research hypothesis would be called the EXPERIMENTAL HYPOTHESIS. Tests of differences or relationships between sets of data are performed using INFERENTIAL STATISTICS (Chapter 15–18). Let me describe two examples OF HYPOTHESIS TESTING, one laboratory based, the other from 'the field'.

*1 In the laboratory: a test of short-term memory theory*    A theory popular in the 1960s was the model of short-term (ST) and long-term (LT) memory. This claimed that the small amount of information, say seven or eight digits or a few unconnected words, which we can hold in the conscious mind at any one time (our short-term store) is transferred to a LT store by means of rehearsal – repetition of each item in the ST store. The more rehearsal an item received, the better it was stored and therefore the more easily it was recalled.

A challenge to this model was that simply rehearsing items is not efficient. Humans tend to make incoming information meaningful. Repetition of words, for instance, does not make them more meaningful. One way an unconnected list of words *could* be made more meaningful is to form a vivid mental image of each one and to link it to the next in a bizarre fashion. If 'record' is followed by 'plane', for instance, imagine a candy striped little aeroplane flying through the centre hole of the previously imaged music record.

From this a prediction can be made:
People asked to learn a list of words using image-linking will recall significantly more items than when they are asked only to rehearse each word of an equivalent list.
This is our hypothesis for testing.

Every time this experiment is conducted the hypothesis is well supported. Most people are much better using imagery. This is not the obvious result it may seem. Many people feel far more comfortable simply repeating things. They predict that the 'silly' method will confuse them. However, even if it does, the information still sticks better. So, a useful method for exam revision? Well, making sense of your notes, playing with them, is a lot better than simply reading and repeating them.

2. *In the field: a test of maternal deprivation*  Bowlby (1951) proposed a controversial theory that young infants have a natural (that is, biological or innate) tendency to form a special attachment with just one person, usually the mother, different in kind and quality from any other.

What does this theory predict? Well, coupled with other arguments, Bowlby was able to predict that children unable to form such an attachment, or those for whom this attachment was severed within the first few years of life, especially before three years old, would later be more likely than other children to become maladjusted.

Bowlby produced several examples of seriously deprived children exhibiting greater maladjustment. Hence, he could *support* his theory. In this case, he didn't do something to people and demonstrate the result (which is what an experiment like our memory example above does). He predicted something to be the case, showed it was, and then related these results back to what had happened to the children in the past.

But remember that continual support does not *prove* a theory to be correct. Rutter (1971) challenged the theory with evidence that boys on the Isle of Wight who suffered early deprivation, even death of their mother, were *not* more likely to be rated as maladjusted than other boys so long as the separation had not also involved continuing social difficulties within the family. Here, Bowlby's theory has to be adjusted in the light of contradictory evidence.

**Hypotheses must be specific!**  The hypothesis for the memory study is written above. Notice just how specific it is. We have stated *precisely* what we are expecting to happen, and no more. We don't say, in the hypothesis, *why* we are making the prediction. We simply predict in the most exact terms.

I have introduced the term 'significantly' here. This is an important term, fully explained in chapter 14. For now, I hope you can accept that, loosely speaking, it means a genuine, not a tiny or 'fluke' difference.

**The null hypothesis**  Rutter didn't want to show that his separated boys differed to any substantial degree from normal boys. He was interested in *dis*-proving Bowlby's hypotheses. With regard to just the boys whose mothers had died, the research hypothesis following from Bowlby's theory would be:

'Ratings of maladjustment will be significantly higher among children who lost their mothers before three years old than among other children.'

The hypothesis which predicts that this *won't* be the case is known as the NULL HYPOTHESIS. In this case it might run:

'There will be no significant difference between maladjustment ratings of normal children and children who have lost their mothers before reaching three years old.'

The null hypothesis predicts that any difference, or relationship, found between two sets of results, is not significant. It states that any differences, or relationship, found are reasonably explained as what would be expected by chance (or 'random') variation alone. The matches in any two boxes will differ slightly in average length but we don't often have a case against the retailer. Any two samples of boys will produce differences in maladjustment ratings. But if we don't demonstrate that a difference is large enough ('significant') we must assume the null hypothesis is true.

> Try writing the null hypothesis for the memory experiment.

(My attempt: There will be no significant difference between the number of items correctly recalled when people use imagery and the number of items correctly recalled when they use rehearsal.)
We don't have to *believe* any particular hypothesis we test. We can propose it in order to disprove it, as happens in the Rutter example. I can say 'Your view that women are less logical than men predicts that they ought to perform less well in computer studies,' and then proceed to show that this isn't true. (It isn't.) I take your theory, deduce a hypothesis from it, test it and demonstrate that the null hypothesis is correct instead.

**One- and two-tailed hypotheses**   It is possible to conduct a study in which we do not predict the direction in which results will go. Will people perform a simple practical task – such as threading a needle – better or worse in front of an audience? If we do not predict the condition – with-an-audience or without-an-audience – in which people will perform better, then we are said to have a TWO-TAILED HYPOTHESIS. If we make the prediction we have a ONE-TAILED HYPOTHESIS.

**When is a hypothesis test 'successful'?**   As we saw above, retaining the null hypothesis may sometimes be just what we want to do and can be highly informative. Students doing practical work often get quite despondent when what they predicted does not occur. It feels very much as though the project hasn't worked. Some students I was teaching recently failed to show, contrary to their expectations, that the 'older generation' were more negative about homosexuality than their own generation. I explained that it was surely important information that the 'older generation' were just as liberal as they were (or, perhaps, that their generation were just as hostile).

If hypothesis tests 'fail' we either accept the null hypothesis as important information or we critically assess the design of the project and look for weaknesses in it. Perhaps we asked the wrong questions or the wrong people? Were instructions clear enough? Did we test everybody fairly and in the same manner? The process of evaluating our design, and incorporating information from the research or null hypothesis, is educational in itself and forms an important part of our research report – the 'Discussion'. The whole process of writing a report is outlined in appendix 1.

## How do psychologists conduct research?
A huge question and basically an introduction to the rest of the book! A very large number of psychologists use the experimental method or some form of well controlled field research, involving strict measurement in the data gathering process.

In chapter 9, however, we shall consider why many psychologists, humanists among them, reject the use of the experiment and may also tend to favour methods which bring in qualitative data – information from people which is in descriptive, not numerical, form. Some of these psychologists also reject the scientific method as I have outlined it. They accept that this has been a successful way to study inert matter, but seek an alternative approach to understanding ourselves.

One thing we can say, though, is, whatever the outlook of the researcher, there are three major ways to get information about people. You either ask them, watch them or meddle. These are covered in 'Asking questions', 'Observational methods' and 'The experimental method (part 1 and part 2)'.

# Planning research

To get us started, and to allow me to introduce the rest of this book, let's look at the key decision areas facing anyone about to conduct some research. I have identified these in figure 2. Basically, the four boxes are answers to the questions:

Variables:        WHAT shall we study? (what human characteristics, under
                  what conditions?)
Design:           HOW shall we study these?
Samples:          WHO shall we study?
Analysis:         WHAT sort of evidence will we get, in what form?

Before looking at these a little more closely, try planning a piece of research which tests the (loosely-worded) hypothesis that 'people are more irritable in hot weather'.

### Variables
Variables are tricky things. They are the things which alter so that we can make comparisons, such as 'Are you tidier than I am?' Heat is a variable in our study. How shall we define it? How shall we make sure that it isn't humidity, rather than temperature, which is responsible for any irritability?

But the real problem is how to measure 'irritability'. We could, of course, devise some sort of questionnaire. The construction of these is dealt with in chapter 9. We could observe people's behaviour at work on hot and cool days.

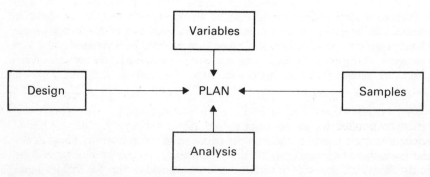

*Figure 2  Key decision areas in research*

Are there more arguments? Is there more swearing or shouting? We could observe these events in the street or in some families. Chapter 7 will deal with methods of observation.

We could even bring people into the 'laboratory' and see whether they tend to answer our questionnaire differently under a well controlled change in temperature. We could observe their behaviour whilst carrying out a frustrating task (for instance, balancing pencils on a slightly moving surface) and we could ask them to assess this task under the two temperature conditions.

The difficulty of defining variables, stating exactly what it is we mean by a term and how, if at all, we intend to measure it, seemed to me to be so primary that I gave it the first chapter in the main body of the book (chapter 2).

## Design
The decisions about variable measurement have taken us into decisions about the design. The design is the overall structure and strategy of the research. Decisions on measuring irritability may determine whether we conduct a laboratory study or 'field' research. If we want realistic irritability we might wish to measure it as it occurs naturally, 'in the field'. If we take the laboratory option described above, we would be running an experiment. However, experiments can be run using various designs. Shall we, for instance, have the same group of people perform the frustrating task under the two temperature conditions? If so, mightn't they be getting practice at the task which will make changes in their performance harder to interpret? The variety of experimental designs is covered in chapter 6.

There are several constraints on choice of design:

*1 Resources*    The researcher may not have the funding, staff or time to carry out a long-term study. The most appropriate technical equipment may be just too expensive. Resources may not stretch to testing in different cultures. A study in the natural setting ('in the field') – say in a hospital – may be too time consuming or ruled out by lack of permission. The laboratory may just have to do.

*2 Nature of research aim*    If the researcher wishes to study the effects of maternal deprivation on the three-year-old, certain methods are ruled out. We can't experiment by artificially depriving children of their mothers (I hope you agree!) and we can't question a three-year-old in any great depth. We may be left with the best option of observing the child's behaviour, although some researchers have turned to experiments on animals in lieu of humans. The ethics of such decisions are discussed more fully in chapter 20.

*3 Previous research*    If we intend to repeat an earlier study we must use the same method. An extension of the study may require the same method, because an extra group is to be added, or it may require use of a different method which compliments the first. We may wish to demonstrate that a laboratory discovered effect can be reproduced in a natural setting.

*4 The researcher's attitude to scientific investigation*    There can be hostile debates between psychologists from different research backgrounds. Some swear by the strictly controlled laboratory setting, seeking to emulate the 'hard' physical sciences in their isolation and precise measurement of variables. Others prefer the more realistic 'field' setting, while there is a growing body of researchers in the humanistic, Gestalt or 'action research' traditions who favour qualitative methods. We shall look more closely at this debate in the methods section.

## Samples

These are the people we are going to study or work with. If we carry out our field observations on office workers (on hot and cool days) we might be showing only that these sort of people get more irritable in the heat. What about builders or nurses? If we select a sample for our laboratory experiment, what factors shall we take into account in trying to make the group representative of most people in general? Is this possible? These are the issues of 'sampling' and are dealt with fairly thoroughly in chapter 3.

One word on terminology here. It is common to refer to the people studied in psychological research, especially in experiments, as 'subjects'. There are objections to this, particularly by psychologists who argue that a false model of the human being is generated by referring to (and possibly treating) people studied in this distant, coolly scientific manner. However, some important terminology assumes the use (as in 'subject variables'). I have used 'subject' where the context would normally support it (mainly experimental work), and 'participant' or just 'people' elsewhere.

## Analysis

The design chosen, and method of measuring variables, will have a direct effect on the statistical or other analysis which is possible at the end of data collection. In a straightforward hypothesis-testing study, it is pointless to steam ahead with a design and procedure, only to find that the results can barely be analysed in order to support the hypothesis.

There is a principle relating to computer programming which goes: '*garbage in – garbage out*'. It applies here too. If the questionnaire contains items like 'How do you feel?', what is to be done with the largely unquantifiable results?

Thoughts of the analysis should not stifle creativity but it is important to keep it central to the planning.

## One last word on the nature of scientific research (for now)

Throughout the book, and in any practical work, can I suggest that the reader keep the following words from Rogers (1961) in mind? If taken seriously to heart and practised, whatever the arguments about various methods, I don't think the follower of this idea will be far away from 'doing science'.

> 'Scientific research needs to be seen for what it truly is; a way of preventing me from deceiving myself in regard to my creatively formed subjective hunches which have developed out of the relationship between me and my material.'

## Key terms for this chapter

| | | |
|---|---|---|
| Data | Hypothetico- | Samples |
| Deduction | deductive method | Scientific method |
| Empirical method | Induction | Statistics |
| Hypothesis | Piloting/pilot trials | Descriptive |
| Research | Qualitative data | Inferential |
| Experimental | Quantitative data | Theory |
| Null | | Variables |
| One-tailed/two-tailed | | |

# Variables and Definitions

A variable is anything which varies. Rather a circular definition I know, but it gets us started. Let's list some things which vary:

1 Height – varies as you grow older
          – varies between individuals

2 Time – to respond with 'yes' or 'no' to questions
         – to solve a set of anagrams

3 The political party people vote for

4 Your feelings towards your partner or parent

5 Extroversion

6 Attitude towards vandals

7 Anxiety

Notice that most of these can vary both within yourself from one time to another, and between different individuals in society.

A variable can take several or many values across a range. The value given is often numerical but not necessarily so. In example 3 above, for instance, the different values are names.

The essence of studying anything (birds, geology, emotion) is the observation of changes in variables. If nothing changed there would be nothing to observe. The essence of science is to relate these changes in variables to changes in other variables.

## Measuring variables

Some of the variables above are easy to measure and we are familiar with the type of measuring instrument required. Height is one of these and time another, though the equipment required to measure 'reaction times' (as in example 2) is quite sophisticated, because of the very brief intervals involved.

Some variables are familiar in concept but measuring them numerically seems a very difficult, strange or impossible thing to do, as in the case of *attitude* or *anxiety*. However, we often make estimates of others' attitudes when we make such pronouncements as 'He is very strongly opposed to smoking' or 'She didn't seem particularly averse to the idea of living in Manchester'.

Variables like *extroversion* or *dissonance* are at first both strange and seemingly unmeasurable. This is because they have been invented by psychologists in need of a unifying concept to explain their observations.

If we are to work with variables such as *attitude* and *anxiety* we must be able to specify them precisely, partly because we want to be accurate in the measurement of their change, and partly because we wish to communicate with others about our findings. If we wish to be taken seriously in our work it must be possible for others to replicate our findings using the same measurement procedures. But what *are* 'attitude' and 'anxiety'?

## Defining Psychological Variables

As an exercise, try to write down your definition of:
(a) intelligence
(b) anxiety
(c) superstition
before reading any further.

You probably found this quite hard, especially for the first term. Why is it we have such difficulty defining terms we use every day with good understanding? You must have used these terms very many times in your communications with others, saying, for instance:

I think Jenny has a lot of intelligence
Bob gets anxious whenever a dog comes near him
Are people today less superstitious than they were?

### Psychological constructs

Suppose I ask you, instead of defining intelligence or anxiety, to give me some examples of them. Have a go at that now just for a few moments . . . .

That was probably a lot easier. Remember, I said in chapter 1 that information about people must come, somehow, from what they say or do. When we are young we are little psychologists. We build up a concept of 'intelligence' or 'anxiety' from learning what are signs of it; biting lips, shaking hand, tremulous voice in the latter case, for instance.

Notice that we learn that certain things are done 'intelligently'; getting sums right, doing them quickly, finishing a jigsaw. People who do these things consistently get called 'intelligent' (the adverb has become an adjective). It is one step now to statements like the one made about Jenny above where we have a noun instead of an adjective. It is easy to think of intelligence as having some thing-like quality, of existing independently, because we can use it as a noun. We can say 'What is X?'. The Greek philosopher Plato ran into this sort of trouble asking questions like 'What is justice?'. The tendency to treat an abstract concept as if it had independent existence is known as REIFICATION.

Some psychologists (especially the behaviourist Skinner, who takes an extreme empiricist position) would argue that such observable events, and, for anxiety, directly measurable internal ones (like increased heart rate or adrenalin secretion), are all we need to bother about. Anxiety just *is* all these events, no more. They would say that we don't need to assume *extra* concepts over and above these things which we can observe and measure. To assume the existence of internal structures or processes, such as 'attitude' or 'drive' is 'mentalistic', unobjective and unscientific.

Other psychologists argue that there is more. That a person's attitude, for instance, is more than the sum of statements about, and action towards, the attitude object. They would argue that the construct is useful in theory development, even if they are wrong in some detail. They behave, in fact, like the 'hard' scientists in physics.

No physicist has ever directly seen an atom or a quark. This isn't physically possible. (It may be *logically* impossible to ever 'see' intelligence, but that's another matter.) What physicists do is to *assume* that atoms and quarks exist and then work out how much of known physical evidence is explained by them. Quarks are HYPOTHETICAL CONSTRUCTS.

Taking a careful path, psychologists treat concepts like intelligence, anxiety or attitude as hypothetical constructs too. They are *assumed* to exist as factors which explain observable phenomena. If, after research which attempts both to support and refute the existence of the constructs, the explanations remain feasible, then the constructs can remain as theoretical entities. A state of anxiety is assumed from observation of a person's sweating, stuttering and shaking. But we don't *see* 'anxiety' as such. Anxiety is, then, a hypothetical construct.

## Organisation of constructs

A construct can be linked to others in an explanatory framework from which further predictions are possible and testable. We might, for instance, infer low self-esteem in people who are very hostile to members of minority ethnic groups. The low self-esteem might, in turn, be related to authoritarian upbringing which could be checked up on. We might then look for a relationship between authoritarian rearing and prejudiced behaviour as shown in figure 3.

If psychologists are to use such constructs in their research work and theorising, they must obviously be very careful indeed in explaining how these are to be treated as variables. Their definitions must be precise. Even for the more easily measurable variables, such as short-term memory capacity, definitions must be clear.

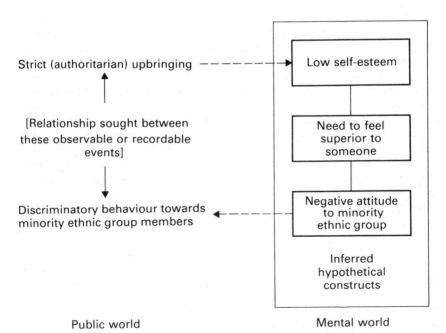

*Figure 3 Explanatory framework of hostility to minority ethnic groups*

One particular difficulty for psychologists is that a large number of terms for variables they might wish to research already exist in everyday English with wide variation in possible meaning.

Discuss with a colleague, or think about, the terms shown below:

Identity    Instinct    Reinforcement    Egocentric    Attitude
Neurotic    Attention    Conformity       Unconscious   Conscience

### Operational definitions

In search of objectivity, scientists conducting research attempt to operationalise their variables. An operational definition of variable $X$ gives us *the set of activities required to measure $X$*. It is like a set of instructions. For instance, in physics, pressure is precisely defined as weight or mass per unit area. To measure pressure we have to find out the weight impinging on an area and divide by that area.

Even in measuring a person's height, if we want to agree with others' measurements, we will need to specify conditions such as what to take as the top of the head and how the person should stand. In general though, height and time present us with no deep problem since the units of measurement are already clearly and universally defined.

In a particular piece of memory research we might define short-term memory capacity as 'the longest list of digits on which the participant has perfect recall in more than 80% of trials'. Here, on each trial, the participant has to try to recall the digit string presented in the order it was given Several trials would occur with strings from three to, say, 12 digits in length. At the end of this it is relatively simple to calculate our measure of short-term memory capacity according to our operational definition.

If a researcher had measured the 'controlling' behaviour of mothers with their children, he or she would have to provide the coding scheme given to assistants for making recordings during observation. This might include categories of 'physical restraint', 'verbal warning', 'verbal demand' and so on, with detailed examples given to observers during training.

The notorious example, within psychological research, is the definition of intelligence as 'that which is measured by the (particular) intelligence test used'. Since intelligence tests differ, we obviously do not have in psychology the universal agreement enjoyed by physicists. It might be argued that physicists have many ways to measure pressure but they know what pressure *is*. Likewise, can't psychologists have several ways to test intelligence? But psychologists aren't in the same position. They are still using the tests to try to establish agreement on the nature of intelligence itself. (See 'factor analysis' in chapter 9).

An operational definition gives us a more or less valid method for measuring some *part* of a hypothetical construct. It rarely covers the whole of what is usually understood by that construct. It is hard to imagine an operational definition which could express the rich and diverse meaning of human intelligence. But for any particular piece of research we must state exactly what we are counting as a measure of the construct we are interested in. As an example, consider a project carried out by some students who placed a ladder against a wall and observed men and women walking round or under it. For this research, 'superstitious behaviour' was (narrowly) operationalised as the avoidance of walking under the ladder.

Imagine you were about to start testing the hypotheses stated below. In each case, try to provide operationalised definitions for the variables involved. If it helps, ask yourself 'What will *count* as (aggression) in this study? How exactly will it be measured?' Think carefully, and then state the exact procedure you would use to carry out the measurement of the variables.

1 Physically punished children are more aggressive

2 Memory deterioration can be the result of stress at work

3 Language development is advanced in infants by parents who provide a lot of visual and auditory stimulation

4 People will be more likely to comply with a request from a person they trust

5 People told an infant is male will be more likely to describe the infant according to the popular male stereotype than will those told it is female.

Here are some ideas:

1 *Physical punishment*: number of times parent reports striking per week; questionnaire to parents on attitudes to physical punishment. *Aggression*: number of times child initiates rough-and-tumble behaviour observed in playground at school; number of requests for violent toys in Santa Claus letters.

2 *Stress*: occupations defined as more stressful the more sickness, heart attacks etc reported within them. *Memory* could be as we defined short-term memory capacity on page 18.

3 *Language development*: length of child's utterances; size of vocabulary, etc. *Stimulation*: number of times parent initiates sensory play, among other things, during home observation.

4 *Compliance*: if target person agrees to researcher's request for change in street. *Trust*: defined in terms of dress and role. In one case researcher dressed smart with doctor's bag. In the other, with scruffy clothes.

5 *Stereotype response*: if subject chooses words on list drawn up from survey of what characteristics the general public thought of as typically masculine and typically feminine.

## Independent and Dependent Variables

Think back to the experiment on memory described in chapter 1. Here, our operational definition of memory performance on the 20 item list is 'Number of items correctly recalled during two minutes, order of recall irrelevant'. The variable in the experiment was mode of learning – imagery or rehearsal – for which the operational definition is really in the instructions given to subjects.

We have two variables here. Mode of learning and number of items recalled. Which of the two following statements makes more sense to you:

1 'The mode of learning depends upon the number of items recalled'

2 'The number of items recalled depends upon the mode of learning'

Not too difficult I hope? Now, one of these variables is known as the DEPENDENT VARIABLE (commonly DV for short) and the other is known as the INDEPENDENT VARIABLE (IV). I hope it is obvious that, since the number of items recalled *depends* upon which learning mode is used, it gets called the 'dependent variable'. The variable it depends on gets known as the 'independent variable', it isn't affected by the DV, it is independent of it. The DV *is*, we hope, affected by the IV.

Suppose we give subjects a list of words to learn under two conditions. In one they have 30 seconds to learn and in the other they have one minute. The time given for learning (IV) will, we expect, be related to the number of words correctly recalled (DV). This is the hypothesis under test.

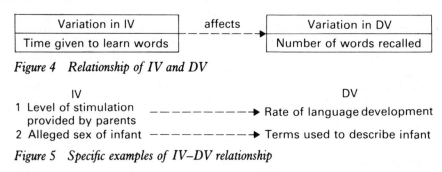

| Variation in IV | affects | Variation in DV |
|---|---|---|
| Time given to learn words | | Number of words recalled |

*Figure 4  Relationship of IV and DV*

|  IV  |  |  DV  |
|---|---|---|
| 1 Level of stimulation provided by parents | – – – – – – – ➔ | Rate of language development |
| 2 Alleged sex of infant | – – – – – – – ➔ | Terms used to describe infant |

*Figure 5  Specific examples of IV–DV relationship*

Try to identify the IV and DV in the other examples given on page 19.

A fundamental process in scientific research has been to relate IV to DV through experimental manipulation, holding all other relevant variables constant while only the IV changes. Some psychology textbooks assume that IV and DV apply only to experiments. However, the terms originate from mathematics, are common throughout scientific research and relate to any linked variation. In an experiment the IV is completely in the control of the experimenter. It is what the experimenter manipulates. In other research, the IV, for instance the amount of physical punishment or sex-role socialisation, is assumed to have varied way beyond any control of the researcher. These points are explored more thoroughly in chapter 5.

In our imagery-or-rehearsal experiment we found that the group using imagery did, indeed, recall far more words than the rehearsal group. Two questions:

1 What would interfere with your ability to perform at your best in either of these memory tasks?
2 Could something *other* than the imagery be responsible for the differences?

**Extraneous variables**
This is a general term referring to any variable at all which might have an effect on the measured DV. It tends to be used in reference mainly to experiments where we would normally be interested in controlling the unwanted effects of all variables except the IV, so that we can compare conditions fairly.

**Random error (or random variable)**   Maybe your answers to question 1 included some of the following:

– the way you were feeling on the day
– the stuffy atmosphere in the room
– the noise of the heater
– the fact that you'd just come from a Sociology exam

The heater may go on and off by thermostat. Experimental apparatus may behave slightly differently from trial to trial. A technician may cough when you're trying to concentrate. Some variables above affect only you. Others vary across everyone. Some people will pay more attention than others. The words presented have different meanings to each person. These 'people' differences are known as SUBJECT VARIABLES – see chapter 3.

All these variables are unpredictable (well, something could have been done about the heater!). They are sometimes called 'nuisance variables'. They are random in their effect. They do not affect one condition more than the other, we hope. In fact, we assume that they will just about balance out across the two groups, partly because we *randomly allocated* subjects to conditions (see chapter 3).

Where possible, everything is done to remove obviously threatening variables. In general though, random errors cannot be entirely eliminated. We have to hope they balance out.

Random errors, then, are unsystematic extraneous variables.

**Constant error**   For question 2, did you suggest that:

– subjects might be better in the imagery condition because it came second and they'd had practice?
– the list of words used in the imagery condition might have been easier?
– in the imagery condition the instructions are more interesting and therefore more motivating?

In these examples an extraneous variable is operating *systematically*. It is affecting the performances in one condition more than in the other.

If the effect of an extraneous variable is systematic it is serious because we may assume the IV has affected the DV when it hasn't.

Suppose babies lying in a cot look far more at complex visual patterns. Suppose though, the complex patterns were always presented on the right-hand side, with a simple pattern on the left. Maybe the cot makes it more comfortable to look to the right. Perhaps babies have a natural tendency to prefer looking to the right. This is a constant error which is quite simple to control for. We don't have to know that left or right *does* make a difference. We just might as well alternate the simple and complex positions from left to right in order to rule out any such possibility.

**Confounding (or confounding variables)**   What we have said in the last paragraph is that something else, *other than the independent variable we were manipulating*, has produced the differences observed in our results. The variable – left- or right-side presentation – was varied systematically with the experimental IV – simple vs. complex pattern – . Left or right side is acting as an uncontrolled IV. By alternating both types of pattern to left and right we would have eliminated it. But we didn't and now it CONFOUNDS our results. Notice in figure 6 that three explanations are possible.

Notice from option (c) that both variables could be responsible. A significant number of babies chose the right-side pattern. This could be because some of them preferred the right side and some of them preferred more complex patterns. It could also be because, in most babies, these variables *together* tip the balance towards preference.

In assuming that an IV causes a DV to change we may make serious errors of interpretation. Recently, at the beginning of the Christmas vacation, I decided to start drinking only coffee which was decaffeinated. I had been told by a friend that this might reduce some unpleasant feelings of tension I had been experiencing, such as palpitations and shaking. To my surprise, after a couple of weeks the feelings subsided.

Can you spot the confounding variable?

Well, I did say it was the start of the Christmas vacation! From experience I can assure you that, after a gruelling winter term, some relaxation was inevitable anyway. A second alternative explanation of the changes could have been that I expected them and this helped them occur – a possibility one always has to consider in psychology when subjects know in advance what aspect of their behaviour is expected to alter. (The 'placebo' effect: see chapter 3).

In the imagery experiment, it may not be the *images* which cause the improvement. It may be the meaningful linkages, amounting to a story, which people create for the words. How could we check this hypothesis? Some students I was teaching once suggested we ask people blind from birth to create the links. I'm absolutely sure this would work. It certainly does work on people with poor visual imagery. They improve as much as others using image-linking.

## Confounding and constant errors

So what's the difference between a confounding variable and a constant error? I'm afraid I have to introduce you to a little academic ambiguity. Some textbooks state that a confounding variable can be anything at all which affects the DV, other than the IV. In other words, constant and radom errors would both count. However, most books (and this is my preference) state that the effect of a confounding variable is *systematic*. It is, in other words, an alternative, or partial, explanation for observed effects. One way in which the terms 'confounding variable' and 'constant error' do differ, however, is that the latter term tends to be used in reference to experiments and the researcher's manipulation and control of variables and conditions. A confounding variable can be present (and very often is) when any difference or relationship between data is demonstrated through non-experimental research. We shall follow up this point after the next exercise.

Look back at the exercise on page 19. Assume that in each example research is carried out which supports the link between IV and DV. (groups under greater stress *do* have poorer memory performance, for example). Can you think of a confounding variable in each example which might explain the link?

*Figure 6 Possible confounding variables*

## Confounding in non-experimental research

In non-experimental work the researcher does not control the IV. The researcher measures variables which already exist in people and in society, such as social class of child and child's academic achievement.

One of the reasons for doing psychological research is to challenge the 'common sense' assumptions people often make between an observed IV and DV. It is easy to assume, for instance, that poor home resources are responsible for low academic achievement when a relationship is discovered between these two variables. But those with low resources are more likely to live in areas with poorer schools which attract less well-trained staff. The relationship is confounded by these latter variables.

One study found that diagnosed schizophrenics tended to excrete less of certain hormones than non-schizophrenics. This was taken as possible evidence for a genetic factor. In a replication study where both groups had been on the same hospital diet, no significant difference in hormone excretion was found. It appeared that in the original comparison, difference in diet had been a confounding variable which later explained the hormone excretion difference.

Similar confounding occurred when Bowlby (1953) observed that children without mothers and reared in institutions often developed serious psychological problems. He attributed the cause of these problems almost entirely to lack of a single maternal bond. Later checks revealed that along with no mother went regimented care, a serious lack of social and sensory stimulation, reduced educational opportunity and a few other variables possibly contributing to later difficulties in adjustment.

## Key terms for this chapter

Confounding variable      Operational definition
Constant error            Random error
Dependent variable        Random variable
Extraneous variable       Reification
Hypothetical constructs    Variable
Independent variable

## Exercises

1 Identify the assumed independent and dependent variables in the following statements:
(a) Attitudes can be influenced by propaganda messages
(b) Noise affects efficiency of work
(c) Time of day affects span of attention
(d) Performance is improved with practice
(e) Smiles given tend to produce smiles in return
(f) Aggression can be the result of frustration
(g) Birth order in the family influences the individual's personality and intellectual achievement
(h) People's behaviour in crowds is different from behaviour when alone

2 In exercise 1, what could be an operational definition of: 'noise', 'span of attention', 'smile'?

3 Two groups of six-year-old children are assessed for their cognitive skills and sociability. One group has attended some form of pre-school education for at

least a year before starting school. The other group has not received any pre-school experience. The pre-school educated group are superior on both variables.

(a) Identify the independent and dependent variables
(b) Identify possible confounding variables
(c) Outline ways in which the confounding variables could be eliminated as possible explanations of the differences

# Samples and groups

## 1 Samples

Suppose you had just come back from the airport with an Indian friend who is to stay with you for a few weeks and she switches on the television. To your horror, one of the worst imaginable game shows is on and you hasten to tell her that this is not typical of British TV fare. Suppose, again, that you are measuring attitudes to trade unions and you decide to use the college canteen to select persons to answer your questionnaire. Unknown to you, the men and women you select are mainly people with union positions on a training course for negotiation skills. In both these cases an unrepresentative sample has been selected. In each case our view of reality can be distorted.

### Populations and samples

One of the main aims of scientific study is to be able to generalise from examples. A psychologist might be interested in establishing some quality of all human behaviour or in the characteristics of a certain group, such as those with strong self-confidence or those who have experienced pre-school education. In each case the POPULATION is all the existing members of that group. Since the population itself will normally be too large for each individual within it to be investigated, we would normally select a SAMPLE from it to work with. A population need not consist of people. A biologist might be interested in a population consisting of all the cabbages in one field. A psychologist might be measuring subjects' reaction times, in which case the population is the times (not the people) and is infinite, being all the times which could ever be produced.

The particular population we are interested in (say, those with strong self-confidence), and from which we draw our samples, is known as the TARGET POPULATION.

### Sampling bias

We need our sample to be typical of the population about which we wish to generalise results. If we studied male and female driving behaviour by observing drivers in a town at 11.45 am or 3.30 pm our sample of women drivers is likely to contain a larger than usual number driving cars with small children in the back.

This weighting of a sample with an over-representation of one particular category is known as SAMPLING BIAS. The sample tested in the college canteen was a biased sample, if we were expecting to acquire from it an estimation of the general public's current attitude to trade unions.

According to Ora (1965), many experimental studies may be biased simply because the sample used are volunteers. Ora found that volunteers were significantly different from the norm on the following characteristics: dependence on others, insecurity, aggressiveness, introversion, neuroticism and being influenced by others.

A further common source of sampling bias is the student. It is estimated that some 75% of American and British psychological research studies are conducted on students (Valentine, 1982). To call these all volunteers is slightly misleading. In many American institutions the psychology student is required to participate in a certain number of research projects. The choice (or 'volunteering') only concerns which particular ones.

### Subject variables

In many laboratory experiments in psychology the nature of the individuals being tested is not considered to be an important issue. The researcher is often specifically interested in an experimental effect, in a difference between conditions rather than between types of person. In this case the researcher needs, in a sense, 'an average bunch of people' in each condition.

> An experimental group searches a word list for words rhyming with 'tree' whilst counting backwards in sevens. A control group does the same thing but does not have to count. The control group performance is superior. Could this difference be caused by anything other than the distraction of counting?

I hope that one of your possible explanations was that the control group might just happen to be better with the sound of words. There may be quite a few good poets or songwriters among them. This would have occurred by chance when the people were allocated to their respective groups. If so, the study would be said to be confounded by SUBJECT VARIABLES. These are variations between persons acting as subjects, and which are relevant to the study at hand.

# 2 Sampling

### Representative samples

What we need then, are samples representative of the population from which they are drawn. The target population for each sample is often dictated by the hypothesis under test. We might need one sample of men and one of women. Or we may require samples of eight-year-old and 12-year-old children, or a group of children who watch more than 20 hours of television a week and one watching less than five hours.

Within each of these populations, however, how are we to ensure that the individuals we select will be representative of their category? The simple truth is that a truly representative sample is an abstract ideal unachievable in practice. The practical goal we can set ourselves is to remove as much sampling bias as possible. We need to ensure that no members of the population are more likely than others to get into our sample. One way to achieve this goal is to take a truly RANDOM SAMPLE since this is strictly defined as *a sample in which every member of the target population has an equal chance of being included.*

## Random samples

> Which of the following procedures do you think would produce a group of people who would form a random sample?
>
> (a) Picking anybody off the street to answer a questionnaire
>    (Target population: the general public)
>
> (b) Selecting every fifth home in a street
>    (Target population: the street)
>
> (c) Selecting every 10th name on the school register
>    (Target population: the school)
>
> (d) Sticking a pin in a list of names
>    (Target population: the names on the list)
>
> (e) Selecting slips from a hat containing the names of all Wobbly College students and asking those selected to answer your questionnaire on sexual behaviour
>    (Target population: Wobbly College students)

The answer is that none of these methods will produce a tested random sample. In item (a) we may well be biased towards avoiding people we don't like the look of. In items (b) and (c) the definition obviously isn't satisfied (though these methods are sometimes known as QUASI–RANDOM SAMPLING or SYSTEMATIC SAMPLING. In (d) we are less likely to drop our pin at the top or bottom of the paper. In (e) the initial selection is random but our sample will end up not containing those who refuse to take part.

Most psychological research does not use random samples. A common method of obtaining participants is to advertise in the local press and commoner is to use students. I have never come across a student practical research project, or many others for that matter, which used truly random samples. Children may be chosen at random from a nursery class but this gives a random sample only of the nursery class as population, not of young children in general (and usually excludes those sick on the day).

What students can reasonably do is attempt to obtain as random a sample as possible, or to make the sample fairly representative, by selecting individuals from important sub-categories (some working class, some middle class and so on) as is described under 'stratified sampling' below. Either way, it is important to discuss this issue when interpreting results and evaluating one's research.

## How to sample randomly

**Computer selection**    The computer can generate an endless string of random numbers. These are numbers which have absolutely no relationship to each other as a sequence and which are selected with equal frequency. Given a set of names the computer would use these to select a random set.

**Random number tables**    Alternatively, we can use the computer to generate a set of random numbers which we record and use to do any selecting ourselves. Such a table appears as table 1 in appendix 3. Starting anywhere in the table and moving either vertically or horizontally a random sequence of numbers is produced. To select five people at random from a group of 50, give everyone a number from 1 to 50 and enter the table by moving through it vertically or horizontally. Select the people who hold the first five numbers which occur as you move through the table.

**Manual selection**    The numbered balls in a Bingo session or the numbers on a roulette wheel are selected almost randomly as are raffle tickets drawn from a barrel or hat so long as they are all well shuffled, the selector can't see the papers and these are all folded so as not to feel any different from one another. You *can* select a sample of 20 from the college population this way, but you'd need a large box rather than the 'hat' so popular in answers to questions on random selection.

These methods of random selection can be put to uses other than initial sample selection:

**Random allocation to experimental groups**    We may need to split 40 participants into two groups of 20. To ensure, as far as possible, that subject variables are spread evenly across the two groups, we need to give each subject an equal chance of being in either group. In fact, we are selecting a sample of 20 from a population of 40, and this can be done as described in the methods above.

**Random ordering**    We may wish to put 20 words in a memory list into random order. To do this give each a random number as described before. Then put the random numbers into numerical order, keeping the word, item or person with it. The words will now be randomly ordered.

### Ensuring a representative sample

If a researcher, conducting a large survey (see chapter 8), wanted to ensure that as many types of people from one town could be selected for the sample which of the following methods of contacting people would provide the greatest access?

(a) Using the telephone directory
(b) Selecting from all houses
(c) Using the electoral role
(d) Questioning people on the street

I hope you'll agree that the electoral role will provide us with the widest, unbiased section of the population, though it won't include prisoners, the homeless, new residents and persons in psychiatric care. The telephone directory eliminates non-phone owners and the house selection eliminates those in residential institutions. The street will not contain people at work, those with a severe disability unless they have a helper and so on.

If we use near–perfect random sampling methods on the electoral role then a representative sample should, theoretically, be the result. We should get numbers of men, women, over 60's, diabetics, young professionals, members of various ethnic groups and so on, in proportion to their frequency of occurrence in the town as a whole. This will only happen, though, if the sample is fairly large as I hope you'll agree, at least after reading the section on sample sizes further below.

### Stratified sampling

We may not be able to use the electoral role or we may be taking too small a sample to expect representatives by chance. In such cases we may depart from complete random sampling. We may pre-define those groups of people from whom we need representation.

If you want a representative sample of students within your college you might decide to take business studies students, art students, catering students and so on, in proportion to their numbers. If 10% of the college population comprises art students, then 10% of your sample will be art students. If the sample is going to be 50 students then five will be chosen randomly from the art department.

The strata of the population we identify as relevant may vary according to the particular research we are conducting. If, for instance, we are researching the subject of racism in education, we would want to ensure proportional representation of minority ethnic group members and of education workers, whilst on abortion we might wish to represent various religions. If the research has a local focus, then the local, not national, proportions would be relevant. In practice, with small scale research and limited samples, only a few relevant strata can be accommodated.

### Quota sampling

This method was popular amongst market research companies and consists of obtaining people from strata in proportion to their occurrence in the general population but with the selection from each stratum being left entirely to the devices of the interviewer who would be unlikely to use pure random methods, but would just stop interviewing 18–21 year-old males, for instance, when the quota for interviewing had been reached.

### Cluster samples

It may be that, in a particular town, a certain geographical area can be fairly described as largely working class, another as largely middle class and another as largely Indian sub-continent Asian. In this case 'clusters' (being housing blocks or whole streets) may be selected from each such area and as many people as possible from within that cluster will be included in the sample. This, it is said, produces large numbers of interviewees economically because researcher travel is reduced, but of course it is open to the criticism of being not representative within the clusters selected.

### Snowball sampling

This refers to a technique employed in the more qualitative techniques (see chapter 10) where a lot of information is required just to get an overall view of an organisational system or to find out what is happening around a certain issue such as alcoholism. A researcher might select several key people for interview and these contacts may lead on to further important contacts to be interviewed.

### Critical cases

A special case may sometimes highlight things which can be related back to most non-special cases. Freud's studies of people with neuroses led him to important insights about the unconscious workings possible in anybody's mind. Researchers interested in perceptual learning seek out cases where people have regained sight dramatically, perhaps through a breakthrough operation.

### The self-selecting sample

You may recall some students who placed a ladder against a wall and observed how many men and women passed under or around it. In this investigation the sample could not be selected by the researchers. They had to rely on taking the persons who walked along the street at that time as their sample. Several studies involve this kind of sample. In one study, persons using a phone booth were asked if they had picked up a coin left in the booth purposely by the researchers. The independent variable was whether the person was touched while being asked or not. The dependent variable was whether they admitted picking up the coin or not.

Volunteers for experimental studies are, of course, a self-selecting sample.

## The opportunity sample

Student practical work is very often carried out on other students. For that matter, so is a lot of research carried out in universities and polytechnics. If you use the other students in your class as a sample you are using them as an opportunity sample. They just happen to be the people you can get hold of.

The samples available in a 'natural experiment' (see chapter 5) are also opportunistic in nature. If there is a chance to study children about to undergo an educational innovation, the researcher who takes it has no control over the sample.

## Sample size

One of the most popular items in many students' armoury of prepared responses to 'Suggest modifications to this research' is 'The researcher should have tested more subjects'. If a significant difference has been demonstrated between two groups this is not necessary unless (i) we have good reason to suspect sampling bias or (ii) we are replicating the study (see chapter 4).

If the research has failed to show a significant difference we may well suspect our samples of bias. But is it a good idea to simply add a lot more to our tested samples?

**The argument FOR large samples**    It is easier to produce a biased sample with small samples. I hope this example will make this clear. If you were to select five people from a group containing five Catholics, five Muslims, five Hindus and five Buddhists, you'd be more likely to get a religious bias in your sample than if you selected ten people. For instance, if you select only five they could all be Catholics, but with ten this isn't possible.

*In general, the larger the sample the less the likely sampling bias.*

Does this mean then that we should always test as many subjects as possible? Another argument for large samples is demonstrated by the following example. Suppose there are somewhat more pro- than anti-abortionists in the country as a whole, the ratio being six to five. A small sampling strategy, producing 12 for and ten against will not convince anyone that this difference represents reality, but a difference of 360 to 300 might. Although we haven't yet covered probability, I hope that your acquired sense of chance factors would agree with this.

**The argument AGAINST large samples**    One reason we can't always take such large samples is economical, concerning time and money. But another limitation is that larger samples may obscure a relevant subject variable or specific effect.

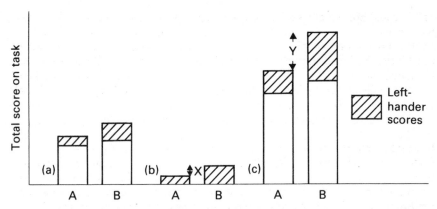

*Figure 7    Task scores for right- and left-handed subjects*

Suppose, for instance, there is a task which, when performed under condition B produces improvement over condition A but only for left-handed subjects (left-handers are disadvantaged when writing left to right with ink which has to dry, for instance). These contributions to the total scores are illustrated by the two left-hand columns in figure 7. Here, the increased total score for all subjects on condition B is due almost completely to the difference for left-handed subjects (distance $X$ shown by the middle two columns (b) in figure 7). If only left-handed subjects were considered, the difference would be seen as significant (not just chance) but the overall difference for all subjects is not. The difference shown by the two right-hand columns (c) of figure 7, where a lot more subjects have been tested is significant. However, the researcher might conclude that there is a slight but significant difference across *all* subjects. A specific and interesting effect (sharp improvements for left-handers) is being obscured by simply taking a lot more subjects, rather than stopping after the first 'failure' to examine possible subject variables (left- or right-handedness) which are hiding the effect.

A large sample, then, may disguise an important subject variable which needs teasing out.

Large samples may also disguise weaknesses in the *design* of an experiment. If there are a large number of uncontrolled variables present then differences between two small groups may seem insignificant (just chance variation). It may take large samples to show that the difference *is* consistent. In field studies (outside the laboratory – see chapter 6) we may have to put up with this lack of control, but in laboratory experiments such random or confounding variables can be controlled so that small samples will demonstrate the real difference.

It has been argued that the optimum sample size, when investigating an experimental IV assumed to have a similar effect on most people, is about 25 to 30. If significance is not shown then the researcher investigates subject variables and the design of the study.

# 3 Subject groups

## Control groups and experimental groups

> Suppose we were interested in attempting to reduce racial prejudice in children by use of a specific training programme. After one year the children's attitudes are indeed more positive than they were at the start. Can we say that the procedure obviously works? Is there an alternative explanation of the prejudice reduction? Where's the confounding variable?

Well, perhaps the children would have reached this greater maturity in thought without the treatment, through the increasing complexity of their encounters with the environment. We need to compare these children's development with that of a group who do not experience the programme. This latter group would be known as a CONTROL GROUP and the group receiving the programme as an EXPERIMENTAL GROUP or TREATMENT GROUP.

In selecting these two groups we must be careful to avoid confounding by subject variables and ensure that they are equivalent in composition. We can select each entirely at random or on a stratified basis. In some studies like this, subjects would be chosen as matched pairs (see chapter 6) so that for each child in one group there was a child to compare with in the other, matched on particular characteristics such as age, sex, social class and so on.

## Placebo group

The experimental group in the example above may have lowered their output of prejudice responses because they knew they were in an experimental programme, especially if they knew what outcomes the researchers were expecting. In trials of new drugs some people are given a salt pill or solution in order to see whether simply the expectation of improvement and knowledge of having been given a cure will produce improvement alone. Similarly, psychologists create PLACEBO GROUPS in order to eliminate the possibility that results are confounded by expectancy variables.

A common experimental design within physiological psychology has been to inject subjects with a substance which simulates the physiological reactions which occur when individuals are emotionally aroused. A control group then experiences everything the injected (experimental) group experience, except the injection. The placebo group receives an injection of a harmless substance with no physiological effects. Performances are then observed and if both the control and placebo groups differ in the same way from the experimental group we can rule out expectancy as the cause of the difference. Some of the children in the prejudice study above could be given a programme unrelated to prejudice reduction, and also informed of expected results, in order to serve as a placebo group.

## Key terms for this chapter

| | | |
|---|---|---|
| Cluster sample | Quasi-random or | Self-selecting sample |
| Control group | Systematic sample | Snowball sample |
| Critical cases | Quota sample | Stratified sample |
| Experimental group | Random numbers | Subject variables |

**Key terms** – *continued*

| | | |
|---|---|---|
| Opportunity sample | Random sample | Target population |
| Placebo group | Representative sample | Treatment group |
| Population | Sample bias | |
| | Sample | |

**Exercises**

1 A researcher shows that participants in a conformity experiment quite often give an obviously wrong answer to simple questions when six other confederates of the experimenter have just given the same wrong answer by pre-arrangement. What else must the researcher do in order to demonstrate that the real participants actually are conforming to group pressure?

2 The aim of a particular investigation is to compare the attitudes of working-class and middle-class mothers to discipline in child rearing. What factors should be taken into account in selecting two comparable samples (apart from social class)?

3 A psychologist advertises in the university bulletin for students willing to participate in an experiment concerning the effects of alcohol consumption on appetite. For what reasons might the sample gathered not be a random selection of students?

4 An adequate random sample of business studies students in the county of Suffex could be drawn by which one of these methods?

   (a) Selecting one college at random and using all the business studies students within it.

   (b) Group all business studies students within each college by surname initial (A, B, . . . Z). Select one person at random from each initial group in each college.

   (c) Put the names of all business studies students at all colleges into a very large hat, shake and draw out names without looking.

5 A psychologist visits a group of 20 families with a four-year-old child and trains the mother to use a special programme for promoting reading ability. Results in reading ability at age six are compared with those of a control group who were not visited and trained. A research assistant suggests that a third group of families should have been included in the study. What sort of group do you think the assistant is suggesting?

6 A psychology lecturer requires two groups to participate in a memory experiment. She divides the students in half by splitting the left side from the right side of the class. The left side get special instructions and do better on the problem solving task. The lecturer claims that the instructions are therefore effective. Her students argue that a confounding variable could be operating. What are they thinking of, perhaps?

# PART II

# METHODS

## Three general themes

### Reliability and validity

These terms will be treated extensively in chapter 9, just after the sections on psychological tests and questionnaires (an area where a variety of reliability and validity assessments are made). Here, however, I would like just to introduce the terms briefly, since, for each of the research methods we are to discuss, the question of general reliability or validity can be raised.

## 1 Reliability

If a psychological research finding can be repeated it is reliable. This finding may be an experimental effect, for instance that anagrams of common words are solved more quickly than anagrams of uncommon words, or it could be an observation made 'in the field' – for instance, that parents who talk to their infants more have children with larger vocabularies at the age of two years.

Repeating a research study in order to check on its reliability is known as 'replication'.

A psychological test or measure, such as an attitude questionnaire, is also known as reliable if it tends to produce the same scores from the same people at different times.

It should be obvious that, if we are going to use measures at all, they should be measures which produce similar results on similar occasions. This is the least we'd ask of a thermometer or timing device.

In traditional scientific method, replication plays a very important role. Recently there was immense excitement in the world of physics when one group of researchers claimed to have successfully produced 'cold fusion' – a process which could potentially release enormous amounts of cheap energy – at normal room temperature. One replication, by different scientists, was announced. But one replication is not enough. Several more attempts failed and, just three months after the jubilant announcements, the effect was back in its place as part of the still imaginary future.

If you tell me you have shown that, with special training, anyone can be trained to telepathise, I should want to see your evidence and experience the phenomenon for myself. It's not that I don't trust you, but we need others to check our wilder claims or to look coolly at processes which, because we are so excited about them, we are failing to analyse closely enough. I may discover an alternative explanation of what is happening or point out a flaw in your procedure.

## Standardised procedure

In the interests of replication, then, it is essential that I can follow your procedure exactly. Not only that, it is essential that you stuck to your procedure with all the people you tested. Suppose you had compared people you'd trained with people you hadn't. The acid test is that your trainees should perform better under *exactly the same circumstances* as your untrained group. It would be quite unsound if you were 'chatty' whilst testing your trainees, because you knew them, and more formal with the others.

Barber (1976) gives an example of what he calls 'the investigator loose procedure effect'. It also includes the problem of what we shall call 'experimenter bias' in the next chapter. The study (Raffetto, 1967) led one group of experimenters (people who conduct research for investigators) to believe that sensory deprivation produces many reports of hallucinations and another group to believe the opposite. The experimenters then interviewed people who had undergone sensory deprivation. The instructions for interviewing were purposely left vague. Experimenters reported results in accordance with what they had been led to believe – more hallucinatory reports from those expecting them.

Even with standardised procedures, experimenters do not always follow them. Friedman (1967) argued that this is partly because experiments are not thought of as involving social interaction and non-verbal communication. Male experimenters, when the subject is female, are more likely to use her name, smile and look directly at her. Procedures do not usually tell the experimenter exactly how to greet subjects, engage in casual pleasantries, arrange seating and how much to smile.

As we shall see in a little while, there are psychological research methods for which the requirement of standardised procedures would stifle the kind of relationship sought with the people on whom (or with whom) the psychologist conducts research. Such methods tend to sacrifice experimental reliability for ecological validity, about to be explained.

# 2 Validity

An effect or test is valid if it demonstrates or measures what the researcher thinks or claims it does. A researcher might claim to have demonstrated that children directly imitate an adult model in a laboratory experiment. In fact, the children might be 'pleasing the experimenter' and doing what they have guessed she or he wants them to do. A questionnaire intended to obtain information on how parents actually treat their children might instead measure what parents think one *ought* to do with one's children. It is therefore an invalid measure of the parents' child-rearing practice. It could still be highly reliable, of course.

We can also produce a seemingly valid measure which has low reliability. By asking observers to rate aggressive behaviour produced by five year olds in the playground, we would appear to be using a more valid measure of aggression than would be the case if we used a questionnaire or observed aggressive behaviour requested from the child in a laboratory situation. The playground aggression is genuine and spontaneous – it would have occurred had no observer been present (we hope). However, observer ratings can be quite unreliable. This could either be because the raters are poorly trained or not rating according to their training, in which case our measure may well be valid but unreliable in this circumstance. On the other hand, it could be the case that the low reliability points to an ambiguous or inadequate rating scale which in turn indicates lowered validity.

### Ecological validity

It has been argued that no laboratory experiment can be a truly valid test since the researcher can never be studying naturally occurring behaviour in an everyday setting. A study is said to become ecologically valid the more it samples such natural circumstances and avoids the artificiality of some psychological research settings.

What counts as a 'natural environment' is sometimes hard to guage. Much human behaviour occurs in what is not, to the individuals concerned, a natural environment. There is, for instance, the doctor's surgery, a visit to the police station or the inside of an aeroplane. For some subjects the laboratory can be no less natural than anywhere else. In Ainsworth's (1971) study of infant attachments, behaviour was observed when mother was present, when she was absent and when a stranger was present. From the infant's point of view it probably wasn't of great consequence where this study was carried out – the local nursery, a park or the laboratory (which looked something like a nursery anyway!). The infant is very often in situations just as strange and what mattered overwhelmingly was whether mother was there or not.

We shall return to this line of discussion when we consider the advantages and disadvantages of the laboratory in the next chapter.

# 3 The quantitative–qualitative dimension

In the chapter on variables, and in chapter 1, I introduced a traditional approach to scientific study and measurement in psychological research. This would include an emphasis on the directly and physically observable, the assumption that cause and effect relationships must be logically analysed, and the use of quantitative methods wherever possible – loosely speaking, POSITIVISM. Not everyone agrees that this is the appropriate method for the study of active human beings rather than inert matter. I mentioned this briefly at the end of chapter 1. Some argue that a QUALITATIVE approach is possible in the investigation of psychological phenomena.

### Quantification and qualitative experience

'Quantification' means to measure on some numerical basis, if only by frequency. Whenever we count or categorise, we quantify. Separating people according to astrological sign is quantification. So is giving a grade to an essay.

A qualitative approach, by contrast, emphasises meanings, experiences (often verbally described), descriptions and so on. Raw data will be exactly what people have said (in interview or recorded conversation) or a description of what has been observed. Qualitative data can be later quantified to some extent but a 'qualitative approach' tends to value the data as qualitative.

It is rather like the difference between counting the shapes and colours of a pile of sweets as against feeling them, playing with them, eating them. Or counting sunsets rather than appreciating them. The difference between each one may be somehow quantifiable but such measurements will not convey the importance and the special impact of some over others.

By strict definition a variable can only be quantitative. As it changes it takes different values. There may only be two values, for instance male and female. A positivist would argue that psychologists can only study variables because contrast and comparison can only be achieved where there is change; what changes is a variable and variables must be quantifiable.

The case against is eloquently put by Reason and Rowan (1981) in a statement on what they call 'quantophrenia':

> There is too much measurement going on. Some things which are numerically precise are not true; and some things which are not numerical are true. Orthodox research produces results which are statistically significant but humanly insignificant; in human inquiry it is much better to be deeply interesting than accurately boring.

This is a sweeping statement, making it sound as though all research not using the methods which the authors prefer is 'humanly insignificant'. Many possibly boring but accurate research exercises have told us a lot about perceptual processes, for instance. However, the statement would not have been made had there not been an excess of emphasis, within psychological research history, on the objective measurement and direct observation of every concept, such that, important topics, not susceptible to this treatment, were de-valued.

On the topic of 'emotion', for instance, in mainstream textbooks you will find little that relates to our everyday understanding of that term. You will find strange studies in which people are injected with drugs and put with either a happy or angry actor, and studies in which people are given false information about events they are normally oblivious of – such as their heart or breathing rate. These things are quantifiable, as are the responses such subjects give to structured questionnaires.

### Varying research contexts

The debate about qualitative research represents, to some extent, differences of interest in the way psychology should be practised or applied. If you're interested in the accuracy of human perception in detecting colour changes, or in our ability to process incoming sensory information at certain rates, then it seems reasonable to conduct highly controlled experimental investigations using a strong degree of accurate quantification. If your area is psychology applied to social-work practice, awareness changes in ageing, or the experience of mourning, you are more likely to find qualitative methods and data of greater use.

But the debate also represents fundamental disagreement over what is the most appropriate model for understanding human behaviour and, therefore, the best way to further our understanding. We shall investigate this point further in chapter 11.

A compromise position is often found by arguing that the gathering of basically qualitative data, and its inspection and analysis *during* the study, can lead to the stimulation of new insights which can then be investigated more thoroughly by quantitative methods. This might still be considered a basically positivist approach, however.

An old example of this reasoning occurred in some research which studied the effects of long term unemployment in Austria in the 1930s (Jahoda–Lazarsfeld and Zeisl, 1932). A small boy, in casual conversation with a research worker, expressed the wish to become an Indian tribal chief but added 'I'm afraid it will be hard to get the job'. The investigators developed and tested quantitatively the hypothesis that parental unemployment has a limiting effect on children's fantasies. Children of unemployed parents mentioned significantly less expensive items in their Christmas present wishes, compared with children of employed parents. (We assume, of course, that the parental groups were matched for social class!)

## Relative values of quantitative and qualitative studies

In general, methods which are tighter and more rigorous give rise to more reliable data, replicable effects and a claim to greater objectivity. However, results are open to criticism of giving narrow, unrealistic information using measures which trap only a tiny portion of the concept originally under study. More qualitative

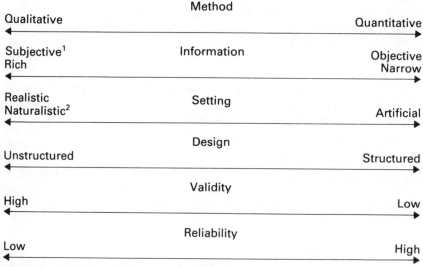

*Figure 8  Variations in construction and control*

**Note:**

1 Some qualitative proponents argue strongly that their methods do not necessarily invoke greater subjectivity at all. Numbers can be used subjectively, as when 'trained raters' use a rating scale to 'code' observed behaviour. A descriptive account of an abused person's experience can be written objectively and can be checked with them for accuracy and true reflection. A person's own, major reasons for objecting to abortion could be counted as more objective data than a number which places them at five on a zero to 30 abortion attitude scale.

2 Naturalistic studies (those carried out in natural surroundings) may use fully quantified data gathering procedures. Qualitative studies however, will almost always tend to be naturalistic.

enquiries, with looser controls and conducted in more natural, everyday circumstances give richer results and more realistic information. They are therefore held to produce more valid data. They suffer the criticisms of being less reliable and more subjective (but see note 2 below figure 8).

Loosely controlled methods will produce unpredictable amounts and types of information which the researcher has to sift, organise and select for importance. Such methods leave more room for the researcher to manouvre in questioning the participants and in deciding what observations are more worthwhile, thus fostering more natural, less stilted human interaction with more realistic results. The price is greater individual bias and less comparability across studies.

Studies can vary in their construction and control across all the dimensions shown in figure 8. The qualitative-quantitative dimension tends to correlate with the other dimensions as shown, and it is worth bearing these in mind as we progress through the research methods commonly in use in psychological investigation today. Qualitative approaches are integrated into the chapters on observation and on asking questions. Others are covered in chapter 11.

### Important terms for this chapter

| | |
|---|---|
| Ecological validity | Reliability |
| Positivism | Standardised procedure |
| Qualitative (data/approach) | Validity |
| Quantitative (data/approach) | |

### Exercises

1 Which is the more valid measure of a person's attitude to the elderly:

   (a) answers to a questionnaire

   (b) what they say to a close friend in conversation

   (c) what they say in an informal interview

   (d) the number of elderly people they have as friends?

Which of these might be the most reliable measure?

2 What is the consequence of having data which are:

   (a) highly reliable but not valid

   (b) highly valid but not very reliable?

3 Two psychologists have recently completed research into the experiences of persons with disabilities in the able-bodied world. One conducted informal interviews and looked for illuminating points brought out by the interviewees. The other used a pre-structured questionnaire and published significant differences in attitude, measured by the questionnaire, between the interviewees and a control group of able-bodied people. Construct the list of criticisms which each might make of the other's procedure and findings. Chapters 8 and 9 contain detailed evaluations of these methods.

# The experimental method I

## The nature of the method

Among the variety of research methods and designs popular with psychological researchers, there is a rather sharp divide. Designs are seen as either *experimental or non-experimental*, the latter often being called INVESTIGATIONS, although, of course, experiments are investigations too, in the general sense. This conceptual divide between methods is further sharpened by the fact that, in various learning institutions, it is possible to take a degree course in 'experimental psychology'.

Table 1 gives some terminology for these two groupings with some indication, I hope, of where some methods lie on the dimension of experimenter control which weakens as studies move away (to the right) from the traditional laboratory experiment.

## Experiments

In experiments an attempt is made to control as many variables as possible whilst altering only the IV. A strong and careful attempt is made to even out random variables and to eliminate constant errors. The reason for this is that, if all other variables are controlled, only the IV can be responsible for changes in the DV. The reasoning here is not confined to scientific experiment but is used as 'common sense' thinking in many practical situations in everyday life. If you're trying to work out what causes interference on your TV set you would probably try turning off one piece of electrical equipment at a time, leaving all others just as they were, until the interference stops.

*Complete control of the IV is the hallmark of an experiment.* As an example, consider a researcher who very briefly exposes one, two and three syllable words to subjects who have the task of recognising them as soon as possible. The IV here (the variable which the experimenter alters) is the number of syllables in each word. The DV is the time taken to recognise each one. When looking for the IV in a straightforward experiment it is helpful to ask 'what were the various conditions which subjects underwent?'

To make this a well-controlled experiment, all other variables, as far as is feasible, should be held constant. Hence the experimenter would ensure that each word was of exactly the same size, colour, print style and so on. Machine settings, ambient light and background noise should not be allowed to vary. Also, the words would need to be of fairly comparable frequency of occurrence in everyday reading, otherwise frequency might act as a confounding variable.

### Investigations which are not experiments
In contrast, consider the study of the effect of early visual stimulation on children's later cognitive development. We can't take a group of children and

deprive them of visual experience under controlled conditions. (If you're not convinced, please read the chapter on ethics now!)

In non-experimental investigations, the researcher gathers data through a variety of methods *but does not intervene* in order to control an independent variable. Other forms of control may well occur in order to enhance the accuracy of measurement, as when children of specific ages take a highly structured test of intelligence in a quiet and uninterrupted environment.

The weakness of non-experimental investigations is that, since the researcher does not have control over all relevant variables, confounding is much more likely.

> Assume it is found that children deprived of good visual stimulation at home are slower in cognitive development. What confounding variables (*not* the lack of visual experience itself) could explain the children's slower development?

*Table 1   Experimental Terminology*

| EXPERIMENT | NON-EXPERIMENT (or INVESTIGATION) |
|---|---|
| Laboratory experiment | (Observational study)[1] |
| Quasi-experiment | (Correlation study)[2] |
| Field experiment | (*Ex post facto* research) |
| Natural experiment | |
| More | Less |
| ←——————— Investigator control ———————→ | |
| | Non-experimental designs include: |
| | Interview |
| | Survey |
| | Observation |
| | Case study |
| Experimental hypothesis[3] | Research hypothesis |

**Notes:**

1  This term is sometimes used for all methods other than experimental. The idea is that, if we aren't manipulating, we can only be observing what occurs or has occurred naturally. Unfortunately, it is easy to confuse this wide use with the sense of observation as a technique (or method) where it literally means to watch and record behaviour as it is produced. This is different from, say, interviewing. Observation, as a technique, may be employed in a straightforward experiment.

2  This term can also be used for non-experimental designs but it only makes sense to use it where changes in one recorded variable (say income) are related to changes in another variable (say, educational standards expected for children). Correlation is explained in chapter 17. Many studies of variables existing in the social world do not, however, use correlation.

3  These are the appropriate terms for the hypotheses. All hypotheses are research hypotheses first, but the experiment earns this special title.

Two reasons I could think of were:

1 Parents who do not stimulate visually might also not stimulate in ways that have an important effect on cognitive development. For instance, they may not talk very much to their children.

2 Lack of visual stimulation may be one of the results of busy working parents who also can't afford good child care facilities. The general lack of resources might in some way affect cognitive development.

The diagram below shows the essential difference between an experiment and a non-experimental investigation:

| Experiment | | Non-Experimental investigation | |
|:---:|:---:|:---:|:---:|
| Manipulated | Measured | Measured | Measured |
| IV ——— | DV | IV ——— | DV |

The control of the IV, and our ability to eliminate as many extraneous variables as possible, gives us greater confidence that changes in the DV are produced by changes in the IV.

## Elimination of hypotheses in non-experimental work

In an experiment we can eliminate alternative explanations of an effect by controlling variables. Where we do not have an experimental level of control we can still eliminate possible explanations. If we wish to investigate my explanation above that children lacking visual stimulation may also be lacking language stimulation, we can conduct a study of parents who are poor visual stimulators but competent in verbal stimulation. If their children are behind in cognitive development then my explanation has to be invalid.

Remember that, in chapter 1, I pointed out that scientific research does not require that experiments be conducted. Astronomers did very well with careful observation and hypothesis testing. A vast amount of psychological research has been carried out using non-experimental methods.

## From non-experiment to experiment

Very often a non-experimental study can lead to experiments being conducted to 'tighten up' knowledge of the variables under study. For instance, the observation has been made that children tend to change their reasoning about 'wrong' and 'right' actions, concentrating their attention at first on the objective consequences of the act rather than taking the actor's intention into account too. This has led to direct (and successful) experimental attempts to alter the child's predominant style of reasoning by observation of an adult model using a more advanced judgement mode.

In many areas of psychological research, children can only be observed, not experimented with. However, some psychologists have performed experiments on animals as a substitute. Monkeys, for instance, have been deprived of their mothers and many animals have been subjected to various forms of physical punishment. These studies obviously raise ethical issues and we shall discuss these in some detail in chapter 20.

## The laboratory

Most studies carried out in laboratories are experiments, but not all. It is possible to bring children into a laboratory simply to observe their behaviour in a play setting without subjecting them to any changes in an IV.

**Control**   If an aim of the experiment is to reduce relevant extraneous variables by strict control then this is best achieved in a laboratory setting, particularly where highly accurate recordings of human cognitive functions (such as memory, perception, selective attention) are required. The IV and DV can be very precisely defined and accurately measured.

Bandura's (1965) research used controlled observation to record amounts and types of aggression shown by children after they themselves had watched an adult model being rewarded, unrewarded or punished for aggression. These three conditions represent the strictly controlled IV of an experimental design. Each child was observed in an identical play setting with an identical (now notorious) Bobo doll.

Consider the difference between this experimental setting and the 'field' setting of raters observing the aggressive behaviour of children in a school playground. In the playground, children may move off, be obscured by others or simply lack energy in cold weather. They may wish to play with the observer if he or she isn't hidden.

Bandura had strict control over timing, position and analysis of filmed records of behaviour. Ainsworth, mentioned on page 000, had complete control over the departure of a mother and arrival of a stranger when testing infants' reactions to separation in a laboratory setting, as well as highly accurate recordings of the infants' behaviour.

**Artificial conditions**   In physical science it is often necessary to study phenomena under completely artificial and controlled conditions in order to eliminate confounding variables. Only in this way would we know that feathers obey gravity in exactly the same way as lead. Critics of the laboratory method in psychology however, argue that behaviour studied out of context in an artificial setting is meaningless, as we shall see below.

Later on we shall discuss various criticisms of the experiment as a research method. Here we shall list some related criticisms of the laboratory as a research focus.

## Criticisms of the laboratory as research location

1 *Narrowness of the IV and DV.*   The aggression measured in Bandura's experiments is a very narrow range of what children are capable of in the way of destructive or hostile behaviour. Bandura might argue that at least this fraction of aggressive behaviour, we are now aware, could be modelled. However, Heather (1976) has argued persuasively:

   'Psychologists have attempted to squeeze the study of human life into a laboratory situation where it becomes unrecognisably different from its naturally occurring form.'

2 *Inability to generalise.*   A reliable effect in the laboratory may have little relationship to life outside it. The concept of an 'iconic memory' or very short-term 'visual information store', holding 'raw' sensory data from which we rapidly process information, has been considered by later psychologists to be an artifact of the particular experiments which produced evidence for it.

   Certainly there is a lot less faith now in the idea that experiments on rats, pigeons or even chimpanzees can tell us a lot about complex human behaviour.

3 *Artificiality.*   A laboratory is an intimidating, possibly even frightening place. People may well be unduly meek and over-impressed by their surroundings. If

the experimenter compounds this feeling by sticking rigidly to a standardised procedure, reciting a formal set of instructions without normal interactive gestures such as smiles and helpful comments, a 'subject' is hardly likely to feel 'at home' and behave in a manner representative of normal everyday behaviour.

## Some defence

In defence of the laboratory it can be said that:

1 In the area of psychological research which looks at human performance, perception or psychological processes, not only does the artificiality of the laboratory hardly matter, it is the only place where highly technical and accurate measurements could be made.

   If we study human vigilance in detecting targets, for instance, does it matter whether this is done in the technical and artificial surroundings of a laboratory or the equally technically and artificial environment of a radar monitoring centre where research results will be usefully applied? If we wish to discover how fine infants' perceptual discriminations are, this can be done with special equipment and the control of a laboratory whereas, when fairly young, an infant is hardly likely to know or care whether it is at home or not.

2 Physicists would not have been able to split atoms in the natural environment, nor observe behaviour in a vacuum. Psychologists have discovered effects in the laboratory which, as well as being interesting in themselves, have produced practical applications. Without the laboratory we would be unaware of differences in hemispheric function, the phenomena of perceptual defence or the extreme levels of obedience to authority which are possible. In each case, the appropriate interpretation of results has been much debated but the phenomena themselves have been valuable in terms of human insight and further research.

3 Research conducted under laboratory conditions is generally far easier to *replicate*, a feature valued very highly by advocates of the experimental method.

## Field experiments

The obvious alternative to the laboratory experiment is to conduct one's research 'in the field'. A field experiment is a study carried out in the natural environment of those studied, perhaps the school, hospital or street, whilst the IV is still manipulated by the experimenter. Other variables may well be tightly controlled but, in general, the experimenter cannot maintain the high level of control associated with the laboratory.

It used to be thought that the laboratory should be the starting point for investigating behaviour patterns and IV–DV links. The effects of such studies could then be tried out in 'the field'. The comparison was with the physicist harnessing electricity in the laboratory and putting it to work for human benefit in the community. In the last two decades many psychologists have become disaffected with the laboratory as appropriate for psychological research and have concentrated more on 'field' results in their own right.

Two examples of field experiments are:

1 Hoffling (1966) showed that 21 out of 22 nurses obeyed a telephone instruction from an unknown doctor to administer twice the maximum permitted dose of a

drug to a patient despite hospital rules stating that signed authorisation was required.

2 An elegant design by Friedrich and Stein (1973) involved observation of nursery school children to obtain a baseline for co-operative, helpful and friendly behaviour for each child. Children were then randomly assigned to two groups. Over a month, at regular intervals, one group watched 'pro-social' television programmes whilst the other (control) group watched neutral films of circuses and farm activity. The children were observed again at the end of the period and there was a significant rise in co-operativeness and peer-directed affection for the experimental group.

### Advantages and disadvantages of the field experiment

By studying effects in the natural environment, the field experiment avoids the criticism that results can't be generalised to real situations, though of course, one may not be able to generalise to real situations markedly unlike this particular field setting. The field experiment therefore has high ecological validity, though control, and therefore reliability, is weaker.

In many cases participants are unaware of being involved in an experiment until effects have been recorded. The extent to which they are aware of the aims of the experiment determines the extent to which it may be queried for subject bias and the effects of 'demand characteristics' (see below). Still, even with some distortion through this awareness, it will not involve the apprehension and artificiality of the laboratory.

The field experiment may be more expensive and time-consuming. The researcher may require skills of tact and persuasion, not needed in the laboratory, in dealing with those who need convincing that the research is necessary and in arranging details of the design which will ensure valid results whilst retaining co-operation with personnel such as the teacher or hospital worker.

The major disadvantage, however, is in the lack of control which the investigator can exert over extraneous variables, over strict manipulation of the IV and over careful, accurate measurement of the DV. All these are vulnerable to far more fluctuation in the field setting, compared with a laboratory.

### Quasi-experiments

Some studies don't quite qualify as true experiments. Remember that the experimenter has to attempt control over all possible confounding and 'nuisance' variables in order that changes in the DV can be attributed confidently to manipulation of the IV. This includes random allocation of subjects to experimental and control groups since, if not, differences in the DV could be attributable to differences between the subject groups. We will discuss this issue further in chapter 6, 'Experimental designs'.

The term 'quasi-experiment' is given to studies in which experimental procedures are applied yet the study does not meet the full requirements of experimental control, namely, random allocation of subjects to conditions.

An example is the pre-test/treatment/post-test design. A group of people with dyslexia, attending one centre, might be tested prior to implementation of a new training programme, and tested again after it has been completed. To eliminate the possibility that the 'treatment group' might have improved anyway, without the programme, a more thorough design would include a control group. These could be other persons with dyslexia attending the centre on a different day or from a quite different centre. This design uses a 'non-equivalent control group', however. The control group might fail to improve, not because they did not receive the 'treatment' but because their centre lacks some other variable associated with the 'treatment' group's centre. Confounding cannot be ruled out.

Note that if the experimenter had been allowed to use people at one centre and allocate these at random to experimental or control groups then the study would qualify for full experimental status.

### Natural experiments

There are occasions when a natural event is about to occur which a psychologist may exploit for research purposes. For instance, a headteacher may be about to introduce a 'discovery learning' approach in one infant class of the school. The regime in one ward of a psychiatric hospital may change to an emphasis on patient autonomy, nurses to guide and train rather than care and guard. In both cases there will be a naturally occurring control group – a similar group not experiencing the change – with which behaviour changes can be compared. The IV, however, is not at all controlled by the experimenter. The experiment is 'quasi' since no control is possible over subject variables.

The advantage here is that participants are not aware that they are part of an 'experiment', though there may still be distortion of normal behaviour as a response to the real-life changes and novelty they are experiencing. However, the investigator is not guilty of interfering, though his or her presence may have some unwanted effects.

### *Ex post facto* research

A researcher might record differences in reaction to a finger-painting exercise between working-class and middle-class children. Males and females might be tested for differences in verbal ability. In cases like these, it is argued, the IV is class or gender and the researcher cannot claim to have controlled these since the people studied were socialised throughout their lives prior to the test.

Sex, class, years of education and so on are variables which the researcher can have no influence over. In studies like this, the dependent variable is measured and we then look backwards, in a sense, to see whether differences in it are *associated* with the independent variable. The problem is that, because the IV is confounded by so many other variables, we cannot state that it is the *cause* of changes in the DV. We can use techniques like matching, and random selection of subjects from the appropriate populations, in order to try to eliminate some confounding variables but there are far too many of these to ever be able to state that a difference is unambiguously the result of sex or class difference.

### 'True' and 'Pseudo' experiments

The term 'pseudo experiment' is sometimes used to refer to the general category of studies which employ various controls and have the design of experiments, yet the experimenter either lacks control over the IV or over allocation of subjects to conditions. One can begin to split hairs over what does and does not count as an experiment. The important point, however, is to recognise limitations in one's design, and the potential for confounding or ambiguity in interpreting results, no matter what the research programme is eventually called.

## CRITICISMS OF THE EXPERIMENT

Many criticisms of the experimental method involve the implicit assumption that the experiment is being carried out in a laboratory. We have already considered the advantages and disadvantages of laboratory research. The following criticisms, then, apply to the experiment as a design, irrespective of where it is carried out, though some carry more weight when applied to the laboratory experiment.

# 1 From within the experimental research tradition

Even those who strongly favour the use of the experimental method have realised that there are very many pitfalls involved in running experiments, some of which are not obvious and have been brought to our attention by sometimes dramatic demonstrations.

Barber (1976) has documented many of these pitfalls and he categorises these into the following groups:

1  Investigator paradigm effect
2  Investigator experimental design effect
3  Investigator loose procedure effect
4  Investigator data analysis effect
5  Investigator fudging effect
6  Experimenter personal attributes effect
7  Experimenter failure to follow the procedure effect
8  Experimenter misrecording effect
9  Experimenter fudging effect
10  Experimenter unintentional expectancy effect

Most of these speak for themselves and several could be applied to non-experimental studies. The 'investigator' is the person with overall control of the research whereas the 'experimenter' is a person carrying out the procedure on each participant, often as a research student or as a paid employee.

Experimenters may fudge results because they are hired for the job and wish to 'succeed' or because they will be compared with others in order to assess EXPERIMENTER RELIABILITY – the extent to which two experimenters' results agree. They may misrecord or fail to follow procedure because the investigator has designed a loose procedure. The personal attributes of experimenters (attractiveness, sex, etc) may well affect participant behaviour. The design which an investigator uses, or their own psychological 'paradigms' (roughly speaking, their theoretical perspective) may well produce different results from other designs. The most notorious investigator fudging in psychological history was conducted by Sir Cyril Burt, as documented by Leon Kamin (1977).

## Experimenter expectancy
Since psychology experiments are carried out by humans on humans, it has been argued that the necessary social interaction which must occur between experimenter and participant makes the psychological experiment different in kind from any other. Is it possible that the experimenter could unintentionally 'give the game away' to the participant? This is Barber's point 10.

Rosenthal (1966) showed that students given groups of 'bright' and 'dull' rats (who were actually randomly mixed for brightness) produced results consistent with the label of their rats. This was originally used to show that experimenter expectancies can even affect the behaviour of laboratory rats. However, Barber argues that the results were almost certainly due to other effects from his list of ten above, such as deviation from procedure.

40 experiments between 1968 and 1976 failed to show evidence of experimenters passing on influence which the investigators tried to produce. However, some studies have shown that experimenters *can* affect participants' responses through facial or verbal cues and that certain participants are more likely to pick up experimenter influence than others, particularly those high in need for approval.

### Demand characteristics

If participants who need approval are affected by experimenter influence, then it suggests that they perhaps wanted to 'please the experimenter' and get the 'right' result. Orne (1962) has talked of DEMAND CHARACTERISTICS as the totality of cues which appear to reveal the experimental hypothesis and which tell the participant what is required of her or him.

In fact, Weber and Cook (1972) found little evidence that participants *do* try to respond as they think the experimenter might wish. Masling (1966) has even suggested that, knowing the experimental aims, behaviour might be altered away from expectancy – the 'screw you' effect. Research suggests, however, that most participants try to appear normal and competent since they are concerned about how their behaviour will be judged. This may well influence them to behave as naturally as possible and show that they cannot be influenced.

It must be emphasised that *any* research study, experiment or not, in so far as participants are aware of the research aims, can be affected by some of the variables implied by 'demand characteristics'. Perhaps the closeness of the researcher, and the awesome surroundings, make their effect more salient in the traditional laboratory experiment.

### Removing bias – blinds and double blinds

Investigators usually do not want their participants to be aware of the experimental aim. Deception may well have to be employed to keep them in the dark and the moral implications of this are discussed in the chapter on ethics. Keeping participants in the dark is known as the employment of a 'single blind' procedure. But it has been argued here that experimenters may transmit cues. Hence, it makes sense to keep experimenters in the dark too. The employment of a 'double blind' procedure does just that – experimenters, or those who gather results directly from the participants, are not told the true experimental aims. Where a placebo group is used, for example, neither the participants, nor the data gatherers may know who has received the real treatment.

## 2 The humanist objection

I pointed out in chapter 1 that people involved in psychology experiments have traditionally been referred to as 'subjects'. Humanist psychologists have argued that this is a reflection of the experimentalists' attitude to humans and human research. It implies that the researcher holds, perhaps implicitly, a 'mechanistic' model of humans. Heather (1976) has claimed that 'Human beings continue to be regarded by psychologists as some kind of helpless clockwork puppet, jerked into life only when something happens to it.' Hampden-Turner (1971) states '. . . power over people in a laboratory can *only* lead . . . to a technology of behaviour control.' (italics in original). Such objectors to the experimental method would normally be found in the qualitative research method 'camp' already introduced.

**Key terms for this chapter**

Single and double blind    Experiment    *Ex post facto* research
Correlational study    Field    Investigation
Demand characteristics    Laboratory    Observational study
Experimenter expectancy    Natural
Experimenter reliability    Pseudo
   Quasi

**Exercises**

1 State whether the following are laboratory experiments, natural experiments, field experiments or other investigations:

   (a) A ladder is placed against a street wall to see whether more males or females will avoid it
   (b) Boys with no brother and boys with two brothers are observed under laboratory conditions to see which group exhibits greater aggression
   (c) A researcher, dressed either casually or smart, approaches passengers at a station to ask for directions. The aim is to see whether smart dress elicits greater help
   (d) Under laboratory conditions, people are asked to make a speech, contrary to their own view, first alone and then in front of others
   (e) The study described in (b) is extended. One group of boys is subjected to frustration and then observed again for level of aggression
   (f) Drug addicts are compared with a control group on their tolerance of pain, measured in the laboratory
   (g) Researchers visit various grades of worker at their place of employment and take them through a questionnaire on their attitude to authority. It is thought the more highly-paid will express greater respect for authority
   (h) One of two very similar homes for the elderly passes from local government to private control. Workers in each are compared on job satisfaction over the following year, using informal interviews.

2 Of the designs outlined in 1:

   (a) Which are not likely to be affected by demand characteristics?
   (b) Which might involve looser procedures?
   (c) Which are subject to researcher bias?
   (d) In which could 'blind' procedures be employed?

3 You are discussing with a colleague two methods of measuring 'conformity'. One involves recording how often people will answer a simple question wrongly when several other people in the room have already answered wrongly (laboratory study). The other involves stopping people in the street who have infringed a traffic light or litter regulation and taking those who agree to it through a short questionnaire (field study). Find arguments for and against each proposal – I hope you can think of at least three for and three against each. Pages 43 to 45 of this chapter should provide the general information you need.

# The experimental method II

## EXPERIMENTAL DESIGNS

Julie:   It really infuriates me. I drive really smoothly on my own, completely in control; then Susie gets in and I do stupid things like crash gears and stall.

Pete:   Yeah?

Julie:   Right! I'm sure people perform worse when someone important's watching them.

Pete:   Well I'm not. I play pool better when Nikki's around.

Julie:   Perhaps it depends on what you're like. Perhaps extraverteds (or whatever you call 'em) do better and intrawhatsits do worse. I wonder if people in the middle aren't affected.

(Julie went on to take 'A' level psychology and a degree!)

Let's suppose we decide to check out Julie's first hypothesis. It predicts that people perform sensori-motor tasks worse in the presence of an audience. Let's set up a laboratory experiment.

We need to operationalise. We need:   a sensori-motor task
                                   an audience
                                   a measure of performance

We could ask people to move a metal ring along one of those wiggly wire contraptions you see at village fêtes. They have to avoid touching the wire with the ring as they move. If they do touch, a buzzer sounds and an error is recorded – this is our measure of performance by which we can assess 'improvement' quantitatively (and our DV). Let's suppose we run the experiment with everyone doing the test in condition A first – performing the task in front of an audience of 12 observers. In the second condition (B) they perform the task in a quiet, soundproof room, alone. There are significantly less errors in the second condition.

## REPEATED MEASURES DESIGN

The design above would be known as REPEATED MEASURES in the language of experimental design. The measure (of doing the wiggly wire test) is *repeated* on each person under the various conditions of the IV. If the subjects are the same for both conditions, and all other variables are controlled, any differences, we assume, (though we could be wrong), must be the effect of the IV.

Just to check, what is the independent variable?

*Table 2   Related and unrelated designs*

| Design | In each condition: | |
|---|---|---|
| | **Same subject(s)** | **Different subjects** |
| **Related** | Repeated measures | Matched pairs |
| **Unrelated** | Single subject | Independent samples |

Well, the recommendation in the last section was to look for the conditions which were varied. In this case then, the IV must be the variation between conditions: presence or not of an audience.

## Related designs

The repeated measures design is one of a set known as RELATED DESIGNS – (see table 2) – 'related' because, when results are presented, a value in one condition is directly related to a value in the other condition, in this case, because both belong to the same person and can therefore be directly compared.

Repeated measures design can also be known as WITHIN GROUPS or BETWEEN CONDITIONS, the latter term displaying the logic of the repeated measures design.

## We've proved it, Pete!

Suppose we report our result to Pete. He is unimpressed. He says 'Well, the way you did it, I'm not at all surprised they did better in the second condition.'

> What is he on about? What has he spotted? What might be responsible for people's improvement in condition B other than the presence of the audience?

## Order effects

You probably realised that there is a possible confounding variable at work here. People might improve on the second condition because they've had some practice (and they may be less anxious about learning a new task). If they had performed worse on the second go this might have been through becoming disheartened by failure, through boredom or through fatigue.

Constant error caused by the order in which subjects participate in conditions is known as an ORDER EFFECT. This is one of the major disadvantages of a repeated measures design.

> Can you make a list now of some solutions to this problem? How can a researcher design an experiment which avoids the contamination of order effects?

## Dealing with order effects

**1 Counterbalancing**   If all subjects' performances on condition B could be improved because of the experience in condition A, it makes sense to have half the subjects perform condition B first. This is known as COUNTERBALANC-ING the conditions.

Would this in fact eliminate the order effect? Well, no it wouldn't. Practice, if it is effective, will still produce improvement, but this will improve half the scores in condition A and half in condition B. Hence the improvements should cancel each other out overall. Suppose that each person improves by making five less errors on average in the condition they took second. If we had four people doing the with-audience/without-audience order, and four taking the conditions in the opposite order we could imagine that this is what was going on:

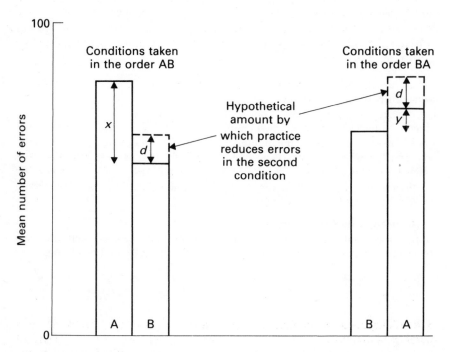

*Figure 9    Counterbalancing*

The overall reduction from condition A to condition B contains an extra component as a result of practice when subjects take the with-audience condition (A) first. The whole difference is shown as X, and the extra component as d. When conditions are taken in the opposite direction, the reduction through practice on condition A causes the overall difference to be smaller than it should be through manipulation of the IV alone. If there is a real difference in performance caused by the audience presence, however, it should show in the combined difference, X + Y, which should represent the average difference for all subjects with practice effects balanced out of this final average. (Because X + Y = (X − d) + (Y + d); the two differences which would have occurred without the practice effect).

Note:   It is easy to get fooled into thinking that, because the design involves splitting subjects into two groups, we have an independent samples design (see below). The splitting is solely for the purpose of counterbalancing. For each subject we still have a pair of scores which are therefore related – one for each condition. Each subject is still taking both conditions.

*Asymmetrical order effects* This perfect sounding arrangement may be upset though if the practice effect occurring when taking one order of conditions is not equivalent to that produced by the other order.

For instance, suppose that in the without-audience condition it is possible to concentrate on improvement and that this transfers to the audience condition. However, when the audience is present in the first condition, all one's concentration goes on coping with the audience and no improvement in technique is transferred to the without-audience condition. Counterbalancing now loses its evening-out effect and we have the constant error of practice affecting the with-audience condition only. If this were the case we would end up with an artificially small difference overall.

Note: 'asymmetrical' just means 'not symmetrical' – the effect is not evenly balanced between the two groups.

## 2 Complex counterbalancing

### (a) ABBA
(Not an ageing Swedish pop group!) All subjects take conditions in the order stated. Their score on A is taken as the mean of the two A conditions and likewise for B. This arrangement can still suffer from an asymmetrical effect, though it should be weakened.

### (b) Multi-condition designs
If an experiment has three conditions we might divide subjects into six groups and have them take part in the following orders of condition:

ABC ACB BAC
BCA CAB CBA

**3 Randomisation of condition order** Some experiments involve quite a number of conditions. For instance, a sensori-motor task may be performed under six different lighting conditions. Each subject would be given the conditions in a different random order.

**4 Randomisation of stimulus items** This is an elegant way to deal with possible order effects in a two-condition experiment. Suppose we want to see whether concrete words are easier to recall than abstract words. Instead of giving the same group of people a list of concrete words to learn and recall, then a list of abstract words, we can give them just one list with concrete and abstract words randomly mixed together. Note that this could be a way to mix even three conditions together but either the list gets rather long or we have less of each item in the list, in which case we might present several such mixed lists in several trials.

**5 Elapsed time** We can leave enough time between conditions for any learning or fatigue effects to dissipate.

**6 Using another design** We may have to give up the idea of using the same group for each condition. We could have separate groups. We would then move to an 'independent samples design', described below, but, since this design has important disadvantages we might try to resist this more drastic solution to the problem of order effect.

### Other disadvantages with repeated measures design

- If each subject participates in both conditions of, say, a memory experiment using word lists, we have to use a different list in each condition. This involves us in the problem of choosing words for each list which are equivalent. It is possible to obtain lists which give the frequency of occurrence of words in the written English language, obtained through literature surveys.

- The aim of the experiment may become obvious to the subject. They may then try hard to 'please the experimenter' by performing in accordance with what they perceive as the research aim or, of course, they just might try to defeat the object!

- Subjects must be available for both conditions. If conditions are weeks apart some subjects may be lost.

When *not* to use a repeated measures design:

1 When order effects cannot be eliminated or are asymmetrical.

2 When people should be naive for each condition. Leeper (1935) showed that people can be influenced to see one or the other of the two women in Boring's ambiguous woman picture (in Gross, 1987) by showing them one unambiguous version first. Obviously these same subjects cannot now be biased to see the other woman in a comparable manner.

3 Research often involves an independent variable which is a category of persons, such as male/female, working class/middle class or extrovert/ introvert. In this case we are comparing the performances of two different groups of people and a repeated measures design is obviously not possible.

4 We administer a 'treatment' to one group and need to compare their subsequent performance with a control and/or placebo group. For instance, we might wish to assess the effect of a programme designed to sensitise children to the needs of persons with disabilities. We need a control group to compare the 'treatment' children's development with.

# INDEPENDENT SAMPLES DESIGN

Suppose then that we select two groups of people (not randomly, but from whom we can get – student colleagues on our course and the biology course who share statistics classes). One group do the with-audience condition, the other group do the task alone. Again we get a significant increase in the without-audience condition.

We are now conducting what is known as an INDEPENDENT SAMPLES design experiment. This title says just what it means. An entirely different group of people take each condition (there could be three conditions or more). It belongs to a category known as UNRELATED DESIGNS, since the scores from one group of subjects, who undergo just one condition of the IV, are quite unrelated to the scores from another group who participate in the other condition of the IV.

Examples of independent samples designs would be:

1 One group are given a list of words and asked to repeat each word several times ('rehearse') before receiving the next item. A second group are asked to form

vivid mental images of each item and to make links between each item and its successor. Both groups are tested for retention in a free recall task.

2 The social skills of children who have experienced an experimental pre-school education programme are compared with a control group who have not. This could be a natural, field experiment, unless the researcher set the programme up.

Unfortunately, this design also comes with a variety of other titles. The ones I have come across, in order of the frequency with which I have encountered them, are: INDEPENDENT SUBJECTS, INDEPENDENT GROUPS, and BETWEEN GROUPS.

## It worked again Pete!
So what could doubting Pete say this time? He certainly has something to say. Before we hear it . . .

> What might now be responsible for the difference between conditions? What might cause one group to do worse, other than the fact that they performed in front of an audience? Also list any other disadvantages you can see in this design.

Pete says, 'Who did the experiment?' We tell him. He smirks, 'Ah! Remember you said, Julie, that introverts might be worse performers in front of an audience? Well, you know how introverted the biology mob are. Did you make sure you had equal numbers of them in each group?'

## Subject variables
The major weakness with the independent samples design is that any differences in the DV between two conditions can be attributed to differences between the two subject groups. This is colloquially known as the problem of SUBJECT VARIABLES.

Suppose, in example 1 above, we accidentally placed more experienced memorisers in the imagery group. Or suppose that our selection of children for the experimental programme just happened to include more socially skilled children.

In other words, rather than the independent variable being responsible for any differences in the dependent variable, the DV differences might be produced by variation between the subject groups.

## Dealing with subject variables
In an independent samples design it would always be difficult to rule out subject variables as a possible source of variation in our results, but there are certain steps we can take to reduce the likelihood that they were the cause of differences found:

## Pre-test of subjects
We can show that both groups were similar in performance before the experimental conditions were applied. For instance, for the pre-school children we would have to ensure that the average social skill performance was about equal in both groups.

In the memory study, both groups could be pre-tested on the same stimulus list, different from that used in the experimental trial. There still could be a subject variable problem. Though both groups might perform equally well on the pre-test list, the list for the experiment trial might contain words more familiar to people in the one group. There might, say, be several geographical terms and more geography students in the imagery group.

### Random allocation of subjects to conditions

We would expect there not to be significantly more geography students in one group because we would allocate subjects to each of the experimental groups (or the control and experimental groups in some experiments) on a random basis only (see chapter 3). However, random allocation being quite unpredictable by definition, odd combinations can still occur.

### Representative allocation

We can ensure that each group contains half the males, a similar age range, a fairly similar range of educational backgrounds and so on. It might not strike us, however, to ensure an equal number of geography students. Inspection of the list might alert us to this possible confounding variable, but we can't balance the groups for every conceivable variable.

We must decide intuitively, given the nature of the research topic and aims, which variables are going to be the most important to balance for. Pete thinks we should have paid attention to his stereotype of the biology students. Within each relevant category chosen (male, female, psychology student etc.) which we decide is relevant, allocation of half the category to one condition and half to the other would be performed on a random basis. The reasoning and method here are similar to that of stratified sampling.

### Other disadvantages of independent samples design

- To obtain as many scores in each condition we have to find and test twice the number of subjects. This can be costly and time-consuming. We do have the advantage (over repeated measures design), however, that we can't lose subjects between conditions and we can run the two conditions simultaneously rather than having to wait until practice effects have worn off.

- If there is too much difference between the statistical variances of the two groups, we may not proceed with a parametric test – the most powerful of statistical tests (see chapters 13 and 16).

## MATCHED-PAIRS DESIGN

We can actually do more than just ensure that the two groups for our research are roughly equivalent on relevant variables like extroversion. We can *pair* one person in the audience condition with a person in the no-audience condition. The two people can be *matched* for extroversion score, age, sex, occupation and any other variable thought to be relevant to wiggly-wire performance.

This compromise between the two designs so far discussed is known as the MATCHED-PAIRS design.

For each member of one group we put a paired subject in the other group. We pair people on the basis of relevant variables, the choice of what is relevant being, as before, based on the nature of the research. We now avoid order effects by having different groups in each condition, but we are also, we hope, keeping subject variables to a minimum.

We might, for example, pair each child who is to receive the experimental pre-school programme with a child in the control group on the basis of, say, exact age, sex, ethnic group, social and economic background of parents and number of children in family.

The matched-pairs design falls into the category of *related designs* since each subject's score or rating in one group can be related to a score in the other group. This obviously can't be done where two sets of scores come from two unmatched groups.

One of nature's most useful gifts to psychological researchers is, some believe, the existence of identical (monozygotic) twins. These represent the perfect matched pair – when they're just born at least. Any differences between them later in life can fairly safely be attributed to differences in environmental experience. The converse is not true, however. Similarities cannot be attributed to common genetic make-up, since identical twins usually share fairly similar environments too.

# SINGLE SUBJECT DESIGN

To hear of just one person being used for experimental research can make the scientifically minded recoil in horror. Surely this must produce quite unrepresentative results, impossible to generalise with? Quite rightly, they assume, one turns to objective psychological research in order to avoid the many generalisations which the lay person often makes from their own limited experience.

However, consider a physical scientist who obtains just one sample of weird moonrock from a returning space mission. The rock could be tested for amount of expansion at different temperatures, in a vacuum and in normal atmosphere, in order to detect significant changes in its behaviour. This would yield valuable scientific knowledge in itself.

Further, from our general knowledge of the world of rocks we could fairly safely assume that similar rock would exist on the moon. In the same way there are some sorts of things which people do which, we know for good reason, are likely to vary according to the same *pattern* (but not necessarily at the same level) for almost everyone. An example of this might be the experimental situation in which someone has to make decisions from an increasing number of alternatives – sorting cards according to colour, then suit and so on.

Ebbinghaus carried out an enormous number of memory experiments on himself using a wide variation of conditions and lists of nonsense syllables. The introspectionists used single subjects – people highly trained to report on feelings and sensations.

### Related or unrelated?
A set of results for a single subject in an experiment, which measures reaction times as the dependent variable, might look like:

Table 3   Single subject design

| Condition A | Condition B |
|---|---|
| 0.579 secs | 0.713 secs |
| 0.621 | 0.615 |
| 0.543 | 0.792 |
| . . . . | . . . . |
| . . . . | . . . . |
| . . . . | . . . . |

*Box 3   Summary of advantages and disadvantages of the various experimental designs*

| Design | Advantages | Disadvantages | Remedy (if any) |
|---|---|---|---|
| **Repeated Measures** | Subject variables eliminated<br><br>More economical on subjects | Order effects<br><br>May not be able to conduct second condition immediately<br><br>Need different stimulus lists etc. | Counterbalance/ randomise conditions<br>Leave long time gap between conditions<br>Do independent samples instead<br><br>Randomise stimulus materials |
| | Homogeneity of variance not a problem (see chapter 15)<br><br>Need fewer subjects | Subjects not naïve for second condition and may try to guess aim<br><br>Loss of subjects between conditions | Deceive subjects as to aim (or leave long time gap) |
| **Independent Samples** | No order effects<br><br>Subjects can't guess aim of experiment<br><br>Can use exactly the same stimulus lists etc.<br><br>No need to wait for subjects to 'forget' first condition | Subject variables not controlled<br><br>Less economical on subjects<br><br>Lack of 'homogeneity of variance' may prevent use of parametric test (chapter 15) | Random allocation of subjects to conditions |
| **Matched Pairs** | No order effects<br><br>Subject variables partly controlled<br><br>No wait for subjects to forget<br><br>Can use same stimulus lists etc.<br><br>Homogeneity of variance not a problem | Some subject variables still present<br><br>Hard to find perfect matches and therefore time-consuming<br><br>Loss of one member of pair entails loss of whole pair | Randomly allocate pairs to conditions |
| **Single Subject** | Useful where few subjects available and/or a lot of time required for training subject | Can't generalise to other subject categories with confidence<br><br>Retraining required if original subject leaves project | Treat subject very nicely! |

Is this data produced from a related design? Contrary to our probable first conclusion of 'yes', the answer is in fact 'no'! Each score in condition A has no *particular* partner in condition B. A particular score in A is related to *all* the scores in B to an equal degree, since the same person produced them all. But, in a related design, the first score in A (0·579) would be *uniquely* related to the first in B (0·713) because this was the only B score which the same person produced or because the B score was produced by the person matched with the first A person. Another way of seeing this is that it would be quite possible to have more scores in condition B than there are in condition A.

## Key terms for this chapter

Asymetrical-order effects
Between conditions
Between groups
Counterbalancing
  AB & BA
  ABBA
Independent groups
Independent samples design
Independent subjects

Matched-pairs design
Order effects
Related and unrelated designs
Repeated-measures design
Single-subject design
Within groups

## Exercises

1  In Fantz's famous 'looking-chamber' experiment, a baby is shown two patterns and the researcher records how much time is spent looking at either pattern. The idea is to see whether the baby prefers complex patterns to simpler ones. What is the independent variable, the dependent variable and what sort of design is this?

2  In one version of the 'visual cliff' experiment, infants are observed while their mothers try to entice them to come to them across a glass sheet with a large drop beneath it. What condition can be added to make this a true experiment and what sort of design would the experiment then be?

3  Your tutor conducts an experiment on your class. Each student is given a set of anagrams to solve and the time to solve each one is taken. You find that some of the anagrams were of concrete words and the others were of abstract words. This was the IV. What design was this, and what special precaution, associated with this design, has your tutor wisely taken and why?

4  Again your tutor conducts an experiment. Students are in pairs. You time your partner while she learns a finger maze, first with the left hand, then with the right. She then times you while you learn first with the right, then the left. What design is this? What special precaution is taken and why?

5  What design was Watson's famous classical conditioning study on 'Little Albert'?

6  A researcher looks for families in which there are two brothers or two sisters born within a year of each other and where one sibling has suffered a certain illness before four years old. They are tested at eight years old to see whether the illness child is poorer than the other on number and reading skills. What sort of design is being employed here?

# Observational methods

## 1  INTRODUCTION

We have seen that there can be fairly serious problems with the use of the experimental method in psychology, particularly in the laboratory where a very narrow, and perhaps artificial, selection of behaviour may be studied, where 'demand characteristics' may distort the procedure and where persons studied are 'dehumanised'. A set of methods which can avoid some, but not always all, of these criticisms is the set known generally as 'observational methods'.

In a sense, behaviour is observed in every psychological study. A researcher makes observations on the participants' reaction times, answers to a questionnaire, memory performance and so on.

The emphasis, in using the term 'observational', however, is on the researcher observing *a relatively unconstrained segment of a person's freely chosen behaviour*.

There is ambiguity in the use of the term 'observational' in research literature. It can refer to the use of observation as a *technique* for gathering data about behaviour in a study which might in general be referred to as an experimental design. On the other hand, 'observational' might refer to the overall *design* of a study, in contrast to a controlled experiment.

### Observation as a technique or as an overall design

**As technique**  Observation may be used as a *technique* within a traditional experimental design, as in Milgram's (1963) work on obedience where, in addition to mechanical recordings of subjects' responses, film record was made in order to observe changes in emotional reactions. We have previously described Bandura's studies on children's imitations of models for aggression. Using observation as a technique for measuring the dependent variable of aggression, Bandura was able to manipulate a variety of independent variables, including the status or role of the model, the consequences of the model's behaviour and the degree of frustration experienced by the child just prior to observing the aggressive model.

The two examples above employ observational techniques in a laboratory setting. Field experiments very often use observation as a technique. Friedrich and Stein's study, described below, is a good example. Observation may also be employed within a role play or simulation study, described below.

**As overall design**  If an investigation is given the title 'observational', this is usually in order to *contrast* it with other designs, particularly the experimental. In this case, the researcher has chosen to observe naturally occurring behaviour and *not* to experiment with it, i.e. no independent variable is manipulated. A hypothesis concerning an independent variable may nevertheless be tested, as when, for instance, an investigator observes the fantasy play of middle- and working-class children and predicts differences in amount or content.

## Weakness of pure observational studies

Where the overall design is observational we have the weakness, outlined earlier, that if we discover a relationship between different sets of data we are not usually in a position to establish cause-effect relationships with any confidence, since manipulated IV has not led to changes in the DV.

Suppose we observe higher levels of aggression among children who choose and watch more violent television programmes. Does the television promote their aggression or does their aggression (arising from some other cause) affect their choice? A controlled experiment might provide enlightenment.

In an earlier chapter we saw that Friedrich and Stein (1972) assigned children to three experimental conditions – violent, pro-social and neutral television viewing programmes. After a month's viewing it was observed that the violent programme group were significantly more aggressive in nursery-school play. Interestingly, the impact was greatest on those children who were initially highest in aggression.

An experiment, then, can back up a hypothesis formed from observation, by showing a fairly clear-cut causal effect. Note that the experiment above uses observation as a *technique* in a natural 'field' setting.

# 2 PARTICIPANT AND NON-PARTICIPANT OBSERVATION

A PARTICIPANT OBSERVER is to some extent a part of the group of individuals being observed, whereas a NON-PARTICIPANT OBSERVER observes from a distance and should have no effect on the behaviour being observed. This is a 'dimension', since there are varying degrees of participation and these are described later on. There is also a dimensional aspect to DISCLOSURE in that persons observed can be more or less aware of the exact extent to which, or reasons for which, they are being observed. Coupling the extremes of these two dimensions, we can obtain the examples of studies shown in table 4.

*Table 4    Chart for data gathering*

| | | | | | Playing with others: | | |
|---|---|---|---|---|---|---|---|
| Child | Inactive | Reading | Playing alone | Looking on | Different activity | Same activity | Co-operative activity |
| A | | | | | | | |
| B | | | | | | | |
| C | | | | | | | |
| D | | | | | | | |
| E | | | | | | | |
| F | | | | | | | |

The discussion of indirect, structured and controlled observation which follows is related entirely to non-participant studies. Participant observation is largely a qualitative approach and will be discussed later in the chapter.

# 3　STRUCTURED (OR 'SYSTEMATIC') OBSERVATIONS

## Data gathering devices
Records of behaviour can be made using any or a mixture of the following devices:

– Film or video recording
– Still camera
– Audio tape (to record spoken observations)
– Hand-written notes, ratings or coding 'on the spot'

Visual recording has the advantage that behaviour can be analysed (rated or coded) after the event at any required pace.

All the methods above might be used discreetly such that the participant is either completely unaware of the recording process (in which case ethical issues arise) or at least unable to see or hear the equipment during the observation session. This can be achieved with the use of screens or 'one-way' mirrors through which observers or the camera, but not the participant, can see.

## Data gathering systems
Observers may often work to a specific 'grid' of behavioural categories, such as that shown below. On the chart in table 4, observers of children's behaviour during a free-play nursery session, might record the amount of time that each child spent in each of the particular activities categorised (in columns).

In addition to simply recording *what* behaviour occurs, and how often, observers may be required to:

RATE behaviour according to a structured scale – for instance one to ten on 'showing interest'
CODE　behaviour according to a set of coding categories – for instance, graphic symbols which represent the positions of parts of the body

In each case, some degree of standardisation would normally be sought by giving observers intensive training prior to commencement of observation sessions.

## Time, point and event sampling
It may not always be possible or appropriate to record complete sequences of behaviour and interaction using video. If a session must be observed 'live', several observers might be required, one or two for each person observed. Where only one or a few observers are available, TIME SAMPLING techniques can be employed, in which observations of each individual are made for several short periods in say, a two-hour session. In some cases, the short periods of, say, 15 seconds, are consecutive, so that a picture of the frequency of behaviour is built up.

In POINT SAMPLING an observer concentrates on each individual in a group just long enough to record the category of their current behaviour before going on to observe the next person.

In EVENT SAMPLING observations are made of a specific event each time it occurs, for instance, each example of a 'fight', however this is operationally defined for the research in progress.

### Reliability of observational techniques

Observers need to produce reliable observational records. The reliability of observers can be established by correlating (chapter 17) their records with those of another observer or team. Such comparison will produce a measure of INTER-RATER RELIABILITY, 'rater' being another term for an observer who 'rates' behaviour.

Reliability may be low because of OBSERVER BIAS. From the psychology of perception we know that each person's view of a situation is unique and that our perceptions can be biased by innumerable factors. An untrained observer might readily *evaluate* behaviour which the researcher wants reported as objectively as possible. Where the trained observer reports a hard blow, the novice might describe this as 'vicious'.

There may be human error in failing to observe some bits of behaviour at all. One is reminded of the 'blind' soccer referee or ice-skating judge. In the study of animals it is easy to 'see' human characteristics in animal behaviour. This is known as 'anthropomorphism' and occurs, for instance, when birds are said to be 'talking' or a cat to be 'smiling'. In human studies, it could be falsely assumed that Jason 'follows' an adult (and is perhaps insecure) when he happens to be walking in the same direction. Or Jenny might be mistakenly described as 'copying' when she looks into a box to see what it was Sarah was looking at.

The problem may not lie with the human observers, however, but with the rating scale they are given which could be too vague or ambiguous. Reliability is enhanced by specifying in advance precisely what behavioural acts are to count in particular categories. Observers have to decide, for instance, when a push counts as aggressive or when a child is 'demanding'. Observers are usually trained to a standard of reliability and accuracy *before* the observational study proper begins.

# 4 CONTROLLED OBSERVATION

Observations can be controlled through structure as outlined above. Control can also be exercised over the environment in which observations take place. A high degree of environmental control can be exercised in the laboratory, though the participant need not be acutely aware that the environment *is* a 'laboratory'. Discussion groups may be observed in a comfortable 'seminar room', for instance. Mary Ainsworth (1971), mentioned earlier, conducted a programme of research into infants' stranger and separation anxiety. In this study, the floor of a carefully organised playroom was marked into squares and trained observers recorded on film (and by speaking onto audiotape) the movements of a child when its mother left and a stanger entered the room. The infant's behaviour was also filmed and the results were related to events of sensitivity in mothers' interactions with their children.

# 5   OBJECTIONS TO CONTROL – NATURALISTIC OBSERVATION

Studies in the laboratory do not escape many of the criticisms of laboratory experiments made earlier, in the sense that the laboratory can be a highly artificial, possibly inhibiting atmosphere. Behaviour in the normal social context cannot be observed here. Some researchers, in order to record more usual, everyday behaviour, go out into the field and make 'naturalistic' observations in, say, the home, the nursery or the workplace. The method was inherited by psychology largely from the ethologists (Lorenz, Tinbergen) who studied animals in their natural habitat but nevertheless made very detailed and accurate recordings of what they showed to be instinctive patterns of behaviour.

The early 'baby biographers', whom we shall encounter when discussing the 'diary method' below, were carrying out naturalistic observations, as did Piaget on his own children. Perhaps these studies also incorporated a certain amount of participative involvement on the part of the observers, however!

Because the behaviour observed in these studies, so long as the observer is discreet, would have occurred anyway, it is said to be very high in ecological validity. In some studies, however, persons are aware that they are being observed. This can mean a video camera following them around the house for instance. In this case we still have the problem of possibly distorted behaviour. As Shaffer (1985) describes:

> 'Consider the experiences of one graduate student who attempted to take pictures of children's playground antics. What he recorded in many of his photos was somewhat less than spontaneous play. For example, one child who was playing alone with a doll jumped up when the student approached with the camera and informed him that he should take a picture of her 'new trick' on the monkey bars. Another child . . . said 'Get this' as he broke away from the kickball game and laid a blindside tackle on an unsuspecting onlooker'

What researchers *can* do is to become a predictable and familiar part of the environment. For instance, Charlesworth and Hartup (1967) made several visits to a nursery school, interacted with the children, learnt their names and so on. This also gave them the opportunity to test out and improve the reliability of the observation scheme they were going to employ.

Examples of research studies, from the general literature, which used naturalistic observation would be:

Brown *et al.* (1964) – study of Adam, Eve and Sarah's speech productions in the home with parents every one or two weeks for several years

Caldwell & Bradley (1978) – developed the Home Observation for Measurement of the Environment (HOME) inventory, which observes parent–child interaction and provision of play materials, to be correlated with levels of intellectual development.

List the advantages and disadvantages of naturalistic observation as you understand it.

*Box 4  Advantages and disadvantages of naturalistic observation*

| Advantages | Disadvantages |
|---|---|
| The behaviour which occurs is more natural and is (if the target is unaware of the observer) unaffected by anxiety or the target's need to impress. | Extraneous variables are poorly controlled, if at all |
| | There is greater potential for observer bias, since both extraneous variables and the observed behaviour are more unpredictable |
| There is high ecological validity | |
| This approach is useful where: | It is difficult to transport and use discretely some of the technical equipment required for good recordings. |
| It would be unethical to experiment with, or intervene in the lives of, children or animals. | |
| Individuals would be unlikely to co-operate with interview or questionnaire methods | It is difficult sometimes for observers to remain hidden. |
| | Thorough replication is harder to achieve |
| The researcher decides that the full social context is necessary for the observed behaviour to carry meaning | If it uses a structured data gathering system it has the disadvantages of structured observation outlined below |

# 6  OBJECTIONS TO STRUCTURED OBSERVATION

Because observation can be so structured and rigid, it would be considered inadequate by groups of (usually social) psychologists who argue against the reduction of behaviour to artificially isolated units. What *is* the smallest unit we can work with? To describe a person as 'lifting an arm' may be objective *physically* but is stripped of social meaning compared with 'she waved', 'he made a bid' or 'she threatened the child'. Reduction to the simplest units of behaviour (the 'molecular' level) can create observations which are numerous, separated and meaningless.

The attempt to firmly categorise interactions or assess responses by number can produce data at the 'reliable but not rich' end of the data-gathering spectrum. This positivist approach would be criticised by, for instance, humanists and phenomenologists, who promote a 'holistic' view of the person in psychology.

Diesing (1972) states that the holist (psychologist) studies a 'whole human system in its natural setting', and says:

'The holist standpoint includes the belief that human systems tend to develop a characteristic wholeness or integrity. They are not simply a loose collection of traits or wants or reflexes or variables of any sort . . .; they have a unity that manifests itself in nearly every part . . . This means that the characteristics of a part are largely determined by the whole to which it belongs and by its particular location in the whole system'

Something is lost, it would be argued, by pigeon-holing responses and simply counting them, or by giving them a rating-scale value. It is more important to record events observed such that the social meaning of actions is preserved for analysis. This may mean recording as much as possible of the social context in which actions occurred. It may also mean making a comprehensive record of an individual's behaviour, such that specific actions are understood and perceived within the pattern of that person's unique experiences and motivation. It is not possible to do this using a highly constraining 'grid' or other pre-constructed framework for observation. We now turn to methods which attempt to generate a richer account of human behaviour in initially unquantified, descriptive form; that is, QUALITATIVE data.

# 7  QUALITATIVE NON-PARTICIPANT OBSERVATION

In Ainsworth's study, described above, some of the observers produced a running commentary on each child's behaviour by speaking into a tape recorder as they watched. The same technique has been used by observers following the interactions of mothers and children in their own home. This generates a lot of raw data in qualitative form. These studies however are not usually conducted under the holistic banner. Rigid structure may be imposed on the data, during analysis, by independent raters trained in the ways already mentioned.

Some studies of this sort, though, do go further along the qualitative route. The unquantified, descriptive data may not be simply categorised or coded. The data may also be analysed for illuminative insights leading to fresh research topics. Or they may be presented alongside quantitative analysis in order to illustrate qualitative differences and issues which numerical reports cannot portray. It is even possible that the *sorts* of observation made might change as the study progresses as a result of FORMATIVE revision of method; where feedback from early observations informs the researcher on optimum ways to proceed. The more the aim of the study tends away from purely positivist analysis, the more the data gathered become susceptible to the qualitative methods outlined in chapter 9.

# 8  ROLE-PLAY AND SIMULATION

Discussion of these methods is situated here because, although some observations of role-play have been relatively pre-structured, the tendency has been to develop categories and models from fairly free-flowing, unrestricted participant behaviour and speech. In some cases, participants *observe* role-plays (non-active role), but, by and large, it is participants' role-playing which is observed (active role).

The techniques have been used for a long time in psychological research, particularly in the area of social psychology, but their use became highlighted when they were advocated as an alternative to the use of gross experimental deception during the 1970s.

### Active role
The study might require active role playing within a simulated social setting, such as being asked to get to know a stranger. Participants may take on a specific role – being chairperson of a group making risky decisions. Participants have been asked to role-play in juries of various sizes, under varying pressures, whilst dynamics of the situation are recorded. These may be, for instance, the informal rules which are developed in the group (Davis *et al.*, 1975).

People have been asked to simulate various emotional feelings and accompanying behavioural expressions.

In all these cases observations may be made at the time or behaviour filmed for subsequent detailed analysis.

## Non-active role

Participants may be asked to watch a role-play or simulated performance and then be asked to report feelings, reactions or suggestions as to how the depicted scene might continue. They may be asked how they would behave in the continuing situation.

In this case, the simulation simply serves as material for what is basically a question-asking method belonging in the next chapter. One approach, the one which started the controversy over experimental deception, is worth mentioning. Mixon (1979) was analysing Milgram's famous studies on 'destructive obedience' – for an account of this experimental paradigm, see chapter 20. Mixon's objection was partly moral but also that the true social situation, for the subject in Milgram's experiment, had not been thoroughly understood.

Milgram described the experiment to many other people, very few of whom said they would expect anyone to continue obeying the experimenter in giving electric shocks to an obviously suffering 'learner'. Mixon argued that Milgram made it obvious to these people that the experiment was really about 'destructive obedience'. Mixon gave his participants scripts of the experiment to read *with no clue* what the real experimental aims were. He asked them to describe how they thought the experiment would continue. He then altered the scripts with different groups. Only when the script included the experimenter seeming a little concerned for the victim did all participants say that they expected the subject to discontinue obedience. Mixon argues that the social context of Milgram's experiment gives strong messages that the norms of scientific professionalism are in place and that no harm can come to the victim (though, obviously, pain is occurring).

In a few cases the participant can be actor *and* audience. Storms (1973) had people engage in a two person interaction which was filmed. They then viewed the film either seeing only their partner or only themselves. This had significant effects upon their attributions of cause to the behaviour observed.

## Purposes of role-play and simulation

Ginsburg (1979) argues that the methods can be used for discovery and verification. In discovery, general observations might be made which lead to more specifically testable hypotheses or models. In verification, hypotheses such as Mixon's can be tested.

Ginsburg thinks that the most valuable use is for illuminating what he calls the 'role/rule framework' under which actions occur. They will not tell us a lot about individuals but perhaps a lot about the rules people assume or invent, and follow, given certain social situations. They may show us how people go about negotiating such rules. They may tell us about sequences and hierarchies of social action.

## Weaknesses of role-play and simulation

Critics, early on, argued that role-play was non-spontaneous and passive; that people would act in socially desirable and superficial ways; and that what people said they would do and what they would do were very different matters.

Proponents argued back that experiments, too, can produce artificial, super-ficial behaviour and that deception itself, of the Milgram variety, introduced unreal conflict, for subjects, between what seemed to be happening and what could be expected to happen in a humane, scientific establishment.

On the issue of spontaneity, several studies are cited as producing very great personal commitment and lack of pretence, perhaps the most dramatic being that of Zimbardo (1972), described briefly in chapter 20, which had to be ended after five of its planned 14 days because 'prison guards' were being so ruthless and callous, whilst 'prisoners' were becoming so submissive and dejected.

# 9  THE DIARY METHOD

Towards the end of the nineteenth century, some academics began to realise that they could not argue endlessly about whether children were born with innate tendencies, 'inherently good' as Rousseau would have claimed, or with Locke's 'tabula rasa' for a mind. They realised that a scientific approach was necessary. The first steps towards this were taken by the 'baby biographers', of whom Charles Darwin (1877) is probably the most notable. The data was a diary of daily observations on the growth and development of his own son. Most diaries were developmental records of the observers' own children. The studies were therefore 'longitudinal' (see chapter 10).

A problem with these diary accounts was that each biographer had their own particular perspective to support and tended to concentrate on quite different aspects of their child's behaviour from other diarists. They also tended not to standardise the intervals between their recordings.

Later, when child development study had become a well-established disci-pline, Piaget kept diaries of the development of his children. He had a thorough model of cognitive development and his observations were used to exemplify aspects of the theory (*not* to 'prove it true'). He developed tests or demon-strations of some characteristics of children's thought at various ages – such as egocentricity – which he then used with other children, employing the CLINICAL METHOD (see chapter 8).

Diaries are also kept during most participant observation studies. Where observation is covert these will be constructed, where possible, at the end of each day, either completely from memory or from any discreetly jotted notes recorded where opportunities have arisen.

In both these uses, the diary method has the great advantage that the observed persons are acting quite naturally, particularly so in the case of babies, since they are at home with their own parents. This must be a source of some of the richest, most genuine and intimate data in the business!

A further, unusual use of diaries has occurred in participative research (see chapter 11) where participants themselves keep diaries of their activities and perceptions throughout a study. The researcher then subjects the diary content to some form of content analysis. Rajesh Tandon (1981) did this in a study aimed at improving peer group organisation and initiative taking in a rural agricultural training and modernisation programme. He found that questionnaire data gathered was often at odds with the diary records, the latter being far more congruent with the researcher's own field notes.

*Box 5   Advantages and disadvantages of the traditional diary method*

| Advantages | Disadvantages |
|---|---|
| Rich, genuine information<br>Natural surroundings<br>Subject of observation completely relaxed<br>Simple to conduct if in observer's own<br>home | Observer bias can be high<br>Comparison with other diary studies<br>difficult because of variation in emphasis<br>Single subject only – can't generalise<br>Commitment to quite long-term study |

# 10  PARTICIPANT OBSERVATION

It follows from the line of argument above that a more authentic observation of people can be made by being involved in their day-to-day interactions within their normal network of human group relationships. The meaning of their behaviour should then be more accessible to the observer for ecologically valid recording. Whether these objectives can be achieved in a manner which would still count as scientific is a matter of heated debate and one which will be evaluated later on.

The degree to which an observer can participate in the group being studied is a continuum according to Patton (1980). He distinguishes between the following:

**Full participant**   The observer's true research role is hidden ('undisclosed') and members take him/her as an authentic member of the group. Hence, secrets may well be disclosed. However, Douglas (1972) argues that a respected and trusted researcher may be handed secrets that a real member might not receive for fear that the real member could use these against the divulger.

**Participant as observer**   The participant's observational role is not hidden but 'kept under wraps'. It is not seen to be the main reason for the participant's presence. Members relate to the participant mainly through roles and activities central to the group. An example here might be that of a researcher who effectively becomes a temporary member of a school's teaching staff in order to conduct research of which other staff are aware in general terms. Alternatively, a teacher might conduct research for a further qualification and use her work setting as a study.

**Observer as participant**   Here the observer role is uppermost and members of the group *accept* the observer in their midst as researcher. If valued, the researcher may be given quite intimate information but will be constrained in reporting it when such information is offered as secret.

**Full observer**   The role of uninvolved observer which we've already discussed as 'non-participant observation'.

### Undisclosed participant observation
Traditional examples of these studies are:

*Festinger (1956):*   joined a religious sect which believed the world would end on a certain date. He and his colleagues followed developments up to and just past the fateful moment, observing reactions during the last moments of life and the subsequent 'reprieve'. An interesting account can be found in Brown (1965).

*Whyte (1943):* studied an Italian street gang in Chicago by joining it. It was obvious Whyte was not a normal gang member. His 'cover' was that he was writing a book about the area. Most famous for his statement that 'I began as a non-participating observer. As I became accepted into the community, I found myself becoming almost a non-observing participant'.

*Frankenburg (1957):* studied a Welsh village and is often quoted for his initiative in solving the problem of not 'blowing cover' yet taking good notes by becoming secretary of the local football club.

*Rosenhahn (1973):* a 'classic' study which promoted controversial criticism of the medical establishment's handling, labelling and diagnosis of psychiatric manifestations. Researchers presented themselves at hospital out-patients' departments complaining of hearing voices making certain noises in their heads. During their subsequent voluntary stays in a psychiatric ward they made observations on staff and patient behaviour and attitudes towards them. Patients often detected the 'normality' of the researchers well before the staff. An excellent example of seeing behaviour as pathological because of its producer's 'label' was the fact that a nurse recorded a researcher's note-taking as 'excessive writing behaviour'. To be fair, the nurse was dutifully carrying out strict instructions to observe and record anything unusual in patients' behaviour.

### Ethical issues in undisclosed participant observation

One of the reasons humanists, for instance, object to many psychological experiments (such as Milgram's (1963) or Asch's (1956)) is that they use DECEPTION of subjects. Participant observation which is undisclosed obviously suffers this criticism too. The researcher has also to decide what, if anything, can be published without the group's or any individual's consent. A particular hazard is that, when the observer 'comes clean' and declares the research role, any one individual studied may not be able to recall what they have divulged, or how they have behaved, since the research began. The individual should be allowed to view material for publication and to veto material which they object to where anonymity does not protect against the nature of the material identifying them.

Lack of consent-seeking leads to a greater mistrust of the distant and elite research body. An answer to the problem of deception is, of course, to disclose one's research role and objectives. These ethical issues are more fully discussed in chapter 20.

### Disclosed participant observation

An example would be the study of Becker (1958) whose observers joined a group of medical students in lectures and laboratory sessions and engaged in casual conversation both in work time and in the social atmosphere of their dormitories. They also joined in ward rounds and discussion groups and spent some time simply watching the students' various activities.

In a strong sense, it could be argued that Whyte's study is disclosed since, for the gang members, writing a book about them and doing some research on them could hardly be distinguished.

What strengths and weaknesses can you see in the use of participant observation? List the advantages and disadvantages of disclosure.

## Strengths of participant observation

**Flexibility**  A pre-set structure for observation, interview or survey question-naire imposes the researcher's framework, assumptions and priorities on those who are to be studied. What is relevant in the target group's social world has already been decided. Participant observation is flexible. What is to be included as data in the study is not formally set in concrete at the outset. Indeed, the extent to which the observer will participate may not be the same throughout the study, as Whyte's famous statement above makes clear. Whyte also found that through participant observation 'I learned the answers to questions I would not have had the sense to ask had I been getting my information solely on an interviewing basis.'

**Relationship with observed group**  Specific groups in the local environment, such as gangs or strongly-identifying cultural groups, are likely to see an establishment researcher as an authority figure and to be consequently sus-picious. Methods for research, other than participant observation, such as interviewing or survey by questionnaire, do not give the researcher long enough to establish trust and to dissipate such suspicions. The research encounter is too brief to ensure genuine co-operation. Participant observation may sometimes be the only way to discover what truly makes such groups 'tick' and to find out which expressed attitudes stem from prior and perhaps deeper values and beliefs.

Kidder (1981) argues that the *longer* the participant observer spends in a research setting, where their aims and purpose are disclosed to group members, the *less* likely it is that their presence will influence or distort the behaviour of the observed persons. This seeming paradox is explained by pointing out that, although group members may wish to appear in a certain light to the observer, if this behaviour is unnatural for them they will not be able to sustain it for long among friends and relatives. Even if the observer does not recognise artificiality, friends and co-workers will, and the observer is likely to hear about it. Kidder adds that it is much easier for experimental, one-day subjects, whose identities remain anonymous, to distort reality by behaving quite uncharacteristically.

Other advantages are summarised below.

## Difficulties with participant observation

The presence of a participant observer must change group behaviour to some degree, if only marginally since, unless the researcher remains mute and passive (and therefore *doesn't* participate), interactions must occur which wouldn't have occurred otherwise. Here is a statement from one of the members of Whyte's gang:

'You've slowed me down plenty since you've been down here. Now, when I do something, I have to think what Bill Whyte would want me to know about it and how I can explain it. Before I used to do these things by instinct.'

Pretty damning for the researcher who claims their presence to be unobtrusive and non-influential. However, researchers like Whyte argue that they blended into and became a part of the activities of the group, rather than changing what happened substantially, supporting Kidder's view above.

As Whyte's statement on page 70 testifies, the researcher obviously becomes socially and emotionally involved in the group and this must cast doubt on their eventual objectivity in reporting. The participant observation supporter would argue, however, that the attempt to be totally objective leads to the artificiality and rigidity we discussed earlier.

The participant researcher can't usually make notes at the time of observation. Most have to rely on diary keeping after the day's events. Frankenburg, as we noted earlier, found a crafty way to record notes under cover of being a club secretary, but this method would not be available to the observer of street-corner gang life. Necessarily then, most participant observers are prey to the psychological factors of memory loss and distortion.

Since the researcher is the only observer present and since events observed are unique, there is none of the usual opportunity to objectively verify results. Conclusions can only be loosely generalised to similar situations and groups.

*Box 6   Advantages and disadvantages of observational study types*

|  | **Advantages** | **Disadvantages** |
|---|---|---|
| **Non-participant** | | |
| Laboratory | More flexible behaviour than that studied in laboratory in experiment | Behaviour can be quite artificial with low ecological validity |
| | Stricter variable control | Subjects can guess what researcher is expecting to see |
| | Can be part of experiment indicating cause-effect direction | Subjects may be affected by knowledge that they are being observed |
| Naturalistic | Higher ecological validity | |
| | Can be used where unethical to experiment, where verbal reports not available and where direct questioning would be rejected | Rarely possible to use in experiment indicating cause-effect direction |
| | | Higher potential for observer bias |
| | Subjects can be unaware of being observed and therefore behave naturally in social context | Difficult to hide observer or equipment |
| | | Thorough replication less likely |
| **Participant** | Extremely high ecological validity | Researcher has to rely on memory |
| | Much richer information from intense and lengthy interaction | Emotional involvement makes objectivity less easy to maintain |
| | Meanings of actors' behaviour more available | Problem of keeping cover if required |
| | Lack of formality, presence of trust gives insights unavailable from any other method | Researcher's behaviour alters that of group members |
| | | Un-replicable and no one can check validity of data gathered |
| | | Difficult to generalise any result |

# 11 INDIRECT OBSERVATION

Some events have already occurred but can serve as empirical evidence for social science theories. Durkheim, a sociologist, made ground-breaking studies of relative rates of suicide, comparing these with varying social conditions.

Many events, like suicide, are of interest to psychologists and are either unpredictable or do not occur often enough for thorough scientific research. Governmental elections are relatively infrequent and make the study of voting behaviour somewhat inconvenient. Behaviour cannot be observed directly in events such as earthquakes and suicide.

Psychological researchers might, instead, use observed social statistics as data. These can be drawn from historical sources ('archival data'), government information or the media. Television programmes might, for example, be observed for examples of gender stereotyping. The fact that young black people obtain fewer interviews and less jobs compared with white youngsters might be attributed to black youngsters having lower qualifications. A researcher can eliminate this hypothesis with an observation of employment statistics which show that this discrepancy occurs among black and white youngsters with *equal* qualifications. This could also be called a SURVEY of labour statistics. The common use of 'survey' is discussed in chapter 8.

Note that, although indirect, these studies do make observations on the behaviour of people and, through some interpretation, prevailing attitudes. Notice also that this is a perfectly legitimate way to test and eliminate hypotheses about causal factors in social phenomena. The observation of electronic or printed media coverage could be subjected to CONTENT ANALYSIS.

# 12 CONTENT ANALYSIS

Originally, the formalised approach called 'content analysis' was a specific method devised for sampling and analysing messages from the media and other recorded material, such as literature, famous people's speeches, or wartime propaganda.

Attempts to analyse media messages can be dated back to the turn of the century, when various writers were concerned about standards, about validity and about the influence of the press on society, crime and morals. In the 1930s and 1940s, however, content analysis 'took off', first because 'weighty' social psychological theory turned towards it for supporting evidence, second because propaganda became a serious threat before and during the war, and third, because the electronic media could no longer be considered an extension of the press.

In this use it was seen as a quantifying instrument for descriptive information, as this definition demonstrates:

'. . . content analysis broadly describes a heterogenous domain of techniques which are focused upon the (more or less) systematic, objective and quantitative description of a communication or series of communications.'

Crano & Brewer (1973)

This, then, is another way of observing, not people directly, but the communications they have produced. The communications concerned were originally those already published, but some researchers have conducted content analysis on materials which they have *asked* people to produce, such as essays, answers to interview questions and so on.

**Examples of analysis of existing materials**   *Shneidman* (1963) analysed the speeches of Kennedy and Nixon in their televised presidential debates, demonstrating differences in their logical argument.

*Ogilvie et al.* (1966) analysed real and simulated suicide notes with some success in discriminating between the two. In this case the simulated notes did not exist naturally but were written by persons matched for the real note-writer's characteristics.

*Bruner and Kelso* (1980) reviewed studies of 'restroom' graffiti spanning thirty years. Most studies analysed the material either at a superficial level – the overt content of statements – or at an interpretive, often psychoanalytic level. Bruner and Kelso analysed the messages 'semiotically', concluding that women's graffiti were more interpersonal and interactive, tending to contain questions and advice about love, relationships and commitment. Men's graffiti tended to be egocentric and competitive, concentrating on conquests and prowess. Their messages served the function of confirming a position of control and the maintenance of power, whereas women's messages reflected the cooperation and mutual help strategies of the dominated.

*Gerbner et al.* (1979) analysed American television for violence in programmes, noting when it increased (weekend, daytime) and decreased (early evening).

**Analysis of specially produced materials**   *Kounin and Gump* (1961) asked children about bad school behaviour. They were in two groups, those of punitive and of non-punitive teachers. As predicted, content analysis of the interview protocols showed that children of punitive teachers were more concerned with aggression. Here, content analysis was used in a traditional hypothesis-testing design.

   Content analysis has been used on plays, folklore, legend, nursery rhymes and even popular music in order to demonstrate differences between cultures and sub-cultures and within cultures over time. The preoccupations of various magazines, newspapers and journals have been linked, through content analysis, with the various political leanings of such publications. Changes in content have been used as indicators of change in public attitude.

### The process of content analysis

*Sampling*   The researcher has the problem of deciding just what material to sample from all that exists. For newspapers, this will mean making a decision based on political leaning, price, target readership and so on. For visual media, a representative sampling of programmes, times, advertising slots and so on, must occur. Advertising is often linked to the content of adjacent programmes.

*Coding Units*   These are the units into which the analysed material is to be categorised. These can be as shown in box 7.

   It became common in the 1980s to investigate children's literature and both children's and adult television programmes for evidence of stereotyping, negative images or sheer omission of women or members of minority ethnic groups. Try the following exercise:

Imagine that you are going to conduct a practical exercise in which the aim is to investigate cultural stereotyping in children's books. We are interested in the extent to which, and ways in which, black people are portrayed. What units (words, themes, characters) might you ask your coders to look out for?

*Box 7   Coding units*

| Unit | Examples |
| --- | --- |
| word | Analyse for sex-related words in different magazines |
| theme | Analyse for occasions, in children's literature, on which boy/girl initiates and gets praised |
| item | Look for whole stories e.g. article on Northern Ireland |
| character | Analyse types of character occurring in TV cartoons |
| time & space | Count space or time devoted to particular issue in media. |

Here are some possible units:

black person in picture
black person in leading role
black person in subsidiary role
European features; face made darker
disappearance from story pictures of black person who appeared earlier
success/failure/trouble – black and white characters compared
inappropriate words:- 'coloured'; 'immigrant'
portrayed as foreign/savage/'primitive' etc.

Note: content analysis can highlight the *omission* of items, themes and characters.

## Procedure

In the traditional model, the researcher will present coders with a pre-constructed system for categorising occurrences. This means that the researcher will have to have become very familiar with the sort of materials likely to be encountered prior to the start of the content analysis exercise.

As with observation, coders may be asked to *categorise* only, thus producing *nominal level* data. Or they may be asked to *rank* items, for instance, a set of open-ended responses on self-image, ranked for 'confidence'. Alternatively, each item might be *rated*: children's drawings could be scored for 'originality'. In the last two cases the measurement level would be *ordinal*. Nominal and ordinal data are levels of measurement introduced in chapter 12. In the interests of removing researcher bias the coding might now be entirely completed by assistants who are unaware of the research hypothesis, if there is one. It has also been common to test for inter-coder reliability using correlational techniques.

## Key terms for this chapter

| | | |
|---|---|---|
| Archival data | Naturalistic observation | Observer rating/coding |
| Content analysis | Non-participant | Participant observation |
| Controlled observation | observation | Role-play |
| Diary method | Observation design | Simulation |
| Disclosure | Observation technique | Structured observation |
| Formative approach | Observer/inter-rater | Time/point/event |
| Holist viewpoint | reliability | sampling |
| Indirect observation | Observer bias | |

## Exercises

1 Outline a research study which would use observation to investigate the following hypotheses:

  (a) During exploratory play, mothers allow their sons to venture further away from them than their daughters
  (b) When asked personal, or slightly embarrassing questions, people are likely to avert their gaze
  (c) Women are safer drivers than men
  (d) There are common patterns of behaviour among individuals in groups which are asked to produce volunteers for an unpopular task

Ensure that:  variables are operationalised
              the *exact* method of data gathering is described, including the location, sample selection, data collection method and equipment used.

2 A student decides to carry out participant observation on her own student group. She is interested in the different ways her classmates cope with study demands and social commitments. Discuss the ways she might go about this work, the problems she might face and the ways in which she might surmount difficulties.

3 Describe ways in which Bandura's hypotheses, including those which investigate the influence of different types of child and adult model, could have been investigated using naturalistic observation rather than the laboratory.

4 A researcher is concerned that the rating scale in use is not producing good inter-rater reliability. The observations of two observers are as follows:

| Observations for child X: altrustic acts in 5-minute intervals: | | | | | | | | |
|---|---|---|---|---|---|---|---|---|
| | 0–5 | 6–10 | 11–15 | 16–20 | 21–25 | 26–30 | 31–35 | 36–40 | 41–45 |
| Observer A | 1 | 3 | 4 | 2 | 5 | 12 | 9 | 4 | 8 |
| Observer B | 2 | 10 | 8 | 7 | 1 | 3 | 5 | 5 | 6 |

Would you say this represents good reliability or not? What statistical procedure could tell us the degree of reliability (see chapter 17)?

5 Work with a colleague and decide on a variable to observe in children or adults. Make the variable something which is likely to occur quite frequently in a short observation period (10 minutes), such as one person smiling in a two-person conversation in the college refectory. Make your observations of the same person at the same time separately and then compare your results to see whether you tend to agree fairly well or not.

# Asking questions I

## INTERVIEWS AND SURVEYS

## 1  INTRODUCTION

So far we have seen that the psychologist who needs information can set up experiments to see what people do under different conditions or use observation techniques to record segments of behaviour in more or less natural circumstances. Perhaps the reader has asked by now 'Why don't psychologists just go and ask people directly about themselves?' So far, it looks as though only the participant observer might have done that. A general term used for any method which asks people for information about themselves is SELF REPORT METHOD.

There are in fact many ways in which psychological researchers ask questions about individuals. This can occur as part of an experiment or observational study, of course, but here we are now concentrating on studies where the gathering of information through FACE-TO-FACE questioning is the primary research mode.

### Structure and disguise
These methods range across two major dimensions. A questioning method can be formally STRUCTURED, in which case every respondent (person who answers questions) receives exactly the same questions, probably in the same order. Or the method can tend towards the UNSTRUCTURED, in which case validity may be high though reliability is low. (This is similar to the difference between controlled and participant observation covered in the last chapter). In the unstructured study, objective comparison of cases and generalisability is weak but the researcher has the advantage of flexibility towards the respondent and asking questions in a more informal, relaxed atmosphere in which genuine and complete answers may be more forthcoming.

However, the more unstructured the interview, the greater the skill required by interviewers and the more the success of the research depends on implementation of these skills. Also greater are the chances of researcher bias and selectivity.

### The Kalamazoo study
Questionnaires may be more or less structured too. The importance of giving respondents the freedom to say what they really think is demonstrated by the results of a piece of applied psychological research conducted by Peronne *et al.* (1976) who were evaluating a new accountability system set up by the Kalamazoo Education Association in its schools. The system had been heavily criticised. Teachers were asked to complete a questionnaire with fixed choice questions – 'agree' or 'disagree'. The researchers also set a couple of open-ended questions to which staff could respond in their own words at any length.

77

School board members were prepared to dismiss the quantitative results from the fixed choice questions as somehow biased but, on publication of the qualitative results they could hardly ignore the clear statements of fear, concern and frustration which dominated replies to the open-ended questions and they were influenced strongly enough to make substantial changes.

A factor which might further enhance production of honest answers will be that of DISGUISE. The ethical principles involved in deceiving persons will be dealt with later, but obviously an aid to obtaining truthful information will be the disguising of the researcher's real aim where information sought is highly sensitive, potentially embarrassing or otherwise felt as a threat to the interviewee if disclosed. Interviewees may also try to 'look' good if they know what exactly is the focus of the study.

A matrix of assessment techniques which fall into four categories formed by these two variables, structure and disguise, is shown in box 8. However, it must be remembered that each variable represents a dimension, not a pair of exclusive opposites. Some methods are only partially disguised and/or only relatively structured. In Hammond's technique, respondents were asked factual questions about days lost through strikes, for instance, and had to tick an answer from two, one of which was far too high and one far too low. Without it being obvious to the interviewee, attitude to trades unions was said to be measured.

Levin used psychoanalytic techniques to assess women's degree of 'penis envy'. The women she studied reported anything they thought they saw in Rorschach ink blots (which are abstract drawings representing nothing in particular).

Eysenck's questionnaire on extroversion and neuroticism gives the respondent some idea of its aim but is not completely transparent.

We have mentioned the Kalamazoo study and we shall mention the Hawthorne studies in a short while.

A further way to disguise research aims is to ask questions about the topic of interest and simultaneously record the respondent's galvanic skin response, an indicator of anxiety if high.

### Effects of interpersonal variables

This chapter is about asking people questions mostly to gather information. We have seen that some research designs, particularly the laboratory experiment, have been criticised for their artificiality and for producing *demand characteristics*. But when we ask people questions, however informally, so long as they are aware

*Box 8  Matrix of assessment techniques*

|  | Structured | Unstructured |
|---|---|---|
| **Disguised** | Hammond's (1948) 'error choice technique' | Use of projective tests as in Levin (1978) |
|  | Eysenck and Eysenck's (1975) EPQ questionnaire |  |
| **Undisguised** | Peronne *et al.* (1976) Kalamazoo study |  |
|  | Most attitude questionnaires | Roethlisberger & Dickson (1939 Hawthorne studies |

that there is a research aim, there will be an element of artificiality and distortion. There is an interaction of roles – interviewer and interviewee. Characteristics of the interviewer's style and presentation will affect the quality of information obtained. Demand characteristics may well operate in that the interviewee may use cues from the interviewer, or from the questionnaire, to try and behave according to perceived research aims. Researcher bias may also operate where the interviewer is aware of expected or desired results.

> The relationship and interaction between interviewer and interviewee will affect the quality and amount of information obtained in an interview. Make a list of all the ways in which you think this could happen.

My list would include all the following points:

In particular, the class, sex, culture or race, and age of either person in the interview may make a lot of difference to proceedings. Cultural difference, here, doesn't have to be great. It could be the difference between Londoner and Scot or simply northerner and southerner.

**Gender**   That gender is an important variable is demonstrated in a study by Finch (1984) where young mothers gave her access to views which a man would have been highly unlikely to obtain. A woman interviewee can assume common understanding with a woman interviewer, as when one of Finch's mothers said '. . . fellas don't see it like that do they?'

**Ethnicity**   That race or ethnic group creates differential interviewing behaviour was shown by Word *et al.* (1974). They observed the behaviour of white interviewers with white and black interviewees. With white interviewees, the interviewers showed significantly higher 'immediacy' – which includes closer interpersonal distance, more eye contact, more forward lean and so on. They followed this up with a demonstration that 'job applicants' in the study reciprocated the low-immediacy behaviour of the interviewers and received significantly poorer ratings for their interview performance.

**Formal roles**   The differences above may have greater effect if the interviewee also views the researcher as an authority figure. This perception will partly depend upon the style the researcher adopts but even a highly informal style may not deter the interviewee from seeing her or him as very important. Their answers then, may lack fluency because they are constrained by the respondent's search for 'correct' language or content. On the other hand, some respondents may feel quite superior to the interviewer and consequently their answers may be somewhat superficial and cursory.

**Personal qualities**   Interacting with these major differences will be other personal qualities and characteristics of both people. The interviewer, instructed to be informal, may find this quite difficult with some people and may therefore behave rather artificially, this being detected by the interviewee. There may be something else about the interviewer that the interviewee just doesn't like.

**Social desirability**   A common problem in asking questions is that of SOCIAL DESIRABILITY. This is the tendency to want to look good to the outside world and to be seen to have socially desirable habits and attitudes. To an esteemed researcher, then, people may give a quite false impression of their attitudes and behaviour. It is notoriously difficult, for instance, to measure prejudice openly. When asked, many people will make statements like 'I believe we're all equal' and 'Everybody should be treated the same', whereas, in their everyday life, and in conversation with friends, other, more negative attitudes towards some groups may well emerge. On issues like child-rearing practice or safe driving people know what they ought to say to an interviewer.

**Evaluative cues**   It is unusual to be asked for one's opinion, in a situation where no criticism or argument can be expected. The interviewer has to be careful not to inadvertently display behaviour, however subtle, which might get interpreted as either disagreement or encouragement since the interviewee may well be searching for an acceptable or desired position.

# 2  INTERVIEWS

One-to-one, or face-to-face interviews range in style across the range of structure from fixed to open-ended questions. Answers to open-ended questions will often be coded by placing them into categories, such as 'left wing' or 'right wing' for political questions or by rating them on a scale of perhaps one to ten for, say, aggressiveness. In some surveys, interviewers code answers on the spot as they are received. In the less structured type of interview, response analysis is a long, complicated and relatively subjective process. In qualitative research studies there may be no interest in quantifying responses at all beyond basic categorising. The emphasis will be on collating, prioritising and summarising all information acquired (see chapter 19) and perhaps suggesting areas and strategies for action. The setting and procedure for interviewing may also be more or less structured and we will consider five categories of interview, starting at the relatively unstructured end of the continuum.

## Types of interview

**1  Non-directive**   Some psychology practitioners use interviews in which the interviewee can talk about anything they like and in which the psychologist gives no directing influence to the topics but helps and guides discussion. The main aim would be to help the 'client' increase self-awareness and deal with personal problems. This method would be used by psychotherapists and counsellors and would not count, therefore, as research in the sense generally used in this book. But, of course, clients do, in a sense, research their own personality and the psychologist may need information, gathered in this manner, in order to help them.

This approach may be used in collecting information which forms part of a CASE STUDY, a topic discussed later on.

The insights derived from such studies often get drawn together into an overall psychological theory, model or approach which adds, in time, to the pool of knowledge and ideas which is a stimulus for further research by other means. Freud's insights, for instance, influenced Bandura in his development of social learning theory which he supported mainly by controlled observation studies.

**2  Informal**   An informal interview has an overall data gathering aim. At the non-structured extreme the session is similar to the non-directive approach just described. This was employed in a large-scale and now famous study of industrial relations at the Western Electric company's Hawthorne works in Chicago, starting back in 1927. Early structured interviews were not successful. Employees went off the topics set by the interviewers' questions. The 'indirect approach' which the researchers then developed involved interviewers listening patiently, making intelligent comments, displaying no authority, giving no advice or argument and only asking questions when necessary. They found employees became far more articulate and, as an overall outcome of the study, management realised that seemingly trivial complaints were only the external symptoms of much deeper personal and social problems, requiring more than the superficial response to employee complaints they had originally envisaged.

In the relaxed atmosphere of the informal, non-directive interview, interviewees can talk in their own terms. They don't have to answer pre-set questions which they might find confusing or which they just don't wish to answer. They are not constrained by fixed-answer questions which produce rather narrow information.

This approach has been used in social science research for some time and has more recently, largely in the 1980s, become popular in areas of applied research, particularly by the proponents of qualitative approaches.

*Box 9   Summary of advantages and disadvantages of the informal interview*

| Advantages | Disadvantages |
|---|---|
| Interview can be moulded to individual, situation and context | Unsystematic and therefore different information from different individuals |
| High validity | Difficult to analyse variety of information gathered |
| Richer, fuller information likely on interviewee's own terms | Strongly influenced by interpersonal variables |
| Interviewee feels relaxed and unassessed | Relative unreliable |

**3   Informal but guided**   One way to retain the advantage of the informal approach is to keep the procedure informal, not to ask pre-set questions in exactly the same order each time, but to provide interviewers with a guide which is an outline of topics to be covered and questions to be asked. The guide leaves the interviewer to decide, on the spot, how to work in and phrase questions on the various topics. In other words, with specific data requirements, the interviewer 'plays it by ear'.

*Box 10   Summary of advantages and disadvantages of the informal but guided interview*

| Advantages | Disadvantages |
|---|---|
| Increase in consistency of information | Different question wordings will create varying interpretations and emphasis |
| Data analysis simpler, more systematic | Interviewer may miss important topics |
| Information still genuinely given | Substantial influence by interpersonal variables |
| Interviewer can still be flexible | Low reliability |
| High validity | |

**4   Structured but open-ended**   To avoid the looseness and inconsistency which accompany informally gathered interview data, the interview session can use a standardised procedure. The interviewer gives pre-set questions in a predetermined order to every interviewee. This keeps the multiplicity of interpersonal variables involved in a two-way conversation to a minimum and ensures greater consistency in the data gathered. The respondent is still free to answer, however, in any way chosen. Questions are open-ended. For instance, 'How do you feel about the company's sales policy?' might be asked, rather than 'Do you approve of the company's sales policy?'

*Box 11    Summary of advantages and disadvantages of the structured, open-ended interview*

| Advantages | Disadvantages |
|---|---|
| Responses far more easily compared | Flexibility of interviewer being able to |
| Data more easily analysed | respond to different individuals, situa- |
| No topics missed or fleetingly covered | tions and contexts is lost |
| Reduction of interpersonal bias | Question wordings may reduce richness |
| Can be used by several interviewers at the | Answers less natural |
| same time | Coding of answers may not be high in |
| Can be reviewed by other researchers | reliability |
| Respondents not constrained by fixed | |
| answer | |

**5  Fully structured**    In this type of interview, as with the last, questions are fixed and ordered. In addition, the respondent may only answer according to a formal system. Three examples of structure, in increasing complexity, might be:

1 Answering questions with either 'yes' or 'no'.
2 Responding to a statement (not a question) with one of the following:
     *Strongly agree   Agree   Neutral   Disagree   Strongly disagree*
3 Selecting from several alternatives a suitable court sentence for a rapist.

In fact, this approach is hardly an interview worth the name at all. It is a face-to-face data-gathering technique, but could be conducted by telephone or by post (which would reduce bias from interpersonal variables still further). The structured method is usually in use when you're stopped on the street by someone with a clipboard. Responses can be counted and analysed numerically but can often be difficult to make because the respondent wants to say 'yes' (for this reason) but 'no' (for that reason) or 'I think so' or 'sometimes'. A sensitive structured system has a list for choosing responses including alternatives such as 'sometimes', 'hardly ever', or, 'certain', 'fairly confident' and so on. The method just described is often that used in a SURVEY.

# 3   THE CLINICAL METHOD (or 'clinical interview')

This method uses a semi-structured interview method in a particular manner. It is usually aimed at testing fairly specific hypotheses or at demonstrating a clear and limited phenomenon. However, it also recognises the unique experience of each interviewee. Initially, each person questioned will be asked the same questions, but further questions are tailored to the nature of initial replies. The

*Box 12   Summary of advantages and disadvantages of the fully structured interview*

| Advantages | Disadvantages |
|---|---|
| Very quick to administer | Respondent completely constrained by |
| Easily replicated |    question and response system |
| Generalisable results | Information gained is narrow |
| Data analysis relatively simple | Information may be distorted by: |
| Quantification without bias |    ambiguous wordings |
| Low influence from interpersonal variables |    complex wordings |
| High reliability |    inappropriate response choice list |
| | Suffers from all the difficulties associated |
| |    with questionnaires |
| | Low validity |

method was extensively used by Piaget. Anyone who has tried to test a child on one of Piaget's conservation tasks will know that the specific language chosen, and the quality of the adult's interaction with the child, are all-important factors in determining the progress of such a test. It is easy to get a four-year-old child to give the 'wrong' (i.e. non-conserving) answer with an injudicious choice of question wording or with 'clumsy' conversation.

'Is there more liquid in this glass?' is a leading question which may well prompt the child into saying 'yes' to please. Anyway, after all, the column of liquid *is* taller (though narrower). The question 'Is there more in this glass, more in this other one, or are they both the same?' is rather demanding on the child's short-term memory!

The clinical method, then, uses a non-standardised procedure but heads for a definite goal. Standardised questions, rigidly adhered to by the interviewer can seem rather artificial to the adult respondent. The problem with children is greater. If they don't understand the particular form of words they may well 'fail' when an alteration in question form may well have revealed that the child has the concept sought after all. Piaget believed, therefore, that he could get the most accurate information about a child's thinking by varying the questioning in what seemed to the child a fairly natural conversation with an adult. Of course, we end up with the alleged weaknesses of unstandardised procedures.

Freud's methods too have been said to involve the clinical method, since the aim of some sessions was to test a specific hypothesis about the client's unconscious network of fears and ideas.

*Box 13   Summary of advantages and disadvantages of Clinical Method*

| Advantages | Disadvantages |
|---|---|
| Leads to accurate assessment of person's thinking and memory | Non-standardised method |
| Interviewer can vary questions in order to check person's understanding | Researcher's theoretical beliefs can influence questions asked and interpretations made of what person understands |
| Information gained fairly rich | |
| Interviewee relaxed | Difficulty in comparing one interview protocol with another |

# 4 THE INDIVIDUAL CASE STUDY

A case study involves gathering detailed information about one individual or small group. Typically this would include a comprehensive CASE HISTORY, usually, but not exclusively, gathered by interview. This would be the person's record to date in employment, education, family details, socio-economic status, relationships and so on, and might include a detailed account of experiences relevant to the issue which makes the person of particular research interest. This reason might be that the person has suffered severe social and physical deprivation, or that their life is particularly affected by, perhaps, illness or criminal background.

Information might also be gathered, as the study progresses, on all these variables. The person would be regularly interviewed, mostly in an unstructured manner, and may be asked to take psychological tests. A case study may not use interviews exclusively. In some cases, particularly where the person is a young child, observation may play a large part in the collection of information, as when, for instance, the severely deprived child's play activities and developing social interactions are monitored for change.

In some instances the individual is selected for a forward-looking case study because they are about to undergo a particularly interesting and possibly unique experience. Gregory and Wallace (1963) for instance studied the case of SB, blind almost from birth, who received sight through surgical operation at the age of 52. The researchers were able to study in depth, not only his visual abilities and development, but also gathered qualitative data on his emotional reactions to his new experiences and progress. This included his initial euphoria and his later depressions, caused partly by loss of daylight and his disillusionment with impure surfaces (flaky paint, old chalk marks on blackboards).

A case study, such as this one, though intrinsically valuable, can also shed light on general psychological issues such as the nature–nurture debate in perception. However, since SB had spent a lifetime specialising senses other than vision, his perceptual learning experiences cannot be directly compared with those of a young infant.

Freud developed his comprehensive psychoanalytic theory of human development using, as fuel and illustration, his records from dozens of patients' case histories.

At the social end of the psychological research spectrum, we would find case studies on groups of individuals such as those conducted by participant observers or the evaluative studies of establishments exemplified by the Kalamazoo work, described earlier.

De Waele and Harré (1979) recommend the construction of assisted autobiographies. In this method, the autobiographical account is conceived as a co-operative effort between the participant and a team of about a dozen professionals (psychologist, social worker, etc.). Their project involved prisoners who, though volunteers, were paid a salary as a research team member. The process involves continuous detailed negotiation among team members about various 'accounts' from the participant. The participant's own life and resources are at all times respected and the professional team must 'stand in a relation of humility' to it.

This method is, of course, extremely time consuming and enormously expensive, though intense in its production of rich, meaningful data. Harré belongs among the 'new paradigm' researchers described in chapter 11 and this type of research project is an example of the collaborative approach.

## The value of case studies

Being a somewhat unstructured, probably unreplicable study on just one individual or group, the case-study design would seem to be of the rich but unreliable type and to be rather suspect in its scientific use. Bromley (1986) has recently argued however, that case studies are the 'bedrock of scientific investigation'. Many psychological studies, he argues, are difficult to replicate in principle and it is the interesting, unpredictable case which has traditionally spurred scientists towards changes in paradigm or theoretical innovation. Bromley feels that a preoccupation with the experiment and psychometrics has led to a serious neglect of the case study approach by most psychologists. He points out that, as in most sciences, psychological evidence can be valid and effective, yet remain unquantifiable. The case study has a variety of specific advantages and useful points which follow.

**1 Outstanding cases**   A phenomenon may occur which is unique or so dramatic it could not have been predicted or studied in any pre-planned way. An example is the study of multiple personality by Osgood *et al.* (1976) in which the very rare but genuine experiences of a person with three quite separate psychological identities is recorded and analysed. Luria (1969) studied a man with astonishing memory capabilities who was originally noticed because he was a journalist who took no notes at briefing meetings.

Such cases may bring to attention possibilities in the human condition which were not previously considered realistic and may prompt investigation into quite new, challenging areas.

**2 Contradicting a theory**   One contrary case is enough to seriously challenge an assumed trend or theory of cause–effect relationship. It has been assumed that humans go through a 'critical period' where language must be heard to be learned, or where attachments must be formed and maintained in order to avoid later psychological problems. One case of an isolated child learning language, or of a maternally-deprived child developing normal adult social skills, after deprivation during much of the critical period, is enough to seriously undermine the critical period hypothesis.

**3 Data pool**   In an effort to identify common factors or experiences, a mass of information from many case studies may be pooled, sorted and analysed. The subjects may be, for instance, psychiatric patients or children with a particular reading disability. As a result, quantitative studies may be carried out, once linking variables appear or are suspected.

**4 Insight**   Whether or not case studies of special circumstances lead to later, more formal, structured and quantitative studies, the richness they provide is their unique strength. Very often we could not possibly imagine the special experiences of the subject, and we could not possibly draw up the appropriate questions to find out.

These experiences may cause us to quite restructure our thoughts on a particular condition, allowing us to empathise more fully, for example, with the AIDS sufferer or to understand the full impact of unemployment on a family. This adds to our overall knowledge pool and comprehension of human psychology though it may not test any specific hypothesis.

**Disadvantages of the case study**

1 **Reliability and validity**    There is an obviously high degree of unreliability involved. No two cases are the same. Many studies are quite unreplicable, indeed, their uniqueness is usually the reason for their being carried out in the first place. Their strength is in richness, their weakness in lack of generalisability.

Some check on reliability can sometimes be made, however, by comparing information gained from different sources; for instance, the person themselves in interview, close relatives' accounts, documentary sources, such as diaries and court reports. This is similar to the notion of 'triangulation' described in chapter 14.

Ecological validity is high. The experiences observed by the researcher are genuine and complex. Historical material, however, often depends on just the subject's own memory. Memory is notoriously error-prone and subject to distortion. Experiences which we claim to recall from childhood are often our original reconstruction from relatives' stories told to us about our life before memory was possible.

2 **Interviewer–subject interaction**    Any interview involves human interaction and information collection is prone to the interpersonal variables discussed earlier on. But the case study necessitates a very close relationship between interviewer and subject over an extended period and many intimate interviews. Though the very depth of this relationship may promote an extremely rich information source, it may also seriously interfere with the researcher's objectivity.

3 **Subjective selection**    There is another possible element of subjectivity. Rather than present everything recorded during a case study, which might take as long as the study itself, the researcher must be selective in what information enters the final report. This may well depend upon the points of background theory or issues which the researcher wishes to raise or emphasise. Further, for every illustrative case study, we do not know how many cases did not deliver the kind of information the researcher wished to present.

# 5   INTERVIEW TECHNIQUES

If the interview is completely structured, the interviewer will be using a questionnaire and the construction of these is outlined in chapter 9. The techniques and procedures described in the following pages apply to any interview which is less structured and, in particular, to interviews in which open-ended, qualitative data is sought.

# Achieving and maintaining rapport

In an unstructured interview, the quality and characteristics of the interviewer's behaviour is of utmost importance and not just the interesting 'extraneous variable' it is often considered to be in the structured interview or survey study. People provide a lot more information about themselves when they are feeling comfortable and 'chatty' than in a strained, formal atmosphere where suspicions are not allayed, or an awkward, 'stiff' or aggressive interviewer may produce little co-operation and even hostility from the interviewee. How may rapport be established?

## Language
It is valuable to spend some time discovering terminology used by the group under study. They may have nicknames and use their own jargon, including sets of initials (such as 'SUDs' – standing for 'seriously under-deprived' i.e. upper class children).

Interviewees will be most comfortable and fluent using their normal language mode (dialect, accent, normal conversational style) and must be made to feel that its use is not only legitimate but welcome and valued.

## Neutrality
Accepting the language style and any non-verbal behaviour of the interviewee will help to assure her/him that the interview is entirely non-judgemental. The interviewee must feel that no moral assessment of what they say is, or will be, involved.

## Giving information
The interviewer can give full information at the start of an interview about the purpose of the research, who it is conducted for, what sorts of topics will be covered and how confidentiality will be maintained. Unlike the case with formal questionnaires, the interviewer can explain the purpose of any particular question. A natural questioning environment should encourage the interviewee to ask what the interviewer has in mind but *offering* this information is courteous and keeps the participant involved.

## Confidentiality
If interviewees are to be quoted verbatim (one of the principles of some qualitative research) there is the problem that individuals can be identified from particular statements. In the 1950s, the people of Springdale village, in the USA, vilified researchers (Vidich and Bensman, 1958) who, though using pseudonyms, made identification of individuals possible because their problems were analysed in the research report. The villagers held an effigy of 'the author' over a manure spreader in their 4th July parade!

Participants should be reminded of their right to veto comments made throughout the project and should be aware of the final format in order to exercise discretion over information divulged.

## Training
In order to establish and maintain rapport, interviewers can undergo some degree of training which might include the following:

**Listening skills**   The interviewer needs to learn when *not* to speak, particularly if they, themselves, are normally quite 'speedy' and talkative. There are various skills in listening, too numerous to detail here, which include:

- not trivialising statements by saying 'How interesting but we must get on'.
- hearing that a 'yes' is qualified and asking whether the interviewee wants to add anything. What follows may well amount to a 'no'.
- not being too quick or dominant in offering an interpretation of what the interviewee was trying to say.

**Non-verbal communication**   The interviewer needs to be sensitive to non-verbal cues, though not to the point of awkwardness. In what position will an interviewee talk most comfortably? What interviewer postures are interpreted as dominating? What is a pleasant tone and manner for questioning? And so on.

**Natural questioning**   This is really the biggest factor of all. How can the interviewer make the discussion feel natural, and therefore productive, whilst getting through a set of major questions? If the interviewer has only four or five target questions then it should not be too difficult to insert these into a freely-flowing conversation. With a larger list it may be necessary to use prompt notes but some formality can be avoided by listing these on paper used for note taking.

**Interest**   It is essential that the interviewer remains interested and *believes* that the interviewee's information, as well as sacrificed time, are valuable. The interviewee needs to feel this is the case. Patton (1980) urges that the concept of the bad interviewee should be ignored, arguing that it is easy to summon up stereotypes (of the hostile or paranoid interviewee, for instance). He suggests that it is the sensitive interviewer's task to unlock the internal perspective of each interviewee by being adaptable in finding the style and format which will work in each case. We are a long way here from the argument that scientific research demands completely un-swerving standardised procedure!

One overall necessity here is practice. Interviews can be made more effective with thoughtful preparation and by practising with colleagues as dummy interviewees until stumbling points and awkwardness have been reduced or ironed out.

# Types of question

It is deceptively simple to ask poor or problematic questions. Some of the common mistakes to avoid are outlined in the principles of questionnaire design described in chapter 9. Items to avoid are double-barrelled, complex, ambiguous, leading and emotive questions. In addition, the following points might be noted:

1 It is easy to ask two or more questions at once if the interviewer gets enthusiastic. 'So tell me about it. What was it like? How did you feel? Did you regret it?', for instance, puts a memory strain at least on the interviewee.

2 Questions like 'Are you enjoying the course?' may well receive a monosyllabic answer. Open-ended questions like 'Please can you tell me what you are enjoying about the course?' will be more likely to produce richer information.

3 'Why?' questions can be wasteful in time. Asking a student 'Why did you join the course?' will produce a variety of replies in quite different categories. For instance:

'It'll get me a decent qualification'
'To meet new people'
'It was nearer than London'
'My mother thought it was a good idea'

are all possible answers. We can decide, during the planning stage, what category of reply we would like and design questions accordingly. What should certainly be avoided is an implication that the answer given is unwanted by saying, for instance, 'No, I didn't mean that . . .'

4 Interest may not be maintained if too many personal background details are asked. This point is valid for surveys too, as mentioned below.

# The sequence and progress of questions

### Feelings and reactions
As with more formal questioning methods, the interviewee will feel more comfortable if the session does not kick off with emotionally-charged or controversial items. Likewise, it will be hard to discuss feelings about or reactions towards an issue or event until the interviewee has had a chance to acclimatise by describing it. Early questions can be aimed at eliciting a description, and later questions can prompt feelings about or reactions towards events described.

### Helpful feedback
An interview will run more smoothly if the interviewee is aware of the position reached and the future direction. In particular it might be useful to let the interviewee know:

1 when the interviewer is about to change topic. For instance, 'Now let's talk about the students on the course'.

2 that the next question is particularly important, complex, controversial or sensitive. For instance, 'You've been telling me what you like about the course. Now I'd like to find out about what you don't like. Can you tell me . . .'

3 about what the interviewer thinks the interviewee has just said, or said earlier, without, of course, reinterpretations which depart far from the actual words used.

This feedback allows the interviewee to realise they are making sense and being productive; also, that they are not being misrepresented. They can alter or qualify what they've said. This process also keeps the interviewee actively involved and confident.

But it is important not to summarise interviewees' statements in a language form which makes them feel that their own statements were somehow inferior and in need of substantial rephrasing.

# Recording data

Interviewers have three common choices for saving data: note taking, audio tape or video tape recordings.

### Note taking
Taking hand-written notes will obviously slow down the procedure. It could be useful to develop some form of personal short-hand – at least short forms of

commonly-used terms and phrases. The note book does have the handy advantage of being a place to store discreetly the interview questions or outline. If used, the interviewer needs to be careful not to give the impression that what the interviewee is saying at any particular moment is not important because it is not being recorded.

### Audio recording
Many people feel inhibited in the presence of a tape recorder's microphone. The interviewer needs to justify its use in terms of catching the exact terms and richness of the interviewee's experiences and in terms of confidentiality. The interviewee has to be free to have the recording switched off at any time. The tape recorder has the advantage of leaving the interviewer free to converse naturally and encourage the greatest flow of information.

### Video recording
A 'live' video camera in the room is a prominent feature and can hardly help retain the informal, 'chatty' atmosphere which a loosely-structured, open-ended interview is supposed to create. It is possible to acclimatise interviewees to its presence over quite a number of sessions, but this is costly in time. The great value, of course, is in the recording of non-verbal communication at a detailed level and the chance to analyse this at a comfortable pace. If this information is not required, however, then video is an unnecessary, intrusive gimmick.

Both video and audio recordings could be conducted unobtrusively by simply not revealing their presence to the interviewee, but, in this case, serious ethical issues must be addressed. Two answers to possible dilemmas here are:

1 Inform the interviewee of the recording process but keep equipment completely hidden

2 Give information about the recording only after the interview has taken place, but emphasise that recordings can be heard or viewed, sections omitted or the whole recording destroyed at the interviewee's request.

Option 2 is of course potentially wasteful and time consuming.

## 6  SURVEYS

A survey consists of asking a lot of people for information. In the informal, loosely-structured interview, each respondent's answers form a small case study. A survey can consist of a set of such small case studies. Much more often, though, it would involve the use of a structured questionnaire, with answers open or closed, as described in interview types 4 and 5 on page 000. Each set of responses forms an equivalent unit in a large sample. Interviewers usually work as a team and procedures are therefore fully standardised. Each will be briefed on the exact introductory statement and steps to be followed with each respondent.

A survey may be used for two major research purposes: descriptive or analytical.

### Descriptive
Here the researcher wants an accurate description of what people, in some target population, do and think and perhaps with what frequency. Bryant *et al.* (1980),

for instance, studied child-minding in Oxfordshire and focused on the minders' behaviour and attitude towards their clients, as well as on the children's development. A more notorious and wide-ranging survey was that of Kinsey (1948, 1953) on American sexual behaviour. A recent, extremely comprehensive survey (Jowell & Topf, 1988) gathered information on current British social attitudes. The issues covered included: AIDS, the countryside, industry's and unions' influences on political parties, the government's current economic policies, education, the north and south divide and which household jobs should be shared – according to married and single persons's opinions.

## Analytic use

Survey data can be used to test hypotheses. Hatfield and Walster (1981) interviewed 537 college men and women who had a regular partner. Those who felt their relationship was equitable were far more likely to predict its continuation over one to five years than were those who felt one partner received or gave too much. This tested hypothesis supported a theory of human interaction based on calculated gains and losses.

In Sears *et al.*'s (1957) wide-ranging study of child-rearing practices, using mothers from two suburbs of Boston, USA, many hypotheses were tested by correlating (see chapter 17) rearing techniques with children's characteristic behaviour. Data was gathered by rating open-ended answers to structured questions given to the mothers. The raters assessed only from the interview recording and didn't meet the mother. The researchers found positive relationships between the use of physical punishment and a child's higher level of aggressive behaviour. Mothers who were rated as warm and used 'withdrawal of love' as a major disciplinary technique had children with stronger consciences. Both these variables, withdrawal of love and strength of conscience, were assessed indirectly from the interview data and are examples of constructs, *operationally defined.*

Often, from a large descriptive survey, hypotheses can be formulated or checked against further information from the same survey. For instance, in the second report of the National Child Development Study (Davie *et al.* 1972), a survey of a large sample of children born in 1958, it was found that children from social class V (unskilled manual) were at a particular disadvantage on reading tests, compared with other manual and non-manual classes. Why might this be? Well, from the same survey data it was found that overcrowded homes and homes lacking basic amenities were related to serious reading retardation *irrespective* of a child's social class, sex, area of the UK or accommodation type. Children from social class V were more likely to live in such homes. So, reading deficiency could be related to factors only indirectly related to, but more prevalent within, one class.

## Survey design

In survey work there are three major areas of decision-making necessary before initiating the contact with respondents. These are the *sample, mode of questioning,* and the *questions* themselves. The first two areas will be dealt with now. Dealing with the actual content of questions I shall leave until the next section on questionnaires and tests in general.

### The sample

Of all methods, the survey throws particular emphasis on the sample since the aim, very often, is to make generalisations about a relatively large section of the

*Box 14    Advantages and disadvantages of the survey over the in-depth interview*

| Advantages | Disadvantages |
|---|---|
| Many respondents can be questioned fairly quickly | Structured questions miss more informative data |
| Can be a lot less expensive than in-depth interviews (which have a lot of information to be transcribed | Large-scale surveys can be expensive in assistants |
| Less influence from dynamics of interpersonal variables | More influenced by superficial interpersonal variables; respondent has no time to come to trust and confide in interviewer |
| Less bias in analysing answers, since questions are structured | More likely to produce 'public responses', not respondent's true ideas |
| | Possibility of social desirability effect higher – see next section |

population, if not all of it. If the sample is the whole population then the survey is known as a CENSUS.

We have dealt with the main methods and issues of sampling in an earlier chapter. Survey work has produced two other forms of sample not used elsewhere. These are the PANEL and the FOCUS GROUP.

**The panel**    This is a specially selected group of people who can be asked for information on a repetitive basis. They are much used by market research companies, government survey units and audience research in broadcasting. It is easier and more efficient to rely on the same, well-stratified group to provide information each time it is required.

One problem can be that panel members become too sophisticated in their reviewing and can become unrepresentative in, say, their viewing habits since they feel they must watch all the programmes mentioned in their questionnaire.

**Focus groups**    The idea here is to bring together a group of individuals with a common interest and to conduct a form of collective interview. Discussion among members may provoke an exchange of views and revelations providing information and insights less likely to surface during a one to one interview. Though not providing much in the way of reliable, quantifiable data, such groups can be a starting point for research into a specific area, as an aid to exposing and clarifying concepts.

### The mode of questioning

There are three obvious ways of communicating with respondents: face-to-face, telephone and letter. Of these, telephones are used rarely, though they will often be used for making initial contact.

The privacy of the postal method is likely to produce more honest answers. Interpersonal variables, discussed above, are reduced to a minimum in postal surveys though the respondent may make assumptions about the researcher from the style of the covering letter. The method is also a good deal cheaper and less time-consuming.

The disadvantages are first, that the questionnaire must be exceptionally clear, and unambiguous instructions for its completion must be carefully written. Still, respondents may answer in an inappropriate way that a 'live' interviewer could have changed. Second, the proportion of non-returners is likely to be higher than the number of refusals by other approaches. This matters a lot when, for instance, it is reported that 75% (300) of respondents agreed that government should continue to substantially finance higher education if it is also true that only 400 out of 1000 persons contacted bothered to complete and return the form. Can we count the missing 600 as neutral or not bothered?

## Key terms for this chapter

| | |
|---|---|
| Case history | Open-ended question |
| Case study | Panel |
| Census | Researcher bias |
| Clinical method | Respondent |
| Content analysis | Self report |
| Disguise | Social desirability |
| Face-to-face | Structure |
| Focus group | Survey |

## Exercises

1 Without looking back at the text, try to think of several advantages and disadvantages the survey has compared to the informal interview.

2 Suppose you decided to conduct a survey on attitudes towards the environment in your area. Outline the steps you would take in planning and conducting the survey, paying particular attention to:

 – the sample and means of obtaining it
 – the exact approach to respondents you would use
 – the types of question you would ask

 To answer this last point in detail you will need to read the next section on questionnaires, at least briefly.

3 A researcher wishes to investigate specific instances of racism (abuse, physical harassment, discrimination) which members of minority ethnic groups have experienced. Four assistants are employed to conduct informal, guided interviews starting with individuals whose names have been provided by local community leaders.

 (a) What kind of sample is drawn?
 (b) One interviewer records far fewer instances than the other three. Can you give at least five reasons why this might be?
 (c) Another interviewer argues that the study should follow up with a structured questionnaire over a far wider sample. Why might this be?

4 You are about to conduct an interview with the manager of the local, large supermarket. He is 43 years old, quite active in local politics and is known to be fairly friendly. Make a list of all the variables, especially those concerning your own personality and characteristics, which might influence the production of information in the interview.

5 A researcher wishes to survey young people's attitudes to law and order. Interviewers complete questionnaires with sixth formers who volunteer from the schools which agree to be included in the study. Families are also selected at random from the local telephone directory. Young people are also questioned at the local youth club. Discuss several ways in which the sample for the complete study may be biased.

# Asking questions II

## Questionnaires, scales and tests

### Questionnaires and attitude scales
Questionnaires, attitude scales and tests are instruments for gathering structured information from people. Questionnaires used in surveys are usually constructed for the specific research topic and tend to test for a current opinion or patterns of behaviour. Attitude scales are usually intended to have a somewhat longer life span. They are seen as technical measuring instruments and therefore require STANDARDISATION and a more thorough preparation in terms of reliability and validity. It is usually intended that they tap a more permanent aspect of the individual's personality, such as attitude towards religion or authority.

However, many of the features of attitude scale construction can be employed by the student who wishes to create a measure of people's views on a current issue, such as preservation of the environment or attitudes towards animals.

Questionnaires, scales, psychometric and projective tests can all be used in experimental situations as well as in the field. One group might be assessed for 'self-esteem' before and after a 'treatment' in which they are made to feel successful. This can be compared with a control group's assessments.

## 1 QUESTIONNAIRES

In the section on attitude scales we will discuss in some detail the issues to be considered when developing scale items. Most of the points included there apply to survey questionnaires as well. If you are constructing a simple opinion questionnaire, it would make sense to check the general points made below and then go on to item 3 on 'Questionnaire and scale items'.

### Some general principles
The following principles are part of the common 'lore' of survey questionnaires. They apply particularly to the situation in which strangers, or people little known to the interviewer, are being asked a big favour in stopping to answer a few questions.

1 **Ask for the minimum of information required for the research purpose** A respondent's time is precious so why ask for information obtainable elsewhere? Personal details may be available from company or school records. The respondent's time spent answering questions has a bearing on mood, and mood will certainly be altered if the interviewer asks what sex the respondent is! Other details, such as whether married and number of children may well be drawn from an introductory relaxing chat and, if not, during final checking.

A further argument concerns the principle of *parsimony*, that is, limiting effort to the necessary whilst maintaining efficiency. Too much information may not be useful. Some questions may have been included only because they 'seemed interesting', which is too vague a basis for inclusion.

**2  Make sure questions *can* be answered**  'How many times have you visited a doctor this year?' may be quite difficult for many people to answer at all accurately.

**3  Make sure questions will be answered truthfully**  The question in point 2 is unlikely to be answered truthfully because of its difficulty. Other difficult or wide ranging questions are likely to receive an answer based more on well-known public opinion, rather than on the individual's own experience and values. Questions on child-rearing, for instance, if not phrased very explicitly, are well known for producing, where wide error is possible, answers more in accord with prevailing 'expert' views on good practice.

**4  Make sure questions will be answered and not refused**  Some sensitive topics will obviously produce more refusals. Most respondents will continue on a sensitive topic, once started, but may baulk at a sensitive question turning up suddenly in an otherwise innocuous context, for instance a sex-life question among political items. The interviewer has to provide a context in order to justify sensitive points, or else avoid them.

### Fixed and open-ended questions
At the least structured extreme, survey questionnaires have open-ended questions. Most questionnaire items are fixed choice, however, where respondents are asked to select an answer from two or more alternatives. Open-ended questions have several advantages, some of which we alluded to earlier.

1  They deliver richer information
2  The respondent does not feel frustrated by the constraint imposed with a fixed choice answer
3  There is less chance of ambiguity, since the respondent says what he or she thinks and doesn't have to interpret a statement and then agree or disagree with it.
4  The questioning is more realistic. We rarely have to simply agree or disagree, or say how strongly, without giving our reasons.

However, open-ended questions are also difficult to code or quantify, whereas fixed choice items make numerical comparison relatively easy. Chapter 19 on qualitative data, discusses methods of dealing with open-ended answers.

Here are a few examples of fixed choice items:

1. I voted in the last election                                              YES/NO

2. I would describe my present dwelling as:
   (a) Fuly owned by me
   (b) Owned by me with a mortgage
   (c) Owned by me as part of a housing association
   (d) Rented from the local council
   (e) Rented from a private landlord
   (f) Provided by employer
   (g) Other (please state)

3. My age is: (a) Under 16 (b) 16–21 (c)22–35 (d) Over 35

4. At what age did your baby start crawling? .......... months

The questionnaire constructor has to be careful to phrase questions clearly and unambiguously, such that the respondent is in no doubt which answer to give. The supreme ideal is that all respondents will interpret an item in the same way. Some questions will permit the respondent to tick or check more than one item but if this is not desired (one response only should be unique to each respondent) then possible overlap must be carefully avoided.

> Is it possible to check more than one answer in any of the items given above?

I would think there might be confusion if I were just 35 and answering item 3. In item 2 (e) and (f) might overlap.

### Features of good questionnaires and measurement scales

Where survey questionnaires are requesting purely factual information (such as occupation, number of children at school, hours of television watched, and so on) the following principles are not so crucial, though all measures should be reliable ones. (Factual questionnaires usually have 'face' validity – see below). Where scales and tests attempt to measure psychological characteristics, the following are extremely important:

1 They should DISCRIMINATE as widely as possible across the variety of human response. They shouldn't identify a few extreme individuals whilst showing no difference between individuals clustered at the centre of any scale. This is referred to as DISCRIMINATORY POWER

2 They should be highly RELIABLE

3 They should be supported by tests of VALIDITY

4 They should be STANDARDISED if they are to be used as general, practical measures of human characteristics.

ITEM ANALYSIS is the name of methods used to deal with 1 and 2. This will be explained later on where validity will also be more thoroughly examined and standardisation will be introduced.

A questionnaire, scale or test will normally be piloted, perhaps several times, before the researcher is satisfied that it meets these criteria. Even an unambitious questionnaire, constructed by students as part of course practical work, should be piloted at least once to highlight pitfalls and possible misinterpretations.

## 2 ATTITUDE SCALES

Attitude scales are quite like questionnaires but do not usually use questions. Most use statements with which the respondent has to agree or disagree.

Remember that questionnaires can vary along the dimension of DISGUISE and that the purpose of the scale could therefore be disguised from the respondent, as in Hammond's technique, mentioned earlier in the chapter. Some attitude scales give some clue to their purpose while others are transparent, as in the case where a limited topic, such as dental hygiene, is involved.

We will look at the techniques of five popular types of attitude scale, along with their advantages and disadvantages.

## Equal appearing intervals (Thurstone, 1931)
To construct a Thurstone-type scale:

1 Produce a large set of statements, both positive and negative towards the attitude object. For instance: 'Companies should provide more crèche facilities'.

2 Engage a panel of judges to rate each item on a scale of one (highly negative on the issue) to 11 (highly positive on the issue). They are urged to use all of the scale and not to bunch items into a few categories.

3 Take the mean value, for each item, of all the judges' ratings. Our item above might get an average rating of 8.7 for instance. This is its SCALE VALUE.

4 In the interests of reliability, reject items which have a high level of dispersion (see chapter 13), as measured, usually, by their standard deviation. These items are those on which judges are least in agreement.

5 In the finished scale, a respondent now scores the scale value of each item agreed with. Hence, people favourable to equal opportunities measures will tend to score only on high scale value items and thus end up with a high overall score.

A sample of items which might appear in a Thurstone type scale is shown below, along with each item's scale value. The values, of course, would not be visible to the respondent.

|  | *Please tick if you agree* |
|---|---|
| Women are less reliable employees because they are likely to leave through pregnancy | (2.1) |
| Interview panels should scrutinise all questions before interviewing to ensure that none are discriminatory | (5.8) |
| Companies should provide more crèche facilities | (8.7) |

*Box 15   Weaknesses of the Thurstone method*

1 The judges themselves cannot be completely neutral, although they are asked to be objective. In an early debate on this issue, Hinckley (1932) was severely criticised for rejecting judges as 'careless' because they sorted a majority of items into a few extreme categories, against the exhortation mentioned in item 2 of the construction process above. It turned out that most of these judges were black (or pro-black whites) who rated as fairly hostile certain statements seen as relatively neutral by white judges unaware of, or unconcerned by, black issues.

2 There is a difficulty in choosing the most discriminating items from among those with the same scale value.

## Summated ratings (Likert, 1932)
To construct a Likert-type scale:

1 Produce an equal number of favourable and unfavourable statements about the attitude object.

2 Ask respondents to indicate, for each item, their response to the statement according to the following scale:

| 5 | 4 | 3 | 2 | 1 |
|---|---|---|---|---|
| Strongly agree | Agree | Undecided | Disagree | Strongly disagree |

3 Use the values on this scale as a score for each respondent on each item, so that the respondent scores five for strong agreement with an item favourable to the attitude object, but one for strong agreement with an unfavourable item.

4 Add up the scores for each item to give the respondent's overall score.

5 Carry out an item analysis test (discussed later) in order to determine the most discriminating items – those on which high overall scorers tend to score highly and vice versa.

6 Reject low discriminatory items, keeping a balance of favourable and unfavourable items.

Step 5 here is the Likert scale's greatest strength relative to other scales. It means that, unlike in a Thurstone scale, an item does not need to relate obviously to the attitude issue or object. It can be counted as DIAGNOSTIC if responses to it correlate well with responses overall. For instance, we might find that respondents fairly hostile to equal opportunities issues also tend to agree with 'Women have an instinctive need to be near their child for the first two to three years of its life'. This could stay in our attitude scale since it might predict negative equal opportunities attitude fairly well.

*Box 16   Weaknesses of the Likert method*

1 For each respondent, scores on the scale only have meaning *relative* to the scores in the distribution obtained from other respondents. Data produced is therefore best treated as ORDINAL (see chapter 1) whereas Thurstone considered intervals on his scale to be truly equal.

2 The 'undecided' score, 3, is ambiguous. Does it imply a neutral position (no opinion) or an on-the-fence position with the respondent torn between feelings in both directions?

3 Partly as a consequence of 2, overall scores, central to the distribution (say 30 out of 60) are quite ambiguous. Central scores could reflect a lot of 'undecided' answers, or they could comprise a collection of 'strongly for' and 'strongly against' answers, in which case, perhaps the scale measures two different attitudes.

## The social distance scale (Bogardus, 1925)

Bogardus' scale was originally intended to measure attitudes towards members of different nationalities. Respondents had to follow this instruction:

'According to my first feeling reactions, I would willingly admit members of each race [respondents were given several races or nationalities] (as a class, and not the best I have known, nor the worst members) to one or more of the classifications under which I have placed a cross.'

They were then given this list to tick, for each race:

1 To close kinship by marriage
2 To my club as personal chums
3 To my street as neighbours
4 To employment in my occupation
5 To citizenship in my country
6 As visitors only in my country
7 Would exclude from my country

It is claimed that, in practice, it is unusual for respondents to accept the race or nationality at a higher level than one at which rejection has occurred, for instance, accepting in one's street, but not to one's occupation. This is known as a 'reversal'.

It is possible to adapt this technique to test attitudes towards any category of persons. The classifications themselves will of course need altering to fit the particular categories of person.

On the equal opportunities theme, it would be possible to grade types of occupation into which respondents felt female workers should be encouraged. Modification, however, will require re-standardisation in order to avoid too many reversals.

*Box 17  Weaknesses of the Bogardus method*

1 Reversals cannot be entirely eliminated. Some people are more protective about their employment than their streets, particularly in cities, I would suspect.

2 The overall scale for scoring is narrow, leaving less room for sensitive statistical analysis.

## Cumulative scaling (Guttman, 1950)

Roughly speaking, the principle of the Bogardus scale is here extended to any attitude object, not just person categories. On a Bogardus scale, if we know a person's score we know just how far up the scale they went, assuming no reversals. Hence, we can exactly reproduce their scoring pattern. This last achievement is the ideal criterion of a Guttman scale. A clear (but not particularly useful) example would be a scale checking height, where you would tick all those items below which are true for you:

1. I am taller than 4' 0"
2. I am taller than 4' 6"
3. I am taller than 5' 0"
4. I am taller than 5' 6"
5. I am taller than 6' 0"
6. I am taller than 6' 6"

A positive response to item 4 logically entails a positive response to items 1, 2 and 3 also. In the same way as this scale measures a unitary dimension (height), so a true Guttman scale is supposed to only measure one finite attitude and is known as a 'undimensional scale'.

In practice, when measuring attitudes rather than height, it is never possible to perfectly reproduce a respondent's exact answering pattern from their overall score. As we shall see below, items can very often be interpreted differently by respondents and it is rarely possible to isolate attitudes such that answers reflect a undimensional scale. For instance, one respondent, who is a member of a particular minority ethnic group, might disagree with 'members of all ethnic groups should be treated equally' since, in his or her view, the group has been treated pretty unequally in the past and requires compensation. Hence, from the tester's point of view this person's answers may seem inconsistent, since they are otherwise strongly favourable to minority ethnic groups, yet a negative response on this item is taken as hostility.

*Box 18   Weaknesses of the Guttman method*

| |
|---|
| 1  Reversals cannot be eliminated. |
| 2  Guttman himself was criticised for not dealing with the problem of representativeness in selecting items. He claimed this could be achieved through intuitive thinking and experience. |

## The semantic differential (Osgood *et al.*, 1957)

The original intention behind this scale was to use it for measuring the *connotative* meaning of an object for an individual, roughly speaking, the term's associations for us. Thus, we can all give a denotative meaning for 'nurse' – we have to define what a nurse is, as in a dictionary. The *connotation* of a nurse may, however, differ for each of us. For me, a nurse is associated with caring, strength and independence. For others, by popular stereotype, he or she may be seen as submissive and practical.

On a semantic differential the respondent is invited to mark a scale between bi-polar adjectives according to the position they feel the object holds on that scale for them. For 'nurse' on the following bi-polar opposites, I might mark as shown:

good    ✓   ___  ___  ___  ___  ___  ___  bad
weak    ___  ___  ___  ___  ___   ✓   ___  strong
active  ___   ✓   ___  ___  ___  ___  ___  passive

Osgood claimed that factor analysis (see later this chapter) of all scales gave rise to three general meaning factors, to one of which all bi-polar pairs could be attached.

'Active' (along with 'slow–fast', 'hot–cold') is an example of the ACTIVITY factor.

'Strong' (along with 'rugged–delicate', 'thick–thin') is an example of the POTENCY factor.

'Good' (along with 'clean–dirty', 'pleasant–unpleasant') is an example of the EVALUATIVE factor.

Adapted to attitude measurement, the semantic differential apparently produces good reliability values and correlates well with other attitude scales, thus producing some CONCURRENT VALIDITY (see page 112)

*Box 19    Weaknesses of the semantic differential*

> 1 Respondents may have a tendency towards a 'position response bias' where they habitually mark at the extreme end of the scale (or won't use the extreme at all) without considering possible weaker or stronger responses. This can occur with a Likert scale too, but is more likely here since the scale points lack the Likert verbal designations (or 'strongly agree' etc.).
>
> 2 Here, too, we have the problem of interpretation of the middle point on the scale.

# 3   QUESTIONNAIRE OR SCALE ITEMS

## What to avoid in statement construction

What do you think is unsatisfactory about the following statements, intended for an attitude scale?

1 'We should begin to take compensatory action in areas of employment and training where, in the past, members of one ethnic group, sex or disability type have suffered discrimination or experienced disadvantages as a direct result of being a member of that category.'

2 'Society should attempt to undo the effects of institutional racism wherever possible.'

3 'Immigrants should not be allowed to settle in areas of high unemployment.'

4 'Abortion is purely a woman's choice and should be made freely available.'

5 'It should not be possible to ask a woman about her spouse's support, when husbands are not asked the same questions.'

6 'Mrs Thatcher and her government are callously dismantling the welfare state.'

7 'Do you agree that student grants should be increased?'

8 'Do you have a criminal record?'

**1   Complexity**   Not many respondents will take this in all in one go. The statement is far too complex. It could possibly be broken up into logical components.

**2   Technical terms**   Many respondents will not have a clear idea of what 'institutional racism' is. Either find another term or include a preamble to the item which explains the special term.

**3   Ambiguity**   Some students of mine used this item once and found almost everyone in general agreement, whether they were generally hostile to immigrants or not. Hence, it was not at all discriminating. This was probably because those positive towards immigrants considered their plight if new to the country *and* unemployed. Those who were hostile to immigrants may well have been racially prejudiced and either mistakenly thought most immigrants were black, or equally incorrectly thought most black people were immigrants.

**4  Double-barrelled items**    This quite simple item is asking two questions at once. A person might well agree with free availability – to avoid the dangers of the back-street abortionist – yet may not feel that only the woman concerned should choose.

**5  Negatives**    In the interests of avoiding response set (see below), about half the items in a scale should be positive towards the object and about half negative. However, it is not a good idea to produce negative statements simply by negating a positive one. It can be confusing to answer a question with a double negative, even where one of the negatives is camouflaged, as in:

'It should not be possible to reject a candidate's application on the grounds of disability.'

This could be rephrased as 'A candidate's disability should be completely ignored when considering an application.'

The item in the exercise has two overt negatives in it and this can easily be confusing.

**6  Emotive language**    A statement such as this may not get an attitude test off to a good start, particularly in many constituencies in the south-east of England! If there are emotive items at all it might be best to leave these until the respondent is feeling more relaxed with the interviewer or with the test itself.

**7  Leading questions**    As I said, most attitude tests don't have actual questions in them. Should this sort of question occur, however, it carries with it an implication that the respondent should say 'yes'. If you don't feel this is so, just try to imagine a friend or colleague opening the day's conversation with such a question. To the respondent it can seem hard to disagree, something which people would usually rather not do anyway. One might begin with 'Weeell . . .'. Respondents may well say 'Yes, but . . .' with the 'but' amounting to disagreement, even though the response is recorded as agreement.

**8  Invasion of privacy**    This is private information, along with sex life and other obvious areas. Many people will find questions about attitude quite intrusive. Certainly the student conducting a practical exercise should be very careful about such intrusion.

## Organisation of items

**1  Response set or bias**    An effect called RESPONSE ACQUIESCENCE SET often occurs when responding to questionnaires. This is the tendency to agree rather than disagree ('Yeah saying'). To avoid a constant error from this effect, items need to be an unpredictable mixture of positive and negative statements about the attitude object. This has the effect either of keeping the respondent thinking about each item or of giving the inveterate yeah sayer a central score, rather than an extreme one. There is also some evidence of a smaller bias towards *disagreeing* with items.

**2 Respondent's interpretation**  With any questionnaire or scale, it is a good idea to make it clear that both positive and negative items will appear. There are several reasons for this.

Respondents are likely to view the interviewer as believing the statements made. A set of statements all contrary to what the respondent thinks may well set up strong emotional defences. We have said already that, for the same reason it would be best to start with less extreme statements.

There are also demand characteristics (see chapter 5) associated with responding to a questionnaire. The respondent may well try to interpret the aim of the research or questions. Again, if all initial items are in the same direction the respondent may form an impression of the interviewer's aims or personality which can distort the respondent's later answers.

**3 Social desirability**  Mentioned in part 1 of this chapter, this factor involves respondents guessing what is counted as a socially acceptable or favourable answer and giving it in order to 'look good'. Some questionnaires attempt to deal with this by including items which only an angel would agree or disagree with. If too many such items are answered in the 'saintly' manner, the respondent's results are excluded from the research. Eysenck calls his set of items a 'lie scale', though an excluded respondent is not necessarily lying. They may be near perfect or they may be distorting the truth just a bit.

A further reason for doing this might be to 'please the researcher' by giving the results it is assumed are required.

### Reliability and number of items
The number of items used in a questionnaire needs to be kept manageable in terms of time and the respondent's patience, but enough items should be chosen for reliability to become acceptably high. With a larger number of items, random error, from respondents' individual interpretations and misunderstandings, should cancel each other out.

*Box 20  Constructing an attitude scale*

---

1 Produce a substantial number of items which are balanced for:
  (a) Strength (some 'weak' statements, some 'hard')
  (b) Breadth: is the whole area covered?
  (c) Direction: in a Likert type scale, some items should be 'pro' the issue and as many 'anti'; half of each of this set should be weak and half strong

2 Pilot this first batch of items for ambiguity, misunderstanding etc.

3 Replace deleted items by new ones, still keeping a balance

4 Repeat 2 and 3 until all items are unproblematic

5 Arrange items in a random or alternating order which will discourage response bias or hostility build up

6 Pilot this arrangement on good-sized sample and conduct item analysis on results

7 Delete unreliable items and replace as before, including steps 2 and 3

8 Keep repeating cycle(s) until reliability is satisfactory

9 Inspect final version to ensure validity has not been sacrificed during this process. Do items still cover main issues, or do some issues now predominate?

---

# 4 PROJECTIVE TESTS

These tests have been developed out of the psychoanalytic tradition of psychological research work. They are based on the principle of *projection* as a 'defence mechanism'.

> The *Rorschach* ink blot test is a set of abstract drawings rather like children produce with 'butterfly' paintings. A sheet of wet ink is turned over on itself to form an ambiguous 'blob'. The test-taker reports what he or she feels they can see in the picture. This is assumed to reflect, in part, that person's projections of inner, perhaps hidden emotions onto the external world.

> Similarly, the *Thematic apperception test* (TAT) is a concrete picture, often of people in some situation, about which, the test-taker is asked, 'What is happening?'

These tests belong in the unstructured, disguised section of the quadrant formed by these two dimensions. It is claimed that their open-endedness produces richer responding and that their disguised nature provides genuine data, un-biased by people guessing the researcher's (or therapist's) intent.

It is argued that the tests can be used to measure such factors as the affective, usually hidden, component of attitudes. They have very often been used to assess concealed aggression, hostility, anxiety, sexual fantasy and so on in hypothesis testing work. Levin's study, mentioned in chapter 8, used Rorschach tests.

*Box 21   Weaknesses of projective tests*

> 1 Being open-ended and initially qualitative, the tests are suspect for their reliability. Some users take great care in checking agreement between raters who code and categorise responses, ignorant of the research hypothesis. The researcher provides a comprehensive and subtle coding scheme. This occurred in Levin's study.
>
> 2 It is quite possible for coders to be highly consistent, compared with one another, yet for the measures to be quite unrelated to any theoretical psychoanalytic principle. A person in Levin's study who said of people seen in the Rorschach blot 'I can't quite tell if they're male or female' may not *actually* be confused about their sexual body-image, for instance. Since the tests are also *disguised* measures of hypothetical concepts, the problem of validity is serious.

# 5 SOCIOMETRY

Sociometry is specifically aimed at analysing the interconnections between people in smallish groups. Typically, group members are asked who their best friends are, with whom they would prefer to work on a problem or with whom they

*Table 5   Sociometric matrix*

|  |  |  | Chosen | | | | |
|---|---|---|---|---|---|---|---|
|  |  |  | A | B | C | D | E |
| Solution | Chooser | A |  | 0 | 1 | 1 | 1 |
| matrix |  | B | 1 |  | 0 | 1 | 1 |
|  |  | C | 1 | 0 |  | 1 | 0 |
|  |  | D | 0 | 0 | 1 |  | 0 |
|  |  | E | 0 | 0 | 0 | 1 |  |

would share a room, and so on. Questions can also ask about least preferred group members or about who should be leader.

Information generated, then, is in the form of person choices, positive or negative. These choices can be represented on a SOCIOMETRIC MATRIX, as shown in table 5. '1' represents being chosen and '0' not. It is possible to subject these matrices to mathematical analysis. Out of this can come measures of group cohesiveness or predictions of internal conflict.

A more obvious and direct product of the matrix is the SOCIOGRAM or, in more general mathematical terms, the DIRECTED GRAPH. An example of the sociogram resulting from table 5 is given in figure 10.

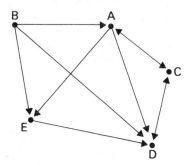

*Figure 10   Sociogram or directed graph*

From this diagram it is immediately obvious that B is an 'isolate', D is very popular, though chooses colleagues carefully, and C only chooses people who reciprocate the choice.

The sociogram tends only to be used in practical applications, rather than in research studies, where interactions are usually too numerous for charts, and detailed mathematical processing is required.

## Applications
Research applications include the study of classroom interactions. Teachers, for instance, have been found to prefer the children most chosen by their classmates, and vice versa. The effect of direct praise to pupils can be assessed in terms of increased popularity among peers.

In general, comparisons can be made between group structures and group effectiveness. For popular individuals, links can be sought with other measures of liking and attraction. The relationship of 'isolates' and 'cliques' to the rest of the group can be further investigated.

*Box 22    Weaknesses of sociometric method*

1  Although small group studies can use the sociogram for illustration, larger studies, and any seeking statistical analysis, require sophisticated and specialised mathematical methods.

2  Choices made alone and on paper can differ markedly from those made in real situations with all group pressures present. On the other hand, the anonymity and distance of the choice might just disclose real attractons, suppressed in the practical group setting.

# 6  PSYCHOMETRIC TESTS

Psychologists have developed many tests which were intended to be standardised instruments of measurement for human psychological characteristics. These are known as PSYCHOMETRIC TESTS and their use as PSYCHOMETRY. The tradition goes back to Galton who began the measurement of mental abilities in the 1890s by testing thousands of people on many sensory and cognitive tasks. Although some attitude scales have become highly refined, and even projective tests are sometimes called 'psychometric', if well standardised, it is intelligence and personality tests which have undergone a high degree of standardisation and scrutiny for validity. This is partly because such tests are used in professional practice where peoples' life chances can be affected.

These tests have also undergone much periodic, revision, since they are highly sensitive to bias from cultural, class and other social factors. It is on these grounds that their validity has been most seriously challenged and thoroughly investigated.

For instance, to the question 'What should you do if you find a stamped addressed envelope in the street?', it might be 'intelligent', in a very poor area, where petty crime is unremarkable, to steam off the stamp – a response which gained no mark in one famous test. A picture depicting a boy holding an umbrella at the wrong angle to falling rain was said by Puerto Ricans to be incorrect, not because of the angle but because the boy was holding the umbrella at all. This is considered highly effeminate in Puerto Rican society!

It is beyond the scope of this book to cover intelligence and personality testing in depth, along with all the weaknesses and criticisms of the tests. This is covered very well in other available texts, in particular R. Gross, *Psychology: The Science of Mind and Behaviour*. The examples given above simply demonstrate the need for standardisation and constant revision from a research method's point of view. They also show the reader, I hope, what is meant by class and cultural bias.

For the student thinking in terms of research methods, however, it is important to recognise that any study, including experimental ones, might include, as data, results of psychometric tests. Most tests will be beyond the scope of student use, since they are closely guarded as technical instruments of the psychological profession. They also usually have quite complex scoring manuals which are even more closely monitored.

## Factor analysis
Researchers often support the development and use of psychometric tests by employing a form of 'construct validity' (explained later in this chapter), which involves a complex statistical procedure known as FACTOR ANALYSIS. The aim is to

find factors (hypothetical constructs) which might explain the observed relationships between subjects' scores on several tests or subtests. The steps involved are these:

1 A large sample of people are measured on several tests or subtests.

2 Correlations (see chapter 17) are calculated between every possible pair of tests or subtests and arranged in a matrix as shown in the example below.

3 The matrix of correlations is fed into the factor analysis programme which looks for 'clusters' – groups of tests or subtests which all correlate well together.

4 The researcher 'asks' the programme to 'solve' the matrix for a particular number of factors. This means the programme attempts to explain the relationship between test results (the 'clusters') using this given number of factors. The factors and the explanation are purely statistical.

5 The programme gets the best solution and states the amount of variation between tests or subtests still unexplained.

6 The researcher might ask the programme to solve for a higher number of factors if the amount unexplained is too high.

To make the concept of factor analysis a little clearer, I hope, imagine the following. We select a few hundred people of average fitness and subject them to various athletic events. We correlate the results of every event with every other, producing a table, part of which might look like table 6:

*Table 6*

| Correlations between various athletic events | | | | | | | |
|---|---|---|---|---|---|---|---|
| | 100 Metres | 200 Metres | 3000 Metres | 5000 Metres | Shot | Discus | Long Jump |
| 100 Metres | × | 0.87 | 0.24 | 0.31 | − 0.65 | − 0.32 | 0.47 |
| 200 Metres | | × | 0.19 | 0.28 | − 0.61 | − 0.29 | 0.39 |
| 3000 Metres | | | × | 0.91 | − 0.16 | 0.03 | 0.13 |
| 5000 Metres | | | | × | − 0.08 | 0.11 | 0.09 |
| Shot | | | | | × | 0.65 | 0.14 |
| Discus | | | | | | × | − 0.02 |
| Long Jump | | | | | | | × |

As we'll see in chapter 17, if people tend to score similarly on two variables, these variables are said to 'positively correlate' and we'd expect a value close to + 1. If there is a tendency to be high on one variable whilst being low on the other we'd expect a value approaching − 1. No relationship at all is signified by a value close to zero.

As we'd expect from common sense prediction, there is a strong correlation between 100 and 200 metres, and between 3000 and 5000 metres. There is a moderate correlation between discus and shot put and between 100 metres and long jump, whereas that between 100 metres and shot put is moderately negative.

Intuition might suggest that the underlying factors responsible for these relationships are *sprinting ability*, *stamina* and *strength*. If we asked the factor analysis programme to solve for just two factors it would probably tell us that, no matter which way the matrix was solved, a lot of relationship between variables was left unaccounted for. For three variables it might well give us a good solution with little variation unexplained. But it is important to note that it would be up to us to name the factors and to debate what real processes they are an indication of.

Roughly speaking, this is what factor analyists do with the scores of large samples on personality and intelligence tests and subtests. The factors emerging are recognised and named intuitively. The factors are said to be responsible for the subjects' variations in performance across the tests.

It is important to recognise that factor analysis does not 'prove' that such factors exist. It simply provides supporting evidence which allows the researcher to claim that intelligence or personality could be organised in a particular way and that the factor analysis results don't refute this. Factor analysis is a purely statistical process. As with all statistical results, researchers, with particular views and theories to defend, interpret and present statistics in a way which gives them the best support.

There is a more extensive discussion of factor analysis and its limitations in Gross (pp. 635–6 and 695–9). An extensive and severe criticism of the use of factor analysis to support models of intellectual structure is provided by Block and Dworkin (1974).

# 7   RELIABILITY, VALIDITY AND STANDARDISATION

It is common in psychological research to attempt the measurement of variables for which there is no universally agreed measure. Examples are attitude, motivation, intelligence. Some variables even appear as invented constructs, examples being: extroversion and introversion or ego-strength. The tests which psychologists construct in order to measure such variables often serve as operational definitions of the concept under research. The attitude scales and psychometric tests which we have discussed would all need to be checked formally for their reliability and validity. They would also need to be standardised for general use. We'll discuss methods for each of these checks in turn.

## RELIABILITY

Any measure, but especially one we have just invented, must be queried as to its accuracy in terms of producing the same results on different occasions. A reliable measuring instrument is one which achieves just this performance. Consider a practical example. If you have kitchen scales which stick you won't get the same reading for the same amount of flour each time you weigh it. The measure given by your scales is unreliable. We can also say that your scales have poor reliability.

A difference between kitchen scales and instruments used for human characteristic measurement is that psychologists often use tests with many items whereas weight is measured by just one indicator – the dial reading. Psychological tests of, for instance, political attitude can be queried as to their INTERNAL RELIABILITY, meaning 'is the test consistent within itself?' This is usually measured by checking whether persons tend to answer each item in the same way as they answer all others. Like scales and other instruments, though, these tests can also be checked for their reliability in producing similar results at different times. Cronbach (1960) has discussed these two rather different uses of the term reliability applied to a psychological measure. Using Cronbach's terms, INTERNAL CONSISTENCY and STABILITY, the difference might be pictured like this.

Imagine you were giving a statement to the police. Your statement might be found to be unreliable in two distinct ways:

1 Internal consistency – you may contradict yourself within the statement

2 Stability – you may alter important details when asked to remake the statement some time later

Internal consistency is the same as internal reliability. Stability may be called EXTERNAL RELIABILITY: does the test produce similar results on (at least two) different occasions?

# Methods for checking internal reliability

### Split half method
A psychological test which consists of several items or questions can be split so that items are randomly divided into two sets comprising half the complete test each. If the test is reliable then subjects' scores on each half should be similar and the extent of similarity is assessed using correlation (chapter 17). Correlations achieved here would be expected to exceed 0.9.

### Kuder–Richardson method
This method estimates the average split half correlation which would occur if the split half method was carried out for every possible splitting of the items into two halves.

### Item analysis
Items are considered good, in a questionnaire, if they *discriminate* well between individuals. There are two common methods for checking the discriminatory power of items.

1 For each item in the test or questionnaire, the correlation is calculated between each person's score on the item and their score on the test as a whole. This system only works where individuals can respond to each item along a scale, such as '1' (for strongly agree) to '5' (for strongly disagree) as in a Likert scale attitude questionnaire. It can't be used where responses are just 'yes' or 'no'.

2 Looking at individuals' scores overall on the test, the highest 10% and the lowest 10% of scores are identified. This 10% is not fixed and could be 15% or 20% if desired. The scores of these two groups of people are then totalled for each item in the test. If these two extreme groups scored very differently then the item is highly discriminative. If not, it is low in discriminating between the two groups and may be discarded.

Both these systems may be accused of some circularity since the scores used to decide whether an item is of poor discriminatory power include the response to that item. That is, the test for reliability uses scores on an as yet unreliable test.

# Checking external reliability

### Test-retest reliability
To check that a psychological test produces similar results each time it is used, we would have to use it on the *same* people on each occasion, otherwise we have no comparison. 'Test–retest' means that a group of people are tested once, then again some time later. The two sets of scores are *correlated*, to see whether people tend to get the same sort of score on the second occasion. If they do, the test has high reliability. Correlations achieved here would be expected to be at least around 0·75–0·8.

> There are several reasons, however, why people may not score the same, second time around, on the same test. Can you think of a few?

1 People may answer differently the second time *because* they took the test before and now wish to alter the image they feel they made.

2 They may also simply recall what they answered on the first occasion and not answer according to their current perceptions.

3 Some external event may have had a significant impact on attitudes. If the questionnaire is on capital punishment and a serious terrorist incident has occurred between first and second test, attitudes may have hardened.

4 The research may have included an attempt to change attitude between first and second test, in which case the attitude scale should have *already* been tested for reliability.

### Replication
The concept of external reliability can be extended from psychological tests to psychological effects. The effect found in an experiment can be said to be reliable if it occurs again in a *replication* of the original study. The use of imagery in memorising a list of words reliably produces superior recall compared with the use of rote rehearsal of each item. A psychologist who claims that a new therapy

reduces tantrums in autistic children will have discovered a reliable technique only if others can replicate the effects claimed. In this form of checking for reliability, unlike that of tests and questionnaires, the same persons are not usually retested. Here we are asking whether an experimental *manipulation* can be repeated reliably. In a crude sense 'will the same trick work on different people?'. We can also ask whether a non-experimental effect is reliably found. For instance, is it a reliable finding that children without pre-school experience are less sociable? Do we get the same difference with different samples of children?

*Table 7   Comparison of tests for internal and external reliability*

| | Test Part A | Test Part B | Whole Test in March | Whole Test in October | Original experiment First Subjects | Condition X | Y | Replication of original experiment New Subjects | Condition X | Y |
|---|---|---|---|---|---|---|---|---|---|---|
| Ian | A1 | B1 | M1 | O1 | Ian | X1 | Y1 | Charles | X1 | Y1 |
| Jan | A2 | B2 | M2 | O2 | Jan | X2 | Y2 | Roberta | X2 | Y2 |
| Hugh | A3 | B3 | M3 | O3 | Hugh | X3 | Y3 | Clara | X3 | Y3 |
| Jane | A4 | B4 | M4 | O4 | Jane | X4 | Y4 | Paul | X4 | Y4 |
| etc | A5 | B5 | M5 | O5 | etc. | X5 | Y5 | etc. | X5 | Y5 |
| | ⋮ | ⋮ | ⋮ | ⋮ | | ⋮ | ⋮ | | ⋮ | ⋮ |
| Do subjects score similarly on both halves of the test? | | | Do subjects score similarly on both occasions? | | | | | Is the significant effect found in the original experiment replicated? | | |
| INTERNAL RELIABILITY OF TEST | | | EXTERNAL RELIABILITY OF TEST | | | | | EXTERNAL RELIABILITY OF EXPERIMENTAL EFFECT | | |
| Split half Kuder Richardson | | | Test-retest | | | | | Replication | | |

NB. A1, M2 etc. are scores.

# VALIDITY

A test or effect may well be rated as excellent on reliability but may not be measuring what was originally intended. This criticism is often levelled at tests of intelligence which, though quite reliable, measure only a narrow range of intellectual ability, missing out, for instance, the whole range of creative thought which the public language definition would include.

Suppose you gave some seven-year-old children a list of quite difficult words to remember and recall. You may actually be testing their reading ability or word knowledge rather than their memory. Early experiments on perceptual defence, which seemed to show that people would take longer to recognise 'taboo', rude or emotional words, were criticised for the validity of the effect on the grounds that what may well have been demonstrated was peoples' unwillingness to report such words to a strange experimenter or their disbelief that such words could occur in a respectable scientific experiment. The effect was nevertheless quite reliable.

There are various recognised means by which validity can be assessed.

### Face validity
The crudest method for checking validity is simply to inspect the contents of a test to see whether it does indeed measure what it's supposed to. This is possible when devising a mathematics test, for example, for clearly the test should contain problems at the intended level and with sufficient breadth.

### Content validity
A researcher may ask colleagues to evaluate the content of a test to ensure that it is representative of the area which the test is intended to cover. They will carry out this task using their expertise in the topic area to judge whether the collection of items has failed to test certain skills or is unduly weighted towards some aspects of knowledge compared with others.

Content validity is, in fact, simply a more sophisticated version of face validity.

### Criterion validity
The validity of a test of neuroticism might reasonably be established by using it on a group of people who have suffered from a neurotic condition and comparing scores with a control group. Use of the neurotic group would be an example of what is called use of KNOWN GROUPS as a CRITERION. There are two types of criterion validity differing only in terms of the timing of the criterion test:

**Concurrent validity**    If the new test is validated by comparison with a currently existing criterion, we have CONCURRENT VALIDITY. Very often, a new IQ or personality might be compared with an older but similar test known to have good validity already. The known group example above is also a case of concurrent validity.

**Predictive validity**    A prediction may be made, on the basis of a new intelligence test for instance, that high scorers at age 12 will be more likely to obtain university degrees or enter the professions several years later. If the prediction is born out then the test has PREDICTIVE VALIDITY.

Both these methods are in fact predictive since, in science, the term 'predict' does not mean 'forecast'. A social scientist may well predict a relationship between *past* events. Used in this sense, then, there is virtually no difference between these two concepts except for the point in time of the prediction.

### Construct validity
This takes us back to our discussion of variables which are not directly observable and the psychologist's tendency to propose hypothetical constructs (chapter 2). Such constructs require some form of validation, otherwise, why should we continue to take them seriously? Typical of such constructs would be: achievement, motivation, extroversion, dogmatism, dependency, ego-strength.

In each case there is no direct evidence for such constructs having any kind of real existence. Construct validity entails demonstrating the power of such a construct to explain a network of research findings and to predict further relationships. Rokeach (1960) showed that his test for dogmatism predictably distinguished between different religious and political groups, as well as having relationships with approaches to entirely new problems and acceptance of new artistic ideas. Eysenck (1970) argued that extroversion was related to the activity of the cerebral cortex and produced several testable hypotheses from his theory.

Intelligence factors and personality variables are supported as valid by the use of factor analysis, as explained earlier, which is an elaborate part of construct validation.

If this all sounds a bit magical consider that no physicist has ever seen an atom directly. What are observed are the effects of what is *assumed* to be an atom. Although the theory of atomic elements is beyond dispute, the construct of an atom is defined mathematically, is difficult for the lay person to understand and keeps changing in exact definition.

## Standardisation

The process of standardising a test involves adjusting it, using reliability and validity tests to eliminate items, until it is useful as a measure of the population it is targeted at, and will enable us to confidently compare individuals. To make such comparisons the test must be used on a large sample of the target population, from whom means and standard scores (see chapter 13) are established. This will tell us what percentage of people tend to score between certain scores and what is the value which most of the population centre around.

Psychometric tests are used in research but also on an applied basis in decisions about people's life chances and opportunities. These may be related to education, psychotherapeutic treatment or job selection. Therefore, it is of the utmost importance that these tests do not discriminate, in a particular way, against some groups of people, which anyway reduces their scientific value. Standardisation has, therefore, both scientific and ethical importance.

## Standardisation to a normal distribution

Many tests are adjusted until testing of a large sample produces a score distribution which approximates very closely to the normal distribution (see chapter 13). One reason for doing this is that the properties of the normal distribution allow us to perform some extremely powerful statistical estimates.

The fact that an IQ test can be devised and adjusted until it produces a normal distribution on large group testing has led some researchers to argue that the test therefore measures a largely innate quality since many biological characteristics are indeed normally distributed through the working of many random genetic processes together.

Critics have argued that the adjustment of the test to normal distribution is artificial and that many biological characteristics are not normal in distribution. Certainly, some psychological phenomena need not be normally distributed. Attitudes to some issues on which people are somewhat polarised in position (for instance, on nuclear weapons or abortion) will be spread, as measured by questionnaire, in a bi-modal (two-hump) fashion (chapter 13).

An extremely important point here is that a test standardised on a particular population can obviously not be used with confidence on a different population. This criticism has been levelled at those who claimed a difference existed between white and black populations in intelligence. There *was* a difference in IQ score but, until 1973, the Stanford-Binet test had not included black persons in its sample for standardisation. Hence, the test was only applicable, with any confidence, to the white population.

## Key terms for this chapter

Attitude scales
  Thurstone method
  Likert method
  Bogardus method
  Guttman method
  Semantic differential
  Scale value
Diagnostic item
Discriminatory power
Factor analysis
Item analysis
Known groups

Psychometric tests
Reliability
  External Reliability/
    Stability
    Test–retest
  Internal Reliability/
    Internal Consistency
  Item analysis
  Kuder–Richardson
    method
  Split half method

Response acquiescence
  set/Response bias
Standardisation
Validity
  Construct validity
  Content validity
  Criterion validity
    Concurrent validity
    Predictive validity
  Face validity

## Exercises

1 A scale measuring attitude towards nuclear energy is given a test–retest reliability check. It is found that correlation is 0·85. However, it is also found that scores for the sample have risen significantly.

(a) Should the test be used as it is?
(b) What might explain the rise in sample scores?

2 A student friend has devised a test of 'Attitude towards the British' which she wants to administer to a group of international students just about to leave the country.

(a) How could the test be validated?
(b) How could the test be checked for reliability?

3 A friend says 'My cat hates Michael Jackson's music'. I've put the record on ten times now and each time she goes out. Is this a reliable test, a valid test, or neither?

4 Comment on any flaws in the following potential attitude scale or questionnaire items:

(a) Do you feel that the government has gone too far with privatisation?
(b) What do you think is the best way to punish children?
(c) How many times were you late for work in the last two months?
(d) People from other countries are the same as us and should be treated with respect.
(e) It should not be possible to avoid taxation and not be punished for it.
(f) Women are taking a lot of management posts in traditionally male occupational areas (in a scale to measure attitude to women's rights).
(g) Cheap literature is pervaded by the heterosexual stereotype.

5 A researcher administers Rorschach tests to a control and experimental group of psychiatric patients. She then rates each response according to a very well-standardised scale for detecting anxiety. Could this procedure be improved?

# Comparison studies

## 1 CROSS-SECTIONAL STUDIES

Both these and longitudinal studies can give information on changes in a psychological variable over time. A cross-sectional study does this by taking groups of children or adults from specific age bands and comparing them at the same moment in time. Comparisons may well highlight age-related changes and developmental trends. Cross-sectional data are often used to support developmental theories such as those of Piaget or Freud.

Two specific examples of cross-sectional studies are:

1 Williams *et al.* (1975) interviewed five-, seven and nine-year-old children. She asked the children to guess the sex of heavily stereotyped story characters. Five-year-olds showed some stereotyping but seven- and nine-year-olds showed far more.

2 Kohlberg (1981) developed his theory of changes in the style of children's moral reasoning from a study of ten-, 13- and 16-year-olds' attempts to solve several moral dilemmas.

A cross-sectional study can also compare groups defined other than by age. A cross-section of classes might be studied, or of occupational or ethnic groups.

## 2 LONGITUDINAL STUDIES

The big disadvantage of cross-sectional studies is that of subject variance, a problem encountered in any study using independent samples. We can't ever be sure that our two or more groups are similar enough for fair comparison. The longitudinal approach surmounts this difficulty since it employs repeated measures on the same group of subjects over a substantial period, often a number of years. In this way genuine changes and the stability of some characteristics may be observed. If intervals between observations are not too large, major points of change can be identified. Examples of longitudinal studies are:

1 Kagan *et al.* (1980) showed that infants in day care during the working week were no worse developed on any measure than home-reared children, so long as care facilities were good.

2 Eron *et al.* (1972) demonstrated a correlation between longer viewing of television violence at age nine and higher aggressiveness at age 19, by following through a study with hundreds of boys.

3 Kohlberg also carried out longitudinal studies, one lasting for 20 years, on groups of children and their moral reasoning.

Every so often, huge longitudinal studies are carried out on a large section of the child population in order to give some idea of national trends. In such cases the large sample of children is known as a COHORT. An example would be Davie *et al.* (1972) who followed almost 16,000 children from birth (one week in 1958) to the age of 11.

# Evaluation of longitudinal and cross-sectional studies

The longitudinal approach can show genuine changes in the children studied. If the sample is small, generalisation has to be tentative, but with larger samples or replicated studies, researchers can be more confident that changes are common to the population sampled from.

Changes inferred from a cross-sectional study could be the result of variation between groups in, for instance, education or local cultural environment. Samples in cross-sectional studies can also be biased by age discrimination. A sample of 14-year-old village children may not include those at boarding school whereas their nine-year-old equivalents are present at the time of the study.

Where the cross-sectional age difference is large (say 20 years), the different social changes experienced by the two groups may interfere with direct comparison on the variables studied. This is known as the COHORT EFFECT.

Because of the expense and time involved, longitudinal research tends to use relatively fewer subjects. Of these, some may get sick, move or otherwise drop out of the study. The remaining sample might consequently be unrepresentative.

Events specific to an era, such as war, massive unemployment or a dramatic rise in divorce rate, might have a specific effect on one generation of children in a longitudinal study such that their particular pattern of development is not characteristic of other generations. This is known as the CROSS-GENERATIONAL PROBLEM.

Decisions made at the start of a longitudinal study are irreversible once the study has begun, unless the study is relatively unstructured (for instance, a case study). A cross-sectional study can sooner be modified and replicated within the same generation.

Both longitudinal and cross-sectional studies may be confounded by maturational changes in children's general development. For instance, difficult questions will be more easily answered by nine-year-olds than by seven-year-olds. We might falsely conclude that the younger children don't have the knowledge or concept which certain questions ask about. Older children might be more capable of guessing what a researcher is after.

# Cross-sectional, short-term longitudinal study

This is a compromise design for the study of age comparison. Three groups, say of 13-, 15- and 17-year-olds may be studied over two years on the effects of a programme designed to reduce drug addiction. Each group would be compared with a control group, as in a longitudinal study using one age group. But here we can determine the age at which the programme has maximum effect whilst investigating the range 13 to 19 in just two years.

*Box 23   Advantages and disadvantages of longitudinal and cross-sectional studies:*

|  | Cross-sectional | Longitudinal |
|---|---|---|
| **Advantages** | Cross-sectional groups are studied at same historical moment so cross generational problem avoided | The development of specific individuals is recorded |
|  | Few subjects lost during study | No subject variables can confound age and stage comparisons |
|  | Relatively inexpensive and less time consuming. Support for theories, modification or replication all achieved more quickly | Useful where the effect of some 'treatment' or programme is to be followed through and results compared with those of a control group |
| **Disadvantages** | Cohort problem if age difference between groups is large | Samples smaller and subjects may be lost during study |
|  | Subject variables may confound results | Once started, modification can be difficult or 'unscientific' |
|  | Does not provide information on the development of specific individuals | Time consuming. Results only after a long period. Replication and modification difficult or impossible |
|  |  | Relatively expensive |
|  |  | Cross-generational problem possible when development of one generation compared with another |

# 3   CROSS-CULTURAL STUDIES

Psychologists who discover reliable effects or who demonstrate strong developmental trends would usually be interested in whether these may be generalised to fairly different cultures. If so, the case for universal psychological features is strengthened. Language development, for instance, seems to occur in stages recognisable in all cultures so far studied, though debates arise around more specific features of each language group.

Differences found are attributed either to cultural variation or genetic difference, though by far the greater number of cross-cultural studies investigate differences in social behaviour, thus indicating socialisation processes as the far more likely variable.

Cross-cultural studies compare samples from two or more cultures on some psychological variable. Those conducted earlier this century often had a distinctively colonial or Euro-centred flavour. The 'natives' were interesting to study, whole societies were described as 'primitive' and the term 'negro' was commonplace, though this latter term still occurs in some 1980s psychology texts.

Typically, psychologists tested members of a tribal community on visual illusions or counting tasks. The emphasis was often on what such tribes 'lacked', and the studies tended to be ETHNOCENTRIC. An example of ethnocentrism is to describe a tribe's religious beliefs as 'superstitious' whilst not recognising that one's own religious beliefs might suffer the same analysis.

To find fairly non-ethnocentric work, it is useful to turn to the work of the social anthropologists, who tend to conduct intense participant observation studies as a member of a village community for many months if not years. These researchers have studied the community in its own right, not as a comparison with the West. They would attempt to record the inter-relationship of local customs, norms, taboos and social interactions such as marriage and trade.

Classic examples include Margaret Mead's studies of female adolescence in Samoa and of sex-role differences in New Guinea. Whorf (1957) studied concept differences conveyed by different language structures. Ruth Benedict (1934) used the term CULTURAL RELATIVITY to underline her view that an individual's behaviour and thinking must be viewed through, and can only be understood using, that person's own cultural environment.

This point has been subscribed to by many psychologists who argue that the independent and dependent variables of controlled studies are difficult or impossible to compare across wide cultural gaps. Several studies, for instance, found rural African tribespeople significantly more affected than Westerners by some visual illusions, and less affected by others. This was explained with the 'carpentered world' hypothesis that a highly structured, sharp cornered Western environment is responsible for the differences. A fierce debate arose when other research highlighted western-style education as the crucial variable, with its emphasis on the interpretation of printed, two-dimensional graphic materials. Several illusions have been found to work similarly on members of non-industrialised cultures when presented using local artistic materials.

Nevertheless, cross-cultural studies continue but have tended to become less ethnocentric in their assumptions. Ainsworth (1967) studied attachment behaviour in the USA and in Uganda. Kohlberg's theories of moral development have been strengthened by comparative studies in Taiwan, Turkey, Mexico, India and Kenya. Asch's (1956) demonstrations of conformity under social pressure have been used to compare France and Norway, Russia and Israel. The emphasis in these studies is again on difference between cultures.

*Box 24   Advantages and disadvantages of cross-cultural studies:*

| Advantages | Disadvantages |
| --- | --- |
| Can demonstrate universal developmental trends and effects | Can support disguised ethnocentric assumptions |
| Gives insight into quite different cultural systems, beliefs and practices | Extremely costly and time consuming |
| | Variables may not be culturally comparable |
| Can provide reassessment of 'home' society's norms in culturally relative terms | Difficulties of communication. Subtle differences between 'equivalent' terms may make large difference |
| Rich data | |
| | Can ignore the fact that the 'home' culture is not homogenous. British society comprises many identifiable cultures which include Afro-Caribbean, Indian (several separable cultures), Pakistani, Scots (highland and lowland), Irish, Welsh (north and south), Geordie, Liverpudlian, and Cornish, to name a few |

### Comparison studies are design frameworks

A research study can have a longitudinal, cross-sectional or cross-cultural design and still be either experimental or not. Given the nature of the comparison designs, and what they are most useful for, most studies using them are non-experimental. They tend to be observational or make use of some test, scale or interview technique in order to compare existing measured variables.

Where two groups are compared (such as working class and middle class) we have a pseudo-experiment. But a true experiment occurs when one group of children are given a 'treatment' (say, special reading training), organised by the investigator, and another group serves as control, whilst both are followed up over several years.

Experiments can be compared across cultures, such as occurred with Asch's design. However, if the IV concentrated on is the two different cultures (rather than the IV of the experiment itself) – and what differences occur between them – then the design is *ex post facto*, since the investigator cannot manipulate the variable of cultural difference.

### Key terms for this chapter

Cross-sectional study
Longitudinal study
Cohort
Cohort effect
Cross-cultural study

Cross-generation problem
Cross-sectional, short-term
   longitudinal study
Cultural relativity
Ethnocentric

# New *paradigms*

## Positivism

There is a debate which has raged on and off within psychology for a long time. It sometimes dies down but has been particularly potent during the last ten to 15 years. It concerns whether psychological research should follow closely the example of the natural and physical sciences which have been so successful in advancing our understanding of natural phenomena. Their method has involved careful observation, accurate measurement and the assumption that what cannot be so measured is not amenable to scientific investigation – a position amounting to POSITIVISM for want of a better term, though not everyone agrees on the precise meaning of this label. The overwhelming paradigm has been use of the *hypothetico-deductive method* described in chapter 1. A 'paradigm' is the generally accepted method for conducting research and theory development. In practice, if you don't follow it you're less likely to get research grants or have your work taken seriously.

## Doubts about positivism

In a nutshell the issue is: if we carry out research using the highly controlled procedures and exact quantification of variables recommended by traditional science and by most psychological textbooks, including this one in many parts, will we not be gaining only very narrow, perhaps artificial, perhaps sometimes useless knowledge of human behaviour and experience? Consider the following table of results from an experiment where the independent variable was 20 common or uncommon words in a list, presented one per second via computer screen, and the dependent variable was the number of words recalled, order irrelevant, in each condition during 60 seconds after exposure of the last item.

*Table 8   Number of common/uncommon words recalled*

| Number of words recalled: | | |
|---|---|---|
| Subject | Common | Uncommon |
| 1 | 12 | 5 |
| 2 | 13 | 10 |
| 3 | 7 | 6 |
| 4 | 5 | 4 |
| 5 | 18 | 12 |
| 6 | 15 | 12 |
| 6 | 12 | 6 |
| 7 | 18 | 10 |
| 8 | 14 | 7 |
| 9 | 7 | 3 |
| 10 | 12 | 6 |

This provides us with the not unsurprising information that infrequently met words are harder to recall. The empiricist argues that, nevertheless, (and in the spirit of the points made in chapter 1 about 'armchair certainties') the research is required to back up what is otherwise only an unsupported, casual observation. A critic might argue as follows: only in psychology experiments do people have to learn a list of 20 unrelated words. How can this relate to the normal use of human memory which operates in a social, meaningful context? The results of the experiment may be significant but they tell us little of relevance. The study gives us no information at all about the subjects' experiences. They all, no doubt, used personally devised methods and found their own unique meanings in the combination of words presented. This information is powerful and 'belongs' to the subjects, yet is unused and is not asked for, which could even constitute something of an insult to 'subjects' who participated in what, for them, was to be 'an interesting experiment'.

It is also argued that memory experiments using unconnected words, out of context, or even sets of nonsense syllables, which restrict the use of natural capacities, give rise to unnecessarily simplistic models of the person and cognitive abilities.

## Examples of narrowness and artificiality
Similarly, many studies measure attitude using a scale of the kind we looked at in chapter 9. On this, each participant ends up with a single numerical value. On political attitude, for instance, a person's position may be represented as 34, where 40 is the highest value a 'conservative' (right-wing) person could score, the other end of the scale being 'radical' (left wing). Using this system, we are assuming political attitudes to lie along a unitary dimension, whereas, in fact, if we asked people in depth about their ideas and principles, we would uncover various unique combinations of left- and right-wing views which couldn't, meaningfully, be averaged down to a midpoint on the scale.

Consider the measurement of your intelligence, and all that it means to you, as a number not too far from 100. Think of the subject asked to judge people he has never heard of on a five point scale, knowing only that the person possesses characteristics in the form of single words like 'confident' written on a piece of card.

Harré (1981) argues that orthodox (positivist) research methods have led to a great deal of irrelevance in, for instance, social psychological research. He analyses an experiment in which women had to sit and look at themselves on a TV monitor for one minute. The independent variable was then applied in that they heard a lecture on venereal disease either straight away or four minutes later. They were then asked whether they would contribute to a venereal disease remedial programme under certain circumstances. The aim was to test the idea that heightened 'self-focus' would facilitate 'helping behaviour'. Harré argues that the 'self-focus' measure (watching themselves) completely trivialised the complex concept of self originally proposed by G. H. Mead.

## The establishment paradigm
Working under syllabus requirements for students to produce strictly quantified data and analyses, I have often been instrumental in helping narrow an originally rich concept down to an empirically measurable one. For example, two teenage students, intensely interested, understandably, in researching the self concept among teenagers, have ended up counting how many more times girls used social terms to describe themselves compared with boys, because this was a numerically verifiable test of a hypothesis.

My own training taught me to treat all non-quantitative evidence with suspicion approaching the hostile, and that information gathered without a pre-arranged numerical scoring system and rigidly adhered to procedure had to be wide open to vagueness, subjectivity and irrelevance.

Some would argue that this is an example of the establishment imposing the traditional paradigm right from the start. Others argue that this focusing is necessary in the interests of objectivity, clarity of thought and replicability. But it certainly seems possible to achieve the requisite clarity of thought without the knee-jerk reduction to numbers. Astronomers chemists and biologists don't always count – they look for patterns. So did Freud, Piaget, Bartlett, and many other psychologists whose insights do not always fundamentally depend on strictly quantified data.

## The major objections to the traditional paradigm

Some of these have already been touched on in covering the more qualitative aspects of interviewing and observing, as well as in the case study chapter. However, let's put together the general case 'against'.

1 Traditional research treats people as isolatable from their social contexts. It even treats parts of people (e.g. their memory or attitude) as separable. 'Subjects' are to be treated as identical units for purposes of demonstrating the researcher's pre-conceived notions about humans which they cannot challenge. They are manipulated in and out of the research condition.

2 Whereas we all realise that to know and understand even one's good friends one has to stay close, the researcher, in the interests of objectivity, strains to remain distant.

3 This objectivity is seen as mythical. The attempt to stay coolly distant, and the quantitative paradigm, blind the researcher to his/her own influence and active role in the research process which is a social context. When students administer structured questionnaires to peers, for instance, the respondents usually want to know what the student thinks and whether they *believe* all those statements which the respondent had to check.

4 The experimental situation or survey interview can only permit the gathering of superficial information. In the study of person perception and interpersonal attraction, for instance, mainly first impressions have been researched with traditional methods.

5 Experimental procedures restrict the normal powers of 'subjects' to plan, react and express appropriate social behaviour in the context of the research topic. Yet the investigator uses the results to make statements about human nature on the same topic. The resulting model of the person is simplistic and mechanistic.

6 Deception can only falsify the research context and give quite misleading results, besides treating the participant with contempt.

7 The relationship between experimenter and subject is like that of employer–employee. It is dominating and elitist. Hence, behaviour exhibited will mirror this particular social context. This will also contribute to the resulting model of the person.

8 Highly structured research methods pre-determine the nature of resulting information. Theoretical frameworks are imposed on the subjects. Questionnaires, for example, singularly fail to extract the most important information from people. Information obtained is narrow, rarefied and unrealistic.

9 Highly structured coding and categorising systems lose sight of the wholeness of the individual.

## So what do new paradigms propose?

Thomas Kuhn (1962) made the term 'paradigm' popular when he discussed ways in which science goes through radical changes in its overall conception of appropriate models and methodology. A 'paradigm shift' occurred when Einsteinian physics replaced Newtonian.

The paradigm which 'new paradigm' psychological researchers are seeking to replace is the positivist one, which embraces the traditional scientific (hypothetico-deductive) model. But there is not just one new paradigm. The term crops up in several contexts. The term is used by several people and groups with varying backgrounds, principles and aims but with most of the objections above in common. They also would agree with most, if not all of the following points:

1 Psychological research should concentrate on the *meanings* of actions in a social context, not on isolated, 'objective' units of behaviour – holism, not atomism.

2 The emphasis should also be upon interaction. Attribution, for instance, is not the work of one person, but the result of negotiation between observer and observed, who attempts to control attributions or contradict them.

3 Meanings and interactions belong to social situations and contexts and can't be sensibly isolated from these.

4 Research is therefore mostly naturalistic and qualitative.

5 Research is conducted as closely as possible *with* the person(s) studied. A quote from Hall (1975) makes this point:

'Social science research often appears to produce a situation in which a medical doctor tries to diagnose a patient's symptoms from around the corner and out of sight. The social scientist uses his "instruments" to measure the response of the patient as though they were a kind of long stethoscope. The focus of the researcher has been on developing a better and better stethoscope for going around corners and into houses when the real need is for the researcher to walk around the corner, into the house and begin talking with the people who live there.'

6 Participants' own terms and interpretations are the most central data. To quote De Waele and Harré (1977):

'By taking participants' interpretations seriously we avoid the falsification of reality which occurs when self-reports are confined to the replies to questionnaires etc, which have been devised in advance by the investigator . . . Participants, if allowed to construct their own interpretations, often present a range of meanings and reveal implicit theories sometimes widely at variance with those imposed by the investigators.'

This approach is exemplified in Marsh's (1978) work on the accounts given by football fans of the 'rules' of football terrace behaviour. Marsh used an approach developed from Harré's 'ethogenic' perspective, the perspective outlined above.

7  Some version of INDUCTIVE ANALYSIS is preferred to the hypothetico-deductive approach. In the former, theories, models and hypotheses *emerge* from the data-gathering process rather than being confirmed by it. (Ironically, this is close to the philosophy of the early empirical method, where one was supposed to gather data from the natural, physical world with no preconceptions).
    Medawar (1963), however, has argued forcefully against the naïve assumption that one can approach any phenomenon, in order to study it, with absolutely no preconceptions as to its modes of functioning – certainly not in the social world anyway.
    Inductive analysis also involves the process of constantly refining emergent categories and models in the light of incoming data.
    The value of this approach is particularly seen in its ability to permit categories, processes, even hypotheses to emerge which might not have been envisaged as present before research began, whereas traditional research strictly defines variables and dimensions before data collection, such that data may be distorted to fit the pre-arranged scheme.

8  Emergent theories are likely to be local, rather than massive generalisations about the nature of human thought or personality.

9  For the more radical departures from the traditional paradigm there is a high degree of participation by those researched in some or all of the development, running and analysis of the research project. The extreme version of this approach involves the target group acting as collaborative researchers with the original researcher as a form of consultant and data organiser/analyst. Any findings or interpretations are discussed and modified by the group as a whole in its own terms.

10  At the very least, though, most methods under the 'new paradigm/qualitative' umbrella involve the notion of a 'research cycle', gone round several times, in which an integral step is to consult with particpants as to the acceptability and accuracy of emergent theories, models and categories.

## Qualitative approaches

I had originally intended to head this chapter 'qualitative approaches' and take you through a distinct set of methods. As it turned out, it made more sense to deal with the quantitative–qualitative dimension as we went through observation, interview and the like. The methods we have encountered so far which could count as qualitative include:

Open-ended questionnaires
Unstructured interviews

Semi-structured observation
Participant observation
The diary method
The clinical method (to some extent)
Role-play and simulation (depending on particular research)
Individual case studies

Although these methods gather qualitative data, they are not all what one might call 'qualitative' in outlook, by which is meant that the research aim is to use the data in their qualitative form and not extract from them just that which can somehow be represented numerically. The data are retained in the form of *meanings*. In chapter 19 we look at ways in which qualitative data can be dealt with. To the extent that data are strictly categorised, coded or content analysed, the approach tends to be positivistic rather than qualitative in outlook.

But it would be tempting to assume that all approaches which are qualitative in outlook would automatically fall into this category of new paradigm. However, the subterfuge and secrecy of much participant observation runs counter to several of the principles outlined above. The people studied are often not participants in the research, only the researcher is. The presentation of results can tend to deliver the message 'what fascinatingly strange people, and they're organised too.'

## Participative research

The idea of people participating in research and collaborating with the researcher in evolving the project is not new. Here is a quote from Madge (1953):

> 'The techniques of experimentation which have so far been discussed are based on those evolved in the natural sciences. Can it be that a radically different approach is required in social science? Can the human beings who constitute the subject-matter of social science be regarded, not as objects for experimental manipulation, but as participants in what is being planned? If this can be so, it requires a transformed attitude towards social experiment. Traditionally, attention is concentrated on the precautions needed to objectify results, and this entails treating the participants as lay figures to be observed before and after subjection to a series of external stimuli. In contrast, the new approach entails the acceptance and encouragement of conscious co-operation by all concerned. There are then no longer an investigator and his passive subjects, but a number of human beings, one of whom is more experienced than the others and has somewhat more complex aims, but all of whom are knowingly collaborating in a research project.'

What is new in the ideas promoted by Reason and Rowan (1981) in their '. . . *Sourcebook of New Paradigm Research*' is the combination of this idea with several other elements. Some of these are:

## Action research

First proposed by Kurt Lewin in the mid 1940s, this approach basically called for research to be applied to practical issues occurring in the everyday social world. The idea was to enter a social situation, attempt change and monitor results. This might be setting up or contributing to a programme designed to raise awareness on dietary needs or the dangers of smoking. More recently, it has involved working in organisations. Instances might be attempting to alter management–

worker relations, helping a community project to better organise itself or working with prisoners to analyse jail violence.

### Endogenous research

This is an import from anthropology, the originators of participant observation on a big scale. In this approach, rather than living with a community for a year or so, coming away, then publishing a report, the researcher involves members of the community in a research project on their own customs, norms and organisation in their own terms.

### Collaborative research

Roughly speaking, putting the last two approaches together, we get the basis for collaborative research, in which participants are involved as fully as possible in research on their own group or organisation. The researcher may have to lead at the beginning but as participants realise the nature of the game they become more centrally involved in the progress of research. In some cases the research is initiated by an already existing member of the organisation or group.

This is particularly suitable where a group is planning or undergoing change and requires evaluation. Participants take up data-gathering ideas, develop their own, consider the researcher's findings or analyse their own, and debate progress, directions and results in group meetings. Collaborative research is not without confrontations, but the idea is to build on these natural differences constructively. The idea is also to end up with participants directing their own change, rather than an outside expert's research findings, about what is wrong and what might be changed, arriving after research has been done *on* people.

Sims (1981) set out to study 'problem-generation' in health sevice teams and found that, as the participants became interested in the issues, they took on their own lines of investigation. This caused them to consider group dynamic issues they'd never thought about and created an atmosphere of awareness raising and constructive change. They were able to develop, with the researcher, many categories of processes in problem construction which could be transferred (not without addition and modification) to other group situations.

### Other roots and sources

Influences on this direction of research philosophy are numerous. Prominent among them would be: humanism; phenomenology; existentialism; marxism; the psycho-analytic tradition; Kelly's repertory grid work; sociology's ethnomethodology.

The approaches in general tend to be somewhat interdisciplinary, borrowing many ideas from sociology and anthropology in particular. The areas tend to be social psychology and, to some extent, the study of personality. The emphasis is always completely practical and the approaches are at their best applied to problems or challenges within the fields of educational, organisational, clinical or criminological psychology.

### A complete alternative?

Patton (1980), an evaluation researcher who advocates the use of a wholly qualitative approach, argues that the hypothetico-deductive method is not bad or wrong, but has simply overwhelmed research in psychology to become not just a major paradigm, but the *only* paradigm of which new researchers are aware. In advocating the qualitative approach he argues that the new paradigm is a 'paradigm of choice' between the traditional hypothetico-deductive and the alternative holistic, inductive one.

## A feminist perspective

A further and more recent new force within psychological research methods has been the arrival of serious challenges to the traditional research paradigm from the point of view of the politics and ideology of the women's movement.

It is about as stunningly inappropriate that a male should author research on *The psychology of women* (I still have the Penguin paperback!) as that white psychologists should conduct studies on 'the negro' (as they once did).

The early stages of women's research involved studies, under a conventional paradigm, which destroyed (or should have) traditional stereotypes of women's nature or deficiencies relative to men. Research literature now contains a fair amount of stereotype challenging and consciousness-raising work. This stage also challenged the lack of female authorship and visible presence within the research community. Parallels with racism occurred in that, even where women had produced scholarship, this had somehow become marginalised or obscured. The overwhelmingly male-oriented and -dominated research community had edged such work to the periphery.

The content-oriented phase just described, however, though continuing, has led on to a realisation by women involved in the research process that the conventional methods which they have been using to develop the content are themselves largely the product of a male research network and thought base.

This is not to say that women would think, reason and conduct their research *utterly* differently, given the opportunity. It would fall back onto old stereotypes to suggest that women didn't *tend* to use quantification or feel happy testing hypotheses statistically. The logic underlying chess, computer programming and the statistical tests in this book are in a major sense neutral. But they have been 'owned' and promoted for so long by men that it is hardly surprising that when women came to assess their values in the research process they were alerted to methods and research relationships neglected or never taken up by male researchers, and felt by many female researchers to be more valid in representing women's experience. The position is exemplified in Sue Wilkinson's *Feminist Social Psychology* (1986).

Recognised as characteristic of a male approach to research and understanding the world are: preoccupation with quantifying variables; an emphasis on control, mastery and manipulation; a tendency to remain distant rather than be involved with the subjects of research; a preference for gadget-oriented research over naturalistic enquiry; competition and ego building.

## Key terms for this chapter

| | |
|---|---|
| Action research | Inductive analysis |
| Collaborative research | Paradigm |
| Endogenous research | Participative research |
| Feminist perspective | Positivism |

# PART III

# Dealing with data

## Measurement

### Measurement assumptions in 'common sense' statements

Let's start with two 'common sense' statements which any two people might make over the dinner table:

'I think attractive people are more successful because they're more likely to be selected at interviews and to be given more attention generally.'

'No. It could be that more attractive people develop better social confidence earlier on in life and that's what gets them through interviews and the like.'

Inside both persons' heads there must be a concept (perhaps vague) of what counts as attractive. It isn't a concept held uniquely by each individual since they are claiming that people in general, and fairly consistently, respond to the attractive qualities. To prove their points through psychological research, each would need to operationalise their concept of 'attractiveness' (and perhaps of 'success' and 'self-confidence'). In some way or other, values must be attached to different levels of attractiveness with which we will be able to make comparisons. Many people will baulk at the idea of reducing concepts like 'attractiveness' to 'mere numbers', yet numbers measure quantity and quality; quantity or quality differences are implied in such statements as:

- Helen is more artistic than Clare
- George is a contemplative type whereas Rick is practical, energetic and impulsive
- Taureans are down-to-earth people
- Jason is far more intelligent than Johnathan

### Quantitative and qualitative differences

It may appear that a difference of quality, such as that expressed about George, does not need numerical values to confirm it, but how exactly do we know Rick is 'energetic' or 'impulsive'? We must be comparing some things he does (how strongly and how often) with their occurrence in others. We must define what counts as energetic and impulsive and show that Rick is like this more often or to a greater degree than is George. Hence, to demonstrate a difference, we would need some numerical measure. This might be achieved by counting how many people assess George or Rick as energetic, for instance.

## Nominal level of measurement

### Categories
For some differences of quality we do not need to count in order to distinguish one item from another. For instance:

> male and female
> red, green and blue objects
> Roman noses and other noses

Here we do not need to count anything to decide which object goes into which category. We simply compare each item with some learnt concept – what counts as green, a Roman nose (shape) or a male. On occasion we may count number of features present before categorising, for instance, when deciding whether to categorise a car as 'luxury' – how many luxury features does it have?

What matters for such categorisation is that we must be able to place each item in just one category, for purposes of comparison. We might decide to categorise people as 'attractive', 'average' and 'unattractive' for instance. A person is either male or female and can't, when we use a nominal scale, be included in both categories because he/she is a bit of both. Difficulties may arise in categorising a person as smoker or non-smoker, extrovert or introvert, optimist or pessimist, but on a nominal scale categories are *mutually exclusive*. People and things are bunched together on the basis of a common feature – Jason is not the same as Jonathan but they have maleness in common. All irrelevant differences are ignored.

### Labels for categories
If we were conducting a survey which investigated use of the college canteen, we might like to count the number of people using it and categorise these. Table 9 might be used:

*Table 9   Categorisation table*

| Category: | 1 | 2 | 3 | 4 | 5 |
|---|---|---|---|---|---|
| | Students | Teaching staff | Non-teaching staff | Visitors | Other |
| | 650 | 34 | 43 | 17 | 2 |

The numbers given to the categories here are Nominal – 'in name only'. Number 1 (students) is not half of number 2 (teaching staff) or in any way prior to or less than the others in quantity. The numbers are simply convenient but arbitrary labels for identifying each type of person. We could have used 'A', 'B', 'C' etc. We are using numerals (the figures 1, 2, 3 etc.) as labels only and not as real numbers – they don't in any way stand for *quantities*. Likewise, numbers on office doors don't represent quantity but places to find people in.

The numbers *within* each category are known as FREQUENCIES. They represent the number of times an event in category 1 occurred – presence of a student. These numbers *are* being used to count, they do stand for quantities and are known as CARDINAL numbers. Note that, from the definition of nominal data above, each person counted can only go in one category. Hence, a member of staff also undertaking a course as a student at the college can only go in one category, student *or* staff.

Some examples of psychological data gathered on a nominal scale are:

*Table 10  Number of children (average age 4.5 years) engaged in type of play*

| non-play | solitary | associative | parallel | cooperative |
|---|---|---|---|---|
| 8 | 5 | 17 | 23 | 6 |

*Table 11  Oldtown by-election: number of voters by political party*

| Communist | Conservative | Labour | SDP | SLP | Other |
|---|---|---|---|---|---|
| 243 | 14,678 | 15,671 | 2,356 | 4,371 | 567 |

*Table 12  Number of people smoking an average of N cigarettes per day*

| $N =$ | None | 1–5 | 6–10 | 11–20 | 21–30 | 31–40 | 41+ |
|---|---|---|---|---|---|---|---|
| | 65 | 45 | 78 | 32 | 11 | 4 | 3 |

This last example is deceptive. The category titles do form a progressive scale (1–5, 6–10) etc. The essential point, however, is that data are represented in the form of frequencies in separate, exclusive categories, and there is no distinction between persons within each category.

### Comparison of the Nominal level with other levels
Suppose I made a rather foolish claim that brown horses run faster than grey horses. Suppose we observed a race in which there were 20 browns and 20 greys. We could present the results of the race like table 13:

*Table 13  Nominal level race results*

| | Colour of horse: | |
|---|---|---|
| | Grey | Brown |
| Finished in top ten | 3 | 7 |
| Finished in last ten | 7 | 3 |

These are data presented at a nominal level. Each horse appears in one discrete category, along with other horses. The columns represent a nominal scale with two values – grey and brown, and the rows have the two values – in top ten and in last ten.

The result shows us that the browns did better overall but the differences aren't convincing enough to rule out the possibility that the greys might be the superior group next time. Suppose the greys had come first, second and third? We don't have enough information. We need to be able to *compare* the performances of the horses in the top and last ten places.

The nominal level of measurement provides the *least* amount of quantitative information.

### Ordinal level of measurement

Ordinal numbers represent position in a group. They tell us who came 1st, 2nd, 3rd and so on in a race or test. They do not tell us how far ahead the winner was from the second placed. They tell us nothing at all about distances between positions. It may be annoying to be beaten by one-tenth of a second in a cycle race when you and the leader were ten kilometres ahead of the rest of the 'bunch', but what goes on your record is just 'second'. To the punter it doesn't matter by what margin Golden Girl won – it won! If we rank the scores of eight people on a general knowledge test we might obtain table 14:

*Table 14    General knowledge scores*

| Person | Score | Rank of Score |
|--------|-------|---------------|
| 1 | 18 | 5.5 |
| 2 | 25 | 7 |
| 3 | 14 | 1 |
| 4 | 18 | 5.5 |
| 5 | 15 | 3 |
| 6 | 15 | 3 |
| 7 | 15 | 3 |
| 8 | 29 | 8 |

The score of 14 is lowest and gets the rank one. In competitions we usually give the winner 'first' but in statistics it is less confusing to give low scores low ranks.

Persons five, six and seven 'share' the next three ranks (of second, third and fourth). In sport we might say 'equal second', but in statistical ranking we add the shared ranks and divide by the number of persons sharing them. So

$$\frac{2+3+4}{3} = \frac{9}{3} = 3,$$

i.e., we take the statistical mean of the shared ranks. For subjects one and four this means that ranks five and six are shared and

$$\frac{5+6}{2} = 5.5.$$

Here we have *converted* data which was at a higher, more informative level (RATIO data, which we will discuss below), into ordinal level data. The scores are ratio level, the ranks are ORDINAL.

## Comparison of ordinal level with other levels
If we presented the results of the grey vs. brown horse race at an ordinal level, they might look like this:

*Table 15   Ordinal level race results*

| Colour of horse | Grey | Brown |
|---|---|---|
| | 1 | 4 |
| | 2 | 5 |
| | 3 | 6 |
| | | 7 |
| | 11 | 8 |
| | 12 | 9 |
| | 13 | 10 |
| | 14 | |
| | 15 | 18 |
| | 16 | 19 |
| | 17 | 20 |

Now the superiority of the brown horses is very much in doubt. If they'd occupied first, second and third, *and* occupied seven of the first ten places we might have been quite convinced. As it is, we certainly can't say the browns are faster overall. Of course, all the first ten horses might have come in very close together, in which case, coming first, second and third doesn't demonstrate substantially greater speed. What we need *now* is the actual times the horses took to run the course. This will tell us whether the first three greys were well ahead of the browns or not.

Ordinal level of measurement provides *more* information than the nominal scale (it tells us what order individuals can be placed in) but *less* information than an interval scale (we do not know how far apart the people at various rank positions are).

## Interval level of measurement
This is a scale using equal intervals, such as minutes, kilograms, number of words recalled in a memory test or percentage scored in an exam. Intervals on the scale are of equal size, so that 10 to 15 minutes is the same interval as 20 to 25 minutes. The interval of $30°$ to $40°$ is twice the interval from $-10°$ to $-5°$ (Centigrade or Fahrenheit). If one of our horses, Golden Girl, is 3 seconds ahead of Jim's Choice who is, in turn, 6 seconds ahead of Make Believe, then Golden Girl is three times as far ahead of Make Believe as she is of Jim's Choice.

Philosophical problems occur around the issue of whether psychological scales measuring such variables as intelligence, strength of attachment or achievement motivation are truly the interval scales they appear to be at first glance. If these were true interval scales, it ought to be true that, for instance:

Two children scoring five and eight respectively on an achievement scale are as far apart in motivation to achieve as two children scoring nine and 12.

Jane, whose IQ is 100, is as far ahead of John (IQ 80) in intelligence as Jackie (IQ 120) is ahead of Jane.

In practice this isn't true of most psychological scales but it is the goal of PSYCHOMETRISTS (those who construct psychological scales of measurement) to approach the criterion of equal intervals for their scales. In part, this approach is made through the process of standardisation explained earlier. By way of comparison, a true equal interval scale is exemplified by temperature °C because each interval of, say, 10° is measured by an equal expansion of mercury. There is an underlying regular physical change, although, of course, each change of 10° is not felt as equal by us. It might be argued the underlying change for IQ is number of items scored correctly and that therefore the interval from 80 to 100 *is* equal to the interval from 100 to 120.

There are two arguments against this:

1 From a score of 80 you don't necessarily need twice as much extra intelligence to score 120 as you do to score 100. In the same way you don't need twice the arm length or twice the muscle to throw a ball twice the distance someone else did. This is a point where we can see the danger of REIFICATION of the concept of intelligence as if, because we can apply numbers to it, it must exist as something with quantity.

2 It cannot be assumed that all items in the test are equally hard to answer, so can we claim that your score of 110 is equal to my score of 110? Likewise, it is sometimes argued, one subject's score of 15 words recalled in a verbal memory test cannot equal another subject's score of 15 because some words are harder to retain and recall than others and some combinations may have special meaning for one person.

This is a somewhat hair-splitting argument. Generally speaking, psychologists use statistical tests and treatments which require interval level data even when they are measuring intelligence, achievement and the like. It is assumed that the measurements are on a scale with *approximately* equal intervals and that the researcher will be able to recognise when the assumption of equal intervals is affecting the treatment of results in a serious way.

When research produces data which are a human estimate, especially if based on an arbitrary scale, it is *safer* to assume that ratings should be reduced to an ordinal level.

Scores given to individuals should be placed in rank order. This will then mean that a less sensitive statistical test must be used, called 'non-parametric' (see chapter 15).

Here are some examples of human estimates on an arbitrary scale:

People are asked to estimate how masculine or feminine they are on the following scale:

1 **Feminine**                      **Neutral**                     **Masculine**
10..9..8..7..6..5..4..3..2..1..0..1..2..3..4..5..6..7..8..9..10

2 Observers rate, on a scale of one to ten, the level of intimacy displayed by two people in a conversation.

### Reducing data from interval to ordinal level

On inspection of a table of data you will often find two columns of figures, one the interval level data, or data which *look* like interval data, and the other being the set of ranks which the first (interval) set has been reduced to. This has occurred in table 16. The data on the left were truly interval; those on the right were, as we said, untrustworthy as interval data. Truly interval data may often be reduced to ordinal level because it is a lot simpler to conduct a non-parametric test.

*Table 16   Reduction of data (internal to ordinal level)*

| Reaction time (sec.) | Rank | Intimacy rating (Max. 10) | Rank |
|---|---|---|---|
| 0.067 | 1 | 7 | 4 |
| 0.078 | 3 | 6 | 2.5 |
| 0.091 | 5 | 5 | 1 |
| 0.089 | 4 | 6 | 2.5 |
| 0.076 | 2 | 9 | 5 |

It is easy to spot the column which is of ordinal data. It will usually have the title 'rank(s)' at the top of it. Anyway, the column of ranks *is* the ordinal data set.

### Reducing data from interval to nominal level

It is quite common to reduce data like that shown in table 17 to a nominal level by grouping together those above and below the overall mean for the whole sample and comparing this with another variable, in this case, high and low competitiveness. The data, reduced to nominal level, is shown in table 18.

Table 18 is obtained by noting that four children in the high competitive group are above 12.3 (the average anxiety score for all ten children) and only one below.

*Table 17   Data prepared for reduction*

| No. of anxiety indicators observed: | |
|---|---|
| High competitive children | Low competitive children |
| 14 | 10 |
| 21 | 6 |
| 7 | 13 |
| 13 | 5 |
| 18 | 11 |
| Mean 14.6 | 9.9 |
| Mean for whole group = 12.3 | |

*Table 18   Reduction of data (interval to nominal level)*

| | Level of competitiveness | |
|---|---|---|
| | High | Low |
| Anxiety indicators | | |
| Above mean | 4 | 1 |
| Below mean | 1 | 4 |

### A limitation of some interval scales

On some equal interval scales, such as temperature (°C), we certainly cannot say that 40°C is twice as hot as 20°C or that (in psychological measurement) 20 is twice as extroverted as ten. This is because the zero point on both these scales is arbitrary. 0°C is not an absolute cold point – it's 32°F for instance. An extroversion score of zero does not signify a 'pure' introvert. What sense would it make to claim that any human had 'zero intelligence' as measured by IQ test?

## Ratio level of measurement

Scales with a true zero are known as RATIO SCALES. Examples are: time, distance, and most measures of physical qualities. Don't worry that time appears here again. All ratio scales are interval scales first. In our horse race, if Golden Girl completed the distance in eight minutes whilst Jim's Choice took 16 minutes then it certainly makes sense to state that Golden Girl ran twice as fast as Jim's Choice. Remember that it wasn't sensible to say that 40°C was twice as hot as 20°C. In this case all the horses are timed from zero minutes and this is the real zero mark. Similarly, if you recall 15 items from a word list and I recall just five, then you have recalled three times as many items as I did. On a ratio scale, negative numbers have no meaning. You can't recall minus three items and the time of 3.29 pm is irrelevant to timing horses from 3.30 pm. The hallmark of a ratio scale is its possession of a true zero point.

In practice, as a student of psychology, you will not need to worry about the difference between interval and ratio scales except to state what the difference is. For the purposes of choosing an appropriate statistical test, covered in chapter 18, they can be treated as the same thing and you need only justify your data as being at *least* interval level status.

### Comparison of interval/ratio level data with other levels

Results of our horse race would look like table 19 if presented at a ratio level of measurement:

*Table 19   Ratio level of measurement*

| Time taken to cover course: (in seconds) (colour of horse) | |
| --- | --- |
| **Grey** | **Brown** |
| 123 | 132 |
| 124 | 136 |
| 125 | 136 |
|  | 137 |
| 143 | 139 |
| 143 | 142 |
| 143 | 142 |
| 144 |  |
| 146 | 153 |
| 146 | 154 |
| 147 | 156 |

Now we have the fullest information we can get (for this race) on how fast the two groups of horses are over this distance.

Notice that, as the level increased from nominal to ratio, we gained more specific information at each level. This might have enabled us to be more confident about my original hypothesis. As it is, we are now, I hope, not at all convinced.

Interval and ratio levels of measurement give us the *greatest* amount of information in measuring a variable. We need at least interval-level data in order to conduct PARAMETRIC TESTS.

### Continuous and discrete scales of measurement

All the scales mentioned can be divided into two categories: continuous or discrete. On discrete scales each point is entirely separate from the next. It is not possible to have two-and-a-half children, for instance. We may, in a memory experiment find that, the *average* number of words recalled per subject is 14.3, but no individual subject could have recalled 14.3 items. On continuous scales there is no limit to the sub-divisions of points which can occur. It is theoretically possible to measure your height to the nearest thousandth of an inch: technically this might be difficult and in practice, hardly likely to be useful.

Interval and ratio scales can be either continuous or discrete. Nominal scales can only be discrete. Ordinal scales generally have 0.5 as the smallest unit.

### Key terms for this chapter

Cardinal numbers
Continuous measurement scale
Discrete measurement scale
Frequency data
Internal scale/level
Nominal scale/level

Ordinal scale/level
Psychometrist
Quantitive and qualitative difference
Ratio scale/level
Reification

*Exercises*

1 Find one example of each level of measurement from any text books (on psychology) you have available.

2 When judges give their marks in an ice-skating contest, what level of measurement is it safest to treat their data as?

3 A set of surgical records classifies patients as 'improved', 'no change' or 'worsened'. What level of measurement is being used?

4 At what level are the measurements in table 20 being made?

5 Which of the boxes, a to d, below, contains the most sensitive level of measurement?

*Table 20   Exercise 4*

| | Placings of top five riders in Tour de France, 20 July, 1989 | | Time taken so far on whole race | | Popularity rating (Max. 20) | | Riders still in race | Riders so far dropped out |
|---|---|---|---|---|---|---|---|---|
| Fignon | 1 | | 77h 55s | | 12 | | 121 | 77 |
| LeMonde | 2 | | 78h 21s | | 15 | | | |
| Delgado | 3 | | 79h 50s | | 18 | | | |
| Theunisse | 4 | | 83h 07s | | 10 | | | |
| Mottet | 5 | | 83h 17s | | 13 | | | |
| | | (a) | | (b) | | (c) | | (d) |

6 Your daughter argues that, since she came top in each of the three maths tests held in her class this year, she must be *far* better than all the other pupils. What might you point out to her? (Would you dare?)

7 Think of three ways to measure driving ability, one using nominal level data, one ordinal and one interval/ratio.

8 Can you change the data in table 21 first to ordinal level, then to nominal level? The blank tables are for you to fill in.

*Table 21   Exercise 8*

| Time taken to read: (seconds) | | |
|---|---|---|
| Consistent story | Inconsistent story | |
| 127 | 138 | |
| 136 | 132 | |
| 104 | 149 | |
| 156 | 158 | |
| 111 | 123 | |
| Mean of all times $(\bar{x}) = 133.4$ | | (a) |

| Ordinal level | | |
|---|---|---|
| Consistent story | Inconsistent story | |
| | | |
| | | |
| | | |
| | | (b) |

| Nominal level | |
|---|---|
| | |
| | |
| | (c) |

# Descriptive statistics

## Statistics are a selection

In this section, we are looking simply at the ways in which statistical information can be presented. Statistical information is the numerical data gathered during quantitative research. Most research gathers far too much information for every little bit of it to be presented. When a survey of voting preference is conducted, or an experiment is run on 35 subjects, it is not useful to be given just the RAW DATA, that is, every individual's answers or scores. We expect to be given a *summary* of the data which highlights major trends and differences. However, it is important to note that the very act of summarising introduces distortions. We will be given what the researcher decides is the most important information and this will be presented in what is believed to be the most appropriate manner. Politicians and companies, among others, are renowned for presenting data in the best possible light. A psychologist should be looking at the best way to present data *only* in terms of what gives the clearest, least ambiguous picture of what was found in a research study.

## But I can't do sums!

As with many ideas in this book, even if you hate maths, dread statistics and have never done any formal work in this area, you have undoubtedly made statistical descriptions many times in your life without necessarily being aware of it. You may believe that only clever, numerically-minded people do this sort of thing, but consider this. Imagine you have just come home from your first day on a new college course and I ask you what your class is like. You would not proceed to tell me the exact age of each class member. This could take far too long. You'd be likely to say something like 'Well, most people in the class are around 25 years old but there are a couple of teenagers and one or two are over 40.' You have in fact summarised the class ages statistically, albeit rather loosely too. First you gave me a rough AVERAGE, the typical age in the group, then you gave me an idea of the actual VARIATION from this typical age present in the group. Let's look at these aspects of description in a little more detail. Have a look at the data in table 22.

*Table 22 Number of seconds five-year-old nursery class children spent talking in a ten minute observation period, by sex*

| Subject | Male | Subject | Female |
|---------|------|---------|--------|
| 1 | 132 | 6 | 332 |
| 2 | 34 | 7 | 345 |
| 3 | 5 | 8 | 289 |
| 4 | 237 | 9 | 503 |
| 5 | 450 | 10 | 367 |

Before looking at the comments, see what conclusions you can come to about the talking of girls and boys.

Overall, the girls speak just about twice the amount that boys do. But not only this, the boys' times vary very widely compared with the girls', from as little as five seconds to nearly the highest girl's time.

We shall now introduce two formal terms which are used to describe these two aspects of group data description.

*Central tendency*   This is the value in a group of values which is the most *typical* for the group, or the score which all other scores are evenly clustered around. In normal language, this is better and more loosely known as 'the average'. In statistical description, though, we have to be more precise about just what sort of average we mean.

*Dispersion*   This is a measure of how much or how little the rest of the values tend to *vary* around this central or typical value.

## MEASURES OF CENTRAL TENDENCY

### The mean

In normal language we use the term 'average' for what is technically known as the ARITHMETIC MEAN. This is what we get when we add up all the values in a group and then divide by the number of values there are. Hence, if five people took 135, 109, 95, 121 and 140 seconds to solve an anagram, the mean time taken is:

$$\frac{135 + 109 + 95 + 121 + 140}{5} = \frac{600}{5} = 120 \text{ seconds}$$

Calculation of the mean
Term used:   $(\bar{x})$

Procedure:   1 Add up all values
           2 Divide by total number of values $(N)$

Formula:   $(\bar{x}) = \dfrac{\Sigma x}{N}$

This is our first use of a FORMULA. A formula is simply a set of instructions and you (or a computer or calculator) just have to follow them faithfully to get the desired result, rather like following a recipe or instructions for Dr Jekyll's magic potion. $\Sigma$ is a Greek letter ('sigma' – similar to our capital 'S') and it means 'add up all the values defined by the term which follows.' In the case above, the term which follows is $x$ so we add up all $x$'s. If the term given were $\Sigma x^2$ then we would square each $x$ (multiply it by itself) and add up the results. An $x$ in this case is any subject's number of seconds to solve the anagram. $N$ is the number of values there were (five). It is always used to mean this and almost always refers to the number of people there were in the group whose results are being analysed.

**Advantages and disadvantages of the mean** *Advantages:* the mean is the statistic used in estimating population parameters (see page 147) and this estimation is the basis for PARAMETRIC TESTS which are highly sensitive tests used, among other things, to show whether two means are significantly different from one another.

Very often the mean is not the same value as any of the values in the group. It acts like the fulcrum of a balanced pair of scales sitting exactly at the centre of all the DEVIATIONS (which we shall investigate further on) from itself, as I hope figure 11 illustrates, using the anagram time scores from the previous example:

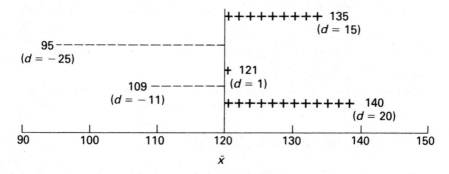

*(d = distance from the mean)*

*Figure 11  Central mean*

The positive distances and the negative distances of the individual scores to the mean exactly cancel out. ($[-25]+[-11]+1+15+20=0$) This can only happen because the mean takes an exactly central position on an interval (and continuous) scale. This makes it the most sensitive of the measures of central tendency covered here.

*Disadvantages:* this very sensitivity, however, can also be something of a disadvantage in certain circumstances. Suppose we add a sixth person's value to our set of anagram solving times. This person had a bad night's sleep and doesn't particularly like doing word games, having had a particularly competitive sister who always won at Scrabble. This person sits and stares at the anagram for exactly eight minutes before getting the answer. Our mean for the six values now becomes:

$$\frac{600+480}{6} = \frac{1080}{6} = 180 \text{ seconds}$$

180 seconds is just not representative of the group in general. It is a highly misleading figure to describe what most of the group did. Five out of six people took a lot less time than this to solve the anagram. A single extreme score in one direction (an 'outrider') can distort the mean (whereas extremes in both directions tend to cancel each other out).

### The median

Using the median gets us around the difficulty for the mean outlined just above. The median is the *central* value of a set. If we have an odd number of values in our set then this couldn't be easier to find. The central value of our first five anagram solution times above is the third one. To find this we must first put all five in numerical order. This gives:

95, 109, 121, 135, 140     The median is 121

If there is an even number of values, as with our sixth person's time added, we take the mean of the two central values, thus:

95, 109, 121, 135, 140, 480     The median is $\dfrac{121 + 135}{2} = 128$

Notice that this value is still reasonably representative of the group of values.

**Calculation of the median**
Procedure:   1 Put all values in rank order
             2 If $N$ is odd, select the central value

$$\left(\text{which is the } \frac{N+1}{2} \text{ th value}\right)$$

             3 If $N$ is even, calculate the mean of the two central values

$$\left(\text{which are the } \frac{N}{2} \text{ th and } \frac{N}{2}+1 \text{ th values}\right)$$

Things are a little trickier if there are any tied values in the set. Consider this set of values:

7,  7,  7,  8,  8,  8,  9,  9,  10,  10

The eights are assumed to be contained somewhere in the interval 7.5 to 8.5. (For clarification on this point, see the remarks just under the heading *The Range*, below, and also under *The normal distribution*, further on.) The median is a point within this interval which would leave two of the eights below it and one above. The best way to estimate this point is to take a value two-thirds of the way along this interval. The interval is one unit so two-thirds along is 0.66. Add this to 7.5, the lower limit of the interval, and we get 8.16 as the median. There is a formula for calculating this value exactly when necessary. It is:

$$\text{Median} = L + \frac{N/2 - F}{f_{\text{m}}} \times h$$

where:

$L$ = exact lower limit of interval containing median
$F$ = total number of values below $L$
$f_{\text{m}}$ = number of values in interval containing median
$h$ = size of class interval
$N$ = number of values

So, substituting here we get:

$$7.5 + \frac{10/2 - 3}{3} \times 1 = 8.16$$

This formula is particularly useful when data are grouped into categories which spread across several values. This occurs in table 13, in the previous chapter on measurement, where smokers are grouped into categories based on how many cigarettes per day they smoke. The categories 1–5, 6–10, 11–20 etc. are called CLASS INTERVALS. Notice that in this example they are not all the same size. Here, it is difficult to see where the median could be. There are 238 cases altogether so the median is the value above and below which 119 of all the cases fall. This must be somewhere in the 6–10 category. We assume that values in this category are evenly spread throughout it. This is what our formula is based on. So $L$ is 5.5, $F$ is 110, $f_m$ is 78, $h$ is 5 and $N$ is 238. The median is 6.08.

### Advantages and disadvantages of the median

Advantages:    Easier to calculate than the mean
Unaffected by extreme values in one direction
Can be obtained when extreme values are unknown

Disadvantages:  Doesn't take into account exact values of each item
Can't be used in estimates of population parameters
If values are few can be unrepresentative; for instance, with 2, 3, 5, 98, 112 the median would be 5.

### The mode

If we had data on a nominal scale, as with categories of play in table 11, we cannot calculate a mean or a median. We can, however, say which type of play was engaged in most, i.e. which category had the highest frequency count. This is what is known as the MODE or MODAL VALUE. It is the most frequently occurring value and therefore even easier to find than the mean or median.

The mode of the set of numbers:

1, 2, 3, 3, 3, 4, 4, 4, 5, 5, 5, 5, 5, 5, 6, 6, 7, 7, 7, 8

is therefore 5 since this value occurs six times in all. For the set of anagram solving times there is no single modal value since each time occurs once only. For the set of numbers 7, 7, 7, 8, 8, 8, 9, 9, 10, 10 there are two modes, 7 and 8, and the set is said to be BI-MODAL. For the table of play categories, the modal value is parallel play. Be careful here to note that the mode is not the number of times the most frequent value occurs but that value itself. Parallel play occurred most often.

### Advantages and disadvantages of the mode

Advantages:    Shows the most important value of a set
Unaffected by extreme values in one direction
Can be obtained when extreme values are unknown

Disadvantages:  Doesn't take into account the exact value of each item
Can't be used in estimates of population parameters
Not useful for relatively small sets of values where there are several modes (e.g. 1, 1, 2, 3, 3, 4, 4, 5, 6, 6, 7, 8)

Can't be estimated accurately when data are grouped into class intervals – we can guess that the mode of smoking figures in table 14 is 19/78-ths into the 6–10 category but this would change if the data were categorised into larger or smaller class intervals, whereas the median would be little affected

### Levels of measurement and central tendency measures

MEAN: The calculation of the mean is an operation on CARDINAL numbers. In other words, the numbers are assumed to have real value on an INTERVAL scale or higher. The mean is therefore the most sensitive measure and uses the most information, though the sensitivity can be a disadvantage.

MEDIAN: Calculation of the median is an ORDINAL operation. As with ordinal data, some information about actual values is therefore lost in the process. However, where data is skewed, the mean is most affected whereas the median gives a fairer estimate of central tendency.

MODE: The mode can only work at a NOMINAL level of measurement. It looks only at the frequency of occurrence of different values and performs no calculation on them. It is useful where no further information about data is available.

## MEASURES OF DISPERSION

### The range

The simplest way to compare the variation in the times spent talking by boys and girls (table 23) is to use what is called the RANGE. This is simply the distance between the top and bottom value of a set.

### Calculation of the range

Procedure: 1 Find top value of the set
2 Find bottom value of the set
3 Subtract bottom value from top value and add 1

Formula: $$(X_{top} - X_{bottom}) + 1$$

For table 24 this gives: Boys $(450 - 5) + 1 = 446$
Girls $(503 - 289) + 1 = 214$

Why add 1?

The addition of 1 may seem a little strange. Surely the distance between 5 and 450 is, straightforwardly, 445? The addition of 1 allows for possible measurement error. When we say that a child spoke for 5 seconds, if our lowest unit of measurement is 1 second, then we can only claim that the child spoke for something between 4.5 and 5.5 seconds, the limits of our lowest measurement interval. If we had measured to *tenths* of a second then 4.3 seconds represents a value between 4.25 and 4.35. Hence, the range is measured from the lowest possible limit of the lowest value to the highest limit of the highest value, in this case, 4.5 to 450.5.

### Advantages and disadvantages of the range
Advantages:     Easy to calculate

Disadvantages: Distorted by, and unrepresentative with, extreme values
Unrepresentative of any features of the distribution of values between the extremes. For instance, the range doesn't tell us whether or not the values are closely grouped around the mean

### The semi-interquartile range
This deals with the last disadvantage of the range. It will be affected by the central grouping of values. It concentrates on the distance between the two values which cut off the bottom and top 25% of scores. These two values are known as the 25th and 75th percentiles, or the first and third quartiles respectively. (We shall deal with these more precisely when we have looked at the features of distribution of data). The semi-interquartile range is, in fact, half of the distance between these two values.

In the following set of values:

$$3, \quad 3, \quad 4, \quad 5, \quad 6, \quad 8, \quad 10, \quad 13, \quad 14, \quad 16, \quad 19$$

4 is the first quartile and 14 the third quartile. The distance between these is 10 and half this, the semi-interquartile range, is 5.

### Calculation of the semi-interquartile range
Procedure:   1  Find the first quartile ($Q_1$) and the third quartile ($Q_3$). A formula for finding percentiles is given later and the first and third quartiles are the 25th and 75th percentiles respectively.
2  Subtract $Q_1$ from $Q_3$
3  Divide result of step two by 2

Formula:   $$\frac{Q_3 - Q_1}{2}$$

### Advantages and disadvantages of the semi-interquartile range
Advantages:     Is representative of the central grouping of values
Fairly simple to calculate

Disadvantages: Takes no account of extreme values
Inaccurate where there are large class intervals

### The mean deviation
In figure 11, we encountered the concept of a DEVIATION VALUE. A deviation value is the difference between any particular value and the mean. It is a measure of how far that value deviates from the mean. In formal terms:

$$d_i = x_i - \bar{x}$$

where $x_i$ means the ith value of the set. $x_1$ is the first value, $x_2$ is the second and so on.

If five people, including yourself, took an IQ test and these were the resulting values:

| Hugh | Helga | Harry | Helena | You |
|------|-------|-------|--------|-----|
| 85   | 90    | 100   | 110    | 115 |

the mean would be 100 and your personal deviation score would be $115 - 100 = 15$. This is how much you deviate from the mean of the group.

The range took no notice, and the semi-interquartile range took only some notice, of the way values deviate from the mean. A sensible way to report dispersion might seem to be, therefore, to report the average (mean) of all the deviations in the set. The set of deviations for the set of IQ scores above is shown in table 23:

*Table 23  IQ score devia-tions*

| Score | Mean | Deviation $(d)$ |
|-------|------|-----------------|
| 85 − 100 = | | − 15 |
| 90 − 100 = | | −10 |
| 100 − 100 = | | 0 |
| 110 − 100 = | | 10 |
| 115 − 100 = | | 15 |

The sum of these deviations is zero and therefore the mean of the deviations would also be zero. This isn't what we wanted. If you look back to figure 11 you can see why this has happened. The means sits precisely in the centre of all the deviations around it. If we use the minus sign to represent direction away from the mean then all the pluses and minuses will cancel each other out. The answer is to take the mean of all the deviation *sizes*, and to ignore any minus signs. This is known as taking the ABSOLUTE VALUE of a number and is represented mathematically by two vertical bars ($|$) either side of a number. So, for the absolute value of a deviation score we would write $|x - \bar{x}|$ or $|d|$.

**Calculation of the mean deviation**

Procedure:  1 Find the mean $(\bar{x})$
2 Subtract the mean from each value $[(x - \bar{x}) = d]$ to obtain a set of deviations
3 Add up all these deviations taking no notice of any minus signs i.e., find $\Sigma|d|$
4 Divide result of step three by $N$

Formula:  $$MD = \frac{\Sigma|x - \bar{x}|}{N}$$

Using this on our IQ data we get:

$$\Sigma|d| = 15 + 10 + 0 + 10 + 15 = 50 \qquad MD = \frac{50}{5} = 10$$

**Advantages and disadvantages of the mean deviation**

Advantages:    Takes account of all values in the set
              Relatively simple to calculate

Disadvantages: Not possible to use in making estimates of population para-
              meters

## The standard deviation and variance

Another way out of the problem of having all the deviations sum to zero is to take
the square of each deviation ($d^2$). This will also make the minus signs all
disappear, but, of course, if we take the mean of all these values ($\Sigma d^2/N$) we will
have a number which is rather large and not at all representative of the set of
deviations. This value is known as the VARIANCE of the set of values. What the
standard deviation then does is to take the square root of the variance in order to
return us to the level the deviations are at. If all that sounds a bit complicated let's
just go through the procedure for our set of IQ scores after giving the formal
details.

**Calculation of the standard deviation**

Term used:   $s$ – for samples
             $\sigma$ – for populations

Procedure:   1 Calculate the mean ($\bar{x}$)
             2 Subtract the mean from each value ($x - \bar{x}) = d$ to obtain a set of
               deviations
             3 Square each deviation ($= d^2$)
             4 Find the sum of the squared deviations
             5 Divide result of step four by $N$ (this result is the *variance*)
             6 Find the square root of result of step five

Formula:    $s = \sqrt{\dfrac{\Sigma d^2}{N}}$        for samples

and   $\sigma = \sqrt{\dfrac{\Sigma d^2}{N-1}}$        for population estimate

The formula for the *variance* is exactly the same, only without the square root
symbols. The terms for variance are $s^2$ or $\sigma^2$.

The reason for the sample–population difference will be explained after we
calculate a standard deviation for our IQ scores (see table 25).

Calculation:

$$s = \sqrt{\left(\frac{650}{5}\right)}$$

$$= \sqrt{130} \qquad \text{(130 is therefore the variance)}$$

$$= 11.4$$

*Table 24 Standard deviation for IQ scores*

| Score | Mean | Deviation (d) | Squared deviation (d²) |
|-------|------|----------------|-------------------------|
| 85 | 100 | −15 | 225 |
| 90 | 100 | −10 | 100 |
| 100 | 100 | 0 | 0 |
| 110 | 100 | 10 | 100 |
| 115 | 100 | 15 | 225 |
| | | | $\Sigma d^2 = 650$ |

Here are two alternative formulae for the sample standard deviation which can make comparison easier:

Alternative 1

$$s = \sqrt{\left(\frac{\Sigma x^2 - (\Sigma x)^2/N}{N}\right)}$$

Alternative 2

$$s = \sqrt{\left(\frac{\Sigma x^2}{N} - (\bar{x})^2\right)}$$

For alternative 1, the $N$ on the bottom line would change to $N - 1$ for population estimates. For alternative 2, the population estimate formula would be:

$$\sigma = \sqrt{\left(\frac{\Sigma x^2 - N(\bar{x})^2}{N-1}\right)}$$

In each case the variance is the value found before taking the square root.

## Population parameters and sample statistics

You may recall that a population is all of a target group from which we may select a sample. Descriptive measures of a *sample* are STATISTICS, whereas the same measures of a *population* are PARAMETERS. The mean and the standard deviation are used to make estimates of population parameters from a sample drawn from that population. This procedure is a very powerful one in statistical analysis, and tests which involve making such estimates are known as PARAMETRIC TESTS. These are the most powerful tests covered by this book. They are highly sensitive and are the most trustworthy in telling us whether the difference between two sample means is significant.

In estimating population parameters, the population mean is assumed to be the same as the sample mean. There will always be some difference between these two and this difference is referred to as SAMPLING ERROR. The sampling error can be estimated using the variance of the sample, so that we can state, say, that there is only a 5% probability that the population mean differs by more than 0.25 in either direction from a sample mean of 6.45. This is known as an ERROR ESTIMATE.

If you recall, in the chapter on sampling, we said that the larger the sample, the less likely is sampling bias. This principle holds good here too. *The larger the sample, the smaller the likely sampling error*, i.e. the closer our estimates will be to the true values.

If our set of IQ scores came from a population with a mean of 100 then the standard deviation of the sample would obviously be the same. However, if the population mean was different, and if we calculated our sample standard deviation using this population mean, the result would always be higher than the sample standard deviation. This is because the sample mean is at the exact centre of all the sample deviations. For instance, if we calculated the standard deviation of our five IQ scores using a mean of 105 we get:

*Table 25   Standard deviation using mean*

| Score | Mean | Deviation | $d^2$ |
|-------|------|-----------|-------|
| 85 | 105 | −20 | 400 |
| 90 | 105 | −15 | 225 |
| 100 | 105 | −5 | 25 |
| 110 | 105 | 5 | 25 |
| 115 | 105 | 10 | 100 |
| | | | $\Sigma d^2 = 775$ |

Calculation: $s = \sqrt{\left(\dfrac{775}{5}\right)} = \sqrt{155} = 12.4$

Because of this, the formula for calculating variance, if it is to be used in estimating the population variance, errs on the side of caution and makes the value a little higher by putting $N-1$, rather than $N$, onto the bottom line (the 'denominator').

Notice that, as $N$, the sample size, gets larger, so this conservative element of estimation gets less important. When $N$ is say, 45, there is very little difference between dividing by this figure or 44.

Note also that, when talking about populations, the term 'variance' is used more often than 'standard deviation'. But 'population variance', although mathematically different from the standard deviation of a population is a reference to the same concept, the amount by which values differ among themselves within a population.

### Advantages and disadvantages of the standard deviation and variance

Advantages:   Can be used in population parameter estimates
Takes account of all values
Is the most sensitive of measures covered
Is the most 'robust' measure. This means that, where samples vary quite widely, the standard deviation is least affected
Can be calculated directly on many calculators

Disadvantages: Somewhat more complicated to calculate (if you don't have an appropriate calculator!)

# DISTRIBUTIONS

When we wish to communicate the nature of our results to others, be it to our tutor, class colleagues or for official publication, we would usually present at least the central tendency and dispersion of any set of numerical data. We might wish, for instance, to report that the mean age at which 'telegraphic' utterances were first noticed by parents was 18.3 months but that there was a wide variation from this shown by a standard deviation of 4.7.

Where possible, we'd usually like to go further than this and present a table of our results, such as table 26.

*Table 26   Result table for small sample*

| Child | Mean age at which telegraphic utterances first noticed (*n* months) |
|:-----:|:------------------:|
| A | 18 |
| B | 21 |
| C | 26 |
| D | 13 |
| E | 11 |
| F | 19 |
| G | 20 |
| | $\Sigma x = 128$ |
| | $\bar{x} = 18.3$ |
| | $s = 4.7$ |

Now we can refer to individual variations and oddities, such as the child who doesn't produce until 26 months and the rather suspicious report of 11 months.

This method of displaying results is useful when the sample taken is relatively small. Had we questioned about 300 parents, however, this approach would be inappropriate and would consume too much space. The individual results – known as the 'raw data' – would be kept safe by the researcher but, for public display, they would be collated into a table known as a FREQUENCY DISTRIBUTION.

We might now end up with a table looking like table 27.

*Table 27   Frequency distribution showing ages at which parents report first noticeable telegraphic utterances*

| Age | 13 | 14 | 15 | 16 | 17 | 18 | 19 | 20 | 21 | 22 | 23 | 24 | 25 | 26 | 27 | Total |
|-----|----|----|----|----|----|----|----|----|----|----|----|----|----|----|----|-------|
| No. of children reported | 1 | 0 | 5 | 12 | 37 | 64 | 59 | 83 | 17 | 41 | 12 | 0 | 4 | 5 | 0 | 340 |

## Percentiles, deciles and quartiles

There are 340 cases in this distribution. We may be interested in finding the age by which 10% of the children were reported as using telegraphic speech. If so we would want to find the tenth PERCENTILE, which is the point which cuts off the bottom 10% of the distribution in the same way that the median cuts off the bottom 50%. The median is in fact the 50th percentile. It is also the fifth DECILE, because deciles cut off the distribution in 10% units; the third decile cuts off the bottom 30% for instance. The median is also the second QUARTILE because quartiles cut off in 25% (or quarter) units.

In the distribution above, the tenth percentile will be the point on the age scale below which 34 children fall (10% of cases). This is somewhere in the 17-month category. Proportionally it must be 16 cases into this category which, in all, contains 37 cases. Hence it's about just under half-way between 16.5 and 17.5 months. We calculate this using a formula which is a general version of that for calculating the median of frequency distributions, seen earlier:

$$\text{Percentile} = L + \frac{N \times p/100 - F}{f_{\mathrm{m}}} \times h$$

where $p$ is the relevant percentile required and the other symbols are the same as for the previous median calculation.

> Try calculating the tenth percentile for this distribution. You should get an answer of 16.93 months.

### Class intervals

Where the scale in use has many points, we can compress the data into class intervals as shown in table 28. This table also introduces the idea of CUMULATIVE FREQUENCY, where the column with that heading shows us how many values fall below the upper limit of the particular class interval.

*Table 28  Number of children and number of daily telegraphic utterances*

| No. of telegraphic utterances | No. of children | Cumulative frequency | Utterances less than: | |
|---|---|---|---|---|
| 0– 9 | 3 | 3 | 9.5 | (These are |
| 10–19 | 0 | 3 | 19.5 | the upper |
| 20–29 | 15 | 18 | 29.5 | limits of |
| 30–39 | 43 | 61 | 39.5 | each |
| 40–49 | 69 | 130 | 49.5 | class |
| 50–59 | 17 | 147 | 59.5 | interval) |
| 60–69 | 24 | 171 | 69.5 | |
| 70–79 | 4 | 175 | 79.5 | |
| | $N = \Sigma = 175$ | | | |

### Graphical representation

To demonstrate to our readers the characteristics of this distribution more clearly, we could draw up a pictorial representation of the data. One of the advantages of doing this is that the mode will be immediately apparent, as will other features, such as the rate at which numbers fall off to either side and any specially interesting clusters of data. A graphical presentation can also be justified by its immediate appeal to the eye.

**The histogram**  A histogram of our distribution would look like figure 12. The width of each column is the same and represents one class interval. If class intervals are combined – it might have been desirable to start with 0–19 since

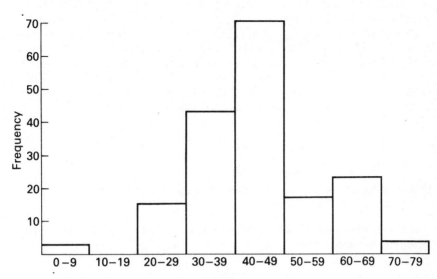

*Figure 12   Histogram of distribution in table 28*

there are so few in this bracket – the interval must be of appropriate width. Hence, 0–19 would be two columns wide. In a histogram, unlike a bar chart, all intervals are represented, even if empty, as for 10–19 in figure 12.

The height of each column represents the number of values found in that interval – the frequency of occurrence. Frequency is always shown on the *y*- (vertical) axis and the scale or class intervals on the *x*-axis. Since columns are equal in width, it follows that the *area* of each column is proportional to the number of cases it represents throughout the histogram. It also follows that the total of all column areas represents the whole sample. If we call the whole area one unit (which is the convention), then a column which represents 10% of the sample will occupy 10% of the total area, that is 0.1 units. The column representing 60–69 utterances represents 24 of the 175 cases. Therefore its area will be $24/175 = 0.138$ of the total area.

*Features of the histogram*
All categories represented
Columns are equal width per equal category interval
No intervals missed because empty
Column areas proportional to frequency represented and these sum to the total area of one unit.

**The bar chart**   The bar chart only has to show columns for the categories of data in which we are interested for comparison. It does not have to show every possible interval. We might, for instance, wish to present a visual comparison of the number of cases of violent crime in London for the years 1987 and 1988.

Notice in figure 13 that the bars are separated and that we do not need to present every column which could possibly exist. We are not presenting a complete sample of data but a specific selection. It would be appropriate to present the means of two conditions in an experiment as a bar chart: for instance, the means for solving anagrams of common and uncommon words.

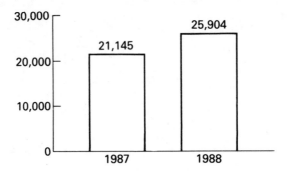

(Source: *Guardian* 7.11.88)

*Figure 13   Bar chart showing no. of violent crimes in London for 1987 and 1988*

It is possible to present highly misleading bar charts and histograms. Have a look at the version of figure 13 shown in figure 14(a). The convention is to show a break in the vertical scale as demonstrated in figure 14(b).

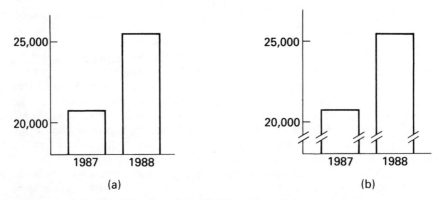

*Figure 14   (a) Misleading bar chart (b) Correct bar chart*

**Frequency polygon**    If we redraw our histogram (figure 12) with only a dot at the centre of the top of each column we would get what is known as a FREQUENCY POLYGON when we joined up the dots, as in figure 15.

This is particularly useful for showing the comparison between progress in two or more conditions of a study. For instance, where two groups of children receive different training-to-read programmes and progress is measured in error frequency over several months of testing. Here, the columns are omitted, as shown in figure 16.

**Ogive**    This is obtained by plotting the cumulative frequency distribution as shown in figure 17. The dots show the number of cases (61, vertical axis) which are below the scale point (39.5, horizontal axis). It is therefore possible to read off the number of cases above or below any scale point, by following this example. The ogive has a distinctive 'S' shape for distributions which are 'normal' (see figure 17), having most cases near the centre and tailing off rapidly and evenly on either side.

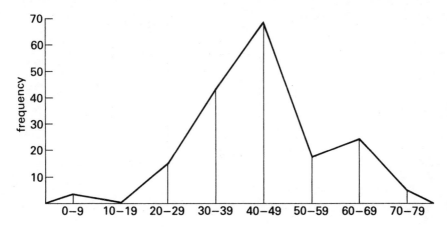

*Figure 15    Frequency polygon*

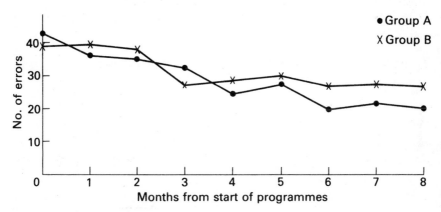

*Figure 16    Frequency polygon for two groups*

## The normal distribution

Earlier in this chapter, I pointed out that a measurement value, such as a person's height of, say, 163 cm is really a statement that the value falls within a class interval. We are saying that the person, for instance, is closer to 163 cm than 162 or 164 cm, rather than that they measure 163 cm exactly. They are in the interval between 162.5 and 163.5 cm. In effect, if we measure to the nearest cm we are placing individuals in class intervals 1 cm wide. It happens that if we take a large enough random sample of individuals from a population and measure physical qualities such as height (or weight, or length of finger), especially if we use a fine scale of measurement (such as to the nearest millimetre), we get a distribution looking like figure 18.

The curve which typically results from such measurements *closely approximates* to a very well-known 'bell-shaped' mathematical curve, produced from a shockingly complicated formula (which you or I need not bother with) devised by Gauss. The curve is therefore known as 'Gaussian' but in statistical work we more commonly refer to it as a NORMAL DISTRIBUTION CURVE.

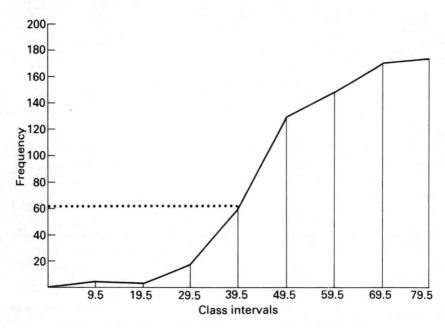

*Figure 17  Cumulative frequency–number of telegraphic utterances*

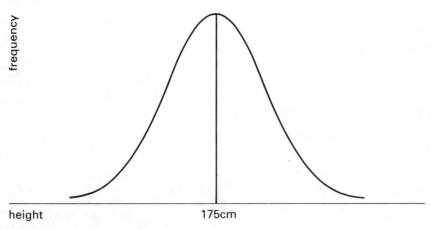

*Figure 18  A normal distribution curve*

## Characteristics of a normal distribution curve

1 It is symmetrical about the mid-point of the horizontal axis

2 The point about which it is symmetrical (175 cm on the curve shown above) is the point at which the mean, median and mode all fall.

3 It is known (for the perfect curve) what area under the curve is contained between the central point (mean) and the point where one standard deviation falls. In fact, working in units of one standard deviation, we can calculate *any* area under the curve (see page 158).

4 The 'asymptotes' (tail ends) of the perfect curve never quite meet the horizontal axis. Although for distributions of real large samples there are existing real limits, we can always hypothesise a more extreme score.

## The normal probability curve

The perfect normal curve is also a curve which gives us the probability of certain events occurring. Although we'll look at probability in more detail in the next chapter, the following discussion is an introduction to the topic. If you are uneasy about probability, however, try reading the first five pages of the next chapter now.

If we toss a coin in a fair (unbiased) manner, we know we are just as likely to get a head as a tail. Hence if we did this many times we would get, on average, an equal number of heads and tails. Every two tosses, on average, we expect one head and one tail. If we toss two coins, four outcomes are possible: two tails, a tail followed by a head, a head followed by a tail, and two heads. So every four tosses, on average, we'd expect no tails once, one tail twice and two tails once. This expectancy is represented on the histogram in figure 19.

If we toss three coins there are the possible outcomes shown in the histogram for three coins. There are now eight possible outcomes of which:

1 is 0 tails
3 are 1 tail
3 are 2 tails
1 is 3 tails

The three outcomes for 1 tail would be: HHT, HTH, or THH.

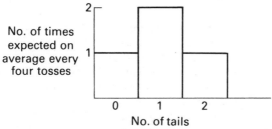

*Figure 19　Two coins*

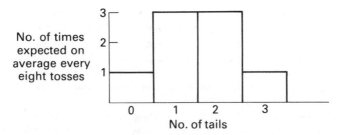

*Figure 20　Three coins*

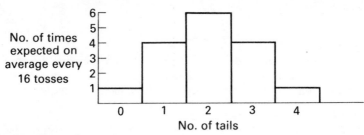

No. of times expected on average every 16 tosses

No. of tails

*Figure 21   Four coins*

With four coins we get the outcomes shown. 16 combinations are possible of which:

> 1 is 0 tails
> 4 are 1 tail
> 6 are 2 tails
> 4 are 3 tails
> 1 is 4 tails

If you look at the famous triangle, devised by mathematician Pascal, you'll see that the numbers within the extreme '1's on each line are obtained by adding the two numbers, one to the left and one to the right, directly above them. You can also see that the fourth line down (1 3 3 1) has the frequencies we expected for the various numbers of tails in the three coin event. The next line has the frequencies for four coins and so on.

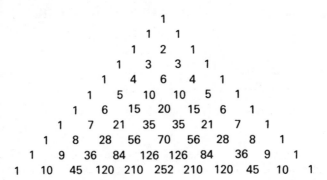

*Figure 22   Pascal's triangle*

We can therefore, without complicated calculation, immediately draw the histogram of expectancies for tossing ten coins together.

Now we might see where all this is getting us. The histogram which represents the number of times we'd expect ten tails, nine tails etc. in a throw of ten coins looks a bit like the shape of a normal curve only very jagged. Note that, if we did indeed throw ten coins, in a bunch, many times over (several thousand) we would get actual frequencies which approximate to this shape.

Imagine now that we build up the probability curve associated with the throwing of 32 coins over and over again. This curve, a rough sketch of which appears in figure 24, begins to look very much like the normal curve. When we

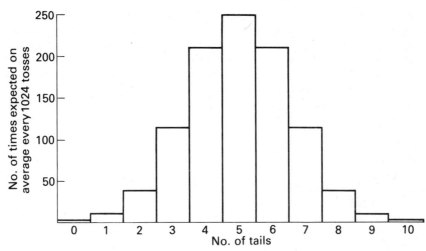

*Figure 23    Ten coins*

chart a frequency distribution of say, height, in reality the curve is not actually smooth but composed of a very large number of columns (little 'organ pipes') whose tops form a slightly jagged version of the familiar curve shape.

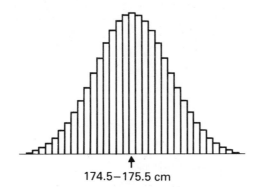

174.5–175.5 cm

*Figure 24*

What is the relevance of all these coins to psychological research? It is argued that variables such as height and weight follow a similar distribution pattern because, like the tossing of a coin many times, a large number of random variables are at work which, overall, produce the familiar bell-shaped frequency curve. Getting a bit closer to human behaviour or experience, if we measured the performance of a dart-player trying to hit the bull, we would find many shots relatively close to the mark and a diminishing number to either side. Similarly, a scale measuring attitude to alcohol use might produce results where very few people are totally opposed to it use, and very few keen on unchecked consumption, with most people on middle ground.

## Standardisation of psychological measurements

An extremely important issue here is the attempt by some psychologists to argue that variables, like intelligence or extroversion, are normally distributed throughout the population. Unlike the case of height, this is *not* based on research which measures intelligence and then *discovers* a normal distribution. In fact, the assumption is made, prior to creating an intelligence test, that, being a human quality, intelligence is likely to be normally distributed. As noted in chapter 8, tests are then STANDARDISED to ensure that, when large numbers are tested, a normal distribution results. In short, whereas height is a naturally-occurring normal distribution, intelligence (and other) tests are constructed to produce one. Usually the scoring of IQ tests is adjusted such that the population mean will be 100 and the standard deviation about 15 points.

### Area under the normal distribution curve

Suppose we devised a reading test for eight-year-olds and the maximum score possible in the test was 80. The test is standardised to a normal distribution such that the mean score, for a large, representative sample of eight-year-olds, is 40 and the standard deviation is 10. I hope it is obvious, for starters, that 50% of eight-year-olds will therefore be above 40 and 50% below. The area for the top 50% is shaded in figure 25.

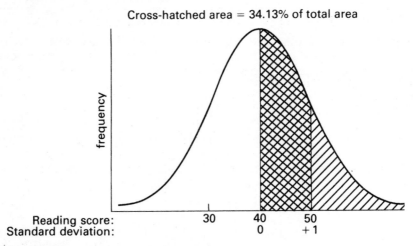

*Figure 25    Reading test distribution curve*

What we know, from the theory underlying the normal curve, is that one standard deviation, on any normal distribution curve, falls at the position shown by the line above 50 on figure 25. This is the point where the downward curve inflects from an inward to an outward direction. We also know that the area trapped between the mean and this point is 0.3413 of the whole. Hence we know that 34.13% of children score between 40 and 50 points on this test, since the standard deviation is 10 points. Figures worth noting are that:

34.13% of all values fall between ($\bar{x}$) and $+1$ (or $-1$) standard deviations
(area $= 0.3413$)

47.72% of all values fall between ($\bar{x}$) and $+2$ (or $-2$) standard deviations
(area $= 0.4772$)

49.87% of all values fall between ($\bar{x}$) and $+3$ (or $-3$) standard deviations
(area $= 0.4987$)

The positions of these standard deviations are shown in figure 26. Note the values above are doubled for areas between $-n$ and $+n$ standard deviations.

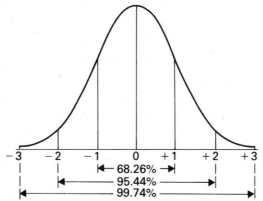

Area between $-n$ and $+n$ standard deviations on the normal curve.

*Figure 26  Positions of standard deviations*

### z-scores (or standard scores)

In the reading test example above, a child with a score of 50 lies one standard deviation above the mean. We could say that the number of standard deviations she is from the mean is $+1$ (the '$+$' signifying 'above'). Thus a child who is $-1.5$ standard deviations from the mean has a score of 25, because $1\frac{1}{2}$ standard deviations is 15 and this we subtract from the mean of 40. If we measure number of standard deviations from the mean in this way we are using z-SCORES or STANDARD SCORES. The formula for calculating a z-score is:

$$z = \frac{x - \bar{x}}{s}$$

where $s$ = standard deviation and $x - \bar{x}$, you'll notice, is the deviation score.

Dividing this by the standard deviation answers the question 'How many standard deviations does this deviation (from the mean) take up?' A z-score is the number of standard deviations a particular score is away from the mean. If the mean for shoe size in your class is 6, with a standard deviation of 1.5, then, if your shoe size is 9 your z-score is 2, or if your size is $4\frac{1}{2}$, your z-score is $-1$. You probably followed the example of the child with 25 points in your head but, in effect, you were using the formula shown. Let's check using the formula:

$$z = \frac{25 - 40}{10} = \frac{-15}{10} = -1.5$$

The formula is needed, of course, when scores aren't as convenient as the ones we've been using as examples.

z-scores cut off various known proportions of the area under the normal curve. Therefore we know the percentage of the population enclosed between the mean and any z-score. For instance, consulting table 2 in Appendix 3 the area between the mean and a z-score of $+1.5$ is 0.4332 of the whole, shown by the right-hand shaded pattern in figure 27:

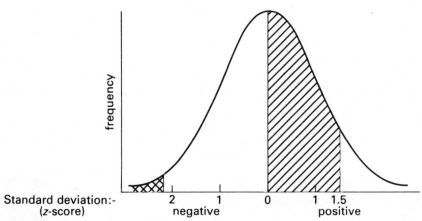

*Figure 27  Area between the mean and z-score of 1.5*

A z-score of $-2.2$ traps 0.486 of the area between it and the mean on the left-hand side. Since the *whole* of the left-hand side of the mean is 0.5 of the area, then only 0.014 (0.5 − 0.486) is left at the left hand extreme after $-2.2$ standard deviations. This is shown by the cross-hatching in figure 27, and by consulting the right-hand column of the table.

## Skewed distributions

Some distributions obtained from psychological measures which might be expected to be normal, in fact turn out SKEWED. That is, they are 'lop-sided', having their peak (mode) to one side and a distinctive tail on the side where more than half the values occur. Have a look at figure 28.

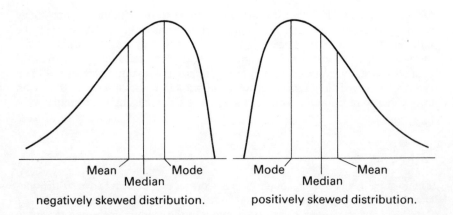

negatively skewed distribution.          positively skewed distribution.

*Figure 28  Positive and negative skews*

Suppose we were measuring reaction time to respond to words displayed one at a time on a computer screen. You have to decide as quickly as possible whether the word is real or non-English. The reaction time, on the majority of trials, is around 0.7 seconds. Over many trials, with perhaps many subjects, which sort of skewed curve might be produced?

It is possible to be very much slower than the majority of scores, but is it possible to be very much faster, when the majority of scores are around 0.7 seconds? This is like the situation in athletics where times can be quite a bit slower than the current good standard but not a lot faster. We would get a positively skewed distribution then. Notice that a positive skew has its tail up the positive end of the horizontal axis.

How would you construct a test which produced a negative skew – make it very easy or very hard to answer?

**Central tendency of skewed distributions**   Notice where the mean, median and mode fall on each distribution. The mode obviously still falls at the top, where the majority of scores are. In each case the mean is furthest from the mode – not surprising really, since we said that it was the most affected by extreme scores in one direction.

### Bi-modal distributions

Some distributions are known as BI-MODAL and, like some camels, have two distinct humps. We noted in the section on standardisation in chapter 9 that some measures of psychological variables may well produce such a distribution. Attitude measurement on a controversial issue (like privatisation of water provision) where not many people are neutral might produce bi-modal distributions. So might a measure of job satisfaction in a company where there are a large number of well-paid white collar workers along with a similar number of poorly-paid manual workers.

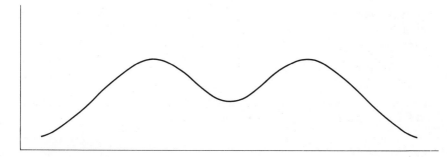

*Figure 29   A bi-modal distribution*

## Key terms for this chapter

| | |
|---|---|
| Absolute value | Mean |
| Average | Median |
| Bi-modal (distribution) | Mode |
| Central tendency | Modal value |
| Class interval | Ogive |
| Decile | (Population) parameter |
| Deviation (score) | Percentile |
| Dispersion | Quartile |
| Distribuiton | Range |
|   Cumulative frequency | Raw data |
|   Frequency | Sampling error estimate |
|   Gaussian curve | Semi-interquartile range |
|   Negative skew | Standard deviaton |
|   Normal distribution | (Sample) statistic |
|   Positive skew | Variance |
| Frequency polygon | Variation |
| Histogram | $z$-score/standard score |
| Mean deviation | |

## Exercises

1 Find the mean and median of the two sets of talking times in table 24.

2 Consider the following set of times, measured in 1/100ths of a second:

62  65  71  72  73  75  76  77  79  80  82  83  92  100  106  117  127

65  70  72  72  74  75  76  77  79  80  82  88  93  102  110  121  128

65  70  72  73  74  76  76  78  80  81  83  90  95  103  112  122  135

2 Sketch a distribution for the data and decide which would be the most appropriate measure of central tendency for it. Calculate this measure and also a measure of dispersion.

3 Draw a histogram for the data in table 27. Calculate the mean for this data.

4 Sketch two roughly normal distributions which have the same mean but quite different standard deviations. Also sketch two normal distributions with the same standard deviation but different means.

5 You are told that a set of data includes one score which is 0.8. The standard deviation for the set is 0. Can you give the mean of the set and say anything else about the six other scores in the set?

6 In an IQ distribution, where the mean is 100 and standard deviation 15,

  (a) what IQ score are 95% of people above?
  (b) what percentage would score less than 90?
  (c) what $z$-score does a person have who scores 120?

7 What sort of skew is present in a distribution which has the following characteristics:

Mean $= 50$      Median $= 60$      Mode $= 70$

# Probability *and* significance

## PROBABILITY

When teaching research methods and statistics in psychology, I always tell my students that they already have many of the important concepts framed in their heads, perhaps somewhat vaguely, developed through years of worldly experience. My job is to illuminate, clarify and name these concepts. This is particularly true of the concept of probability and yet it is the area which causes a relatively higher degree of anxiety and confusion compared with others. Most people do have a very good sense of how probable various events are and yet many people are also loathe to get involved in giving such probabilities a numerical value, either because it seems complicated or because one then seems committed to mysterious 'laws of chance'. A typical conversation goes:

> 'The chances of that happening are about 10,000 to one.' 'But it could happen!' 'Yes, about one time in every 10,000 it will.' 'Yes, but it *could* happen!'

. . . and so on, as if one were disagreeing with the other when both are saying roughly the same thing. Here is someone who *seems* to agree with what I'm saying:

> Probability is an obvious and simple subject. It is a baffling and complex subject. It is a subject we know a great deal about, and a subject we know nothing about. Kindergarteners can study probability, and philosophers do. It is dull: it is interesting. Such contradictions are the stuff of probability.
>
> (Kerlinger, 1969)

Probability works out in peculiar ways. What do you think are the chances of four tossed coins all coming up tails? How many people do you think would have to be in one room before there is a 50–50 chance that two people among them have the same birthday? The answer to the first question is 1 in 16 yet many people respond initially with 1 in 4. The answer to the second question is that, surprisingly, just 20 people will do.

163

### Giving probability a value

Have a look at the statements below. For most of them, you'll find you have some idea of how likely or not it is that these events will occur. Try to give a value between zero (not at all likely) and 100 (highly likely) to each statement, depending on how likely you think it is to occur:

1 It will rain on Wednesday of next week
2 You will eat breakfast on the first day of next month
3 Your psychology tutor will sneeze in the next lesson
4 You will be given a million pounds next year
5 The sun will rise tomorrow morning
6 You will think about elephants later today
7 Someone will bump into you later today
8 A coin tossed fairly will come down showing tails
9 Two coins tossed fairly will both come down tails

For number one, if you live in the UK, whatever the time of year, you may have answered with 50, whereas if you live in Bombay, and the month is October, you'd say about 3. Numbers two and seven depend on your habits and the time of day it is. I would be interested in what happens with number 6, now I've said it!

Now divide all the values you gave by 100. So, if you answered 20 to number seven, for instance, then divide 20 by 100 and you get 0.2.

Probability is always officially measured on a scale of:

$$0 \longleftarrow \qquad \text{to} \qquad \longrightarrow 1$$

NOT possible                                      MUST happen

. . . usually in decimal values, like 0.3, 0.5 and so on. I shall try to explain now why this makes sense.

### Logical probability

Your answer to number eight in the exercise above should have been exactly 50 which converts to 0.5. If you answered 25 (converts to 0.25) to number nine, either you can already calculate probability or you picked something up from the discussion of coin tossing in the last chapter.

Statements eight and nine are quite different from the rest. We can calculate the probability involved from *logical* principles. We can use the values worked out in the last chapter. The reasoning for statement eight runs as follows:

There are two possible outcomes – a head or a tail

> (We discount occasions when it falls on its edge!)

One of these is the outcome we want
There is therefore one chance in two that tails will come up.

This can be expressed as a fraction $(\frac{1}{2})$ or as a decimal (0.5).

The formula for logical probability is:

$$p = \frac{\text{number of ways desired outcome can occur}}{\text{total number of outcomes possible}}$$

(where $p$ stands for 'probability')

There were two possible outcomes and just one of these was 'desired' by us. With two coins there are four possible outcomes (see page 155). If we are interested in two tails as the result (our 'desired' outcome), then only one of the four possible outcomes will do and the probability of our result occurring is $\frac{1}{4}$ (0.25). Another way of looking at this is to say we want the probability that:

1 tail will occur for one toss $(p = \frac{1}{2})$ *AND* 1 tail $(p = \frac{1}{2})$ for the other

When 'and' is involved (we want both to happen), we multiply probabilities. Hence, we get $\frac{1}{2} \times \frac{1}{2} = \frac{1}{4}$ (0.25). When we use 'or', we *add* the probabilities. For instance, if we want to know the probability of *either* two tails $(p = \frac{1}{4})$ *or* two heads being the result, we add: $\frac{1}{4} + \frac{1}{4} = \frac{1}{2}$. So there is a probability of 0.5 that the two coins tossed will come up with the same side showing.

Notice that if we say 'What is the probability of obtaining *either* a head *or* a tail from one toss of a coin' the calculation is: $\frac{1}{2} + \frac{1}{2} = 1$. A head or a tail *must* occur. When events are absolutely certain, we use the value 1. If absolutely impossible, 0. For instance, no heads *and* no tails can't happen (we excluded coins falling on an edge).

> If there were 20 students in your class and the tutor was about to pick one of you to talk about this week's reading, how likely is she to pick you (assuming her choice is random)? How likely is it that she will pick someone else?

The tutor has 20 possible choices and you're just one of them. Your chances of being picked are therefore $\frac{1}{20}$, which is 0.05, fairly close to zero. The chances of someone else having to talk are $\frac{19}{20}$ since there are 19 ways she can make this happen. This comes out at 0.95 (note that the two probabilities added together make 1 – she's going to pick *someone*!).

Although fractions like $\frac{1}{4}$ and $\frac{1}{20}$ can be read as 'one in four' (chances), most probability figures will not be so simple. In fact, for interpreting statistics in psychology, you will need to be fairly agile in converting between decimal values (like 0.05) and *percentage values* (like 5%, the equivalent of 0.05 on the scale of 0 to 1). This is what you were doing in the exercise just above. For those who really get muddled commuting between one and the other, box 25 should help you.

## Empirical probability

With simple events, like tossing one or two coins, we can work out probability *theoretically* in pure, logical terms. We don't bother that an actual coin might be biased, or that it might fall on its edge. Where only two equally likely events are possible, the probability of just one of them occurring is exactly $\frac{1}{2}$ (0.5) and the probability of neither occurring is exactly 0.

With normal life, events or possibilities (which give rise to empirical facts), such as those described by items one to seven in the first exercise above, it is far too complicated, or impossible, to work out what all the logical possibilities are.

*Box 25   %/decimal conversion*

| From percentage to decimal | From decimal to percentage |
|---|---|
| 5% to $p = 0.05$ | $p = 0.05$ to 5% |
| 1 Remove the '%' sign ($= 5$) | 1 Move the decimal point *two* places to the right (005.) |
| 2 Put decimal point after the whole number ($= 5.$)* | 2 Lose any zeros to the left of the first left hand whole digit ($= 5.$) |
| 3 Move the decimal point *two* places to the left, inserting zeros as you go where necessary (i.e. first move 0.5, second move 0.05) | 3 Lose the decimal point if there is nothing to the right of it ($= 5$) |
| | 4 Add the '%' sign ($= 5\%$) |
| * If there already *is* a decimal point, leave it where it is, and go straight to step 3, e.g. $2.5\% \rightarrow 2.5 \rightarrow 0.25 \rightarrow 0.025$ | e.g. for 0.025: $0.025 \rightarrow 00.25 \rightarrow 002.5 \rightarrow 2.5 \rightarrow 2.5\%$ |

The probability of such events just can't be calculated from logical principles. We can attempt to calculate the EMPIRICAL PROBABILITY of (at least some of) items one to seven on the basis of how often similar events have occurred in the past.

Sometimes, our feeling of SUBJECTIVE PROBABILITY (what we *feel* is more or less likely) contradicts empirical probability. Air travel is statistically far safer than travel by road, yet it is hard to be comforted by this when a plane lurches at 33,000 feet!

The principle for estimating empirical probability is similar to that for estimating logical probability except that it is backward, rather than forward, looking. To find the probability of your tutor sneezing next lesson we need:

$$\frac{\text{number of lessons in which tutor has sneezed so far}}{\text{total number of tutor's lessons so far}}$$

In general, the probability of an $x$-type event occurring (like a rainy day) is:

$$\frac{\text{number of } x \text{ type events which have occurred}}{\text{total number of relevant events which have occurred}}$$

where 'relevant events' are the whole category of $x$-type and non-$x$-type events, such as:

– number of lessons tutor sneezes in and number of lessons tutor doesn't sneeze in (i.e. all lessons)
– rainy and non-rainy October days (i.e. all October days)

Where the total number of $x$-type and non-$x$-type events is very large, we might wish to select an appropriate sample. We might then arrive at:

$$\frac{\text{number of times tutor sneezed in sample lessons}}{\text{total number of lessons in sample}}$$

We might take all Octobers this century or just those in the last ten years. We can take the average (mean) number of rainy days per October over this period and arrive at:

$$\frac{\text{average number of rainy days in previous Octobers}}{\text{total number of days in October}}$$

If the average number of rainy days per October is 17, we get 17/31 and the probability of rain, on any particular day = 0.55.

# SIGNIFICANCE

We are often faced with making a decision as to whether a difference is one which matters or not. For instance, suppose you received 62% for your last essay and 60% for the essay which you've just had marked. Are you doing worse or is this just forgettable fluctuation in your tutor's grading? If you got 45% next time, you'd know there was a difference which mattered. The current difference (62%–60%), however, is not likely to bother you. So, we are often certain that a difference signifies a real change and often certain that it doesn't. That's the easy part. When do we change from one decision to the other? At what mark, below 62%, would you decide that your essay standard really had dropped?

In statistical language this is known as a decision of STATISTICAL SIGNIFICANCE. A decision that a difference is significant is made when it is unlikely to have been caused by chance fluctuation (random variables) alone. But how do we decide what counts as unlikely?

A common television advertisement shows the promoted washing-up liquid dealing with far more tables of crockery than an unnamed competitor. The viewer isn't given the chance, though, to discover whether the difference is statistically significant. Similarly, we often see just one person successfully choosing the promoted margarine rather than its anonymous rival. How many people would you want to see making this rather fortunate choice before you were convinced that the result you see is not a fluke? For situations like these we need a formal test.

There will always be *some* difference between the results of two conditions in an experiment or investigation. It is not enough to show that a difference occurred in the direction we wanted or predicted, which is all the television advertisements do. We have to show that the difference is significant. Have a look at the results of the two memory experiments in table 29.

### The 'eyeball test'

An 'eyeball test' is an inspection of results prior to formal testing. Without yet knowing the formal rules of significance decisions we can come to some pretty safe conclusions about the results in table 29. On the right, considering the variance in individual scores, we can see that the difference between means is quite unimpressive. On the left, it seems equally obvious that something has happened. Surely these differences could not be caused by chance fluctuation alone?

One can never *rely* only on an eyeball test. A formal statistical test must always be applied to the main data. It is useful, though, where there are a lot of possible differences to test, and some of these can be ruled out as unworthy of testing because obviously insignificant.

What we are seeking now, however, is a formal cut-off level. How unlikely does a difference have to be before we can call it a 'significant' one?

*Table 29   Memory experiment results*

| No. of words recalled out of 20: | | | | No of words recalled out of 20: | | |
|---|---|---|---|---|---|---|
| S | Common words | Uncommon words | | S | 6 letter words | 7 letter words |
| 1 | 15 | 10 | | 1 | 14 | 13 |
| 2 | 14 | 7 | | 2 | 13 | 14 |
| 3 | 10 | 6 | | 3 | 10 | 12 |
| 4 | 18 | 11 | | 4 | 15 | 13 |
| 5 | 16 | 4 | | 5 | 9 | 7 |
| 6 | 12 | 7 | | 6 | 11 | 15 |
| 7 | 9 | 2 | | 7 | 12 | 13 |
| 8 | 16 | 9 | | 8 | 16 | 15 |
| | Mean = 13.75 | 7 | | | Mean = 12.5 | 12.75 |
| Difference between means = 6.75 | | | | Difference between means = 0.25 | | |

## Significance decisions – an illustrative example

Suppose a friend said she could reliably forecast the sex of unborn babies by swinging a stone pendulum above the mother's womb. Suppose she guessed your baby's sex correctly. Would you be impressed? Your personal involvement might well cause you to react with 'amazing!' or at least, 'well, it *is* interesting that she got that correct.' Stepping back coolly from the situation you realise she had a probability of 0.5 of being correct. Nevertheless, most people would begin to think she had something by the time she'd correctly predicted the sex of two or three more friends' babies.

Suppose she attempted to predict ten babies' sexes in all. How many would you expect her to predict correctly in order for her to be convincing? Would you be impressed if she got five correct? I hope not. This is the performance you'd expect if she had no particular ability to predict at all. But ten out of ten *would* be impressive. It *could* still be a fluke though. We need to know just how unlikely ten out of ten is, *if* the friend is guessing at a chance level.

From our discussion of probability so far, and from table 30, you can work out that her chances of getting three out of three correct are 1/8 or $p = 0.125$. We can treat her predictions like the tossing of a coin – for each guess there are two equally likely outcomes. She *has* to guess male or female and these are (just about) equally likely. There are eight outcomes possible when three guesses are made.

*Table 30   Possible outcomes of guessing the sex of three babies*

| | Outcome number: | | | | | | | | |
|---|---|---|---|---|---|---|---|---|---|
| | 1 | 2 | 3 | 4 | 5 | 6 | 7 | 8 | |
| Baby 1 | √ | √ | √ | × | √ | × | × | × | where √ means she is correct |
| Baby 2 | √ | √ | × | √ | × | √ | × | × | and × means she is wrong. |
| Baby 3 | √ | × | √ | √ | × | × | √ | × | |

She has to end up with outcome number one. Since there are eight outcomes possible, the probability of her achieving number one is 1/8.

When we do the same calculation for ten guesses, we don't have to write out all the possible combinations. We can look at Pascal's triangle. The row for ten gives 1024 possible outcomes (the addition of all the numbers in the ten row). Of these, our friend must again end up with just one. Her chances of pulling this off are therefore 1/1024 ($= 0.00098$). Another way of calculating this would have been to say that she has to get the first sex right ($p = 1/2$), *and* the second right ($p = 1/2$) and so on. Hence, we have to multiply 1/2 by 1/2 ten times. We need $(1/2)^{10}$ which comes to: 1/1024.

## Rejecting the Null Hypothesis
So, with five out of ten predictions correct we are unimpressed. With ten out of ten there was less than one chance in a thousand that this was a fluke result, and surely we'd accept that our friend seemed able to predict sex correctly? If you recall from chapter 1, when we are involved in hypothesis testing, we have the choice of accepting the null hypothesis or rejecting it.

Here, the null hypothesis is that our friend's predictions are at a chance level only. In a sense, the null hypothesis says she's only guessing.

We want to reject this if she makes ten correct predictions. Would we want to reject it if she gets nine correct, or only eight?

> Moving from five to ten, at what number of correct predictions would you accept that our friend is not just guessing? In other words, what is the least number of correct predictions out of ten at which you would reject the null hypothesis?

## Significance levels
Social scientists have several levels at which they reject null hypotheses. They calculate the probability that differences in their results could have occurred by chance alone. If this probability is less than the set level they reject the null hypothesis that the results did occur by chance alone and they claim support for the research hypothesis. They say that the results are *significant* and the significance level is a measure of how confident they are that the results are not a fluke.

There is, however, one level of probability which is a standard. If the probability of a difference occurring were higher than this value then, by convention, no researcher would claim significance for the result. Now what is this level? Should probability for a difference always be below 0.001 (1/1000), 0.01, 0.05 or what?

> Let's see if you already have a sense of where this limit might lie. Suppose I hand you a pack of cards. There are only two possibilities: *either* all the red cards are on top *or* the pack is randomly shuffled. The second alternative is equivalent to the null hypothesis. Your job is to decide which of these two alternatives is the truth by turning over one card at a time from the top. There is a catch. You start with £1000. Every time you turn over a card this amount halves. If you take a guess after turning over two cards, then, you stand to win £250. After turning over how many red cards would you decide, fairly, confidently, that the reds are all on top? If you wait till 17 reds are turned over, you'll win just 1p! Even after ten reds you'll only get £1. Make your choice now.

## The 5% significance level

The probability that four red cards would turn up in succession off the top of a shuffled pack is 1/16 (1/2 × 1/2 × 1/2). For five red cards it is 1/32. A large number of people say they would feel fairly sure of rejecting the shuffled pack theory (the null hypothesis) at five reds (quite a large number of people are also more conservative).

Social scientists call a difference significant, and reject the null hypothesis, when the probability of it occurring by chance alone is less than 0.05. This is popularly known as the 5% SIGNIFICANCE LEVEL.

Because 0.05 is the same as 1/20, in the cards example, a run of five would be significant, and a run of four would not. A run of five will occur less often than one time in 20 by chance alone, whereas a run of four will occur more frequently than one time in 20.

If the result of a psychological investigation would be likely to occur, by chance alone, more often than one time in 20, social scientists do not have confidence in it. It is too likely to have been just a fluke. If the probability of the result occurring by chance is *under* one in 20, it is taken, with temporary confidence, as valid support for the research hypothesis.

> If a result is significant ($p \leqslant 0.05$) the null hypothesis is rejected
> If a result is not significant ($p > 0.05$) the null hypothesis is retained

## But couldn't it still be a fluke?

If we kept shuffling a pack and turning over the top five cards, about one time in 32 we'd get a succession of five reds on top. This is the empirical prediction from our logical calculation of probability. So, yes, this *could* be a fluke. The probability of obtaining the differences in recall for common and uncommon words shown in table 30 is less than 0.01. This could also be a fluke. However, the researcher hypothesised a difference, found that the probability of the difference occurring by chance was less than 0.05, so the result is considered significant and would justify publication.

> What steps can be taken to ensure that, when a researcher finds results significant at the 5% level, the pattern of results which has occurred is not a fluke?

What researchers do is to REPLICATE studies. If an effect is taken as significant, and therefore published, someone else would try to obtain the same results in a repeat of the original study. The chances of the same difference occurring twice by chance alone are smaller than when it occurs first time. This is a test of the RELIABILITY of the effect as explained in chapter 4.

## Critical value

We need to apply the 5% significance level to the baby-sexing results. We want to know the number of correct predictions our friend must make in order that the probability of her doing so is less than 0.05. From row ten of Pascal's triangle we can calculate the probability of her getting different numbers of predictions correct (see table 31).

Figure 23 shows the histogram of expected frequencies which matches this table. The chart can also be seen as a histogram of probabilities for ten coin tosses or ten

*Table 31  Probabilities from Pascal's triangle*

| No. of correct predictions (N) | Probability of N occurring by chance (guessing) alone: | |
|:---:|:---:|:---:|
| | Fraction | Decimal |
| 0 | 1/1024 | 0.001 |
| 1 | 10/1024 | 0.01 |
| 2 | 45/1024 | 0.044 |
| 3 | 120/1024 | 0.117 |
| 4 | 210/1024 | 0.205 |
| 5 | 252/1024 | 0.246 |
| 6 | 210/1024 | 0.205 |
| 7 | 120/1024 | 0.117 |
| 8 | 45/1024 | 0.044 |
| 9 | 10/1024 | 0.01 |
| 10 | 1/1024 | 0.001 |

trials of any event for which there are just two equally likely outcomes. A small version of it is shown as figure 30.

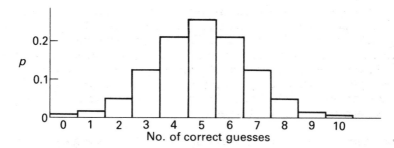

*Figure 30  Histogram of expected frequencies*

The probability of our friend making nine correct predictions by chance is 0.01 and for ten it is 0.001. Hence, the probability of her getting *either* nine *or* ten predictions correct by chance is 0.011, since we add probabilities (see page 165). The chance of her getting eight *or* nine *or* ten correct is therefore 0.055.

We did not predict that our friend would get a particular number of sexes correct. We expected her to get a lot correct. Hence, if she gets eight correct, we do not say that the probability of her doing this was 0.044. We say that the probability of her doing *this or better* was 0.055. Since this value is greater than 0.05, the result would not count as significant. If she gets nine correct, however, the probability of her doing this or better is just 0.011 – well under 0.05 and therefore significant. We would reject the null hypothesis if she makes nine or more correct predictions. The value nine here, is the CRITICAL VALUE for this particular test. It is the value she must equal or beat for us to accept that the effect is significant.

## One- and two-tailed hypotheses

Suppose our friend had got every single prediction wrong. Would we say she was a hopeless baby-sex guesser? Or wouldn't this be a particularly interesting result? After all, the probability of her doing *this* by chance alone is also 0.001. We might suspect that she has indeed got a valid method but that she has her instrument round the wrong way or is reading it incorrectly!

A ONE-TAILED HYPOTHESIS is made when we predict the *direction* of our results. For instance, we might predict that subjects will recall more common than uncommon words. A test of this hypothesis is known as a ONE-TAILED TEST.

A TWO-TAILED HYPOTHESIS is made when we predict a difference but do not state any expected direction. We might predict that males and females will differ in their attitude to male homosexuality, but we do not make a statement about who will be more positive. The test of this hypothesis is TWO-TAILED.

If we test a one-tailed hypothesis and the results go in the opposite direction to that predicted, we cannot reject the null hypothesis, *even if* the probability of their occurrence is below 0.05. With a two-tailed test we can reject the null hypothesis whichever direction the results take, so long as the probability of their occurrence is below 0.05. So why not always make two-tailed predictions then?

One reason is that the one-tailed hypothesis will usually be a specific prediction from a theory. If results are extreme in the opposite direction from that predicted we do not have support for our theory and must return to the drawing board to look for one of several things: a confounding variable in the design or procedure, a fault in our logic predicting the result, or a way to revise our theory to take account of conflicting results.

Another reason is that significance with two-tailed predictions is harder to achieve as I shall try to explain.

## Tails of a distribution

Figure 31 shows an expanded version of the right-hand 'tail' of the probability

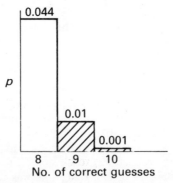

*Figure 31  Expansion of right-hand three columns of figure 30*

histogram in figure 30. For significance, a result must be in the shaded area. If the sex guesser made only eight correct predictions, the area involved would be 5.5% of the total – just too much for significance.

The probability of our sex guesser getting *either* nine or more of her predictions right *or* nine or more wrong is the addition of the following probabilities:

| 10 right | $p = 0.001$ |
|---|---|
| 9 right | $p = 0.01$ |
| 10 wrong | $p = 0.001$ |
| 9 wrong | $p = 0.01$ |
| Total | $p = \overline{0.022}$ |

We have added the probabilities at each tail of the distribution. Even if we'd predicted that she'd get a lot right *or* a lot wrong, her result of nine or ten correct would count as significant, because the probability of this occurring is 0.022 and still well below 0.05. But in other cases this doubling of probabilities for a two-tailed test would cause total probability to rise above 0.05 and leave the result non-significant. In other words, if you hedge your bets, probability rises. A bookie lowers your odds if you change your prediction from 'first' to 'first *or* in the first three'.

The area of probability involved for a two-tailed hypothesis where ten predictions are made is shaded in figure 31. The two tails are added together and produce the totals given above.

If the number of outcomes is very many, as we saw in the last chapter, a normal distribution emerges, with much finer steps between outcomes. Have a look at figure 32. On this distribution it is possible to cut off the exact top 5% of possible results, or the exact top and bottom 2.5% – that is, the most *extreme* 5%, shown by the cross-hatched area. The positive and negative $z$ scores (1.96) leave 95% of the area in the middle and cut off the remaining 5% (2.5% at either end). In table 2, Appendix 3, you can check that a $z$ of $+1.96$ leaves 0.025 of the whole area on its right. Use the right hand of the two area columns in the table.

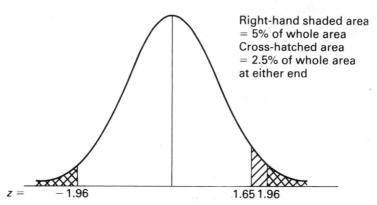

Right-hand shaded area
= 5% of whole area
Cross-hatched area
= 2.5% of whole area
at either end

$z =$    $-1.96$            1.65   1.96

*Figure 32  5% distribution*

Therefore, with a two-tailed test, any result we get must be associated with a $z$ score higher than 1.96 or lower than $-1.96$ to count as significant, because our result must fall in the cross-hatched area – the most extreme 5% of possible outcomes.

For a one-tailed test our result has to fall within the *top* 5% of the curve only, not within the top 2.5% or bottom 2.5%. Therefore the result we get need only be associated with a $z$ score greater than 1.65. In other words, with a one-tailed test we say, *before testing*, 'either our result will be in the area where the top 5% unlikeliest results would fall or we'll retain our null hypothesis'. Any result in the bottom 95% of possible results, then, is a failure to support our research hypothesis.

I hope it's now fairly clear that, for a significant two-tailed test, we would always have to achieve a result which is further out towards the extreme of unlikely results than we would with a one-tailed test. The price paid for this greater ease of achieving one-tailed significance is that, should we get a huge difference in the direction opposite from that which we predicted, we can't claim it as significant for this *particular research study*.

## Other levels of significance

If the baby sexer had got all ten predictions correct it would seem necessary to say that she didn't produce a result which was *just* significant at 5%. Her result was less likely than 0.001, which is 0.1%. When this happens, psychologists point out the level obtained in their final report. There is a tendency to use the following language in reporting results:

| | |
|---|---|
| Significant at 5% | 'Results were significant' |
| Significant at 1% | 'Results were highly significant' |
| Significant at 0.1% | 'Results were very highly significant' |

**The 10% level ($p \leqslant 0.1$)**   A researcher cannot be confident of results, or publish them as an effect, if the level achieved is only 10%. But if the level is in fact close to 5% (like the sex guesser's results if she gets eight predictions correct) it may well be decided that the research is worth pursuing. Procedure would be tightened or altered, the design may be slightly changed and sampling might be scrutinised.

**The 1% level ($p \leqslant 0.01$)**
Sometimes it is necessary to be more certain of our results. If we are about to challenge a well established theory or research finding by publishing results which contradict it, the convention is to achieve 1% significance before publication.

**Lower than 1% ($p < 0.01$)**
In research which may produce applications affecting human health or life changes, such as the testing of drugs for unwanted psychological or behavioural effects, we'd want to be even more certain that no chance effects were being recorded.

**Above 5% ($p > 0.05$)**
Yes, it seems we covered this with the 10% level. But the emphasis here is different. A researcher may be replicating a study which was a challenge to their work. It may be that showing there *isn't* a difference is the research aim. This would be the case with a lot of modern studies aimed at demonstrating a *lack* of difference between men and women on various tests and tasks. In this case the prediction is that the null hypothesis will be retained. The probability associated with results must now fall in the less extreme 95% area under the probability curve.

## Critical values at various significance levels

Notice that for significance at 1% (one-tailed) $z$ would have to be 2.33 or above, because a $z$-value of 2.33 leaves just 0.01 of the area lying on the right-hand side of the distribution. Check in table 2, Appendix 3, using the right-hand 'area left' column.

Just to make sure you've got a fair understanding of what critical levels are and how they work, try the following exercise. If you find it tricky, please don't bang your head against the wall, give up psychology or feel inadequate. Most people find this fairly tricky at first. Do the exercise with a friend, stick at it and/or pester your tutor for examples until you get the hang of it!

What is the critical value of $z$ which obtained $z$-scores would have to beat if results were to be counted as significant at the following levels:

| | | | |
|---|---|---|---|
| Two-tailed | 10% | 2% | 1% |
| One-tailed | 2.5% | 1% | 0.01% |

Answers:

| | | | |
|---|---|---|---|
| Two-tailed | 10% $= 1.65$ | 2%$= 2.33$ | 1% $= 2.58$ |
| One-tailed | 2.5%$= 1.96$ | 1%$= 2.33$ | 0.1%$= 3.11$ |

## Type One and Type Two error

When we have finished analysing research results, and we have tested for significance, we make a statement that we must accept or reject the null hypothesis at the set level of significance, usually 5%.

We may be right or wrong. We can never be *absolutely* certain that an apparent effect is not a fluke. Sometimes it seems crazy to challenge. Say, for instance, we ran an experiment in which there were two conditions: recall of common words, like 'cat', and recall of uncommon words, like 'otiose'. A significant difference at 0.1% ($p < 0.001$) would appear unassailable. However, within psychological research, results are rarely as unambiguous as this, though high levels of significance are what good research aims at.

If a researcher claims support for the research hypothesis with a significant result when, in fact, variations in results are caused by random variables alone, then a TYPE ONE ERROR would be said to have occurred.

Through poor design or faulty sampling, researchers may fail to achieve significance, *even though the effect they were attempting to demonstrate actually does exist.* In this case it would be said that they had made a TYPE TWO ERROR. These outcomes are summarised in table 32.

*Table 32   Outcome summary*

| | Null hypothesis is: | |
|---|---|---|
| **Null hypothesis is actually:** | Accepted | Rejected |
| True | √ | Type one error |
| False | Type two error | √ |

Obviously, if we set a stringent (low) significance level, such as 1%, we may well make a type two error. At 10%, a type one error is much more likely.

## Key terms for this chapter

Critical value
Eyeball test
One-tailed hypothesis/test
Probability
  Empirical
  Logical
  Subjective

Significance levels
  (a) 10%
  (b) 5%
  (c) 1%
Significance decision
Two-tailed hypothesis/test
Type one error/type two error

## Exercises

1 State whether the following values of $z$ (on a normal distribution) are significant or not for:

  (a) One-tailed tests
     1.32  1.75  $-1.9$  $-0.78$
  (b) Two-tailed tests
     $-2.05$  1.89  $-1.6$  1.98

2 State whether tests of the following hypotheses would require one- or two-tailed tests:

  (a) Diabetics will be more health conscious than other people
  (b) Extroverts and introverts will differ in their ability to learn people's names
  (c) Job satisfaction will correlate negatively with absenteeism
  (d) Self-esteem will correlate with outward confidence

3 A student sets out to show that attitude change will be greater if people are paid more to make a speech which contradicts their present attitude. Her tutor tells her that this runs directly counter to research findings on 'cognitive dissonance'.

  (a) What would be a safe significance level for her to aim for?
  (b) If she had originally intended to use the 5% level, is she now more or less likely to make a type two error?

4 A $z$-score of 2 is significant (two-tailed), with $p \leq 0.05$ because it is greater than the critical value of 1.96 for $p \leq 0.05$. This is why the first line of the table below is marked 'true'. Can you complete the rest of the table with ticks or crosses?

|     |      | One- or two-tailed test | $p \leq$ | True or false |
|-----|------|-------------------------|----------|---------------|
| (a) | 2.0  | Two                     | 0.05     | true          |
| (b) | 1.78 | One                     | 0.05     |               |
| (c) | 2.3  | Two                     | 0.025    |               |
| (d) | 2.88 | One                     | 0.002    |               |
| (e) | 3.35 | Two                     | 0.001    |               |
| (f) | 2.32 | One                     | 0.01     |               |

# Inferential statistics I

## NON-PARAMETRIC TESTS OF DIFFERENCE

## TESTS AT NOMINAL LEVEL – Related data

In the last chapter we calculated, from basic probability principles, the CRITICAL VALUE our baby-sexing friend needed to equal or beat for a significant result at the 5% level.

Normally, you'll be pleased to hear, we don't have to find the critical value through such a direct and detailed process. Tables are written for us to consult after doing some fairly straightforward calculations on our results.

As a simple example, take our baby-sexing results and turn them around. How many mistakes (incorrect predictions) can our friend make and still have her results counted as significant? We know she must get at least nine right. She can therefore get only one wrong. Let's call this value 's'. It is the highest number of 'wrong' results we can have whilst calling our overall result significant.

Now look at table 3 on page 283. This is for something called the sign test which we look at formally below. Look down under the column headed 'N' for the value 10 – the ten predictions our friend made. Go across now to the column headed '5%' (one-tailed) on the $N = 10$ line. You should find the value 1. This is the critical value. It tells us (what we know already from our calculations) that 1 is the maximum number of wrong results we can have whilst still treating our results as significant at 5%.

We have actually been through our first test of statistical significance! Some are harder than this but for all tests we go through the same basic procedure, shown in table 33. Let's now look at the sign test in a formal manner.

*Table 33   Procedure to find statistical significance*

| |
|---|
| Decide which test to use (see 'Choosing an appropriate test', page 230) |
| Calculate and obtain a test STATISTIC ('s', in our example above) |
| Obtain critical value from tables |
| Decide whether result is significant (depends on significance level originally set) |

## The binomial sign test (usually shortened to 'sign test')

### Conditions for use
Operates at the NOMINAL level of measurement
Uses pairs of scores from a RELATED design

## Data

A psychotherapist wishes to assess the therapeutic process. One way is to ask clients whether, after three months of therapy, they feel better about themselves. They are asked to rate their self-image by giving a score out of twenty.

*Table 34   Therapy data*

| | A | B | C | D |
|---|---|---|---|---|
| | Rating | | | |
| Client (N=9) | Pre-therapy | After three months therapy | Difference (B−A) | Sign of Difference |
| A | 3 | 7 | 4 | + |
| B | 12 | 18 | 6 | + |
| C | 9 | 5 | −4 | − |
| D | 7 | 7 | 0 | |
| E | 8 | 12 | 4 | + |
| F | 1 | 5 | 4 | + |
| G | 15 | 16 | 1 | + |
| H | 10 | 12 | 2 | + |
| I | 11 | 15 | 4 | + |
| J | 10 | 17 | 7 | + |

## Procedure

## Calculation on our data

1 Calculate the difference between A and B, always subtracting in the same direction. If a one-tailed hypotheses has been made, it makes sense to subtract the score expected to be lower from that expected to be higher. Enter difference in column C.

See column C.

2 Enter sign of difference in column D. Ignore any zero values (i.e. cases where there is no difference in score pairs).

See column D. N becomes 9 because one result is zero.

3 Add up the number of times the less frequent sign occurs. Call this 's'.

Negative signs occur less frequently, so s = 1

4 Find the relevant line of critical values from table 3, Appendix 3 where N = total number of positive and negative signs (not zeros). Decide whether to pay attention to one- or two-tailed 'p' values.

Consult table and look at the horizontal line next to N=9. Since therapy was supposed to *improve* people's self-image, we are conducting a one-tailed test.

5 Compare *s* and the critical values. Find the one with least probability for which our calculated *s* is still not greater. If *s* is greater than all critical values, results are not significant.

Our *s* is 1. This value appears under the column headed '$p < 0.05$' so we know the result is significant. But 1 is also the value under '$p < 0.025$'. Since *s* doesn't exceed this either, and since 0.025 is the lower probability, we take this as our result.

6 Make statement of significance found.

Our result is significant at 2.5%, $p < 0.025$ (one-tailed).

## Summary

The test looks only at the *direction* of differences. The critical value tells us the maximum number of differences in the unwanted direction we can have and still call our results significant at a particular level.

## Explanatory notes

The level is nominal because we started with interval (or interval-like) data and then lost any information about size of difference between each pair of scores. All we know, for each result, is that there *was* a difference and the direction it went in. For each result we have just three categories to put it in: ' + ', ' − ' or '0'. Results given the category ' + ' are all identical as far as the test is concerned.

   The null hypothesis is that any differences occurred at a chance level. In this case, it is the claim that our ten clients are no different from any other ten people asked to rate their self-image with a three-month interval and no therapy. If we selected many random samples of ten and repeated the self-image ratings, less than one sample in 20 would differ between pre- and post-therapy as much as our clients have done. Therefore we are rejecting the null hypothesis.

# TESTS AT NOMINAL LEVEL – UNRELATED DATA

The $\chi^2$ test (also written as 'Chi-square' and pronounced 'ky square')

## Conditions for use

Uses NOMINAL level data.
All data are frequencies.
The data are UNRELATED.

There are other limitations on the use of $\chi^2$, outlined at the end of this section on $\chi^2$.

## Data

The results in table 35 were actually obtained at a psychology workshop by students observing male and female drivers at a pedestrian traffic light. They observed whether a driver stopped or not when approaching the light as it turned to amber.

## Procedure

1 Call the raw data in the table OBSERVED FREQUENCIES.

2 Give each cell a letter as shown: A, B, C and D.

Table 35   Observed frequencies

|  | Sex of driver | | Total |
|  | Female | Male | |
|---|---|---|---|
| Driver stopped | 90  A | B    88 | 178 |
| Driver didn't stop | 56  C | D    89 | 145 |
| Total | 146 | 177 | 323 |

3 Calculate an EXPECTED FREQUENCY for each cell as follows:

Formula:   $E = \dfrac{R \times C}{T}$      where:

$R$ = total of row cells $(A + B)$ or $(C + D)$
$C$ = total of column cells $(A + C)$ or $(B + D)$
$T$ = total of all cells $(A + B + C + D)$

Call data in observed cells 'O' and in expected cells 'E'.

4 Calculate DEGREES OF FREEDOM. For a $\chi^2$ test this is always: (Number of rows $- 1) \times$ (Number of columns $- 1$) except for one special case to be discussed.

5 (a)   *If degrees of freedom = 1*

$$\chi^2 = \sum \frac{(|O - E| - 0.5)^2}{E}$$

For each cell:

1 Subtract $E$ from $O$
2 Ignore any negative sign from the result of step 1
3 Subtract 0.5 from result of step 2
4 Square the result of step 3
5 Divide result of step 4 by $E$

Compute for all cells and then add all step 5 results.

(b)   *If degrees of freedom > 1*

$$\chi^2 = \sum \frac{(O - E)^2}{E}$$

For each cell:

1 Subtract $E$ from $O$
2 Square the result of step 1
3 Divide the result of step 2 by $E$

Compute for all cells, then add up step 3 results.

NB The deduction of 0.5 from the absolute value of $O - E$ is known as YATES' CORRECTION.

6 Find relevant critical value line from table 4 on page 284.

NB All $\chi^2$ tests should be taken as two-tailed except for one exception to be discussed later.

7 Compare calculated $\chi^2$ with critical values and take the highest value which is still not greater than our calculated $\chi^2$ value. (Ask the question, 'which is the highest ours has beaten?') If $\chi^2$ is less than all critical values, results are not significant.

8 Make statement of significance.

**Calculation on our data**
Steps 1 and 2: see table 35.

*Table 36   Expected frequencies*

|  | Sex | |
|---|---|---|
|  | Female | Male |
| Driver stopped | 80.46  A | B  97.54 |
| Driver didn't stop | 65.54  C | D  79.46 |

3 Calculation of expected frequencies

$$\text{Cell A:} \quad E = \frac{178 \times 146}{323} = 80.46$$

$$\text{Cell B:} \quad E = \frac{177 \times 178}{323} = 90.54$$

$$\text{Cell C:} \quad E = \frac{145 \times 146}{323} = 65.54$$

$$\text{Cell D:} \quad E = \frac{177 \times 145}{323} = 79.46$$

4 Degrees of freedom $= (2-1) \times (2-1) = 1$

5 Use formula (a) because degrees of freedom $= 1$

|  | Step 5.1 $(O-E)$ | Step 5.2 $\|O-E\|$ | Step 5.3 $(\|O-E\|-0.5)$ |
|---|---|---|---|
| Cell A | $90-80.46$ $=9.54$ | 9.54 | 9.04 |
| Cell B | $88-97.54$ $=-9.54$ | 9.54 | 9.04 |
| Cell C | $56-65.54$ $=-9.54$ | 9.54 | 9.04 |
| Cell D | $89-79.46$ $=9.54$ | 9.54 | 9.04 |

|  | Step 5.4 $(\|O-E\|-0.5)^2$ | Step 5.5 $\dfrac{(\|O-E\|-0.5)^2}{E}$ |
|---|---|---|
| Cell A | $9.04^2$ $=81.72$ | $81.72 \div 80.46 = 1.016$ |
| Cell B | $9.04^2$ $=81.72$ | $81.72 \div 97.54 = 0.383$ |
| Cell C | $9.04^2$ $=81.72$ | $81.72 \div 65.54 = 1.247$ |
| Cell D | $9.04^2$ $=81.72$ | $81.72 \div 79.46 = 1.028$ |

$$\chi^2 = \text{Total} = 4.129$$

6 The relevant line is the one by 1 degree of freedom.

7 Our 4.129 exceeds 3.84 but not 6.64. Therefore, 3.84 is the critical value and this is under the $p < 0.05$ column (two-tailed).

8 Therefore, our result is significant at the 5% level.

## Summary
The test looks at the variation between observed frequencies and those to be expected if, given row and column totals, there was absolutely no association between the vertical and horizontal variables i.e. no difference at all between the categories of one variable as measured on the other variable.

## Explanatory notes
If you consider our data, it is obvious that, of the 177 males observed, just $\frac{1}{2}$ (50%) of these stopped on the amber, whereas 90 out of 146 females (62%) did.

The $\chi^2$ test looks at these relative proportions. Let's take a simpler fictitious example.

50 high extroverts and 50 high introverts were asked whether they would feel comfortable on a nudist beach. Here are the results.

*Table 37    Observed frequencies*

| Would feel: | Extrovert | Introvert | |
|---|---|---|---|
| Comfortable | 40 | 10 | 50 |
| Uncomfortable | 10 | 40 | 50 |
| | 50 | 50 | |

Note that, of all 50 subjects asked, 50 said they would be comfortable and 50 said they wouldn't. But these 50 aren't evenly spread between the two types of person. A large proportion of extroverts would feel comfortable.

If there were absolutely no difference between extrovert and introvert on this variable (feeling comfortable when nude) then I hope you'll agree that we should expect the data to take this pattern:

*Table 38    Expected frequencies*

| Would feel: | Extrovert | Introvert | |
|---|---|---|---|
| Comfortable | 25 | 25 | 50 |
| Uncomfortable | 25 | 25 | 50 |
| | 50 | 50 | |

The null hypothesis predicts that, if we took many samples this size, we would get cell totals fairly close to these on most occasions. The question is, do the cell totals in table 37 depart significantly from these expected (under the null hypothesis) totals?

Here is an imaginary example to demonstrate the essence of what $\chi^2$ does. Imagine dropping ball bearings onto the spot in the centre of the box above, where all cells meet. The balls bounce away from there in random fashion. We stop when all rows and columns add to 50 (which means the whole process isn't random but this is only an illustrative example). Each time we did this, we'd get results not varying far from those shown in figure 39 – the 'expected' frequencies. Now and again, however, under probability 'laws', freak variations quite far from this would occur. As we did for tossing coins, it is possible to calculate the number of possible combinations of frequencies that will give these row and column totals. The combinations giving low $\chi^2$ values, because observed data do not vary much from expected, are relatively numerous. The combinations giving high $\chi^2$ values, where observed values differ greatly from expected, are relatively few. $\chi^2$ tells us just how often we could expect a result as extreme as the one we actually have.

The null hypothesis here claims that the probability of introvert or extrovert saying they would feel comfortable is equal. Statistically, since 50 out of 100 people in all said they'd feel comfortable, we would expect 50% (50/100) of introverts to say this, i.e. 50/100 × 50. I hope you can see here why the expected frequencies are calculated as $R \times C$. If you followed the last point quite smoothly, then, in a sense, you used this formula without bothering to think about it.

Actually, our sample differed a lot from this expectation. The probability of getting 40 extroverts reporting $X$, and only 10 introverts reporting $X$, on the basis of the null hypothesis, is extremely low ($p < 0.0001$). Hence, we could safely assume, if these results were real, that the null hypothesis can be rejected, and that feeling comfortable when nude is a variable *associated* with being an extrovert. The $\chi^2$ test is known as a TEST OF ASSOCIATION of one variable with another.

Returning to our original data, we can say that, since 145 drivers in all didn't stop, out of a total of 323, then we would expect 145/323 of any category of driver not to stop if they are 'average' drivers on the whole. So, we expect 145/323 of the 146 female drivers not to stop. This gives 65.54. But actually, only 56 women failed to stop.

We assume from this data that stopping on amber *is* associated with being a woman driver. (I might add that other students have failed to replicate this finding, usually finding no difference).

One word of warning. It is easy to get the idea of expected frequencies wrong. When asked what they are it is tempting to respond with 'what is expected to happen' or 'what the researcher expects to happen'. I hope you can see that, since they are what the *null hypothesis* predicts, they are usually the very opposite of what the researcher is predicting will happen.

## The $R \times C \chi^2$ test

We can extend this test to situations where either of the two variables being tested for association has more than two values. There can be $R$ rows and $C$ columns. For instance, four different colleges might be compared for their students' performances in a psychology 'A' level exam:

*Table 39  Comparison of results*

|  | College A | College B | College C | College D | Total |
|---|---|---|---|---|---|
| Passed | 32 | 46 | 34 | 23 | 135 |
| Failed | 5 | 12 | 18 | 1 | 36 |
| Total | 37 | 58 | 52 | 24 | 171 |

The test will tell us whether these ratios of pass and fail are significantly different among the four colleges. Degrees of freedom here would be 3 ([Rows − 1] × [Columns − 1] = 1 × 3). One way of looking at degrees of freedom is to see that, if we knew all the row and column totals, we would only need to know three of the internal cell totals before we could calculate all the rest. In other words, only three of the internal cells are free to vary. Once their values are established, so are all the others.

Since degrees of freedom exceed 1, we would use the simpler $\chi^2$ formula above – (b) – with no Yates' correction.

## $\chi^2$ 'Goodness of fit' test

A special use of $\chi^2$ occurs when we want to investigate a set of data measured on only one variable. For instance, suppose we weren't interested in sex differences for stopping at an amber light. However, we are interested in how all drivers behave at a variety of traffic stopping points. Consider this table:

*Table 40   'Failure-to-halt' offences for county of Undershire*

| A | B | C | D | E | |
|---|---|---|---|---|---|
| Roundabout | Junction stop sign | Traffic light | Pedestrian crossing | Police controlled junction | Total |
| 47 | 17 | 19 | 12 | 3 | 98 |

An 'eyeball test' of this data surely leads us to suspect that drivers are far more careless or disrespectful of driving laws at roundabouts than elsewhere (and, of course, obedient with police officers!). We can treat this as a $R \times C$ test with just one row but five columns. We have to calculate degrees of freedom from first principles because $R - 1 = 1 - 1 = 0$, which isn't allowed! But, there are five cells and, knowing the row total, four of these are free to vary before the last is fixed. So degrees of freedom for a 'goodness of fit' test is given by $C - 1$.

## Calculation

1 Call these data the 'observed frequencies'

2 Cell A $= 47$; Cell B $= 17$; Cell C $= 19$; Cell D $= 12$; Cell E $= 3$

3 Expected frequencies:   Each cell should have the mean of all frequencies per cell (because the null hypothesis predicts no difference across the cells)

   Therefore: $E = 98/5 = 19.6$ for each cell

4 Degrees of freedom $= 4$ (as explained)

5 Use formula (b) as shown on page 180

|        | Step 5.1 $(O-E)$ | Step 5.2 $(O-E)^2$ | Step 5.3 $(O-E)^2/E$ |
|--------|------------------|--------------------|-----------------------|
| Cell A | $47-19.6$ $= 27.4$ | $27.4^2$ $= 750.76$ | $750.76/19.6 = 38.30$ |
| Cell B | $17-19.6$ $= -2.6$ | $-2.6^2$ $= 6.76$ | $6.76/19.6 \quad = \quad 0.34$ |
| Cell C | $19-19.6$ $= -0.6$ | $-0.6^2$ $= 0.36$ | $0.36/19.6 \quad = \quad 0.02$ |
| Cell D | $12-19.6$ $= -7.6$ | $-7.6^2$ $= 57.76$ | $57.76/19.6 \quad = \quad 2.95$ |
| Cell E | $3-19.6$ $= -16.6$ | $-16.6^2$ $= 275.56$ | $275.56/19.6 = 14.06$ |

$$\chi^2 = \text{Total} = 55.67$$

6 Relevant line is by 4 degrees of freedom. Use two-tailed values.
7 Our $\chi^2$ of 55.67 exceeds all values in the line and therefore the relevant critical value is 18.47 which is under the $p < 0.001$ column.
8 The results are significant at the 0.1% level, i.e. $p < 0.001$.

Our result is far higher than this highly significant level. So there is an extremely significant 'lump' in the distribution of scores. Notice that the calculation of cell E contributes quite a lot to the overall $\chi^2$ value, but nothing like that contributed by cell A. Roundabout misbehaviour is far *further* from the average number of misdemeanours per category than is obedience at police-controlled crossings.

### 'Goodness of fit' and normal distributions
This test can be used to decide whether a large sample closely approximates to a normal distribution or not. In this case, our expected frequencies would be calculated according to table 2 (Appendix 3) which shows what proportion of a normally distributed population falls between different $z$-scores. For instance, for a normal distribution we expect 34.13% of all values to fall between the mean and 1 standard deviation ($z = +1$) and 13.59% should fall between 1 and 2 standard deviations from the mean (between $z = +1$ and $z = +2$). $\chi^2$ 'goodness of fit' compares the proportions of our actual distribution with these ideal proportions.

### One variable – two categories only
This is a special case of the 'goodness of fit' $\chi^2$ where we have data measured on just one variable and have only split it into two cells. Suppose, for instance, we told subjects that a fictitious person was 'warm' and asked them to decide whether the person would also be happy or unhappy. We might ask them to rate several such 'bi-polar opposites' but let's just deal with one result shown in table 41.
If subjects are choosing at random (the null hypothesis) then we should get about half the total in each cell, that is, 25. So expected frequencies are 25 for each cell. The calculation then proceeds as normal, including Yates' correction because, I

*Table 41* 'Warm' ratings

|  | Happy | Unhappy | **Total** |
|---|---|---|---|
| **No. of subjects choosing:** | 42 | 8 | 50 |

hope you'll agree, these data have just one degree of freedom – when one cell total is known, given that the total is 50, the other must be known too. The $\chi^2$ value in this case would be 21.78. I hope you'll find this very highly significant.

This is the 'special case' referred to earlier when we can take the test to be one-tailed, so long as our hypothesis predicted the direction of any difference.

### Limitations on the use of $\chi^2$

Observations must appear in one cell only. For instance, if we looked at male and female swimmers and hurdlers, one person could appear in both the swimmers *and* the hurdlers category if they enjoyed both sports. This would make use of $\chi^2$ invalid.

Actual frequencies must appear in the cells, not percentages, proportions or numbers which do anything other than count. For instance, the mean of an interval scale variable cannot appear.

If more than 20% of expected cell frequencies have a total of less than five then a $\chi^2$ test is unreliable. An appropriate alternative is Fischer's exact test. For a $2 \times 2$ $\chi^2$, therefore, where each cell is 25% of the total number of cells (one of four), we should not proceed if *any* cell is less than five. Where individual expected frequency cells do fall below five we can combine categories such that the new expected value is above five. Hence, the categories 1–5 and 6–10, on a table of 'cigarettes smoked per day', might be converted into a category of 1–10.

With one degree of freedom, Yates' correction need only be applied if any expected frequency falls below 10. If the value of $\chi^2$, *with and without* Yates' correction, is significant then the test is reliable. If one result is not significant then a Fischer's exact test should be used.

# TESTS AT ORDINAL LEVEL – RANK TEST ON RELATED DATA

## The Wilcoxon (T) signed ranks test

This is one of two major tests used at the ordinal level for testing differences. One is for *related* and the other for *unrelated* designs. There are two points to be careful of:

1 The Wilcoxon statistic is known as '*T*' and this is extremely easy to confuse with the (little) '*t*' test to be met later as a parametric test.

2 There is also a Wilcoxon 'rank sum' test which works on unrelated data and can be used instead of the Mann–Whitney test, which we'll look at after this one.

### Conditions for use

Data of at least ORDINAL level.
Data from a RELATED design.
In cases where $N$ is large ($>25$) see 'When $N$ is large', below.

## Data

Students were asked to assess two teaching/learning methods, experienced for one term each, using a specially devised attitude questionnaire.

*Table 42  Student assessment data*

| Student (N=15) | Rating of traditional lecture A | Rating of assignment based method B | Difference (B−A) C | Rank of difference D |
|---|---|---|---|---|
| Abassi | 23 | 33 | 10 | 12 |
| Bennett | 14 | 22 | 8 | 9.5 |
| Berridge | 35 | 38 | 3 | 3 |
| Chapman | 26 | 30 | 4 | 5 |
| Collins | 28 | 31 | 3 | 3 |
| Gentry | 19 | 17 | −2 | 1 |
| Higgs | 42 | 42 | 0 | |
| Laver | 30 | 25 | −5 | 6 |
| Montgomery | 26 | 34 | 8 | 9.5 |
| Parrott | 31 | 24 | −7 | 8 |
| Peart | 18 | 21 | 3 | 3 |
| Ramakrishnan | 25 | 46 | 21 | 14 |
| Spencer | 23 | 29 | 6 | 7 |
| Turner | 31 | 40 | 9 | 11 |
| Williams | 30 | 41 | 11 | 13 |

## Procedure

1 Calculate the difference between the pairs of scores (in columns A and B), always subtracting in the same direction. As with the sign test, with a one-tailed hypothesis it makes sense to subtract in the direction differences are predicted to go, i.e. predicted smaller from predicted larger value.

2 Rank the differences in the usual way (see page 000). Ignore the sign of the difference. For instance, Laver's score (−5) is given rank 6 because it is the next largest, in absolute size, after the value (+)4. Also ignore any zero values. These results are omitted from the analysis.

3 Add the ranks associated with the least occurring sign. Call this sum $T$.

## Calculation on our data

See table 42

See table 42. Note that Higgs' results are dropped from the analysis

Least frequent sign is negative. Therefore add ranks: $1+6+8$. These are the ranks associated with the scores of $-2$, $-5$ and $-7$ in the table. Hence $T=15$.

4 Find relevant line (using $N$ which doesn't include subjects with zero differences) in table 7 (appendix 3) and decide whether to pay attention to one- or two-tailed values.

Relevant line is $N = 14$ (remember one result has been dropped). Assume preferred teaching method not predicted. Therefore two-tailed test is appropriate.

5 Find lowest critical value which $T$ does not exceed. If $T$ exceeds all critical values, results are not significant.

$T$ does not exceed 25 or 21 or 15, but it does exceed 6. 15 is therefore the relevant critical value. It is under $p$ 0.02.

6 Make statement of significance.

Differences are significant at the 2% level.

## Summary

The Wilcoxon test looks at the differences between related pairs of values. It ranks these according to absolute size, ignoring the direction of the difference. Statistic $T$ is calculated by adding the ranks of the differences in the least frequently occurring direction (negative or positive). Critical values are the maximum value $T$ can be for the particular significance level. In a sense it asks 'How likely is it that differences this size, relative to all other differences, would occur in the 'wrong' direction?'

## Explanatory notes

Like the sign test, the Wilcoxon looks at differences between paired values. The sign test looked only at the probability of the *number* of differences in the less frequent direction being so low. The Wilcoxon also looks at the *position* of the size of these differences relative to the other differences. If we've made a one-tailed prediction that scores in one condition will be higher than scores in the other, we can say, loosely, that the smaller number of (negative) differences are 'unwanted'. The test asks, in effect, 'what positions in the whole set do these unwanted differences take relative to the wanted ones?'

Suppose we asked several subjects to recite the alphabet both forwards and backwards and timed their performance. We would surely predict a set of positive differences if we subtracted forwards time from backwards? Random sampling may have introduced a poor English speaker or a person who has developed reverse alphabet recital as a party trick or even someone who just loves fouling up psychology experiments. This sort of subject might produce a faster reverse time. Some subjects might take the task really carefully in both directions, in which case differences could be marginally in favour of reverse or forwards. But, overall, we should find most differences in the direction of forwards faster. We can tolerate a very few large differences in the other direction, or rather more moderate ones. The table for critical values of $T$ will reflect this.

For instance, with $N = 10$, $T$ must be less than or equal to 11 for significance at 5%, one-tailed. Therefore the *lowest* score (rank 1) and the *highest* score (rank 10) can be in the unwanted direction (and only these). $T$ will then be 11 and we still have significance. On the other hand, the scores ranking 2.3 and 6 can be in the wrong direction, as can those ranking 1, 2, 3 and 5, since, in each case, $T$ is just 11 and therefore significant.

This demonstrates the weakness of ordinal data where we do not take into account the amount of difference involved. Have a look at the data in table 43.

*Table 43   Therapy data*

|  | Decrease in aggressive responses after therapy | Rank | Increase in co-operative responses after therapy | Rank |
|---|---|---|---|---|
| Archie | 17 | 8 | 16 | 7.5 |
| Bill | 13 | 2.5 | 2 | 3 |
| Colin | −12 | 1 | −14 | 5 |
| Derek | 18 | 9 | 1 | 1.5 |
| Eric | 13 | 2.5 | 1 | 1.5 |
| Francis | 15 | 6 | 4 | 4 |
| George | 14 | 4.5 | 19 | 10 |
| Hugh | 14 | 4.5 | 18 | 9 |
| Ian | 16 | 7 | 16 | 7.5 |
| John | −43 | 10 0 | −15 | 6 |

In both cases $T = 11$ and makes the result significant. The negative sign means the child has gone in the opposite direction to the trend. John and Colin have increased in aggressiveness and decreased in co-operation. John's increase is far more than anyone's decrease in aggression but the ordinal level of data just puts him 10th in absolute size of change.

Whereas a Wilcoxon $T$ would lead us to reject the null hypothesis for both these results, a parametric ($t$) test would not, thus suggesting that to reject the null hypothesis would be a type one error, since parametric tests are the more sensitive and trustworthy tests.

# TESTS AT ORDINAL LEVEL – rank test for unrelated data

## The Mann–Whitney (*U*) Test

### Conditions of use
Data of at least ORDINAL level
(This will very often be data which were originally in cardinal number form, i.e. looked like interval data, but were considered untrustworthy as interval data)
Data from an UNRELATED design

### Data
Children's tendency to stereotype according to traditional sex roles was observed. They were asked questions about several stories. The maximum score was 100, indicating extreme stereotyping. Two groups were used, one with mothers who

had full time paid employment and one whose mothers did not work outside the home.

Table 44   *Sex-role stereotyping*

| Scores of children whose mothers: | | | |
|---|---|---|---|
| had full time jobs N=7 | Rank | had no job outside home N=9 | Rank |
| 17 | 1 | 19 | 2 |
| 32 | 7 | 63 | 12 |
| 39 | 9 | 78 | 15 |
| 27 | 4 | 29 | 5 |
| 58 | 10 | 35 | 8 |
| 25 | 3 | 59 | 11 |
| 31 | 6 | 77 | 14 |
| | | 81 | 16 |
| | | 68 | 13 |
| Rank totals | 40 ($R_a$) | | 96 ($R_b$) |

Note that, since the design is independent samples, there is no requirement for both groups to hold the same number of subjects.

## Procedure

1 If one group has fewer subjects call this group A

2 Rank all the scores as one group

3 Find the sum of the ranks in group A ($R_a$) and group B ($R_b$)

4 Use the following formula to calculate $U_a$:

$$U_a = N_a N_b + \frac{N_a(N_a+1)}{2} - R_a$$

5 Then calculate $U_b$ from:

$$U_b = N_a N_b + \frac{N_b(N_b+1)}{2} - R_b$$

## Calculation on our data

The full time job mothers are group A

See table 45

See table 45   $R_a = 40$; $R_b = 96$

$$U_a = 7 \times 9 + \frac{7 \times (7+1)}{2} - 40$$

$$= 63 + \frac{56}{2} - 40 = 63 + 28 - 40$$

$$= 51$$

$$U_b = 7 \times 9 + \frac{9 \times (9+1)}{2} - 96$$

$$= 63 + \frac{90}{2} - 96 = 63 + 45 - 96$$

$$= 12$$

6 Select the smaller of $U_a$ and $U_b$ and call it $U$

Since $12 > 51$ then $U = 12$

7 Check this in table 5, appendix 3. $N_S$ is the smaller sample number and $N_L$ is the larger sample number. Try the $p < 0.01$ values in the bottom left section first. If $U$ is too high, try the $p < 0.05$ values. For a one-tailed test, the probabilities shown are halved

$N_S$ is 7 and $N_L$ is 9. Where these two meet on the $p < 0.01$ table we have the value 7, which is too low. On the $p < 0.05$ table we find the value 12. Our $U$ equals this. Assuming a one-tailed test, $p$ at this level is 0.05/2. Hence, $p < 0.025$

8 Make statement of significance

The differences are significant at 2.5%

## Summary
The test looks at differences between the sums of two sets of ranks. The value $U$ is calculated from the two rank sums. The critical value gives the value of $U$, for the particular subject numbers in each group, below which less than 5% of $U$s would fall if members of each group acquired their rank on a random basis.

## Explanatory notes
This test can be related to a very familiar situation in which we look at the performance of two teams. Suppose you were in a five-person school cross-country team, competing against a local school. You would have to be impressed if the other school took, say, the first four places with the last of their team coming seventh. The sum of their places is $1 + 2 + 3 + 4 + 7 = 17$. The total sum of places (1 to 10) is 55. Our rank sum must be 38.

Imagine, instead, that members of the two teams each drew from the numbers one to ten placed in a hat. The Mann–Whitney, in a sense, looks at all the combinations of rank sums which are possible when doing this. By comparing our result (for $U$) with tables, we know whether our split in rank sums (17 against 38) is one which would occur less than 5% of the time, if we repeated the number drawing many times. In other words, the critical value is the point below which we start saying 'The other school's apparent superiority was not a fluke!', something which of course we would rush to admit!

Again we have the weakness that the test deals only with relative positions and not absolute scores. If all the first eight runners were neck and neck at the tape (rare in cross-country), then we would not feel so ashamed, at least, not in front of those watching the race. This is the point made in the chapter on 'Measurement', page 132.

As we said above, this is because we are losing information in dealing with ordinal, rather than interval level data. If we knew the runners' times, we could carry out a more sensitive test of significance. The tests which deal with interval level data are known as PARAMETRIC and we shall look at these in chapter 16.

## Mann–Whitney and one-tailed tests
Annoyingly, the tables for the Mann–Whitney do not give us the critical values for a one-tailed test at 5%. The unfortunate student with a $U$ which is only just above the value for a two-tailed test at 5% thinks 'Aha! Since my test is one-tailed and one-tailed values are higher, I've got a significant result. Now just where are the values for 5% one-tailed?' They then read a statement above the table which

says 'The significance levels for one-tailed tests are half those for two-tailed tests', or something similar. The table in this book gives two significance levels but still the best we can know is that a one-tailed result is significant at 2.5%. The 5% one-tailed values never seem to appear in tables. We can work them out with a very complicated formula which converts our result into a $z$-score. However, there is a simpler alternative which follows.

## The Wilcoxon rank sum test

The procedure here is the same as for the Mann–Whitney up to and including the ranking of the data. From this point we simply take the lower rank sum (40 in our example of children and stereotyping), call this $T$, and check this against the critical values in table 6 (Appendix 3) for $N_1 = 7$ and $N_2 = 9$. We find, for a one-tailed test at $p < 0.05$ our $T$ needs to be under 43. Notice that the value at $p < 0.025$ is just 40 which checks with the way our value of 12 for $U$ just met the value in the Mann–Whitney table. But if the rank sum had been 41, 42 or 43, the Wilcoxon would have told us we were still significant at 5%, one-tailed, whereas with the Mann–Whitney we'd have suspected it but couldn't have said so from tables, because our $U$ would have been more than 12.

So why not use the Wilcoxon all the time? No reason why not. I went into some detail on the Mann–Whitney simply because it appears in the content of several syllabuses! The Wilcoxon not only gives you one-tailed 5% values, it's much quicker too!

Beware getting this test mixed up with the Wilcoxon SIGNED RANKS test! If you remember there's only one of these two Wilcoxon tests in which signs are relevant, you should be OK.

When $N$ for the larger sample is greater than 20, use the $z$-score conversion for large samples shown below.

### When *N* is large
Non-parametric rank tests use tables in which $N$, for either group, only goes up to a modest value of 20 or 25. For larger values there is usually a conversion formula which gives a $z$-score. For large samples, the values of Mann–Whitney $U$ and Wilcoxon $T$, if performed many times on two sets of randomly produced ranks, would form near normal distributions. For any particular $U$ or $T$, we can find out where it would fall on that distribution in terms of a $z$-score. We want to achieve a $z$-score which cuts off the last 5% (one-tailed) or 2.5% (two-tailed) of the distribution. From the normal distribution table on pages 280–2 (and see figure 32, on page 173), I hope you'll agree that a $z$-score of 1.65 does the former and 1.96 the latter.

The relevant formulae are:

**Mann–Whitney**

$$z = \cfrac{\dfrac{U - N_a N_b}{2}}{\sqrt{\left(\left[\dfrac{N_a N_b}{N(N-1)}\right] \times \left[\dfrac{N^3 - N}{12} - \Sigma T\right]\right)}}$$

where $N =$ the sum of $N_a$ and $N_b$ and

$$T = \frac{t^3 - t}{12}$$

each time a number of values are tied at a particular rank and $t$ is the number of times the value occurs. For instance, for the data on page 203, the score 8 appears three times. $t = 3$ and $T = (3^3 - 3)/12 = 2$. This would then be repeated for 9, which occurs twice. This time $T = (2^3 - 2)/12 = 0.5$. This would be repeated for 10, 12 and so on. Of course, for these particular data, the $z$-score conversion would not be appropriate, since $N$ is not large.

**Wilcoxon signed ranks (related)**

$$z = \frac{N(N+1) - 4T}{\sqrt{\left(\dfrac{2N(N+1)(2N+1)}{3}\right)}}$$

where $T$ is Wilcoxon's $T$ calculated in the usual way.

**Wilcoxon rank sum (unrelated)**

$$z = \frac{2T - N_1(N+1)}{\sqrt{\left(\dfrac{N_1 N_2(N+1)}{3}\right)}}$$

where $T$ is calculated as explained in the rank sum method, $N_1$ is the number of values in the smaller sample and $N_2$ is the number in the larger sample.

**Key terms for this chapter**

Binomial sign test/sign test
$\chi^2$ test of association
  Expected frequencies
  'Goodness of fit' test
  Observed frequencies
  Yates' correction

Degrees of freedom
Mann–Witney '$U$' test
Test statistic
Wilcoxon rank sum test
Wilcoxon signed ranks test

**Exercises**

1 Should a $\chi^2$ test be carried out on the following data?

| Observed frequencies | 20 | 6 |
|---|---|---|
| | 4 | 10 |

Hint: You should have to do some calculating to find out.

2 A (fictitious) survey shows that, in a particular sample of 100, 73 people are against the privatisation of water provision, whereas 27 support the idea.

   (a) What test for significance can be performed on this data?

   (b) Would this test be one-tailed or two-tailed?

   (c) If, for a larger sample, we knew only that 71% of people were against the idea, and 29% for, could we carry out the same test to see whether this split in opinion is significant?

3 A field study produced the following matrix of results:

**Taste preferred**

|  | 1 | 2 | 3 |  | | | |
|---|---|---|---|---|---|---|---|
| Under 14 | 3 | 8 | 4 | | 2.5 | 5.25 | 7.25 |
| 14–30 | 4 | 6 | 2 | | 2 | 4.2 | 5.8 |
| Over 30 | 3 | 7 | 23 | | 5.5 | 11.55 | 15.95 |

              **Observed frequencies**            **Expected frequencies**

   (a) How many degrees of freedom are involved here?

   (b) Will the result of a $\chi^2$ test be trustworthy?

4 Find out whether the following test statistics are significant, and at what level, for the one- or two-tailed tests indicated. You can put the probability value ($p$) achieved in the blank columns under 'sig'.

| No. in each group | | | Sig. | | T | Sig. | | | T | Sig. | |
|---|---|---|---|---|---|---|---|---|---|---|---|
| $N=$ | $N=$ | $U=$ | One-tail | Two-tail | (WRS)= | One-tail | Two-tail | $N=$ | (WSR)= | One-tail | Two-tail |
| (a) 15 | 14 | 49 | | | 158 | | | (c) 18 | 35 | | |
| (b) 8 | 12 | 5 | | | 68 | | | (d) 30 | 48 | | |

*Note*: WRS = Wilcoxon rank sum      WSR = Wilcoxon signed ranks

5 Nine people are sent on an interpersonal skills training course. When asked whether they found it worthwhile or not, seven said they didn't, one did and one couldn't decide. Using a sign test, decide whether this negative evaluation of the course is significant.

# Inferential statistics II

## PARAMETRIC TESTS OF DIFFERENCE

## PARAMETRIC TESTS

Some way back we discussed 'parameters'. Perhaps you'd like to try and remember what these are before reading any further, or to remind yourself by looking back to page 147. Here, anyway, is a redefinition. Parameters are measures of populations, in particular the mean and standard deviation. Parametric tests are so called because *their calculation involves an estimate of population parameters made on the basis of sample statistics*. The larger the sample, the more accurate the estimate will be. The smaller the sample, the more distorted the sample mean will be by the odd, extreme value.

### Power efficiency
Parametric tests are the most powerful tests covered by this book. What does 'power' mean? It's a tricky concept to define exactly. With the same data, a non-parametric test may give a significant difference, where a parametric one wouldn't (so type one errors can be more likely) or, with other data, the reverse might occur, increasing the likelihood of type two errors. This greater power in correctly rejecting the null hypothesis (making a more accurate probability estimate) is known as 'power efficiency'. There is a mathematical approach to this concept which you would encounter in more advanced texts.

You can see examples of the superior power of parametric tests at the end of this chapter on pages 206 and 207.

The greater power of parametric tests comes from their greater sensitivity to the data. This in turn is because they use *all* the information available. They look at *size* of differences and values involved, not just ranks (order of sizes). They are more subtle, then, in their analysis of data.

This power and accuracy, however, has to be paid for. The tests make estimates of underlying population parameters. These estimates are made on the assumption that the underlying population has certain characteristics, mainly that it has a normal distribution. Such a distribution only occurs if the level of measurement we are using is at least interval. With interval-level data, certain sophisticated mathematical operations can be carried out which can't be done on ordinal data (ranks). These are the assumptions we must satisfy before proceeding with a parametric test:

### Assumptions underlying the use of parametric tests
1 Level of measurement must be at least interval
2 The sample data are drawn from a normally distributed population
3 The variances of the two samples are not significantly different – this is known as the principle of HOMOGENEITY OF VARIANCE.

Notes:

1 We must make a decision about our dependent variable. Is it truly interval level? If it is an unstandardised scale, or if it is based on human estimation or rating, would it be safer to make it ordinal? Remember, data don't often get collected as ordinal. They often appear interval-like but we *reduce* them to ordinal by ranking them.

2 This principle is often written in error as 'the sample must be normally distributed'. This is not so. Most samples are too small to look anything like a normal distribution, which only gets its characteristic bell-like shape from the accumulation of very many scores. A largish sample can be tested for the likelihood that it came from a normal distribution using the $\chi^2$ 'goodness of fit' test covered in the last chapter.

In practice, for small samples, we have to assume that the population they were drawn from is a normal distribution on grounds of past experience or theory. It may be known, from other research, that the variable tested is normally distributed, or it may be possible to argue that, given what we do know, the assumption is reasonable.

3 Statisticians have further investigated this requirement, which used to demand very similar variances. Fortunately, we can now largely ignore it when dealing with related samples, without any great risk of distortion in our result. For unrelated samples we need to be more careful where sample sizes are quite different.

A simple check for variance difference between two samples can be made by checking the two ranges. A thorough check involves use of the $F$-test, which we don't cover in this book, but which tests for the difference between two sample variances in much the same way as a $t$-test (see below) checks for a significant difference between the two means.

## Parametric tests are robust
The principles above are not set in concrete. One can do a parametric test on data which don't fit the assumptions exactly. The fact that the tests, under such conditions, still give fairly accurate probability estimates has led to them being called ROBUST. They do not break down, or become untrustworthy, unless the assumptions are quite poorly met.

## Summary of advantages and disadvantages of parametric tests
Advantages:    More power efficient
More sensitive to features of data collected
Less chance of type one or type two errors
Robust

Disadvantages:  More complicated to calculate
Limitations on types of data which can be tested

**Parametric tests and their non-parametric equivalents**

| | **Related design** | **Unrelated design** | **Correlation** |
|---|---|---|---|
| **Parametric** | Related (or 'correlated')* $t$-test | Unrelated (or 'uncorrelated')* $t$-test | Pearson product-moment correlation coefficient |
| **Non-parametric equivalent** | Wilcoxon signed ranks | Mann–Whitney $U$ (or Wilcoxon rank sum) | Spearman rho ($\rho$) |

* Keep this distinct in your mind from tests of correlation. This unfortunate wording is sometimes used. Think of it as a $t$-test on the *difference* between two groups of scores which are in co-related pairs.

# THE $t$-TEST FOR RELATED DATA

## Conditions for use
Level of measurement in use must be INTERVAL OR ABOVE
Design must be RELATED
Parametric assumptions must be met

## Data
Subjects were given two equivalent sets of 15 words to memorise under two conditions. In condition A they were instructed to form visual imagery links between each item and the next. In condition B they were instructed only to rehearse the words as they heard them. Subjects had two minutes immediately after list presentation, to 'free recall' the words (recall in any order).

*Table 45   Word recall data*

| Number of words recalled in: | | | | |
|---|---|---|---|---|
| Subject number | Imagery condition (A) | Rehearsal condition (B) | Difference $d$ | $d^2$ |
| 1 | 6 | 6 | 0 | 0 |
| 2 | 15 | 10 | 5 | 25 |
| 3 | 13 | 7 | 6 | 36 |
| 4 | 14 | 8 | 6 | 36 |
| 5 | 12 | 8 | 4 | 16 |
| 6 | 16 | 12 | 4 | 16 |
| 7 | 14 | 10 | 4 | 16 |
| 8 | 15 | 10 | 5 | 25 |
| 9 | 18 | 11 | 7 | 49 |
| 10 | 17 | 9 | 8 | 64 |
| 15 | 12 | 8 | 4 | 16 |
| 12 | 7 | 8 | −1 | 1 |
| 13 | 15 | 8 | 7 | 49 |
| | $\bar{x}_a = 13.38$ | $\bar{x}_b = 8.85$ | $\Sigma d = 59$ | $\Sigma d^2 = 349$ |
| | $s_a = 3.39$ | $s_b = 1.61$ | $(\Sigma d)^2 = 3481$ | |

Mean of differences $\bar{d} = 4.54$

(or difference mean) $s_d = 2.50$

## Justification of use of *t*-test
- The data are of interval level status (though not continuous)
- It is commonly assumed that recall totals in a free recall task such as this would form a near normal distribution
- The standard deviations are quite different. However, this is a related design and therefore the homogeneity of variance requirement is not so important.

## Formula

$$t = \frac{\Sigma d}{\sqrt{\left(\dfrac{N\Sigma d^2 - [\Sigma d]^2}{N-1}\right)}}$$

Note: There are several variations of this formula so don't get worried if you find another which looks different. I've found this the easiest to work with overall.

| Procedure | Calculation on our data |
|---|---|
| 1 Calculate the mean of the scores in each condition | See table 45 |
| 2 Arrange final results table such that the first column has the higher mean and call this group (or column) A. Call its mean $x_a$. Call the other mean $x_b$ and the group (or column) B | See table 45 |
| 3 Subtract each subject's B score from their A score. Call this $d$ | See table 45 |
| 4 Square the $d$ for each subject | See table 45 |
| 5 Add up all the $d$s ($\Sigma d$) and all the $d^2$s ($\Sigma d^2$) | $\Sigma d = 59$   $\Sigma d^2 = 349$ |
| 6 Square $\Sigma d$. Note this is $(\Sigma d)^2$. *Be careful to distinguish between* $\Sigma d^2$ *and* $(\Sigma d)^2$! | $(\Sigma d)^2 = 3481$ |
| 7 Multiply $N$ (the number of pairs of scores there are) by $\Sigma d^2$ | $13 \times 349 = 4537$ |
| 8 Subtract $(\Sigma d)^2$ from the result of step 7 | $4537 - 3481 = 1056$ |
| 9 Divide the result of step 8 by $N-1$ | $1056 \div 12 = 88$ |
| 10 Find the square root of step 9 | $\sqrt{(88)} = 9.38$ |

11 Divide $\Sigma d$ by the result of step 10 to give $t$

$59 \div 9.381 = 6.289$   $t = 6.289$

12 Find degrees of freedom $(df)$. For a related design this is $N - 1$

$13 - 1 = 12$

13 Find the largest value of $t$ in table 8, Appendix 3, given the degrees of freedom and appropriate number of tails, which does not exceed our obtained value of $t$. Make significance statement

Critical value for $p < 0.01$ is 3.055, assuming a two-tailed test. The table goes no higher than this. Our value of 6.298 easily exceeds it. Therefore, the probability of our $t$ value occurring by chance alone is at least as low as 0.01 and probably a lot lower. The difference is therefore highly significant.

## Procedure with automatic calculation of standard deviation

If your calculator gives you the standard deviation of a set of values directly there is a far easier route to $t$:

1 Find the standard deviation of the differences, using the $\sigma_{n-1}$ version (not $\sigma_n$), which is the version for population estimates. Call this value $S$. In the example above $S = 2.602$

2 Find $S^2$ (This is the *variance* of the differences) $(= 6.769)$

3 Divide $S^2$ by $N$ $(= 0.521)$

4 Find the square root of step 3 $(= 0.722)$

5 Divide the mean of the differences $(\bar{d})$ by the result of step 4 $(t = 6.289)$

The formula for this is $t = \dfrac{\bar{d}}{\sqrt{S^2/N}}$

## Explanatory notes

The basis of this test can be understood by assuming the position of the null hypothesis. This says, in effect, that there is no difference between conditions. Let's look at what would happen if there really *were* no difference. Then we can see whether our result looks similar to those expected when there is no difference between conditions.

Since this is rather a complex argument, I would suggest that you take it in small steps, stopping every so often to review where we've got to.

1 First, let's find a situation where a null hypothesis *is* true. We have two equally difficult word lists. We test a sample of people on their ability to learn and recall both lists, using counterbalancing of course.

2 If there is no difference between the lists, then people's performance should theoretically be exactly the same on each. But in real life there are always minor differences. We find that list one is recalled marginally better. We

show this by looking at the mean of the differences, (from now on we'll call this a 'difference mean') just as in table 45. Theoretically, the difference mean should be zero.

3 We take a second group and test them. This time there is a minor difference in the opposite direction. The difference mean is negative instead of positive.

4 We repeat this process over and over again on perhaps 200 samples of people. (Don't worry, this is statistical talk – no one ever really does this or needs to. We work from estimates!) Very many of the difference means will be small, half one side and half the other side of zero. Fewer will be large but these will still occur evenly either side of zero.

5 We plot the distribution formed by all the difference means and obtain the curve shown in figure 33. This is called a SAMPLING DISTRIBUTION of difference means.

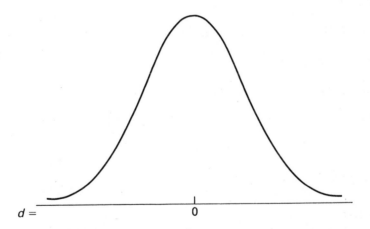

*Figure 33   Sampling distribution of difference means*

6 The standard deviation of a sampling distribution is known as the STANDARD ERROR. If we knew this value we could compare any particular difference mean with it and get what amounts to a $z$-score. We could see how many standard deviations (or 'errors') our *particular* difference mean was from the theoretical mean of zero.

7 Statisticians reckon they can *estimate* the standard error of such a distribution, from a particular sample, by taking the square root of $S^2/N$, where $S^2$ is the sample variance. This is what we did in the quick formula for $t$ above, in fact. The operation there went on to divide *our* difference mean by the standard

error to give *t*. *t* is therefore the number of standard errors our difference mean is from zero in the middle of the theoretical distribution.

8 As you may well have guessed, the objective is to see whether our particular difference mean falls within the most extreme 5% of difference means which could be expected. For a one-tailed test, that's the right-hand 5% of the curve in figure 33.

9 Suppose for every one of the 200-odd samples we took the calculated *t*. These values (which are quite like *z*-scores) would themselves form a distribution. The curve formed would be a familiar shape. If *N* for our samples was fairly large, the curve would look normally distributed. For lower *N* the curve would be a bit flatter and a bit wider. The important thing is that the *t*-curve is the same shape and has the same values, no matter what value the actual variables measured were. It's shape depends solely on *N*. It is, after all, based only on a *ratio* between standard deviations and particular deviations.

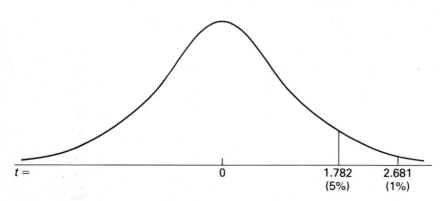

*Figure 34   t-curve for N = 13*

10 The *t*-curve for *N* = 13 (*df* = 12) will look something like figure 34, with the one-tailed values for 5% and 1% significance shown on it. We simply want to compare our *t* with this as we would a *z*-score on a normal distribution. The job is one of consulting tables rather than actual curves, however. The values for *t* with different *N* are given in table 8 in Appendix 3. Notice how similar the values for *t* are to *z* when *N* becomes relatively large.

 The table shows us the distribution expected when the null hypothesis is true. *t*-tests for people performing on our two equivalent lists should fall into this pattern. However, if, as in our experiment, we are predicting that the operation of an independent variable will create a significant difference between two recall conditions, our $t$ must simply beat the one at the 5% or 1% end of the distribution.

# THE $t$ TEST FOR UNRELATED DATA

### Conditions for use
Level of measurement in use must be INTERVAL OR ABOVE
Design must be UNRELATED
Parametric assumptions must be met

### Data
12 subjects were asked to use visual image linking in memorising a list of 15 words. 13 subjects were asked to use only rehearsal on the same list of words. Subjects used free recall to demonstrate retention.

*Table 46   Imagery/rehearsal recall data*

| Number of words correctly recalled in: | | | |
|---|---|---|---|
| Group A (N=12) (score=$X_a$) | $X_a^2$ | Group B (N=13) (score=$X_b$) | $X_b^2$ |
| 12 | 144 | 12 | 144 |
| 18 | 324 | 9 | 81 |
| 12 | 144 | 12 | 144 |
| 10 | 100 | 8 | 64 |
| 10 | 100 | 10 | 100 |
| 14 | 196 | 8 | 64 |
| 14 | 196 | 7 | 49 |
| 18 | 324 | 13 | 169 |
| 12 | 144 | 16 | 256 |
| 8 | 64 | 11 | 121 |
| 14 | 196 | 15 | 225 |
| 14 | 196 | 13 | 169 |
| | | 9 | 81 |
| $\Sigma X_a = 156$ | $\Sigma X_a^2 = 2128$ | $\Sigma X_b = 143$ | $\Sigma X_b^2 = 1667$ |
| $\bar{X}_a = 13$ | | $\bar{X}_b = 11$ | |
| $(\Sigma X_a)^2 = 24336$ | | $(\Sigma X_b)^2 = 20449$ | |
| $SD_a = 2.887$ | | $SD_b = 2.689$ | |

### Justification of use of $t$-test
- The data are of interval level status (though not continuous)
- It is commonly assumed that recall totals in a free-recall task such as this would form a near normal distribution

– The standard deviations are not very different. Even if they were, subject numbers are very close and therefore the homogeneity of variance requirement is not so important.

## Formula

Unrelated $t =$

$$\frac{|\bar{x}_a - \bar{x}_b|}{\sqrt{\left[\frac{\left(\sum x_a^2 - \frac{(\sum x_a)^2}{N_a}\right) + \left(\sum x_b^2 - \frac{(\sum x_b)^2}{N_b}\right)}{(N_a + N_b - 2)}\right] \times \left[\frac{N_a + N_b}{(N_a)(N_b)}\right]}}$$

This is the most complex formula with the greatest number of steps, in the book, so do try to be careful and patient!

| Procedure | Calculation on our data |
|---|---|
| 1 Add up all scores ($X_a$) in group A to give $\sum x_a$ | See table 46 |
| 2 Add up all the squares of group A scores ($X_a^2$) to give $\sum x_a^2$ | See table 46 |
| 3 Square the result of step 1 to give ($\sum X_a$)$^2$. Again, be careful to distinguish this from $\sum x_a^2$ | See table 46 |
| 4 Divide the result of step 3 by $N_a$ (number of results in group A) | $24336 \div 12 = 2028$ |
| 5 Subtract result of step 4 from result of step 2 | $2128 - 2028 = 100$ |
| Steps 6–8 Repeat steps 1 to 3 on the group B scores to give: $\sum x_b$ (step 6), $\sum X_b^2$ (step 7) and ($\sum x_b$)$^2$ (step 8) | See table 46 |
| 9 Divide the result of step 8 by $N_b$ (number of results in group B) | $20449 \div 13 = 1573$ |
| 10 Subtract result of step 9 from result of step 7 | $1667 - 1573 = 94$ |
| 11 Add the results of steps 5 and 10 | $100 + 94 = 194$ |
| 12 Divide the result of step 11 by ($N_a + N_b - 2$) | $194 \div (12 + 13 - 2) = 194 \div 23 = 8.435$ |
| 13 Multiply the result of step 12 by $\frac{N_a + N_b}{N_a \times N_b}$ | $8.435 \times \frac{(12 + 13)}{12 \times 13} = 8.435 \times \frac{25}{156}$ $= 8.435 \times 0.16 = 1.35$ |

| | | |
|---|---|---|
| 14 | Find the square root of the result of step 13 | $\sqrt{1.35} = 1.162$ |
| 15 | Find the difference between the two means: $\bar{X}_a - \bar{X}_b$ | $13 - 11 = 2$ |
| 16 | Divide the result of step 15 by the result of step 14 to give $t$ | $2 \div 1.162 = 1.721$ Therefore $t = 1.721$ |
| 17 | Calculate degrees of freedom when $df = N_a + N_b - 2$ | $12 + 13 - 2 = 2$ |
| 18 | Consult table 8, Appendix 3 and make significance statement as for related $t$ | For a one-tailed test, with $df = 23$, the critical value of $t$ is 1.714 for significance at 5% ($P < 0.05$). Hence, our result is significant (by the narrowest of margins!). Note, for a two-tailed test significance would not be achieved. |

## Explanatory notes

Much of the reasoning here is similar to that for the related $t$. It might help to clarify the reasoning behind the unrelated $t$ with a concrete, non-psychology example.

Suppose you have recently bought two lots of a dozen or so screws from a local shop. You suspect that the second lot are, on the whole, shorter than the first lot. You return to the shopkeeper who assures you that the two lots are from the same stock. This position is that of the null hypothesis. It proposes that the difference between the means of the two samples is caused by random fluctuations in screw length alone, all screws being from the same population. Your position is like that of the experimental hypothesis which holds that the second lot of screws came from a population with a lower mean. The $t$-test result tells us to what extent our two samples need to differ in order to reject the null hypothesis.

Suppose we did this many times:

1 Take two random samples from one population of screws (i.e. all those in one stock carton)
2 Take the mean of each sample
3 Take the difference between these two means taking the second from the first mean
4 Repeat steps 1 to 3 very many times, always taking the second from the first mean.

If we plotted all the differences between the two means we would obtain a *sampling distribution of the difference between two means*, looking pretty much like figure 33, again.

The differences would mostly be small, rarely large, and could be in either direction, negative or positive. They would centre around zero then. The distribution has a standard error, estimated from the variances of the two samples. The difference we obtained is divided by this to find out how many standard errors our difference is from the hypothetical mean difference of zero. This division gives us our $t$ statistic. Again, we reject the null hypothesis when $t$ is large enough. If you look at the monstrous unrelated $t$ formula, you can see that the difference between means is on top and therefore, underneath, is the estimate of standard error for the hypothetical distribution.

If the null hypothesis is rejected, after carrying out a test on the two shop samples, we assume that the two samples do indeed come from two separate distributions arranged something like figure 35.

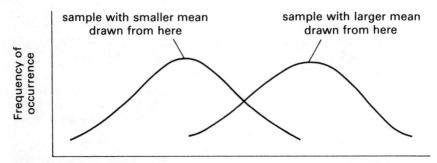

*Figure 35    Frequency of occurrence*

We might now question our shopkeeper further and he or she might of course claim that your discrepancy is 'just one of those things'. It might be a coincidence, of course, but we have shown the probability of it being so is less 0.05. If the shopkeeper plays by the rules of social science a further investigation might be made. Perhaps an assistant made a mistake. Perhaps a newly opened carton really does have a lower mean than the previous carton. We could take another sample from here, and one from the old one, in a replication attempt.

### Summary – related *t*-test
This looks at the mean difference between pairs of related values. Using the variance of the differences, it estimates the standard error of a sampling distribution of similar differences. The null hypothesis assumes that the mean of this sampling distribution would be zero. The *t*-value given is the number of standard errors the obtained mean difference is from zero. The critical value from tables is the value *t* must reach or exceed for significance.

### Summary – unrelated *t*-test
This looks at the difference between the two means of two sets of unrelated values. It estimates, using the variances of both sets, the likely standard error of a sampling distribution of differences between two means drawn from the hypothetical distribution implied by the null hypothesis, which has a mean of zero. *t* is the number of standard errors away from zero the obtained difference between means is on this distribution. The critical value from tables is the value *t* must reach or exceed for significance.

### Power efficiency revisited – comparing our *t*-test result with a non-parametric test
We looked at power efficiency earlier in the chapter. We said that parametric tests had greater power and that the probability estimates given by them have greater validity. Where the margin of significance is quite small (our obtained

value only just exceeds the critical value), the non-parametric test equivalent may not show significance, hence we may make a type two error with the latter test.

If you rank the values in table 47, and then add the ranks up for each group, you will find that the lower of these two sums is 140. If you look in the tables for the Wilcoxon rank sum test, with smaller $N$ being 12 and larger $N$ being 13, you'll find that we must not exceed 125 for significance at $p = 0.05$, one-tailed. Yet the $t$-test we conducted told us that the result was just significant.

In some circumstances it is also possible for a non-parametric test to show significance when a parametric test wouldn't.

As an exercise for the end of this chapter, try conducting the appropriate $t$-test and a Wilcoxon rank sum test on the table of data shown here which is for two unrelated samples.

| | |
|------|------|
| 13.4 | 13.1 |
| 13.6 | 13.1 |
| 13.2 | 13.1 |
| 13.7 | 13.6 |
| 13.7 | 13.4 |

You'll find that here the non-parametric test gives significance where the $t$ value just fails to reach the critical value. What kind of error could a researcher be making if the null hypothesis were rejected after use of the Wilcoxon?

Notice that this error is possible because the rank test doesn't 'know' that the actual values are so close. Again we see the value of interval level data in taking account of actual distances between values, rather than mere positions.

## Key terms for this chapter

Homogeneity of variance
Parametric test
Power efficiency
Robust tests

Sampling distribution
Standard error
$t$-test
    related/correlated $t$-test

## Exercises

1 Comment on the wisdom of carrying out a $t$-test on the following two sets of data:

(a)

| | | |
|----|----|-------------|
| 17 | 23 | |
| 18 | 9  | (unrelated |
| 18 | 31 | data) |
| 16 | 45 | |
|    | 16 | |
|    | 18 | |
|    | 17 | |
|    | 6  | |

(b)

| | | |
|----|----|-----------|
| 17 | 23 | |
| 18 | 11 | (related |
| 18 | 24 | data) |
| 16 | 29 | |
| 12 | 19 | |
| 15 | 16 | |

If, in either case, you feel that conducting a $t$-test would be unwise, what would be the alternative non-parametric test?

2 A report claims that a $t$-value of 2.85 is significant ($p < 0.01$) when the number of people in a repeated measures design was 11. Could the hypothesis tested have been two-tailed?

3 At what level, if any, are the following values of *t* significant? The last three columns are for you to fill in. Don't forget to think about degrees of freedom.

| *t =* | *N* | Design of study | One- or two-tailed | *p* ≤ | Significant at (%) | Reject Null hypothesis? |
|---|---|---|---|---|---|---|
| 1.750 | 16 | related | 1 | | | |
| 2.88 | 20 | unrelated | 2 | | | |
| 1.70 | 26 | unrelated | 1 | | | |
| 5.1 | 10 | unrelated | 1 | | | |
| 2.09 | 16 | related | 2 | | | |
| 3.7 | 30 | related | 2 | | | |

4 Two groups of children are observed for the number of times they make a generous response during one day. The researcher wishes to conduct a parametric test for differences between the two groups on their 'generosity response score'. A rough grouping of the data shows this distribution of scores:

Number of generous responses:

| Group | 0–3 | 4–6 | 7–9 | 10–12 | 13–15 | 16–19 | 20–22 |
|---|---|---|---|---|---|---|---|
| A | 2 | 16 | 24 | 8 | 3 | 0 | 1 |
| B | 5 | 18 | 19 | 10 | 5 | 1 | 3 |

Why does the researcher's colleague advise that a *t*-test would be an inappropriate test to use on this occasion?

# Inferential statistics III

## CORRELATION

### Positive and negative correlations
Have a look at the following statements:

1 The older I get, the worse my memory becomes
2 The more you give kids, the more they expect
3 Taller people tend to be more successful in their careers
4 The more physical punishment children receive, the more aggressive they become when they're older
5 Good musicians are usually good at maths
6 People who are good at maths tend to be poor at literature
7 The more you practice guitar playing, the less mistakes you make

These are all examples of relationships known as CORRELATION. In each statement it is proposed that two variables are co-related, i.e. they go together in the sense that either:

    (a) as one variable increases so does the other. For instance:

        The further you walk, the more money you collect for charity
        The more papers you have to deliver, the longer it takes you

or (b) as one variable *increases* the other variable *decreases*. For instance:

        As temperature increases, sales of woolly jumpers decrease
        The more papers you have to carry, the slower you walk

The correlations of the type stated in (a), are known as POSITIVE and those in (b) as NEGATIVE (someone once suggested the following memory 'hook' for negative correlation: 'as rain comes down so umbrellas go up', a common enough *negative* experience for British people!).

> Decide which of the proposed correlations above are positive and which are negative.
> Think of other examples of positive and negative correlation, in particular, two of each from the research you have studied so far.

### Setting up a correlational study
It is fairly easy to see how we could check out the validity of statement number six, above. We could have a look at school class-test grades or exam results for people who have taken both subjects. To test statement three we have a straightforward measure of variable one (height) but how do we go about

209

measuring the second variable, 'career success'? Do we measure only salary or should we include a factor of 'job satisfaction' – and with what sort of weighting? We would need to operationalise our variables.

> Describe *specifically* the two variables to be compared in each of statements 1 to 7 above, and how exactly you would *operationalise* them for precise measurement.

## Measurement of a correlation

Statements like 'there is a correlation between severe punishment and later delinquency in young boys' or 'severe punishment and delinquency in young boys tend to correlate' are often made in theoretical literature. Actually the golden word 'significant' is missing from the first statement and 'significantly' from the second. We can actually calculate the degree of correlation between any two measurable variables under the sun so long as there is some way of pairing values. Values are often paired because they belong to the same individual in a group (for instance, maths and literature mark for each class member), or on the basis of time (for instance, average temperature for the week and number of suicides). When a correlation is announced in the manner above, however, it is assumed that the relationship is not coincidental or likely by chance alone.

The *calculation* of correlation between two variables is a *descriptive* measure. We measure the 'togetherness' of the two variables. Testing the correlation for significance is *interpretive*.

The STRENGTH of relationship between two variables is the degree to which one variable *does* tend to be high if the other variable is high (or low, for negative correlation). This strength of relationship is expressed on a scale ranging from − 1 (perfect negative) through zero (no relationship) to + 1 (perfect positive). The figure arrived at to express the relationship is known as a CORRELATION COEFFICIENT or COEFFICIENT OF CORRELATION. This figure can be calculated for the relationship between any two variables and, as explained above, when it is stated that there is a correlation, what is meant is that the coefficient calculated is strong enough not to be considered likely by chance alone. Oddly enough, a fairly weak coefficient, as low as 0.3, can be counted as significant if the number of pairs of values is quite high, a point to be explained below.

It is not possible to obtain a coefficient less than − 1 or greater than + 1. If you do obtain such a value there is a mistake somewhere in your calculations (but this can't indicate an error in your raw data). The interpretation of the correlation coefficient scale is, in general:

*Figure 36  Scale of correlation*

Something might jar here. How can something getting more negative be described as getting stronger? Well it can. The sign simply tells us the *direction* of the relationship. To assess strength ignore the sign! Beware this one – it's very easy to read '– 1' as representing no relationship.

## Scattergrams

One way to investigate the relationship between two variables is to plot pairs of values (one on variable A, the other on variable B) on a graph known as a SCATTERGRAM, so named because it shows the scattering of pairs. The extent to which pairs of readings are not scattered randomly on the graph, but do form a consistent pattern, is a sign of the strength of the relationship. I hope the following scattergrams will demonstrate this. They represent data from one person taken after each trial on a simulated driving task:

Data

| Number of trials | Points scored |
| --- | --- |
| 1 | 27 |
| 2 | 54 |
| 3 | 78 |
| 4 | 105 |
| 5 | 120 |
| 6 | 149 |

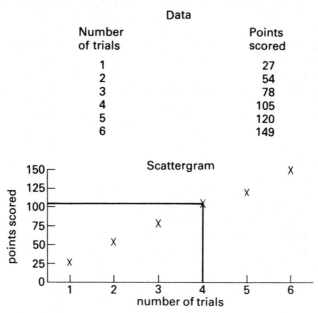

*Figure 37    Driving task–points*

In the first example (figure 37) you'll see that the cross for the pair of values 4 trials/105 points is placed on a vertical line up from 4 on the 'trials' axis and on a horizontal line from 105 on the 'points' axis. All points are plotted in this way. For trials/points we get a picture of a strong positive correlation, for trials/time taken (figure 38) a strong negative, and for trials/number of words spoken (figure 39) throughout the trial we get no relationship at all. Perfect correlations would take the shapes shown in figures 40a and 40b.

If there were no relationship at all between two variables, we could end up with scattergrams as shown in figure 41.

In figure 41(a) we have no relationship because variable $Y$ does not change in any way that is related to changes in variable $X$. Another way of putting this is to say that changes in $Y$ are not at all predictable from changes in $X$.

In figure 41(b) we have no relationship because variable $Y$ stays the same value no matter what changes occur in variable $X$. If $X$ were time and $Y$ were body temperature, this is the relationship we might expect in a healthy, calm and motionless person.

### Data

| Number of trials | Time to complete route (secs.) |
|:---:|:---:|
| 1 | 127 |
| 2 | 118 |
| 3 | 106 |
| 4 | 98 |
| 5 | 85 |
| 6 | 76 |

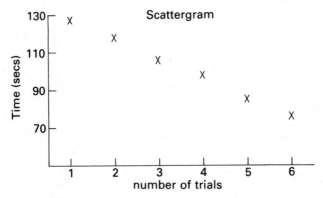

*Figure 38   Driving task–time*

### Data

| Number of trials | Number of words spoken |
|:---:|:---:|
| 1 | 20 |
| 2 | 4 |
| 3 | 13 |
| 4 | 24 |
| 5 | 5 |
| 6 | 15 |

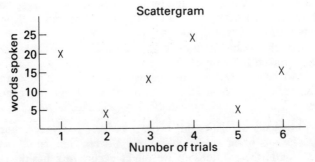

*Figure 39   Driving task–words spoken*

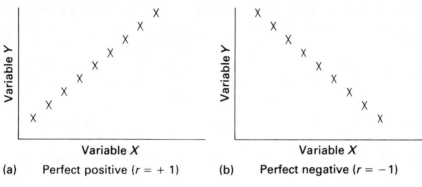

Figure 40 *Perfect correlations*

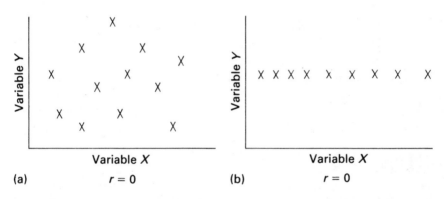

Figure 41 *No-relationship patterns*

## Does *r*=0 always mean no relationship?
Why bother to plot the values if the size of *r* tells us the strength of the relationship? There are several patterned relationships which might show up on a scattergram when our calculation of *r* gives us near zero. Look, for instance, at figure 42:

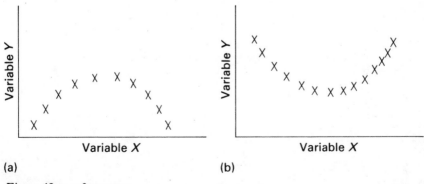

Figure 42 *r=0 patterns*

These are called CURVILINEAR relationships for obvious reasons. What might show this relationship? What about temperatures and months of the year? Is there a good psychological example? Freud argued that the more one was *under* gratified or the more one was *over* gratified, the more likelihood there was of fixation at a psychosexual stage. People perform worse on memory tasks both when there has been extreme sensory deprivation and with sensory overload. One's interest in a task might increase then wane with increasing practice.

1 Draw the scattergrams for the other tables of data in this chapter (tables 47, 48 and 50).

2 Can you think of other relationships between variables which might be curvilinear?

## Calculating correlation coefficients

The two most frequently used coefficients are:

| Name | Symbol | Level of data used with |
|------|--------|------------------------|
| Pearson | *r* | Interval/Ratio (i.e. a PARAMETRIC test) |
| Spearman | ('rho')* | Ordinal (i.e. NON-PARAMETRIC test) |

* both are often written as 'r' but Spearman's should really be written either as '$r_s$', to be clear, or properly as the Greek letter '$\rho$'.

# SPEARMAN'S RHO

## Conditions for use

Data must be at, or converted to, ORDINAL level
Data must be in the form of RELATED PAIRS

## Data

The following fictitious data give students' maths and music class-test grades. Columns D and E give the results in rank order form:

*Table 47    Class-test results*

| Column | A | B | C | D | E | F |
|--------|---|---|---|---|---|---|
| Student | maths mark | music mark | maths rank | music rank | difference between ranks d | $d^2$ |
| John | 53 | 34 | 3 | 6 | −3 | 9 |
| Julia | 91 | 43 | 1 | 5 | −4 | 16 |
| Jerry | 49 | 73 | 4 | 3.5 | 0.5 | 0.25 |
| Jean | 45 | 75 | 5 | 2 | 3 | 9 |
| Jill | 38 | 93 | 6 | 1 | 5 | 25 |
| Jonah | 17 | 18 | 7 | 7 | 0 | 0 |
| Jasmine | 58 | 73 | 2 | 3.5 | −1.5 | 2.25 |

$\Sigma d^2 = 61.5$

Before starting on the Spearman procedure take a look at the squared rank differences in column F. If we are expecting people to score about the same on both tests, what size would we expect these values to be, large or small? What size would we expect $\Sigma d^2$ to be if there is to be a strong positive correlation?

| Procedure | Calculation on our data |
|---|---|
| 1 Put values on variable $X$ in rank order | See column C, table 47 |
| 2 Put values on variable $Y$ in rank order | See column D, table 47 |
| 3 Subtract rank $Y$ from rank $X$ for each pair of ranks | See column E, table 47 |
| 4 Square of step 3 | See column F, table 47 |
| 5 Add the results of step 4 | Total of column F = 61.5 |

6 Insert the result of step 5 into the formula:

$$r_s = 1 - \frac{6 \times \Sigma d^2}{N^3 - N}$$

where $N$ is the total number of pairs*

$$1 - \frac{6 \times 61.5}{7^3 - 7} = 1 - \frac{369}{336}$$

$$= 1 - 1.098 = -0.098$$

7 Calculate $r$ and consult table 9, appendix 3**

$r_s = -0.098$

8 $r_s$ has to be equal to or greater than the table value for significance

Critical value for $p \leqslant 0.05$, where $N = 7$ and test is two-tailed is 0.786

9 Make significance statement

Coefficient is not significant

* *Do* watch the figure 1 here. I've often had students reporting wonderfully successful results, about which they are understandably pleased, only to find that their result of, say, 0.81 has yet to be subtracted from 1.

** Note that in all the other tests, the test statistic value ($t$, $U$, etc) was only required on route to determining significance. Correlation coefficients, however, may be required in their own right, for instance as an indicator of the strength of the relationship. Although they usually are tested for significance this is not always a requirement.

### When $N$ is greater than 30

The table of critical values for $r_s$ stops at $N = 30$. If $N$ is larger than 30, $r_s =$ can be converted to a $t$ value using:

$$t = r_s \sqrt{\left( \frac{(N - 2)}{(1 - (r_s)^2)} \right)}$$

$t$ is then checked for significance with $N - 2$ degrees of freedom.

## Summary
Spearman's Rho $(r_s)$ shows the degree of correlation between two sets of ranks where each rank in one set has a related partner in the other set. The higher the value of $r_s$, the more positive the correlation. The lower the value (past zero) the more negative the correlation.

## Explanatory notes
There is a similarity here between this exercise and the calculation of Wilcoxon's $T$ (see page 189). In that exercise, we wanted all the positive differences to be large, and any negative differences to be small. Here, we want *all* differences to be small, irrespective of direction. A strong positive correlation occurs when, for each pair of values, the rank of each value is very similar. Therefore we'd expect, for a strong positive, that all differences between ranks would be small. Consequently all *squares* of differences should be fairly small too and so, finally, $\Sigma d^2$ should be small. Looking at the formula, all other values can't change: 1 is 1, 6 is 6, and $N$ is the number in our sample.

## Does the formula work?
Let's look at a perfect negative correlation. Here we compare the number of anagrams solved with the time to solve the first anagram for a group of participants in a problem-solving experiment. Here, the fictitious data show that order in solving the first anagram is a perfect predictor of final rank in number of anagrams solved.

*Table 48   Anagram-solving results*

| Participant | Anagrams solved | Rank | Seconds to solve first anagram | Rank | Rank difference $d$ | $d^2$ |
|---|---|---|---|---|---|---|
| 1 | 19 | 5 | 8 | 1 | 4 | 16 |
| 2 | 17 | 3 | 24 | 3 | 0 | 0 |
| 3 | 18 | 4 | 15 | 2 | 2 | 4 |
| 4 | 15 | 1 | 45 | 5 | −4 | 16 |
| 5 | 16 | 2 | 32 | 4 | −2 | 4 |
| | | | | | $\Sigma d = 0$ | $\Sigma d^2 = 40$ |

Inserting $\Sigma d^2 = 40$ into the Spearman formula we get:

$$r_s = 1 - \frac{6 \times 40}{125 - 5} = 1 - \frac{240}{120} = 1 - 2 = -1$$

We get the value $-1$ for a perfect negative correlation.

> The demonstration for a perfect positive correlation $(+1)$ is even simpler and you might like to try it on the first data table in this chapter (table 47). Since there is obviously a perfect correlation here, your calculation should end up with the value $+1$ for $r_s$.

## Advantages and disadvantages of Spearman's Rho
The disadvantages are that the test is *non-parametric* and therefore suffers all the associated weaknesses of these tests outlined in the last section.

The great advantage is that it is quick and simple to calculate!

We now turn to the far more powerful, most popular, parametric measure of correlation.

# PEARSON'S PRODUCT-MOMENT CORRELATION COEFFICIENT

## Conditions for use

Data must be at INTERVAL or RATIO level.

Data must be in the form of RELATED PAIRS.

The grand title of this coefficient might make you feel that this could just be a little more complex . . . and you'd be right! There is, however, a simple way of starting out. One formula for Pearson's *r* is:

$$r = \frac{\Sigma(z_x \times z_y)}{N-1}$$

where $z_x$, for each pair of values, is the standard score (or *z*-score) for the first value (variable $X$), and $z_y$ is the *z*-score for the second value (variable $Y$).

Suppose we were testing the validity of a new reading test by comparing it with an older version. We are expecting children to score roughly the same on both tests.

*Table 49   Reading test results*

| Child No. | Score on old test (X) | Deviation from mean (d) | z-score* | Score on new test (Y) | Deviation from mean (d) | z-score | z×z |
|---|---|---|---|---|---|---|---|
| 1 | 67 | 10.4 | 0.87 | 65 | 5.7 | 0.41 | 0.36 |
| 2 | 72 | 15.4 | 1.29 | 84 | 24.7 | 1.78 | 2.29 |
| 3 | 45 | −11.6 | −0.97 | 51 | −8.3 | −0.60 | 0.58 |
| 4 | 58 | 1.4 | 0.12 | 56 | −3.3 | −0.24 | −0.03 |
| 5 | 63 | 6.4 | 0.54 | 67 | 7.7 | 0.55 | 0.30 |
| 6 | 39 | −17.6 | −1.48 | 42 | 17.3 | −1.24 | 1.84 |
| 7 | 52 | −4.6 | −0.39 | 50 | 9.3 | −0.67 | 0.26 |

$\bar{X} = 56.6 \quad sd_x = 11.9$ $\qquad \bar{Y} = 59.3 \quad sd_y = 13.9$

$\Sigma(z_x \times z_y) = 5.6$

Pearson's $r = \dfrac{5.6}{6} = 0.93$

---

\* Just to remind you: a *z*-score is the number of standard deviations a particular value is away from the mean. On the old test, the *sd* is 11.9, Child number one's score of 67 is 10.4 points from the mean of 56.6 and this is 10.4/11.9 standard deviations. Think in units of 11.9 – how many 11.9 s is it away from the mean? This gives the standard (*z*) score of 0.87

So Pearson's *r* just takes each pair of *z*-scores and multiplies them, adds this lot up and then divides by $N-1$. There is a complicated-looking formula for doing this which removes the problem of calculating *z*-scores, however, and which can be used straight away (with a calculator) from table 51.

(a)  $$r = \frac{N \times \Sigma(X \times Y) - \Sigma X \times \Sigma Y}{\sqrt{[N \times \Sigma X^2 - (\Sigma X)^2][N \times \Sigma Y^2 - (\Sigma Y)^2]}}$$

but if you have already calculated your deviations and standard deviations:

(b)  $$r = \frac{\Sigma(X - \bar{X})(Y - \bar{Y})}{(N - 1)sd_x \times sd_y}$$

is a lot easier.

Let's go through version (a). The values we need are:

*Table 50   Reading test values*

| Column:<br>Child number | A<br>Score $X$ | B<br>(Score $X$)$^2$ | C<br>Score $Y$ | D<br>(Score $Y$)$^2$ | E<br>($X \times Y$) |
|---|---|---|---|---|---|
| 1 | 67 | 4489 | 65 | 4225 | 4355 |
| 2 | 72 | 5184 | 84 | 7056 | 6048 |
| 3 | 45 | 2025 | 51 | 2601 | 2295 |
| 4 | 58 | 3364 | 56 | 3136 | 3248 |
| 5 | 63 | 3969 | 67 | 4489 | 4221 |
| 6 | 39 | 1521 | 42 | 1764 | 1638 |
| 7 | 52 | 2704 | 50 | 2500 | 2600 |
| | $\Sigma X = 396$ | $\Sigma X^2 = 23256$ | $\Sigma Y = 415$ | $\Sigma Y^2 = 25771$ | $\Sigma XY = 24405$ |
| | $(\Sigma X)^2 = 156816$ | | $(\Sigma Y)^2 = 172225$ | | |

| Procedure | Calculation on our data |
|---|---|
| 1 Find $\Sigma X$ and $(\Sigma X)^2$ | See column A |
| 2 Add all $X^2$ to get $\Sigma X^2$ | See column B |
| 3 Multiply $\Sigma X^2$ (step 2 result) by $N$ | $23256 \times 7 = 162792$ |
| 4 Subtract $(\Sigma x)^2$ from step 3 result | $162792 - 156816 = 5976$ |
| 5 to 8 Repeat steps 1 to 4 on the $Y$ data | See columns c & D<br>$25771 \times 7 = 180397$<br>$180397 - 172225 = 8172$ |
| 9 Multiply step 4 result by step 8 result | $5976 \times 8172 = 48835872$ |
| 10 Take square root of step 9 result | $\sqrt{48835872} = 6988.27$ |
| 11 Multiply $\Sigma X$ by $\Sigma Y$ | $396 \times 415 = 164340$ |
| 12 Find $\Sigma XY$ | See column E |
| 13 Multiply step 12 result by $N$ | $24405 \times 7 = 170835$ |
| 14 Subtract step 11 result from step 13 result | $170835 - 164340 = 6495$ |
| 15 Divide step 14 result by step 10 result<br>For the significance check, $df = N - 2$. | $6495 \div 6988.27 = 0.929 = 0.93$ |

As an exercise, try checking that Formula B produces the same result. You could also try calculating Spearman's Rho for this data too. They won't be the same, necessarily. Each has its own table of critical values and, so saying, we now move to a look at the significance of a correlation coefficient.

## Significance and correlation coefficients

Now we return to a familiar theme. Consider the results for maths and music results in table 48 and the reading test results in the table above. I hope you'll agree that, whereas for maths and music it's pretty obvious (by an 'eyeball test') that nothing at all is going on in terms of a relationship, for the test scores above it's equally obvious that there *is* a relationship. The scattergrams in figure 43 show this too.

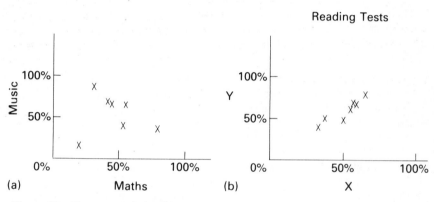

*Figure 43   Test score relationships*

The theme is that we can tell when a correlation is obviously significant (just as you could tell when the baby-sexer was successful) and you can tell when there is obviously nothing going on. How do we decide when a coefficient of correlation becomes significant? We need to know, for a particular number of score pairs (i.e. $N = 7$ above) the value of $r$ above which just 5% of coefficients would occur if we were doing our calculations on randomly associated pairs. Let me clarify.

Suppose we have obtained from some participants a piece of writing on 'Myself and my family'. You are to rate each piece for *self-confidence* whereas I will rate them for *warmth* in the feelings expressed by each participant towards their parents and siblings. We are predicting that the two ratings will be positively correlated. We rate by placing the pieces of writing in rank order on our two variables. We get the results shown in table 51 with just three participants.

*Table 51   Rankings of participants' writing*

|  | Self-confidence | Warmth |
|---|---|---|
| Participant A | 1 | 1 |
| Participant B | 2 | 2 |
| Participant C | 3 | 3 |

The *strength* of the correlation is $+1$, perfect. But is it *significant?* How likely is it that my rankings would agree exactly with yours? In other words, what is the probability that I would produce my rankings by chance alone, for instance, by simply picking from a hat containing these three numbers?

$$\text{Remember that probability is } \frac{\text{number of desired outcomes}}{\text{number of possible outcomes}}$$

The rankings I could have produced are shown in table 52.

*Table 52  Possible rankings*

|  | Your ranking on self-confidence | The possible rankings I could have produced: |
|---|---|---|
| Participant A | 1 | 1  1  2  2  3  3 |
| Participant B | 2 | 2  3  1  3  1  2 |
| Participant C | 3 | 3  2  3  1  2  1 |

The probability that I would produce the order I did (by chance) is therefore 1/6, because there were 6 possible rankings for me to produce.

Expressed in the usual way, probability was therefore 0.167. This is not low enough to be significant. We require a value less than 0.05.

What happens if there are *four* participants and our two sets of rankings match perfectly? The ranks one to four can be arranged in 24 different ways. Therefore, the probability of a perfect match is now 1/24 and this gives $p = 0.042$ – a value low enough for significance.

In the case of five participants, the probability of a perfect match is 0.008. The probability of being just one rank out, as in table 53, for instance, is $p = 0.033$.$^{\star}$

*Table 53  Five-participant correlation*

|  | Self-confidence | Warmth |
|---|---|---|
| Participant A | 1 | 1 |
| Participant B | 2 | 2 |
| Participant C | 3 | 4 |
| Participant D | 4 | 3 |
| Participant E | 5 | 5 |

$N=5$   Correlation=0.9

Probability of correlation of 0.9=0.033
Probability of correlation of $+1$=0.008

Therefore, total probability of
either 0.9 or $+1$ occurring is: 0.041

$\star$ There are just four ways in which the warmth ranks can be arranged such that they are only one rank out from the self-confident ranks. There are 120 ways of arranging ranks one to five altogether. 4/120=0.033

Hence, the probability of getting either a correlation of $+1$ *or* of 0.09 is a total of 0.041. We can count the correlation in table 53 as significant then, since the probability of it, or a higher correlation, occurring by chance is, in total, less than

0.05. The next possible value for the coefficient is 0.8 and the probability of this value occurring is far higher than 0.05.

The CRITICAL VALUE for Spearman's *r* when $N=5$ then, is 0.09 (one-tailed)

When $N=6$, tables give the critical value as 0.829 (one-tailed). If we had numbers one to six in two separate hats and drew one from each hat to create six pairs, the probability of achieving a correlation between these pairs of more than 0.829 is 0.05 or less. Another way of saying this is that if we were perverse enough to repeat this pairing operation very many times we would get a great number of low correlations and only 5% of results would be 0.829 or above.

For $N=20$, however, the value which only 5% of results would exceed is as low as 0.38. As $N$ increases so the distribution of the frequency of correlations lessens or 'bunches up', as I hope figure 44 makes clear. The values for $N=6$,

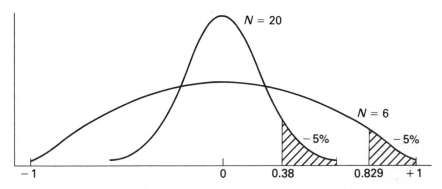

*Figure 44   Distribution of correlations when $N=6$ and $N=20$*

particularly, would not form such a smooth curve in fact. There would actually be a discrete number of steps – values which $r_s$ can take. But the rough outline of the shape the curves would take is as in figure 44.

Notice that as $N$ increases so the critical value for 5% significance decreases. This is, in itself, a negative correlation.

Note, too, that if, with $N=6$, you predicted a negative correlation, as you might between say, self-confidence and feelings of dependence, then your calculated correlation coefficient must be *absolutely* greater than 0.829. For example, $-0.93$ would count as significant since it is more extreme, on the negative end of the curve, than $-0.829$.

### But surely a *strong* correlation must be *significant*?

Our natural inclination, I'm sure, is to feel this must be so. But reconsider what we've been looking at. It's *easy* to get a high-valued coefficient with low $N$. With three pairs we'd get $+1$ or $-1$ every one time in three trials so, by the rules of social science research and of common sense, we can hardly call these results *significant*, even though they're perfect. On the other hand, as we saw just above, for the moderate sample size of 20, correlations above 0.38 will not be expected more than 5% of the time, and are therefore significant when they do occur.

### The guessing error, variance estimate or coefficient of determination

We have two problems now. One is that a rather low coefficient can tell us that two variables are significantly but only weakly connected. What does this weak relationship mean? What can we infer from it? The other is that correlation coefficients don't lie on a ratio scale. A correlation of 0.6 is not twice as 'good' or predictive as one of 0.3.

One way of converting these figures to a ratio scale is to square the value of the coefficient i.e. take $r \times r = r^2$ Statisticians use this as a VARIANCE ESTIMATE, arguing as follows:

> Any set of scores (for instance, the set of reading test $X$ scores) has a variation within it – what we know as the *variance*. The reading test $Y$ scores also have a variance. Our $r$ for these two sets of scores was 0.93 and $r^2$ would therefore be 0.86. It is now said that 86% of the second set of scores are predictable from the first. More concretely (and roughly speaking), if you were guessing reading test $Y$ scores from reading test $X$ you'd be right (or close) about 86% of the time. 14% of the variance in the second set of scores is left 'unexplained'. It could be the result of differences between the new and the old test or random variations in the children's performances from one test to the next.
>
> The variance estimate is made using the COEFFICIENT OF DETERMINATION. This value is: $r^2 \times 100$, which is simply our value $r^2$, above, expressed as a percentage.

### What you can't assume with a correlation

### Cause and effect

Let's leave statistics now and return to the concept of correlation.

> See if you can detect flaws in the following statements:
>
> Research has established a strong correlation between the use of physical punishment by parents and the development of aggression in their children. Parents should not use this form of discipline then, if they don't want their children to end up aggressive.
>
> There is a significant correlation between early weaning and later irritability in the infant, so don't hurry weaning if you want a good-tempered child.
>
> Poverty is correlated with crime, so, if you can achieve a higher income, your children are less likely to become law-breakers.

In each case above it is assumed that one variable is the cause of another.

With any significant correlation there are several possible interpretations:

1 Variable A has a causal effect on variable B
2 Variable B has a causal effect on variable A
3 A and B are both related to some other linking factor(s)
4 We have type one error (i.e. a fluke coincidence)

A good example of situation 3 would be the perfect correlation of two adjacent thermometers, one in °C and the other in °F. The common factor is of course heat and one thermometer cannot affect the other. Similarly, physical punishment may be a method of control used to a greater extent by parents who are also those more likely to encourage or fail to control aggression *or* who tend to live in environments where aggression is more likely to flourish. There again, interpretation 2 is interesting. Perhaps aggression has a substantial hereditary base and children born with more aggressive dispositions *invoke* more physical methods of control from their parents – not an explanation I endorse, but simply a possibility which can't be dismissed.

When you are asked: 'A researcher concludes from a correlation result that . . . (A is the cause of B) . . . Could there be an alternative interpretation? – try B causes A as the alternative. Then try looking for common causes of both A and B. Visually, with the arrows representing causal direction:

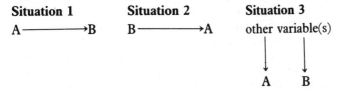

**When cause is more likely**   *1 The prior variable*   One variable may be *prior* to the other. For instance, if tall people were found to be more successful, success could hardly have affected their height. It may of course make them 'walk tall' and it certainly affects others' *perception* of their height as shown by American research indicating that people tend to significantly overestimate the winning candidate in presidential elections. But later success can't influence the genetic blueprint for the physical development of height.

A type 3 explanation is possible, however. Other genetic qualities of tall people might contribute to success in later life, not the height factor itself.

*2 In experiments*   In a non-experimental correlation between two measured variables it is hazardous to claim that one of the variables is the cause of the other.

When a researcher conducts a highly controlled experiment in the laboratory, for instance on hours of food deprivation in rats and their errors in learning to run a maze, the independent variable can take several values and hence a scattergram of results like those shown in figure 45 might emerge:

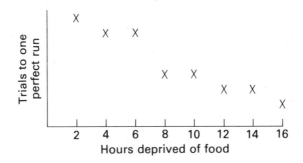

A positive or negative correlation?

*Figure 45   Scattergram of rats' results*

Similarly, we might test human subjects for the primacy effect in memory using several different rates of presentation. As presentation rate increases what might happen to the primacy effect and what sort of correlation might therefore occur between it and the presentation rate?

Here we can be more confident that A causes B, even though we've used a correlation. The correlation simply serves a statistical purpose – it demonstrates a trend between IV and DV. The *design* is still experimental. We can make the same assumptions we make in a traditional two condition experiment about the independent variable affecting the dependent variable. Since the IV is altered first, the DV can't be causing changes in the IV, though, of course, a confounding variable could be.

**The missing middle**    By selecting certain groups to be included in a correlational study a researcher could appear to demonstrate a strong correlational effect. For instance, such a correlation might be announced between financial status and unwanted pregnancies, in that more unwanted pregnancies were reported from lower income households. This could be used politically *either* to blame the poor for a higher birth rate (along with the sin of being poor) *or* for a campaign against low incomes and for better sex education.

The actual facts, however, may have been obscured by biased sampling of only particularly low- and high-income families. Have a look at figure 46:

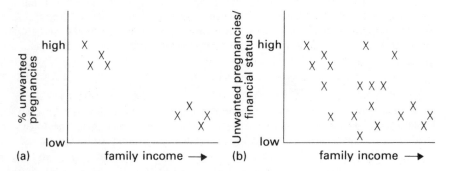

*Figure 46    Unwanted pregnancies/financial status*

The selective samples drawn (figure 46(a)) may show a strong correlation, but a more representative sample (figure 46(b)) won't.

**Nominal type variable**    A correlation cannot be carried out if one variable is nominal. Consider table 54:

*Table 54    Nominal variable in correlation*

| Hair colour | % rating on trustworthiness |
|---|---|
| White | 78 |
| Blonde | 65 |
| Ginger | 51 |
| Chestnut | 62 |
| Auburn | 49 |
| Black | 56 |

The variable of hair colour is nominal. We could turn it into ordinal data by ranking according to colour somehow. If we don't, though, we can't conduct a correlation on these data. We cannot compare pairs of scores or ranks.

Even if we can, at a stretch, put hair colour on an ordinal scale, we can't do this for a two-value nominal variable like sex. If we wanted to see whether smoking was significantly more related to one sex than another we should have to collapse the scale on which smoking is measured and end up with a table like table 55.

*Table 55   Number of cigarettes smoked per day*

|  | Below the mean | Above the mean |
|---|---|---|
| **Females** | 27 | 35 |
| **Males** | 28 | 24 |

. . . and what statistical test would we perform on data like these usually? This is why Chi-squared is called a TEST OF ASSOCIATION and can be classed as a nominal test of relationship, although it appears as a test of difference on the test-choice chart (figure 47).

## Common uses of correlation in psychology
Apart from the several uses already described, there are particular areas of research where a correlation is especially useful and popular.

**Reliability**   When testing for reliability, the test–retest method would involve taking a set of measurements on, say, 50 subjects at one time, then retesting *the same subjects* at a later date, say six months later. Then we perform a correlation between the two sets of scores. Tests between raters (people who rate) for their reliability of judgement would also use correlation, as would a comparison between two halves or two equivalent forms of the same test (see chapter 9).

**Factor analysis**   This uses a matrix of all correlations possible between several tests (a 'battery') taken by the same individuals. Factors statistically derived from the analysis are said to 'account for' the relationships shown in the matrix.

**Twin studies**   Identical twins (and to some extent, fraternal twins) form an ideal MATCHED PAIRS design. Very often scores for twin pairs are correlated, particularly in the IQ inheritance debate where a strong correlation between twins reared apart was powerful evidence for a genetic contribution. It was the *strength* of correlation for high numbers of twin pairs which first encouraged Leon Kamin to investigate Sir Cyril Burt's famous flawed data, but it was the uncanny coincidences in getting *exactly* the same coefficient, with differing numbers of pairs, which led to allegations of fraud.

## Key terms for this chapter
Correlation
  Positive
  Negative
  Coefficient
  Strength vs. significance
Curvilinear relationship

Guessing error
Pearson's product moment coefficient
Scattergram
Spearman's Rho
Variance estimate

### Exercises

1 (From an article in the *Times Educational Supplement*, 3 June 1988)

> . . . teaching the sound and shape of letters can give pre-school children a head start . . . children who performed best at the age of seven tended to be those who had the most knowledge and understanding of the three Rs at the age of four.
>
> In the case of reading, the strongest predictor of ability among seven-year-olds was 'the number of letters the child could identify at the age of four-and-three-quarters' . . . Tizard concludes that nursery teachers should give more emphasis to literacy and numeracy skills . . .

(a) What conclusion, other than the researcher's, could be drawn here?
(b) Briefly describe a study which could help us decide between these alternative interpretations.
(c) What sort of correlation must the researchers have found between number of letters identified at four and number of reading *errors* at seven – *positive* or *negative*?
(d) Suppose the correlation between adding ability at five and mathematical ability at seven were $+0.83$ (Pearson). How would you describe the strength of this coefficient verbally?
(e) How significant would the correlation of 0.83 be (one-tailed) if the sample of children had numbered 33?

2 Several students in your group have carried out correlations, got their results, know what significance level they need to reach, but have sadly forgotten how to check in tables for significance. They agree to do calculations on your data if you'll just check their results and tell them whether to reject or accept their null hypotheses. The blank column is for you to fill in.

*Table 56 Exercise 2*

|  | Coefficient obtained | $N=$ | Significance level required | Direction predicted | Accept or reject $H_0$? |
|---|---|---|---|---|---|
| (a) | $r=\ 0.3$ | 14 | $p<0.01$ | + | |
| (b) | $r=-0.19$ | 112 | $p<0.01$ | − | |
| (c) | $r_s=\ 0.78$ | 7 | $p<0.05$ | + | |
| (d) | $r=\ 0.71$ | 6 | $p<0.05$ | + | |
| (e) | $r_s=\ 0.9$ | 5 | $p<0.05$ | + | |
| (f) | $r=\ 0.63$ | 12 | $p<0.01$ | no prediction made | |
| (g) | $r=\ 0.54$ | 30 | $p<0.05$ | − | |

3 Spearman's test can always be used instead of Pearson's. Is the reverse of this true? Please give a reason.

4 A researcher correlates scores on a questionnaire concerning 'ego-strength' with measures of their anxiety level obtained by rating their verbal responses to several pictures. Which measure of correlation should be employed?

5 If a student tells you she has obtained a correlation coefficient of 2.79, what might you advise her to do?

# Inferential statistics IV

## CHOOSING AN APPROPRIATE TEST

Choosing the appropriate test can leave you with a floundering feeling, since there are so many tests and there can be a lot of data and several hypotheses. The first golden rule is *not to panic*! Stay calm. Next . . .

Take one hypothesis at a time
Choose the test for this hypothesis
Calculate the test
Decide whether the result is significant.

All but one of the tests in this book assume you have just *two* samples and that you want to test for a difference between these or for a correlation between them. The exception is $\chi^2$ which can be used where there are several samples measured on several nominal variables.

Otherwise, if you want to look for differences among more than two samples, you can take groups two at a time and conduct the appropriate test. Say you had a control group, placebo group and experimental group. You can conduct a test between the control and placebo groups, the control and experimental groups and between the placebo and experimental groups. There *are* methods for testing several groups at a time but they are beyond the scope of this book. Cohen and Holliday (1982) will take you through these and they also provide computer programmes (in BASIC) so that, once you've written it to disc, you only have to feed in your data and need never go through all the laborious calculations again!

So how do we choose the appropriate test? This really should be quite simple if you follow the three steps in box 26 and use the flow chart in figure 47. Notice that the decision you have to make at each step is indicated on the flow chart.

*Box 26  Steps in choosing the appropriate statistical test*

> 1  Does the hypothesis predict difference or correlation?
>
> 2  At what level of measurement are the data?
>   *Note:* If the level is interval and you wish to conduct a parametric test, check that your data satisfy the parametric test assumptions before proceeding. If the assumptions cannot reasonably be met, you will have to convert your data to ranked data.
>
> 3  Is the design related or unrelated?

### Parametric test assumptions
Remember (from part II) these are:

1  Interval level data required
2  Samples drawn from a normally distributed population

3 Homogeneity of variance

( . . . with some digression from these allowed)

## Examples of choosing a test

Take a look at table 57. The data were produced by asking male and female 17-year-olds to estimate their own IQ, by measuring their actual IQ, measuring their height and measuring their mothers' IQs.

*Table 57  Male and female IQ data*

| Males | | | | Females | | | |
|---|---|---|---|---|---|---|---|
| Estimated IQ | Measured IQ | Height (cm) | Mother's IQ | Estimated IQ | Measured IQ | Height (cm) | Mother's IQ |
| 120 | 107 | 160 | 100 | 100 | 97 | 155 | 105 |
| 110 | 112 | 181 | 105 | 95 | 92 | 165 | 97 |
| 95 | 130 | 175 | 102 | 90 | 104 | 177 | 115 |
| 140 | 95 | 164 | 97 | 110 | 112 | 162 | 96 |
| 100 | 104 | 163 | 120 | 85 | 130 | 173 | 100 |
| 120 | 92 | 158 | 131 | 100 | 95 | 159 | 120 |
| 110 | 97 | 172 | 115 | 105 | 107 | 164 | 102 |
| 105 | 101 | 171 | 96 | 100 | 101 | 165 | 131 |

Assume that mother and offspring can be treated as matched pairs.
Assume that estimated IQ cannot be treated as interval data.
Assume that this researcher will treat measured IQ as interval level data (though as explained earlier, there is debate about this).

> Using the decision chart (figure 47), try to select the appropriate test for each of the following hypotheses:
>
> 1 Male IQ estimates are higher than female estimates
> 2 Female measured IQs are higher than male measured IQs
> 3 The taller people are, the higher is their IQ
> 4 Female measured IQs are higher than their mothers' measured IQs

**Hypothesis 1**  Decision 1: we are looking for a *difference*
Decision 2: we shall have to convert the estimated IQs to ranked, *ordinal* data
Decision 3: the design is *unrelated*; we have separate groups of males and females

Our choice is therefore **Mann–Whitney** (or **Wilcoxon rank sum**).

**Hypothesis 2**  Decision 1: we are again looking for a *difference*
Decision 2: these data are being treated as *interval* level
Decision 3: the design is *unrelated*, as before

Our choice is therefore a *t*-**test for unrelated samples**

Parametric assumptions must be met:

The interval level data assumption has been made.

IQ tests are standardised to ensure that scores for the general population are normally distributed on them. Hence, the samples must come from a normally distributed population.

Using an 'eyeball' test, variances are not too different. This is not a big problem anyway since, although we have an unrelated design, the numbers in each group are equal.

**Hypothesis 3**  Decision 1: a positive *correlation* is predicted between height and IQ. We can treat male and female as one group
Decision 2: IQ is being treated as *interval*. Height is ratio level and therefore, at least *interval* level
Decision 3: correlations are automatically related designs

Our choice is therefore **Pearson's correlation coefficient**

Parametric assumptions must be met:

Arguments are the same as above but include the fact that height is typically normally distributed.

**Hypothesis 4**  Decision 1: a *difference* is predicted
Decision 2: measured IQ is being treated as *interval* level data
Decision 3: matched pairs produce a *related* design

Our choice is therefore a *t*-test for related samples

Parametric assumptions must be met:

Arguments are the same as above.

For each of the cases where a parametric test is chosen you could of course have chosen a non-parametric test, if you just wanted to use a simpler test. This would be safe where the difference was either obviously significant or obviously not. However, where the outcome is close to the significance level, it is wiser to use the more power-efficient, informative parametric alternative.

Here are some general hints to keep in mind when choosing:

- Correlations must always be, logically, related designs.
- $\chi^2$ tests the *difference* between *observed* frequencies and *expected* frequencies. This is why it is placed where it is on the chart. However, the net result is to tell us whether there is a significant association between one variable (say, being a smoker [or not] and having poor health [or not]). It is called a 'test of association'.
- If data appear as frequencies, in categories, a $\chi^2$ test is indicated. Even though the numbers in the categories are cardinal numbers, if it means that *all* you know is that, say, 22 people are in one category, and you know no more about them and can't separate them in any way (by rank or score) the data are in frequency form and the categories concerned will can be treated as a nominal frequency form and the categories concerned can be treated as a nominal scale.
- If a test or other psychological measure has been *standardised*, it can be treated as producing interval level data.
- If the results in question are in the form of scores or numbers produced by humans estimating or 'rating' events or behaviour, on some arbitrary scale, it is

almost always safest to convert the numbers to ordinal level (by ranking them). The same goes for scores on an unstandardised questionnaire or opinion survey.
– Ordinal data appear as a set of ranks ('ord' for order).

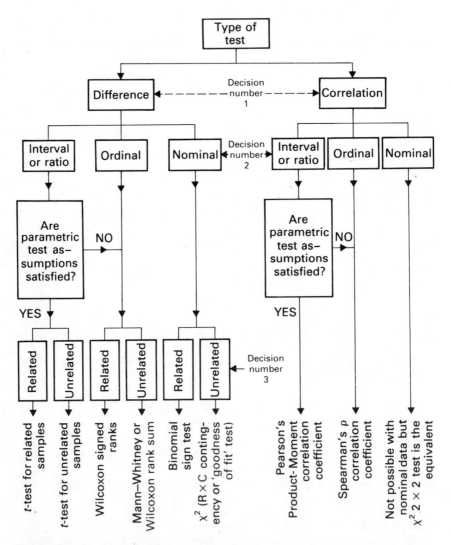

Figure 47   Chart for choosing the appropriate test

## Exercises

What tests should be used on the following data? Where there is a choice, which is the more powerful test and which would be the simplest to conduct?

1 Height (in cm) of girls bred on:

| All Bran | Bread and dripping |
|----------|--------------------|
| 172      | 162                |
| 181      | 172                |
| 190      | 154                |
| 165      | 143                |
| 167      | 167                |

The researcher was interested in whether one of the diets tended to produce taller girls.

2

*Table 58*

| Snooker players – Position in League Table | | | |
|------------------------------------------|----|--------------------|----|
| Smoking and Drinking Players | | Abstemious Players | |
| Terry Davis | 2 | Steve Griffiths | 8 |
| Alex Hendry | 6 | Steve Higgins | 1 |
| Fred Longpole | 10 | Chris Cushion | 5 |
| Alf Garnett | 9 | Betty Baulk | 3 |
| Bob Black | 4 | Susan Swerveshot | 7 |

In this case, we want to know whether abstemious players get significantly higher placings.

3

|          | No. of businessmen standing on window ledges | No. of businessmen *not* standing on window ledges |
|----------|:--------------------------------------------:|:--------------------------------------------------:|
| Tokyo    | 46                                           | 598                                                |
| New York | 103                                          | 524                                                |

If this was what happened when the stock market crashed in 1987, was the crash far worse in the USA? What test will tell us?

4 Students observe whether males or females do or don't walk under a ladder. They want to see whether one sex is more 'superstitious' than the other. What test do they need to use?

5 Ten out of ten nine-year-old boys report that they do not expect to do the washing-up when they are older. Each boy is matched with a boy from a single-parent family. Only two of the single-parent family boys say they do not expect to wash up when older. What test can we use to show that this difference is significant?

6 20 people perform a sensori-motor task in two conditions, one in a quiet room, on their own, the other in a brightly-lit room with a dozen people watching them. An electronic timer takes an accurate record of the number of errors they make in each condition.

(a) What test would be appropriate for investigating the significance of the differences in performance between the two conditions?
(b) What test would be appropriate for seeing whether people all tend to deteriorate or improve by about the same amount in the second condition?

7 A psychologist claims to have a very well standardised measurement scale. What statistical test would be used to check its test–retest reliability? What test would be used to check its validity on a criterion group who should score higher than a control group?

8 A set of photos of couples are rated for attractiveness by a panel of judges who rate the males separately from the females. The hypothesis tested is that people in couples tend to be of a similar level of attractiveness. What test would be used to compare the similarity of the two sets of ratings for male and female partners?

9 Question four in the section on parametric tests shows two distributions of scores. Suppose the researcher felt that these departed significantly from the pattern of a normal distribution. Which test could settle the matter?

10 Two groups of people are selected. One has a very high 'initiative-taking' score, the other group's score is quite low. They are asked to select just one of three possible activities which they would prefer to do. The choices are: rock-climbing, dancing or reading a book. What test would demonstrate significant differences between their choices?

11 The time is recorded for the same group of subjects to read out loud a list of rhyming words and a list of non-rhyming words. What test is appropriate for showing whether the rhyming words take significantly less time to read?

12 A group of management personnel undergo an intensive course on race issues. Essays written before and after the course are content analysed and rated for attitudes to race. What test would be appropriate for demonstrating a significant change of attitude as expressed in the essays?

# Qualitative data

Qualitative data consists of any information, gathered during research, which has not (yet, at least) been quantified in any rigorous way.

## Qualitative data and hypothesis testing

Because of the over-powering paradigm of natural science, it is often assumed that hypotheses can only be tested with quantified, empirical data. But we use qualitative data very often in supporting or contradicting our predictions and explanations.

Much of our reasoning about people's motivations and decision making is based on qualitative evidence. We may explain the unusual or depressive behaviour of a friend in terms of her unique situation in being a single parent and having just lost a supportive parent.

We can predict that persistent young offenders will feel more alienated from middle-class society. We can demonstrate this with the sheer strength and animosity of the content of their accounts. We are not limited to simply counting the number of aggressive responses.

The positivist may well feel tempted to create a standardised questionnaire from the offenders' data for use on offenders elsewhere, or on a control group.

The point being made, however, is that some psychological researchers have argued forcefully for the need to use the qualitative content gained in their research. They might argue, too, that insights gained in interviewing a group of offenders can be generalised with as much validity as questionnaire results. A perspective on the world, quite novel and unexpected, may emerge from the interview and give another interviewer a new range of ideas to broach with different offenders, or with 'control' teenagers who don't share the ideas.

We have seen elsewhere that individual case studies can add important information to the pool of knowledge and ideas which constitutes our understanding of humans and their behaviour. The value of Watson's study of 'Little Albert' was not that it was entirely quantitative. In a single-subject study we learnt just how easy it was to condition a child's fears and we acquired interesting information about how these generalised and failed to extinguish.

## Two approaches to qualitative data

Looking through the literature on qualitative data, two general views seem to emerge on what to do with it. These correspond to the positivist–non-positivist dimension but it must be stressed that this *is* a dimension – there are not just two views but a wide variety.

For the positivist, unquantified data is accepted in a subsidiary role. It is seen as having the following uses:

– it can illuminate and give a context to otherwise neutral and uninspiring statistics, as when Asch tells us *how* his conforming subjects behaved and looked uncomfortable.

– it can lead us to hypotheses testable in quantitative terms, as with the children of unemployed parents mentioned in chapter 4.

The qualitative researcher, however, sees qualitative data as meaningful in its own right. In fact, the use of the term 'qualitative method' usually indicates a commitment to publish the results of research in qualitative terms, remembering, of course, that such a researcher is not averse to looking at things quantitatively, should the opportunity arise and be found illuminating.

## Qualitative analysis of qualitative content

We saw earlier that content analysis can be used to deal with originally qualitative information. The data is rigorously analysed and reduced to quantified units, susceptible to statistical significance testing.

The qualitative researcher too has to categorise data. The whole data set may have been produced from any of the following sources:

Participants' notes and diaries
Participant observer's field notes
Informal or part-structured interviews
Open-ended questions (interview or questionnaire)
In-depth case study (mixture of interviews, observations, records)

and might consist of speech, interactions, behaviour patterns, written or visual recorded material. They might also include the researcher's own ideas impressions and feelings, recorded as the research project was progressing.

The set of data will need order imposing upon it. It has to be organised so that comparisons, contrasts and insights can be made and demonstrated. The qualitative researcher however, will not be categorising in order to count occurences. Instead, data will be categorised in order to analyse and compare the various *meanings* produced in any one category. From interviews with drug addicts, for instance, on their experiences in trying to break the habit, various fears and perceptions of the 'straight' world may emerge which are unique and qualitatively different from others. Each has a special value in painting a picture of personal experience, invisible to non-addicts, but of great utility to a rehabilitation therapist.

The richness of the unique qualities of category items is therefore preserved in qualitative analysis. To use an analogy, at home I may file articles on 'travelling in India' in one category, but hardly because I need to count how many I have!

## Methods of analysis

It is not possible to give precise guidelines on the analysis and presentation of qualitative data. There is no universally accepted paradigm. The decisions will be influenced by the theoretical background or model from which the researcher is working. Several quite specialised methods of analysis have been developed for different sorts of data (conversations, non-verbal communication, pedestrian behaviour and so on). What follows is a set of points applying to collections of data produced from the types of source mentioned above. After that, the reader will be directed to several specialised texts which have more to say on various qualitative or 'new paradigm' methods.

**Categorising**     The qualitative researcher will inevitably begin with a large quantity of written notes and material (audio and video recordings will have been transcribed).

As the notes are read and re-read it should be possible to start grouping items together. As a simple example, if you had asked student colleagues to discuss, during informal interviews, reactions to their college course, statements they make might fall into the following groupings:

| | | |
|---|---|---|
| social contacts | quality of teaching | available resources |
| link to career | timetable | facilities (canteen, etc.) |

. . . and so on.

Some statements will fall into more than one category. Traditionally, the analyst would make several copies of all data so that items can be cut and pasted into various categories and clusters. The modern, labour-saving way is to use the computer and a flexible data base system.

**Indigenous categories**    Prior to development of the researcher's own categories and groupings, the analyst usually looks at those used by the participants themselves. An example would be a group of students who call themselves 'the brains' whilst others get called 'the Neanderthals' by staff. Later on, the analyst might compare these titles and propose explanations of their derivation.

**Researcher's categories**    Some categories may emerge quite clearly on analysis or during data collection. In studying the organisation of a school, for instance, it might emerge that teachers are split into those who do and do not get involved in after-school activities. More likely, though, will be *dimensions* along which people vary, for instance, teachers in their attitude towards student discipline. These could range from the severe, through moderate to lax. This might sound like a quantitative dimension. However, the qualitative researcher is more interested in the *perspective* of each person. So the positions along the dimension from severe to lax are only roughly ordinal but are determined by specific reasons given. People are in a category along the dimension. 'Severe' would be those who say 'you have to show them who's boss' and the like. 'Moderate' teachers might say 'It's no good being the strict parent with them. They get enough of that at home and they don't respect it.'

**Typologies**    Where categories and dimensions are descriptions of people, some researchers may cross these in order to produce a matrix of 'types'. A teacher who is 'lax' on the discipline dimension, but also 'caring' rather than 'distant' may turn out to have an identifiable approach to students, different from all other staff, in that she particularly tries to raise self-esteem and enable students to take control of their own lives. Researchers sometimes give names to these types. In this case the type might be 'therapist'. It is important to remember, however, that the type is mere analogy. Any types created are products of the researcher's current scheme of looking at the data and not lasting realities.

All sciences use analogy and metaphor. In order to tell us what atoms are *like*, physicists describe electrons and neutrons as little balls. Electrical theory borrows the analogy of current 'flowing' like a river. Analogy is necessary in order to communicate under these circumstances. It tells us what something unique and novel is like, not what it *is*.

Creating the matrix of types, however, is useful in several ways. The reasons why a person fits none of the types created might well be worth investigating and lead to fresh insights. Conversely, a type might be produced which no one fits.

**Quotations**    The final report of qualitative findings will usually include verbatim quotations from participants which will bring the reader into the reality of the situation studied. At times, the researcher will, of course, be summarising the perspectives and understandings of participants in the study. But it is important that these summaries, which must, to some extent, be interpretive, or at least selective, are clearly identified as such. The quotes themselves are selections from the raw data which 'tell it like it is'. Very often comments just stick with us to perfectly encapsulate people's position, on some issue or stance in life, which they appear to hold. Here are a few:

> Everybody else out there seems to be having a great time except me'
> 'I just want everyone to like me'
> 'It's no use me speaking out. Nobody wants to listen and they'd tell me it was wrong anyway'
> 'Live for tomorrow, that's what I always say. You can't undo what's been done'

Most researchers see it as important that quotations, especially those intended for publication, are checked out first with the original producer.

## Separating report components
A qualitative research report will contain raw data and summaries of it, analysis, inference and, in the case of participant observation, perhaps feelings and reactions of the observer at the time significant events occurred. These are all valid components for inclusion but it is important that analysis, inference and feeling are clearly separated and labelled as such.

## Early and final analysis
Most qualitative researchers agree that some analysis of data can occur *during*, rather than after, the collection stage. This can direct the researcher to areas and avenues of questioning not originally prepared for. Obviously it is important that such early analysis does not produce blindness to some other areas. In comparison to quantitative research, however, it is possible to construct hypotheses *after* the data collection has begun rather than before it starts. Patton (1980), an evaluation researcher, states:

> 'The cardinal principle of qualitative analysis is that causal relationships and theoretical statements be clearly emergent from and grounded in the phenomena studied. The theory emerges from the data; it is not imposed on the data.'

**Grounded theory**   Patton's statement is very close to the basic principles of 'grounded theory' advocated by Glaser and Strauss (1967). This publication was a forceful presentation of the 'unstructured' approach to observations of human behaviour discussed in chapter 7. These writers argued that observers should (a) enter a research situation with no prior theoretical preconceptions, and (b) create, refine and revise theory in the light of further data collected.

The result expected is that 'grounded' hypotheses, generated through actual observation, would be more true to life than those deduced by prior commitment to, say, behaviourism or Piagetian theory. In fact, grounded theory is an import from sociology, but several of the qualitative or 'new paradigm' social psychologists have incorporated its principles.

The final qualitative research report, then, should give an account of early hypotheses that were formed and the extent to which these guided or changed the direction of further enquiry. Very often, in this sort of research, a point emerges in one interview and the researcher might think 'If only I could go back and ask all the other interviewees about this'. Where possible, this is just what does happen. To some extent, the final report can be a diary of insights and question development.

## Reliability and validity

Qualitative researchers argue that their methods produce more valid data for reasons already discussed (chapters 4 and 11). They would also argue that they have developed safeguards against lack of reliability. Some of these follow.

**Triangulation**    Borrowed from surveying, and used in evaluative research, this means comparing two different views of the same thing: interview with observational data, open with closed questions or one researcher's analysis with another's.

**Analysis of negative cases**    This is the consideration of why certain cases just don't fit the major patterns outlined as a result of analysis. The willingness to do this openly is held to be a validity check. Others can accept the proffered explanation or not, and can call for re-analysis, analyse raw data themselves or attempt some form of replication.

**Repetition of the research cycle**    Qualitative researchers go around the 'research cycle' several times. The researcher checks and re-checks the early assumptions and inferences made. As patterns and theories are developed, so the researcher goes back in again to gather more information which should confirm tentative hypotheses and/or help to further refine, deepen and clarify categories.

**Participant consultation**    Participants are consulted and provide feedback. Qualitative researchers 'at the non-alienating end of the [research] spectrum' (Reason) involve the participants in evaluation of tentative conclusions and refine these in the light of feedback from this process. Reason (1981) makes the point:

> Once we start to do research which does not conform to the general requirements of experimental method, we run the risk of being accused of being mere journalists; indeed we run the risk of *being* mere journalists.

Reason's answer to this criticism is an eloquent argument summarised in the last two safeguards, above. Journalists, he argues, tend to do one round, depart and write fairly impressionistic accounts, with little, if any, feedback process.

## Specialist texts

Burgess (1984) discusses the taking and organising of field notes in great detail. Patton (1980) discusses in depth the content analysis of qualitative data. Potter and Wetherell (1987) include a step-by-step guide to discourse analysis – a highly popular contemporary social psychological approach. Bromley (1986) declared the partial aim of setting out rules of procedure for gathering and analysing case study data.

## Key terms for this chapter

| | |
|---|---|
| Categorising | Negative case analysis |
| Early analysis | Triangulation |
| Grounded theory | |

# PART IV

# Ethics

## Ethical issues in psychological research

# 1 INTRODUCTION

The British Psychological Society (BPS) and the American Psychological Association (APA) have both agreed guidelines on the ethical issues involved in psychological research. The BPS currently has a long statement (1978), covering a wide range of issues, and also a code of conduct (1985) adopted through a postal ballot of all its members. The APA (1987) has a more comprehensive set of ethical principles comprising ten major categories, each with several sub-principles. The general public can bring complaints to the ethics committee who then adjudicate. The psychologist concerned can be reprimanded, dismissed or required to alter behaviour or attend relevant training. This breadth of principles and disciplinary power reflects the far wider application of psychology to the general public as consumers in the USA. Most of the major principles are similar to those which are relevant in the doctor–patient relationship.

One of the APA's major principles deals with research involving human participants and another with animal research. For human research, there are ten sub-principles which are very similar to the categories in the BPS statement, which begins with:

'Psychologists are committed to increasing the understanding that people have of their own and others' behaviour in the belief that this understanding ameliorates the human condition and enhances human dignity.'

The USA ethical principles are prefaced with:

'Psychologists respect the dignity and worth of the individual and strive for the preservation and protection of fundamental human rights. They are committed to increasing knowledge of human behaviour and of people's understanding of themselves and others and to the utilization of such knowledge for the promotion of human welfare.'

Both statements stress the need for an atmosphere of free enquiry in order to generate the widest, most valid body of knowledge. But both also stress that this free atmosphere requires a commitment to responsibility on the part of the psychologist in terms of competence, objectivity and the welfare of research participants.

## 2 PUBLICATION AND ACCESS TO DATA

Before taking a look at the rights and protection of individual participants, we can consider how psychologists are expected to commit themselves to freedom of information.

In general, a psychologist cannot claim to have demonstrated an effect and then withold raw data or information on procedures and samples used. Persons who do this are generally considered to be charlatans. Where psychologists are prepared, as most are, to be completely open with their data, they should still not allow the alleged results of their work to affect people's lives, by policy formulation for instance, before the research community has thoroughly verified, evaluated and replicated results where possible. They should not 'rush to publish'.

There are occasions, in fact, when any scientist may feel that publication of results is potentially harmful or even dangerous. (One is reminded of the persons who first became awfully aware of the horrendous power of the nuclear fission process.) In such cases, the investigator is expected to seek the opinion of 'experienced and disinterested colleagues', an option recommended several times in the BPS statement for various dilemmas.

A significant example of the dangers avoided by these principles is that of Cyril Burt's work on separated identical twins which appeared to show clear evidence of a strong genetic role in human intellectual abilities. The findings played a substantial part in the political debate which produced the British '11-plus' examination and a two (originally three) tier secondary education system, wherein the successful 20% of children passing the exam received a grammar school education. Only after his death did Leon Kamin (1977) establish beyond doubt that Burt's data was inconsistent, to a degree way beyond acceptability and probably fraudulent. Kamin demonstrated that Burt was persistently vague about the exact tests in use and had not made it at all easy to check his raw data. The cult of the 'great expert' had also inhibited investigation of Burt's work by 'lesser' researchers.

Joynson (1989) has recently re-opened this debate, arguing that these accusations are ill-founded and that Burt should be exonerated.

Findings on racial difference (in intelligence or personality, for instance) almost always stir up controversy, which is hardly surprising. For this reason some psychologists have been led to argue that a moratorium should be held on publication. They argue that, since race is always inextricably bound up with culture, most responsible researchers would announce results with great qualification. However, they cannot then stop the lay racist or ignorant reader from using the unqualified information in discriminatory or abusive practices.

Psychologists have also discussed the problem of projective or personality tests being used by the lay selector for jobs or other positions.

They have also argued that professional psychological researchers should exercise integrity over the sources of their funding, increasingly likely to come from industry with an interest in the non-academic use of findings.

# 3  CONFIDENTIALITY AND PRIVACY

Apart from any ethical considerations, there is a purely pragmatic argument for guaranteeing anonymity for participants at all times. If psychologists kept publishing identities along with results, the general public would soon cease to volunteer or agree to research participation.

An investigator can guarantee anonymity or request permission to identify individuals. Such identification may occur, through the use of video recordings as teaching materials for instance, as in Milgram's film *Obedience to Authority*. Research participants who have been seriously deceived have the right to witness destruction of any such records they do not wish to be kept. If records are kept, participants have the right to assume these will be safeguarded and used only by thoroughly briefed research staff. Usually, though, results are made anonymous as early as possible during analysis by using a letter or number instead of a name.

There are very special circumstances where an investigator might contravene the confidentiality rule and these are where there are clear, direct dangers to human life. An investigator conducting participant observation into gang life would have a clear obligation to break confidence where a serious crime was about to be committed. A psychiatric patient's plan to kill himself or a room-mate would be reported. The ethical principles involved here are broader than those involved in conducting scientific research.

The participant obviously has the right to privacy, and procedures should not be planned which directly invade this without warning. Where a procedure is potentially intimate, embarrassing or sensitive, the participant should be clearly reminded of the right to withhold information or participation. Particular care would be required, for instance, where participants are being asked about sexual attitudes or behaviour.

This principle is difficult to follow in the case of covert participant observation, and serious criticism has been levelled at users of this approach on these grounds.

Investigators would usually send a copy of the final research report to all participants, along with a justification of it in terms of its contribution to scientific knowledge and benefit to society in general. This procedure can be difficult where covert observation in a field situation has occurred, and expensive where a survey has used a very large sample.

# 4  MILGRAM – THE CLASSIC EXPERIMENT FOR ETHICAL DEBATE

Any discussion of ethical principles in psychological research inevitably throws up Milgram's work fairly early on in the proceedings. Several ethical issues are involved in this study so let me just describe it briefly and then ask you to think about what these issues are. Almost certainly you will have already heard about the experiment and fuller details are given in, for instance, Gross (1987).

> Volunteers were introduced to another 'participant' who was actually an experimental confederate. The volunteer became a 'teacher' who was asked to administer electric shocks, increasing by 15 volts for each mistake made by the confederate. 375 volts was described as 'Danger: severe shock'. A tape recording of screams and refusals deceived the teacher–participant into believing the confederate was experiencing great pain and wished to end the session. The teacher–participant was pressured into continuing by 'prods' from the experimenter such as 'The experiment requires that you continue' and 'You have no choice but to go on'. To Milgram's surprise, 65% of participants delivered shocks to the end of the scale (450 volts) even though the confederate had ceased responding at 315 volts. Milgram had consulted 'experienced and disinterested colleagues' – psychiatrists predicted that no more than 0.1% would obey to the end. The teacher–participant often displayed extreme anxiety. One even suffered a seizure. An observer wrote:

> 'I observed a mature and initially poised businessman enter the laboratory smiling and confident. Within 20 minutes he was reduced to a twitching, stuttering wreck, who was rapidly approaching a point of nervous collapse. He constantly pulled at his ear lobe and twisted his hands. At one point he pushed his fist into his forehead and muttered, 'Oh God, let's stop it.'
>
> Milgram (1974)

The results of this experiment were used to argue that many ordinary people are capable of behaving in a manner, under pressure, which is retrospectively considered cruel. Atrocities are not necessarily carried out by purely evil persons.

> List the aspects of this experiment which you consider to be unethical. Should the research have been carried out at all? Do the ends (scientific and surprising knowledge) justify the means?

# 5 DECEPTION

Milgram's participants were quite grossly deceived. Not only did they believe they were shocking an innocent victim and that the victim suffered terribly, but also the whole purpose of the research was completely distorted as concerning the effects of punishment on learning.

Deception is exceedingly common in psychology experiments. Menges (1973) reviewed about 1000 American studies and found that 80% involved giving participants less than complete information. In only 3% of studies were participants given complete information about the independent variable, and information about the dependent variable was incomplete in 75% of cases.

Some of this deception seems fairly innocuous. Some participants are told a baby is male, others that it is female, and their descriptions of it are compared. Participants performing a sensori-motor task, where the true aim is to record the effect of an observer on performance, are told that the observer is present to note details of the skilled behaviour involved. Children are told not to play with a toy because it belongs to another child who is next door. Students are told their experimental rats are 'bright'. Even the use of placebos is a deception.

Some deception is more serious. Participants have been told that test results demonstrate that they are poorly adjusted. Female participants are given feedback that they are considered attractive or unattractive by the men who will later interview them. Bramel (1962) gave male participants false feedback about their emotional reaction to photographs of men such that their responses seemed homosexually related. Participants in Latané and Darley's (1976) experiments thought they were overhearing an authentic epilectic seizure. The dependent variable was the speed or occurrence of reporting the seizure.

So what can the investigator do if deception has been used?

# 6 DEBRIEFING

In all research studies, the investigator has a responsibility to DEBRIEF each participant. The true purpose and aims of the study are revealed and every attempt is made to ensure that participants feel the same about themselves when they leave as they did when they arrived. Where participants have been seriously deceived, this responsibility must obviously be taken very seriously and quite some time may need to be spent in reassuring them. The debriefing itself may have to involve a little more deception, as when children are told they 'did very well indeed' whatever the actual standard of their performance and when any suspicion that a participant really is 'poorly adjusted' is not communicated to them.

Applying this to Milgram's experiments, participants who went to the end of the scale were told that some people did this quite gleefully, in order that they could then compare their own unwillingness to proceed, along with their felt anxiety, fairly favourably. (Milgram has never reported that any participant *did* proceed at all happily). However, at least 26 out of 40 participants knew, when they left, that they were capable, under pressure, of inflicting extreme pain, if not death, on an innocent human being. It seems hardly possible that these people left the laboratory feeling the same about themselves as before they entered. In Asch's (1956) classic paradigm too, participants find they have 'conformed' to silly answers to simple problems because a group of confederates gave the answers first. These participants also exhibited great anxiety during the experimental sessions.

## Does debriefing work?

Milgram sent a questionnaire to his participants after the study and 84% said they were glad to have participated, whereas only 1% regretted being involved, the remainder reporting neutral feelings. 80% believed more research like Milgram's should be carried out. 75% found the experience meaningful and self-enlightening.

Some writers discounted this broad range of appreciative and illuminating comments as an attempt by Milgram to justify an ethically unacceptable study. Ring *et al.* (1970) decided to evaluate the consequences to the participant in a study which, even though the investigators were critical of Milgram, not only included the deceptions of the original study but also used a dishonest primary debriefing before a second honest one. They showed that an initial, superficial debriefing dramatically reduces any negative participant evaluation of the research. However, they also found that one third of participants reported residual anger and disappointment with themselves even after the second, complete debriefing.

The fact that even a few participants feel quite negative about themselves well after the experiment, and that many participants felt extremely upset during it, has led many researchers to the position that deception and stress this extreme are ethically unacceptable.

Besides the question of ethics, it is unwise of investigators to indulge in a great deal of deception. Students very often suspect that the manifest structure and explanation of a study in which they participate is false. Ring found that 50% of their participants claimed they would be more wary and suspicious of psychology experiments in the future.

As Reason and Rowan (1981) put it 'Good research means never having to say you are sorry.'

### If you won't deceive, what can you do?

Several investigators, finding gross deception at the Asch or Milgram level quite unacceptable, have turned to role-play or simulation. A description of successful findings by Mixon, (1974) who used the heading above for his title, is given in chapter 7.

Ring was among the advocates of role-playing whereas Aronson and Carlsmith (1968) argued that essential realism would be lost. Horowitz and Rothschild (1970) conducted a replication of Asch's design using a 'forewarned' group, who were told that the experiment was a fake but were asked to play the part of a naïve participant, and a 'pre-briefed' group who knew the experimental aim in detail. The forewarned group 'conformed' at a similar level to the traditionally deceived group, whereas the fully informed group did not conform at all.

These participants seemed to behave in accordance with what most people believe would actually occur in the Asch set up. This is, after all, why Asch's study is so renowned, gripping and well recalled by the psychology student. It defies common sense. The prognosis for role-play, on this evidence, in demonstrating such counter-intuitive effects, therefore, seems not so good. However, the capacity in normal students during role-play for aggressive authoritarianism and subservience, was demonstrated convincingly and against prediction in Zimbardo's classic study described briefly below.

This does not mean that deception of the Milgram intensity is therefore ethically acceptable. Both the BPS and the APA ask that the uncertain investigator seek opinion, again, from those 'experienced and disinterested colleagues' who are not fervently committed to the investigator's desire to confirm theory with the particular hypothesis to be tested.

## 7  STRESS AND DISCOMFORT

There is no argument against the principle that psychological investigators should guarantee the safety of their participants and that everything possible should be done to protect them from harm or discomfort. The difficulty comes in trying to decide what kind of stress or discomfort, physical or mental, is unacceptable. Humanists and others might argue that *any* traditional experimental research on 'subjects' is an affront to human dignity. At a lesser extreme, those who see value in the human experimental procedure have nevertheless criticised some investigators for going too far.

## Mental stress

Examples of studies involving a possibly substantial degree of mental stress were given above. These involved deterioration of a person's self-image or the strain of feeling responsible for action (Latané and Darley). A further example, causing some dissent, is that in which a child was asked to guard the experimenter's pet hamster, which was removed from its cage through a hole in the floor when the child wasn't looking.

But not all mental stress necessitates deception. Participants may be exposed to pornographic or violent film sequences. Extreme psychological discomfort, in the form of delusions and hallucinations, was experienced by participants undergoing 'sensory deprivation' (deprived of sound, touch and sight) such that they often terminated the experience after three days. Zimbardo's (1972) simulation of authority and obedience had to be stopped after six days of the 14 it was supposed to run. Students played the part of aggressive, sadistic and brutal prison guards far too well. Their 'prisoners' (other students) became extremely passive and dependent. Within two days, and on the next few, participants had to be released, since they were exhibiting signs of severe emotional and psychological disorder (uncontrollable crying and screaming) and one even developed a nervous rash.

There is an obligation for investigators, not only to debrief, but also to attempt to remove even long-term negative effects of psychological research procedures. 40 of Milgram's participants were examined, one year after the experiment, by a psychiatrist who reported that no participant had been harmed psychologically by their experience.

## Physical discomfort

Many psychological experiments have manipulated the variables of, for instance, electric shock, extreme noise level, food and sleep deprivation, anxiety or nausea producing drugs and so on.

Watson and Rayner (1920), as is well known, caused 'Little Albert', a young infant, to exhibit anxiety towards a white rat he had previously fondled quite happily, by producing a loud disturbing noise whenever he did so. Apparently Albert even became wary of other furry white objects.

This procedure developed into that of 'aversive conditioning'. Where this is used in the practice of psychotherapy, to rid willing clients of unwanted or destructive behaviour, its use may be justified on the grounds of overall benefit to the client. Where the use is purely for academic research, enhanced knowledge must be weighed against participant discomfort.

Once again, the investigator is expected to seek opinions from professional colleagues. Should the research go ahead, an investigator has to accept another set of responsibilities, which follow.

# 8  THE RIGHT TO NON-PARTICIPATION

The investigator is obliged to:

1 Give the participant full information as to the likely level of discomfort and to emphasise the voluntary nature of the exercise and right to withdraw at any time.

2 Remind the participant of this right to withdraw at any point in the procedure where discomfort appears to be higher than anticipated.

3 Terminate the procedure where discomfort levels are substantially higher than anticipated and/or the participant is obviously disturbed to an unacceptable level.

Now we can see one of the most objectionable aspects of Milgram's study. His experimenter flagrantly contravened all three of these principles. The duty to respect the participant's right to withdraw and to remind the participant of this right are both stressed by the APA. Yet, contrary to this, each participant wishing to stop was commanded to continue in the interests of the research programme. Continuance was 'absolutely essential' and the participant had 'no choice but to go on'. The APA even stresses special vigilance when the investigator is in a position of power over the participant. This was, of course, the very position forcefully exploited in the Milgram study.

It is usual to obtain the informed consent of research participants. As we shall see below, this isn't actually always possible before the research is conducted, though for laboratory experiments consent can always be obtained. In research with children, the informed consent of parents must first be obtained. For obvious reasons, children cannot be subject to great stress, even in the unlikely instance that parents agree (though there was little Albert).

Two factors working against informed consent are the investigator's need to deceive on some occasions, and the significant power attaching to the investigator *role*.

## 9   THE SPECIAL POWER OF THE INVESTIGATOR

In general, then, the investigator is obliged to give the participant every chance not to participate, both before and during the experimental procedure. Working against this, as we have just said, is the position of influence, prestige and power of the investigator. Torbert (1981) says:

'. . . the unilaterally controlled research context is itself only one particular kind of social context and a politically authoritarian context at that. It should not be surprising that some of its most spectacularly well-conceived findings concern persons' responses to authoritarianism.'

An additional dimension to this power emerges when we consider the common position of the United States psychology undergraduates who often face an obligatory participation in a research project of their choice. In some cases an exemption is offered but it costs one additional term paper, making the choice more apparent than real.

A further issue for ethical concern has been the practice of obtaining prison inmates or psychiatric patients for stressful experimental studies, where inducements, such as a pack of cigarettes or temporary release from daily routines, are minimal and would not normally 'buy' participation outside the particular institution.

## 10   INVOLUNTARY PARTICIPATION

In participant observation studies, and in naturalistic (covert) observation, the persons observed are quite often unaware of their participation. This seems fairly unobjectionable where completely unobtrusive observation is made and each observee is just one in a frequency count; for instance, when drivers are observed in order to determine whether more males or more females stop at a 'stop' road sign.

In participant observation people's private lives may be invaded. Humphreys (1970) investigated the behaviour of consenting homosexuals by acting as a public washroom 'lookout'. Persons observed were completely unaware of the study and of the fact that their car registration numbers were recorded in order to obtain more background information later on.

Some field studies carried out in the public arena involve manipulations which interfere with people's lives. A street survey obviously delays each respondent but here consent is always sought first. In Piliavin *et al.*'s (1969) studies on bystander intervention, a person looking either lame or drunk 'collapsed' in a subway train. In one version the actor bit a capsule which produced a blood-like trickle on his chin. Predictably, the 'lame' person got more help than the drunk, with the 'blood' condition having a lowering effect on helping. Piliavin's study, in fact, contravenes the principles of openness (no deception), stress avoidance and informed consent before participation.

Doob and Gross (1968) delayed drivers at a traffic light in either a very smart, new car or an older, lower status one. Effects were predictable in that it took drivers longer to honk at the smarter car.

If these results are fairly unsurprising, couldn't willing participants simply be asked to imagine the situation and consider their likely response? Would simulation work here? Doob and Gross used a questionnaire as well, and found no difference between the reports of how long independent samples of students thought it would take them to honk at each car. Oddly, of the 11 students who said they would not honk, all six of those who would not honk at the low status car were male, and all five of those not honking at the high status car were female.

The 'as if' findings were so different from actual behaviour that the defenders of field research seem vindicated in their claim to more realistic data.

# 11 INTERVENTION

Some aspects of brief intervention with naïve participants we have dealt with above. Several studies have involved intervention on a substantial scale but with willing participation. For instance, psychologists have worked with parents and children in the home in an effort to demonstrate the beneficial effects of parental stimulation on the child's learning and intellectual performance. In these studies a control group is necessary for baseline comparison. In hospital experiments with new drugs, trials are halted if success is apparent on the grounds that it would be unethical to withold treatment from the placebo and control groups. Unfortunately, in psychological intervention research, even if success is apparent, there would not usually be the political power and resources to implement the 'treatment' across all disadvantaged families. Ethical issues arise, therefore, in selecting one group for special treatment.

Where intervention occurs for research purposes only, and involves the production of behaviour usually considered socially unacceptable, ethical principles need very careful consideration. Leyens *et al.* (1975), for instance, raised levels of aggression in boys shown a series of violent films. They were observed to be more aggressive in daily activities compared with a control group shown non-violent films. Several other studies have produced the same effect, some with adults. It is quite difficult to see how debriefing alone could leave the boys just where they were before the study began.

# 12 RESEARCH WITH ANIMALS

There is nothing more certain of producing a lively debate among psychology students than the discussion of whether or not it is necessary to experiment on defenceless animals. Many students are far more emotionally outraged about animal research than about some of the more questionable human studies, on the grounds that humans can refuse whereas animals have no such chance.

One cannot deceive animals, though one can fool them. Nor can they give their informal consent, be debriefed or ask for a procedure to be terminated, though only the most callously inhumane experimenter could ignore severe suffering. Animals can, however, be subject to exploitation, extreme levels of physical pain and mental stress.

Many students spend the whole of an essay on ethics discussing the plight of research animals, though Milgram will often be a secondary focus of attention. I don't intend to go through the innumerable examples of animals in pitiful situations in the psychological research laboratory. To list the kinds of situation is enough:

– severe sensory deprivation

– complete to severe social deprivation

– extirpation or lesion of the nervous system or body parts

– use of extremely aversive physical stimuli including electric shock, noise, poisonous or otherwise aversive chemicals, mood or behaviour altering chemicals

– starvation

Why have psychologists found it useful or necessary to use these methods?

**The case FOR animal research**
1 Animals can be used where humans can't. For instance, they can be deprived of their mothers or reared in complete darkness. This point of course completely begs the question of whether such procedures are ethical.

2 Great control can be exerted over variables. Animals can be made to feed, for instance, at precise intervals.

3 The whole process of development can be observed.

4 Several generations can be bred where species have short gestation and maturation periods. This is useful in studying genetic processes.

5 An effect shown or insight gained in animal studies, although not directly applicable to humans, may lead to fresh and fertile theories about human behaviour. Animal studies have contributed ideas to the debate on human adult–infant bonding and maternal separation, for example.

6 Comparisons across the phylogenetic scale are valuable for showing what humans *don't* have or *can't* do – what we have probably evolved away from or out of. Comparison is invaluable in helping us develop a framework for brain

analysis based on evolutionary history. A seemingly useless or mystical piece of the nervous system may serve, or have served, a function disclosed only through the discovery of its current function in another species.

7 At a very elementary, physiological level, animals and humans have things in common. The nature of the synapse, neural connections and firing for instance, are similar among higher primates.

8 Skinner argued that elementary units of learning would also be similar across most higher species. Hence, he mostly used rat and pigeon subjects in his research work, arguing that patterns of stimulus–response contingencies, schedules of reinforcement and so on were generalisable to the world of human behaviour.

**The case AGAINST animal research**    Theorists have argued that too much extrapolation from animal to human has occurred. Here are some reasons why such extrapolation is considered inappropriate.

1 Seligman (1972) has argued the concept of 'preparedness' which implies that some animals are born especially prepared, through evolutionary processes, to learn easily certain behaviour patterns of survival value to the species. Likewise, some patterns are difficult or impossible to learn at all – the animal is 'contra-prepared'. This makes comparison between one species and another hazardous, let alone comparison between human and animal.

2 Kohler (1925) demonstrated in apes what he referred to as 'insight' learning – solving a novel problem with a sudden reorganisation of detail, much like we do when we spontaneously solve one of those annoying match-stick problems. If apes can do what humans certainly can, then the validity of comparing human learning processes with those of the rat seems questionable.

3 The ethologists have shown that quite a lot of behaviour, subject to cultural variation and slow developmental learning in humans, is instinctive in animals, demonstrated as 'fixed action patterns'. Mating preludes and territorial defence are quite rigidly organised in a large number of species yet quite ungeneralised across the breadth of human cultures.

4 The ethologists, among others, have also questioned the validity of demonstrating that animals do abnormal things in the laboratory and have concentrated on behaviour in the natural environment, only testing animals in the laboratory with variations of the stimuli which would be encountered normally outside it.

5 Language, strongly defined in terms of syntax and symbol, appears to be unique to humans. Language is the vehicle for transmission of cultural values, meanings and the individual's social construction of reality. Very much psychological research, consciously or not, assumes these values and meanings as integral to human awareness. The comparison with animals seems at its weakest here.

The points above are all aimed at the rejection of animal research on *practical* grounds. It is argued that such research will not tell us what we want to know. Other arguments take a moral or humanitarian line.

6 Some argue that it is just categorically wrong to inflict pain and suffering on any living creature.

7 A more profound argument is that the experimenter's 'attack' on nature typifies the 'controlling' model of humankind associated with the psychologist as hard, objective, neutral scientist. This image of the scientist is currently rejected, not just by humanist psychologists and many others, but often by scientists in general who wish to project a model of environmental care.

Supporters of the arguments above would argue that kittens need not be deprived of visual experience in order to study the nature–nurture issue in perception. Field studies on children who unfortunately *happen* to have been so deprived would be considered more valid and more ethical. Likewise, monkeys do not need to be deprived of their mothers. Plenty of children have been. The great debate in attachment theory has been over the number and quality of bonds necessary for optimum development and here, monkey studies can hardly help us.

Whatever the rationale for animal studies, or the fierce, impassioned objections, it seems likely they will continue as an adjunct to psychological research, though perhaps not at their earlier intensity.

British research is carried out under guidelines issued by the BPS (1985). In these the following points are made:

- knowledge to be gained must justify procedure; trivial research is not encouraged; alternative methods are

- the smallest possible number of animals should be used

- no members of endangered species should ever be used

- caging, food deprivation, procedures causing discomfort or pain should all be assessed relative to the particular species studied. A procedure relatively mild to one can be damaging to another

- naturalistic studies are preferred to laboratory ones, but animals should be disturbed as little as possible in the wild

- experimenters must be familiar with the technical aspects of anaesthesia, pharmacological compounds and so on; regular post-operative medical checks must be made.

The guidelines also direct the psychologist to the relevant laws under which animal research is conducted and to the need for various licences.

## Conclusion

All in all, it looks difficult to conduct much research at all without running into ethical arguments. Certainly it seems impossible to proceed with anything before considering possible ethical objections. But this is as it should be. Other natural sciences too have their associations and committees for considering social responsibility in scientific research. They argue about the use to which findings might be put or the organisations from whom it would not be prudent to accept sponsorship. They consider the likely impact of their work on society as a whole.

Similarly, psychology has to make these considerations. But, since humans, as individuals in society, are also the focal point of research, it is hardly surprising that psychology, as a research society, has to be far sharper on its toes in spotting malpractice, abuse, thoughtlessness and unprofessionalism. If psychologists prefer not to have people take one step backwards at parties and say things like 'I bet you're testing me' or 'Is this part of an experiment?', they need to constantly reassure the public that some excesses of the past cannot now happen and that deception really *is* only used when necessary.

The humanists and 'new paradigm' researchers appear to have gained the moral high ground on these ethical issues, not just because they put dignity and honesty first, but because they see their collaborative or non-directive methods as the only route to genuine, un-coerced information. As Maslow puts it:

'. . . if you prod at people like things, they won't let you know them.'

Well, what do you think? You'll probably discuss quite heatedly, with co-students or colleagues, the rights and wrongs of conducting some experiments. I can't help feeling that the information from Milgram's work is extremely valuable. It certainly undermined stereotypes I had about whole cultures being inherently cruel. But I also can't help thinking immediately about those participants who went all the way. Can we be so sure we'd be in the 30% who stopped? Not even all these stopped as soon as the victim was clearly in trouble. How would we feel the rest of our lives? Should we inflict such a loss of dignity on others? I haven't made any final decision about this issue, as about many other psychological debates and philosophical dilemmas. Fortunately, I'm not in a position where I have to vote on it. But what do you think . . . ?

### Key terms for this chapter

Debriefing

Deception

Intervention

Invasion of privacy

Involuntary participation

# Appendix 1 Planning practicals and writing reports

---

| A   Planning your practical |
| --- |

If you are going to be devising and running your own practical work in psychology, good luck! It is great fun, and highly satisfying, to be presenting a report of work which is all your own, rather than of a practical which your tutor sets up and sends you all off to do. However, beware! Your tutor almost certainly has a lot of experience in planning such exercises such that you do not waste all your efforts and end up with useless data or find yourself running a project with hopeless snags or a completely inappropriate design.

Below I have jotted down most of the things I can think of which need attention before you start your data gathering. I've almost certainly missed some things but I hope these will be of some help.

*Nothing I've written, however can substitute for very careful planning, preferably in a small group, before you start your data collection.*

Remember that the 'practical' doesn't start when you actually begin running your trials and testing your participants. That is a tiny part of the whole process. There is a large portion of time to spend planning and another large portion to spend analysing and (dare I say it) writing up your report!

I have written these notes with the traditional, 'tight' hypothesis test in mind. Hence there is emphasis on strict definition of variables and thinking about the system of analysis before starting. This obviously runs counter to the tenets of qualitative and 'new paradigm' research. However, most students will find that, through syllabus requirements or other forces, they will need to be familiar with this traditional design. Besides, since the 'old paradigm' is hardly likely to disappear overnight, I believe it is necessary to understand the approach fully in order to understand its weaknesses and to be able to take off in other directions.

The student wishing to conduct something more qualitative in design would need to consult thoroughly with their tutor in order to avoid ending up with a report which is fascinating but is seen as the work of a 'displaced novelist' and mainly anecdotal.

## NOTES ON PLANNING THE PRACTICAL PROJECT

### The overall aim
– Did the idea just pop up in your head? Is it worth checking to see if there is *related theory*? This might give you firmer ideas. You may be working to a syllabus which wants you to 'embed' the research aims in some background

theory. There is nothing wrong in principle, however, in testing a personal idea which came to you unaided. Creativity is encouraging. However, it is likely that there *is* some related work on it, though perhaps hard to find in your college library. You can always phone up or write to other institutions or libraries, however, such as your local polytechnic.

– *Now* is the time to state your hypotheses very carefully, not when you come to write up the report!

## The design

– Do you need to quantify your variables? Can this be done sensibly? How will 'self-concept', for instance, be measured?

– In thinking of variables it will be useful to think about any *statistical analysis* you are going to employ. For instance, if you want to correlate variable A with variable B, *both* must be measurable on at least an ordinal scale. If you said 'I want to see whether sex correlates with fast driving', you can easily measure how fast individuals drive but how will this be related to sex? You can't say 'the faster people drive, the more male they will be' because sex is a *nominal* variable – it only has two values. Therefore you can't correlate, but you can look for differences.

Will you be able to develop a plausible rating scale for your variable(s)? Can people rate a photograph of a face on a scale of one to ten for 'happiness', for example? Using this approach, you will only be able to do a non-parametric test.

If you measure driving ability by whether a driver stops or not, you can only achieve nominal level data. Is that what you want? Similarly, compare asking whether people passed their test first time with asking how long it took them to learn.

– Are you dealing with too many variables to keep statistical analysis simple enough? Say you wanted to see whether introverts improve on a task without an audience, whereas extroverts deteriorate. You'd like to see whether this is more true for males than for females and perhaps whether age has an effect too. Admirable thinking on interacting variables, but the statistical analysis will get very complicated.

– The last example would be very costly on subjects. Could you get enough? In general, will you be able to get enough subjects for your chosen design? Remember, independent samples designs need twice the number of subjects for the same number in each condition as the equivalent repeated measures design. Will you be able to match pairs appropriately? You may not be able to obtain the information you need for this (e.g. social class). If you are going to use repeated measures, with tests on two different occasions, will your subjects all be available second time around?

– Have you got all the control conditions or groups you need? A pair of students once planned a test of the matching hypothesis. They wanted to see whether people tended to pair photos of couples when they didn't know, out of a set of ten men and ten women, who was married to whom. They conducted the test and reported how often each of their subjects had been successful in making a match. It suddenly struck them that this wasn't a test of the hypothesis that 'people tend to marry people physically similar to themselves'. They had no baseline comparison. They got the people to do the matching test again, this time with the pictures face down.

So, will you need a *condition for comparison*? Think of how you will statistically support your hypothesis.

- Is there a likelihood of any obvious confounding variables? If the general public are to be approached by researchers, will it matter that most of them are female? Some students I taught recently were going to say 'hello' to passers-by under two conditions. It struck them that all of them were female and that there could be a differential response from male and female passers by!

- Are conditions *equivalent*? If the experimental group have longer, more intricate instructions and introduction to their task, could this act as a confounding variable? Should the control group get equivalent but 'dummy' introduction and instructions, and/or equivalent time with the experimenters?

## The sample(s)
- Will you have to use the same old 'friends and acquaintances' or students in the college canteen? If so, will they be too much aware of your previous deceptions?

- Will they reveal the nature of the research to naive subjects you still wish to test?

- Even though the sample can't be truly random or representative, can you balance groups for sex, age etc.?

- Should you ask whether they've participated in this before? You can't ask beforehand, in many cases, for instance, when you're showing an illusion. You'll have to ask afterwards and exclude them from the results if they weren't 'naive'.

- If you suspected some participants of 'mucking around' or of already knowing the aim and perhaps trying to 'look good', you'll have to decide, having asked them afterwards, whether it is legitimate to drop their results. You can discuss this with colleagues.

## The materials
- Are they *equivalent* for both conditions? Some other students were doing a version of the Asch 'warm–cold' study. People in one group were shown a set of terms: *intelligent, shy confident, warm, practical, quick, quiet*. The other group were shown the same terms except that '*cold*' was substituted for '*warm*'. The people had to judge other characteristics of the hypothetical person. One student had missed a class and had no '*cold*' forms, so she changed the word 'warm' in ink and photocopied. This gave a not-too-subtle clue to her second group as to what the important word in the set was.
  Can two memory word-lists be equivalent? Can you say that the words in each are equally frequent in normal language use, or that two sets of anagrams are equally hard to solve? You can use *pre-testing* of the materials to settle this question.

- Are instructions to participants *intelligible*?

- Are there too many units in the material? Will it take too long to test all on each participant? Can they be shortened?

- If you want to construct a questionnaire, see chapter 9. Remember, a test of an attitude is often made, not with questions but with statements for people to agree/disagree with or say how it represents their view. Don't say 'Do you believe in abortion/nuclear power/strikes?' These things exist! We want to know what people think about them.

- If you're unsure of the wording in the questionnaire, get the help of someone who's good with language. Respondents will not respect or take seriously a badly-written questionnaire

- In all cases, *pilot*! Try materials out on friends and relatives

It takes many years to train in the psycho-analytic interpretation of projective tests, such as the Rorschach and TAT. Their validity is very much questioned within the academic world. Therefore it would be unwise to attempt to incorporate the use of these instruments in a student practical.

## The procedure
- There may well be several of you going out to gather data. *Make sure you standardise your procedure exactly before you start.* The most common problem I have seen amongst a group of students doing a practical together is that they didn't have a final check that they had all got exactly the same steps of procedure. Don't be shy to ask your friends to do a final check before they rush off after a lot of hurried changes. Don't feel stupid if you don't feel confident about exactly what you have to do. Ask your friends or the tutor where appropriate. It's better to take a little more time, and admit you're not perfect, than to end up with results that can't be used or, worse, having to do things over again.

- Decide what *extra data* is worth recording (sex, age of subjects) because it might show up a relationship which wasn't part of the original hypotheses.

- *Record all the information on the spot.* If you decide to wait till later to record age or occupation of your interviewee, you may well forget. Then the result may be wasted.

- Work out the *exact* instructions to participants. Have a simulated run through with one of you as subject. What have you failed to explain? What else might the subject need/want to know?

- Decide how you will answer questions your participants might ask. Will you have stock answers or will you ask them to wait until after the testing?

- If the study is an observation:
(i)   Will the observations really be unobtrusive? Check out the recording position beforehand.
(ii)  Will recording be easy? Does talking into a tape recorder attract too much attention for instance? Does the coding system work? Is there time and ample space to make written notes?
(iii) Will more than one person make records simultaneously in the interests of reliability?

## Ethics
As a student it is unlikely that you have been trained sufficiently to be able to conduct satisfactory debriefing sessions. Professional research psychologists themselves often argue these days about the adequacy of debriefing in returning people to normal and 'undoing' any psychological harm done. It is also unlikely

that you'll have the time or resources to debrief properly. You almost certainly won't have the finances to send a copy of your report to each of your participants. Therefore it is extremely important that your proposed research project will not involve any of the following:

- invasion of privacy
- causing participants to lose dignity
- causing participants to think less of themselves
- deception which causes resentment or hostility (check that deception is absolutely necessary)
- unnecessary witholding of information
- pain or discomfort
- breaking of local prohibitions (for instance, drinking alcohol on college premises)
- anything at all about which participants feel uncomfortable.

Assure participants that anonymity will be maintained, and *maintain it*! It is discourteous and bad practice even to talk with close colleagues in the project, or very best friends, in a derogatory manner about participants, even if anonymous. It develops an elitist, manipulative approach to people who have tried to help you in your work.

Also assure participants that they will not feel or look stupid, or reveal anything they don't wish to about themselves.

On approaching unknown members of the public, tell them who you are, where you're from and the reason for doing research (part of your required coursework, for instance).

Make sure your tutor and college are happy about your approach to the public, since they will receive any complaints if you use the college name.

If you have any doubts at all discuss the proposal with your tutor and/or another responsible person whose opinions you respect.

NOW HAVE FUN!

## B  Writing your practical report

If you carry out some practical work, you will find yourself faced with the onerous task of writing it all up. My first piece of advice is *don't put it off*! You'll find it much harder to come back to when any enthusiasm you had for the project will have worn off, and you won't be able to understand why certain precautions were taken or just what certain conditions were all about. You'll find essential details of data and analysis are missing and you may need to ask your class colleagues who've now lost their raw data or are too busy to help much.

### What is the purpose of a report?
There are two main purposes, neither of which is to do with keeping your tutor happy. First, you are telling your reader just what you did, why you did it and what you think it adds to the stockpile of knowledge and theory development. Second, you are recording your procedures in enough detail for some of those readers, who are so inclined, to *replicate* your work. We have seen elsewhere why this is so important to scientific method.

Golden rule number one for report writing, then, is:

Make sure you write with enough depth and clarity for a complete stranger to repeat exactly what you did in every detail.

## What are the rules?

There are none. However, your tutor will often act as if there are when commenting on your work. This is because there *are* conventions fairly generally accepted. Most of these make sense and work in the interests of good report organisation and communication between researchers. Have a look at some journals in your college library, if that's possible, or ask to borrow a copy of one volume from a local academic institution. Your tutor may well have copies of old student work, though very often only the poorer work gets left. Why this systematic bias? The Associated Examining Board (now part of the Southern Examining Group) will send examples of marked work. If all else fails, write to me – I'll send you copies of work which was too bulky to include in this book.

What follows, then, is the generally accepted format, around which most articles vary just a bit. Qualitative, inductive work will follow much the same format but will not have a specific hypothesis to test. However, it will have overall aims clearly set out. Another major difference will be that the 'results' section will tend to merge with the discussion. Otherwise, reporting of procedures and evaluation of findings, overall design and method should all be similar.

Box 27 shows a skeleton scheme of the various sections.

*Box 27    Dissection of a practical report*

```
         Title
    Abstract/summary
    Introduction/aims
       Hypotheses
    Method:   Design
              Subjects/Participants
              Materials/Apparatus
              Procedure
    Results:  Description/Summary
              Analysis/Treatment
    Discussion
    Conclusion
    References
    Appendices
```

### The title

This should be as concise as possible. You don't need 'An investigation to see whether . . .' or similar. You just need the main variables. Very often, in an experiment, you can use the IV and DV. For instance, 'The use of imagery and rehearsal methods in recall of verbal material' will adequately describe a (probably familiar) study. For a field investigation using correlation, 'The relationship between age and attitude to environmental issues' says enough.

### Abstract
Also known as the 'summary'. But why on earth does a summary come at the *beginning*? Well, suppose you were interested in whether anyone had done work on your proposed topic: anxiety and jogging behaviour in red-bearded vegetarian East Londoners. As you flip through dozens of journals looking for related work, how much easier it is to see the summary of findings right at the beginning of the article, without having to wade through to the end. The abstract contains the main points of the research report, 'abstracted' from it. Most of this century, volumes have been produced each month called *Psychological Abstracts*, containing only abstracts from articles in a huge variety of research journals. This speeds up the job of finding relevant work. It's a good idea to make your abstracts stand out by being in a different writing form or typestyle.

### Introduction
I like to think of this as a funnel.

Start with the general psychological subject area. Discuss
theory and research work which is relevant to the
research topic. Move from the general area
to the particular hypotheses to be tested
via a coherent and logical argument
as to why the specific predictions
have been made. State
the specific
HYPOTHESIS

If you recall, way back in chapter 1, we went through, very briefly, the reasons why a prediction was made that, when 'image linking' was used, more items from a word list would be recalled than when rehearsal only was used.

The introduction to a study testing this hypothesis need not contain a five-page essay on the psychology of memory, including Ebbinghaus' work and the performance of eye-witnesses in court. The hypothesis test belongs within a specialised area of memory research.

We can move our reader through the introduction in the following steps:

- the concepts of short- and long-term memory stores
- outline of the two-process memory model
- some evidence for the two-process model
- phenomena the model explains, such as primacy and recency in free-recall tasks
- focus in on the model's emphasis on rehearsal as the process by which material is transferred to the long-term store
- introduce the 'cognitive' objection that humans always attempt to construct meaning out of incoming sensory data. Give examples of what this means
- from this theory it follows that an attempt to give an unconnected word list some 'life', by visualising the items and connecting them, should be more successful in storing the information than simple rote repetition of each word

– additional support could be given here, referring to previous similar studies and the work on imagery in the literature.

We have argued through to our specific prediction. It only remains to state the hypothesis in the clearest terms so there can be no doubt over what exactly were the results we expected.

**Stating aims**   One aim of our research is to demonstrate our hypothesis to be valid, using a free recall experiment under two conditions. An overall aim is to challenge the traditional two-store memory model. Aims are what the research project is *for*, what it is supposed to do. In qualitative projects, aims may be far more wide ranging and less specific than those in a hypothesis-testing project. For this reason, particular care would be taken to specify aims at this point in qualitative research.

**The hypothesis**   This must be very precisely stated. It is simply a clear statement of what is expected to happen. It helps here to concentrate on IV and DV again. I stated the hypothesis for the memory experiment in chapter 1. What the hypothesis does not contain is any of the theory about *why* the prediction is made. It does contain variables precisely identified. Fuller definition of variables will follow in the report, such as the precise meaning of 'rating' in exercise 8 of box 28.

> Below, in box 28 I have stated on the left the hypotheses from some of the exercises at the end of chapter 18. I have, however, stated them too loosely. Try to write out your correct, precise version before checking my final versions on the right (cover the right-hand side up!)

*Box 28   Hypotheses from exercises (Chapter 18)*

| **Too loosely/Incorrectly** | **Correctly** |
|---|---|
| Exercise No. | |
| 4 'More people of one sex will avoid the ladder because they are super-stitious' | 'The difference between the number of men and the number of women not walking under the ladder will be significant' |
| 5 Boys of single parents will show less traditonal sex-role sterotyping' | 'Significantly less one-parent boys will report not expecting to do the washing-up when older' |
| 6 'People will perform worse on the sensori-motor task in front of an audience' | 'Subjects will make significantly more errors on the sensori-motor task in front of an audience than when they are alone' |
| 8 'Ratings on attractiveness will be similar for each member of a couple' | 'There will be a significant, positive correla-tion between ratings of male and female partners on attractiveness' |
| 11 'Non-rhyming words are harder to read' | 'Times for reading non-rhyming words will be significantly longer than times for reading rhyming words' |
| 12 'Subjects will improve in their atti-tude to race as a result of the training course' | 'Post-course essay ratings will be significantly higher than pre-course ratings' |

**The null hypothesis**    The research hypothesis is often given the symbol $H_1$ and the null hypothesis gets $H_0$. Further hypotheses being tested get numbered logically, $H_2$, $H_3$ etc., each with their accompanying $H_0$. The null hypothesis gets stated directly after each hypothesis.

## The method
It is customary and convenient, but not absolutely necessary, to break the method used down into the following four sub-headings. Materials and procedure may often be one heading.

**Design**    This describes the 'skeleton' outline of the study – its basic framework. For instance, is it an experiment or not? If it is, what design is used (repeated measures, etc.)? What conditions are there, and how many groups are used? What is the purpose of each group (control, placebo etc.)? How many subjects are in each group (though this information can go in the 'subjects' section below)? In many cases, describing the groups will be a way of describing the independent variable. In any case, both the IV and DV should be outlined here.

What controls have been employed? Is there counterbalancing and, if so, of what form?

In our experiment on imagery and rehearsal, we could say 'we used a repeated measures design with one group of 15 subjects who were presented with a 20-item word list in two conditions, one with instructions only to rehearse each item, the other with instructions to use image-linking. Order of taking conditions was reversed for half the subjects. The dependent variable was number of items recalled under free recall conditions.' . . . and that's about enough.

You don't need to ,ive any details of procedure or materials used, otherwise you'll find yourself laboriously repeating yourself later on.

If the study is non-experimental, its overall approach (e.g. observational) can be stated along with design structures such as longitudinal, cross-sectional etc. Again there may be (uncontrolled) IV and DV, for instance sex and stopping at an amber traffic light. Controls, such as measures of inter-observer reliability, may have been incorporated. Don't mention details here, just that the control was employed.

**Subjects/Participants**    Give numbers, including how many in each group, and other details relevant to the study. If someone wishes to replicate your findings about 'adolescents' and their self-concepts, it is important for them to know exactly what ages and sex your subjects were. These variables are less important in technical laboratory tasks, though general age range is usually useful and handedness may be relevant. Other variables, such as social class or occupation might be highly relevant for some research topics. Certainly important is how naive to psychology subjects were. Otherwise, keep details to a minimum.

How were subjects obtained? How were they allocated to the various experimental groups (if not covered in your 'design')?

**Materials/Apparatus**    Again, apply the golden rule. Give enough detail for a proper replication to be possible. This means giving specifications of constructed equipment (finger-maze, illusion box) and source (manufacturer, make, model) of commercial items (tachistoscope, computer). Exact details of all written materials should be given here or in an appendix, including: word lists, questionnaires, lists subjects had to choose from, pictures and so on. You *don't* need to give details of blank paper or pencils!

In our memory study we would need two lists of words because we can't have people learning the same list twice without a mammoth confounding variable. We would state in this section how we justify our two lists being equivalent – selected from word frequency list, same number of concrete and abstract terms, etc.

It may be useful to include a diagram or photo of an experimental set-up or seating arrangements.

**Procedure**    The rule here is simple. Describe exactly what happened from start to finish of testing. This must be enough for good replication. Any standardised instructions should be included here or in an appendix, including any standard answers to predicted subject questions.

The exact wording used in training subjects to use imagery in our memory experiment should be included, together with any practice trials and words used for these.

It is very tempting to 'skim' the materials and procedure sections and give far too little detail. My advice if you're not sure you've written enough is:

## GIVE IT TO A FRIEND/RELATIVE TO READ!

If your mother or boyfriend can understand exactly what happened, then it's clear and enough. (They might not get on too well with the other sections without some psychological knowledge).

### Results

**Description**    Large amounts of raw data go in an appendix. A summary table of these is presented in the results section, including frequencies, means, standard deviations or their equivalents. Any tables (appearing here *or* in the appendix) should be well headed. For instance, a table for our experiment starting like table

*Table 59   Incorrect experimental results table*

| Subject | Imagery | Rehearsal |
|---------|---------|-----------|
| 1 | 12 | 8 |
| 2 | 15 | 12 |
| etc. | etc. | etc. |
| : | : | : |

59 is inadequate. What do the numbers stand for? We need a heading 'Number of words recalled in the stated condition'. If results are times, state 'seconds' or 'minutes'; if they are distance measurements, state the units.

You might wish to present a graphical representation of your data, such as a histogram or scattergram. Make sure these are clearly headed too, and that the vertical and horizontal axes have titles.

Tables and charts will need numbering for reference purposes.

**Analysis or treatment**    If there are several hypotheses to test, or different treatments, take one at a time and divide this section into sub-sections ((a), (b), etc.) with a heading for each one stating what is being tested.

State which statistical test is being applied and *justify* this using the decision procedures outlined in chapter 18.

State the result clearly and compare this with the appropriate critical value. Justify the choice of this critical value including $N$ or degrees of freedom, number of tails, and the corresponding level of probability ('$p < . . .$'). Box 29 is a quick exercise in noting what can be missing from statements of significance.

*Box 29  Incomplete significance statements*

| Statements | What's missing? |
| --- | --- |
| 'The *t*-test showed that differences were significant' | At what level? How many degrees of freedom? How many tails? |
| 'There was a strong correlation between the two variables' | But was it significant, and at what level? Was the correlation positive or negative? Was the prediction one- or two-tailed? |
| 'There was a significant difference between the two conditions at the 1% level' | How many degrees of freedom? How many tails? |

State whether the null hypothesis is being rejected or retained.

Calculations of your tests, if you wish to include them, should appear only in the appendix. Many calculations these days will be performed by computer or dedicated calculator. The software used, and intermediary results, can be mentioned in an appendix.

If there are a number of test results, these could be presented in a clear summary table.

### Discussion

The first step here is to explain in non-statistical language just what has happened in the results section. These results must then be related to the hypotheses you set out to test, and to the original aims of the research. These in turn are then related to the background theory, showing support or a need to modify theory in the light of contradictory or ambiguous findings.

Unexpected findings or 'quirks' in the results can also be discussed as a secondary issue. From time to time, such 'oddities' lead to novel research directions. You can try to offer some explanations of these if you have good reasons.

**Evaluating the method**   The conscientious researcher always evaluates the design and method, picking out flaws and areas of weakness. This isn't just to nit-pick. A reader of the report might well come back and accuse the researcher of not considering such weaknesses. The researcher can forestall such criticism by presenting a good argument as to why the weakness should not have serious effect.

The emphasis of the evaluation depends partly on the outcome:

If we got the result we expected, we should look carefully at the design for possible confounding variables producing a type one error. If we were predicting that the null hypothesis would be supported, we should look for ways in which the design and procedures may have hidden differences or relationships.

If we failed to get what we predicted, we should look for sources of random variables (though research with a successful outcome may also have been affected by these). What aspects of the design, procedures and materials used did we find unsatisfactory? There could even be a confounding variable stopping our predicted effect from showing up.

Not everything in an experiment or investigation can be perfect. There is no need to talk about not controlling temperature or background noise unless there is good reason to suppose that variations in these could have seriously affected results. Usually this is quite unlikely.

**Suggest modifications**     Most research leads on to more research. From the considerations made so far you should be able to suggest modifications of this design, or quite new directions, which will follow up on, or check the points made.

### Conclusion

Part of the 'lore' of people teaching psychology is that the main report should end with a conclusion containing a summary of the main statistical conclusions. Looking through two recent copies of *The British Journal of Psychology*, I find that no one does this. There is no section called 'Conclusion', even though there is sometimes one called 'Final Comment'. This is probably the best thing to do – make some summarising comment in terms of overall findings, their relationship to the relevant model or theory and implications for the future. Avoid repeating the abstract or the beginning of your discussion, however. A statistical (verbal) summary may be useful where several tests in the results analysis were talked about one by one in the discussion.

It is worth pointing out that actual journal articles never show calculations or include raw data and rarely justify the statistical test chosen. However, this information is always available through private correspondence. Students doing practical work are usually asked to substitute for the real life situation by including these with their reports.

### References

This is one of the most tedious aspects of writing a report, especially if you've referred to a lot of different research in your work. There is also often a lot of confusion over what exactly counts as a reference, what should be included.

> Golden rule number 2 is:
>
> If you referred to it directly somewhere in your text, include it. If you didn't refer to it, don't include it!

If you wrote, '. . . Gross (1987) argues that . . .', this *is* a reference. The date means you're telling the reader where you got the information from. If you happened to read Gross' textbook whilst preparing your practical or trying to write it up – it may be where you got Bower (1977) from, for instance – then this will *not* be a reference (but Bower will be, if you included it). If you want to tell your reader what you read but didn't specifically refer to in your text, put these titles under 'Bibliography' if you like. In other words, your 'references' are what your text refers to, not what you read in total.

Write references in the way they appear at the back of this book. Notice that *journal articles* have the journal title in italics, underlined or bold. The article is in ordinary print. For *books* the book title gets special treatment. There can be a few awkward ones which were articles in someone else's collection of articles, government reports and so on.

## Appendices

These might contain: calculations, instructions given to subjects, memory list items, questionnaires and so on. These continue your normal page numbering. Separate topics go in separate, numbered appendices ('appendix 1', 'appendix 2', etc.).

## General presentation

It is useful to have page numbering throughout. You might find it convenient to refer to pages in your text.

A title page sets the whole project off well and an index helps the reader go to specific sections. If you have presented a set of projects together, it might help to begin the whole set with an index and to have a 'header' on each page telling the reader what particular practical we're in.

# CHECKLIST FOR WRITING A PRACTICAL REPORT

(Note: some of these points will not apply to non-experimental or qualitative work)

TITLE Does your title give a brief, but clear indication of the content?

CONTENTS Have you numbered every page?
Have you included a contents page listing main sections of the report?

ABSTRACT/SUMMARY Does your summary cover the aims, IV, DV, subjects, design, measures and principle (statistical) conclusions of the research project?
Does it convey a brief, essential impression of the research in less than 200 words?

INTRODUCTION Have you given a brief general overview of the issues and concepts that are relevant to the topic which places the research in context?
Is there an account of similar or related studies?
Have you explained why your study was undertaken?
Have you explained the main aims of the investigation?
Are hypotheses (if any), including null, clearly stated in a straight-forward, predictive form?

METHOD Will your readers have enough detail to repeat the study exactly as you did it?
Have you chosen a suitable set of sub-headings which organise the information clearly?

DESIGN Have you stated the main design form (field observation, repeated measures experiment, etc.)?
Have you explained briefly why this design was selected?
Have you explained the purpose of the different groups and given numbers in each?
Have you identified the IV and DV and described conditions?
Have you listed controls introduced ('blinds', counterbalancing).

SUBJECTS/PARTICIPANTS Is it clear who they were and how they were chosen or obtained?
Have you provided any additional information which may be relevant to the research (age, sex, first language, naïvety)?

MATERIALS/APPARATUS Have you described these in sufficient detail for replication?

Have you made use, where necessary, of drawings and diagrams?

Have you described any technical apparatus?

Have you included word lists, questionnaires etc?

**PROCEDURE** Have you explained, in sequence, exactly what the experimenter/researcher did and what each subject experienced?

Have you reported in full any important instructions given to subjects? (Copies in appendix.)

Have you given a clear impression of the layout and arrangement of events?

**RESULTS** Is there a summary table of results giving totals, means, standard deviations or their equivalents?

Are lengthy, raw data in an appendix?

Have you exploited opportunities for visual presentation?

Are all tables, graphs and charts fully and clearly labelled and numbered?

Have you given each a title and are units clearly shown?

**ANALYSIS/TREATMENT** Have you explained and justified your choice of statistical test for analysis?

Have you listed the results of the tests, their significance, the degrees of freedom, number of tails?

Are calculations in the appendix, or an explanation of how they were done (e.g. computer)?

Are statements made about rejection or not of each null hypothesis?

**DISCUSSION** Is there a verbal (not statistical) description of results?

Do you explain how the results relate to your hypotheses and any background theory or prior research?

Can you explain any unexpected results?

Have you evaluated the design and procedures used?

Have you considered alternative explanations of results?

Have you suggested modifications, extensions or new research to deal with these last three points?

**REFERENCES** Have you listed *all* the studies which you referred to (with a date in brackets) in your text?

Have you used the standard format for references? i.e. last name, initials (date) *book title*. Place published: publisher *or* last name, initials (date). Article title, *journal title*, Vol, pp.

**APPENDICES** Have you labelled each appendix clearly?

Do the appendices continue the page numbering?

Are the appendices included on your contents page and referred to at appropriate points in the text?

# *Appendix 2 Structured Questions*

The following structured questions will give the reader practice in answering exam-type questions whilst noting that marks available indicate where longer answers are required.

## QUESTION 1

A group of 20 five-year-old children on one housing estate have attended a special early-years education project since they were three years old. At the time their parents volunteered for the programme, a control group of 20 children was found by selecting every tenth family from a list of the 200 other families on the estate. The two groups were fairly similar in intelligence at the start of the project. The researchers predict that, among other things, the IQ scores of the project group will be higher than that of the control group. The IQ of the two groups at age five, is measured using a standardised test. The mean of all 40 children is 100. The following results are found:

|  | Special project children | Control group children |
|---|---|---|
| Above Mean | 16 | 12 |
| Below Mean | 4 | 8 |

**Questions**

|  | *Marks* |
|---|---|
| 1 What is the independent variable in this study? | 1 |
| 2 What is the purpose of the control group? | 2 |
| 3 Has the control group been randomly selected? Give reasons for your answer. | 2 |
| 4 In what way do the two groups differ, other than being in the project or not? Why is this important? | 2 |
| 5 At what level of measurement are the data in the table? | 1 |
| 6 What statistical test would be appropriate for deciding whether the experimental group are significantly higher in IQ? Give reasons for choosing this test. | 3 |
| 7 When would it be unwise to use the statistical test you have chosen? | 2 |

8 If we knew the individual IQ score for each child,

(a) what statistical test might then be more appropriate?    1
(b) why would this test be preferable?    2

9 The researchers decide to reject their null hypothesis after analysing
the results. What does this statement mean?    1

10 If the researchers had made a 'type one error' what would this mean?    1

11 (a) What is meant by a test being 'reliable'?
(b) Describe how the IQ test would have been standardised.    3

12 What variables, other than the project itself, might be responsible for
the experimental group's higher IQ?    2

13 What ethical considerations might be made before publishing the
results of this research?    2

# QUESTION 2

The same group of nine children are given an IQ test at ages three, nine and 15
years. The children were selected at random from all children attending a local
playgroup who were likely to remain in the area for the duration of the study.
    The researcher believed that IQ is a relatively stable factor across development.

The correlation between the children's IQ values at ages three and nine is
0.41.
The correlation between the children's IQ values at ages nine and 15 is
0.78.

## Questions

*Marks*

1 Name two important features of the design used in this study.    2

2 Give one disadvantage for each of the features you have mentioned
in question 1.    2

3 State one source of bias in the sample selected.    1

4 Why is it important for the children to stay in the same area, apart
from convenience to the researcher?    1

5 The researcher tests all the children herself. Why might this introduce
a constant error in the results? How might this be easily avoided?    2

6 On the diagrams below, show *roughly* the shapes you would expect
to be produced by:

(a) the scattergram for 0.78    1
(b) a correlation of $-0.95$    1

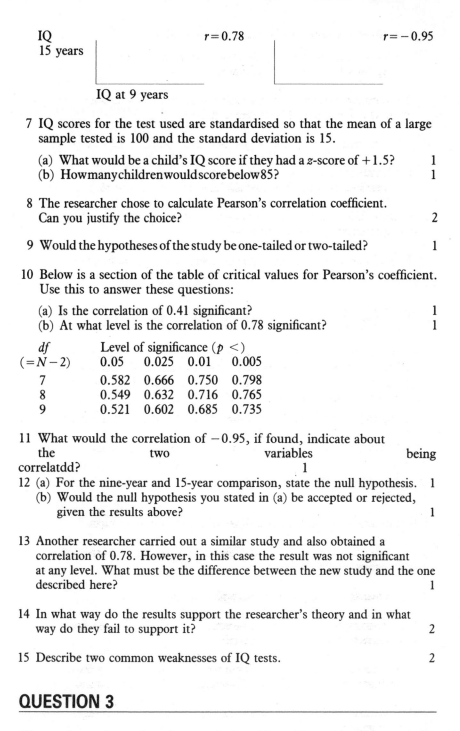

IQ
15 years          $r = 0.78$                    $r = -0.95$

IQ at 9 years

7 IQ scores for the test used are standardised so that the mean of a large
  sample tested is 100 and the standard deviation is 15.

  (a) What would be a child's IQ score if they had a $z$-score of $+1.5$?      1
  (b) How many children would score below 85?      1

8 The researcher chose to calculate Pearson's correlation coefficient.
  Can you justify the choice?      2

9 Would the hypotheses of the study be one-tailed or two-tailed?      1

10 Below is a section of the table of critical values for Pearson's coefficient.
   Use this to answer these questions:

   (a) Is the correlation of 0.41 significant?      1
   (b) At what level is the correlation of 0.78 significant?      1

| $df$ ($=N-2$) | Level of significance ($p <$) | | | |
|---|---|---|---|---|
| | 0.05 | 0.025 | 0.01 | 0.005 |
| 7 | 0.582 | 0.666 | 0.750 | 0.798 |
| 8 | 0.549 | 0.632 | 0.716 | 0.765 |
| 9 | 0.521 | 0.602 | 0.685 | 0.735 |

11 What would the correlation of $-0.95$, if found, indicate about
   the                          two                          variables                          being
correlatdd?                                                1
12 (a) For the nine-year and 15-year comparison, state the null hypothesis.   1
   (b) Would the null hypothesis you stated in (a) be accepted or rejected,
       given the results above?      1

13 Another researcher carried out a similar study and also obtained a
   correlation of 0.78. However, in this case the result was not significant
   at any level. What must be the difference between the new study and the one
   described here?      1

14 In what way do the results support the researcher's theory and in what
   way do they fail to support it?      2

15 Describe two common weaknesses of IQ tests.      2

## QUESTION 3

An experiment is conducted on a single subject. The subject has to decide
whether a word, when it appears on a specially devised screen, is a real word or a
nonsense word. Presentation is arranged such that, on each trial, the word

appears either only in the left visual field or only in the right. The subject cannot predict, on each trial, which side the word will occur.

From past research it is predicted that words appearing to the right will be recognised faster since they go directly to the left ('language specialised') brain hemisphere.

Recognition speed is measured by having the subject press a reaction timing switch when the word has been judged real or not. If an error is made an extra trial is given.

The results, over many trials, form a positively skewed distribution. Differences are significant at 5%, but times for words appearing to the left are faster.

## Questions

Marks

1 Give two advantages and two disadvantages of using a single subject design such as this one.    4

2 What are the independent and dependent variables?    2

3 What should the researcher take into account when choosing the real and nonsense words for stimulus display?    2

4 Can you think of a reason for giving an extra trial each time the subject makes an incorrect judgement?    1

5 (a) Why are the trials presented in a random order?
  (b) How could a random order be selected?    2

6 At what level of measurement (nominal/ordinal/interval/ratio) would a set of reaction times be?    1

7 The researcher would like to conduct a parametric test but finally decides not to. Why might this be?    1

8 Which non-parametric test would be used?    1

9 Roughly sketch a positively skewed distribution and mark on it where the mean and median of the scores would fall.    2

10 It is found that, for this subject, times for words appearing to the left are significantly faster than for those appearing to the right.

  (a) What might explain this subject's times going contrary to prediction?
  (b) What should happen to the null hypothesis?    3

11 This odd result causes the researcher to form a new hypothesis which runs contrary to established research theory in this area. What significance level should be set for the new hypothesis test?    1

12 For the new hypothesis the researcher tests two groups, one in each condition.

    (a) What type of design is this?
    (b) Give one advantage and one disadvantage of this design.
    (c) What can be done to deal with the disadvantage you have stated in (b)?          5

# QUESTION 4

A psychologist carries out research in two teaching departments of a college. The departments are of roughly equal size, one specialising in catering subjects and the other in social work. The catering department is run on fairly traditional leadership lines, where the Head of Department takes all major decisions and consults with her senior staff who pass on management decisions to more junior lecturers. The social work department is organised into small team units which take responsibility for quite major decisions within their area of work.

The researcher is interested in job satisfaction and staff–management relationships. She uses the following methods:

– Unstructured interview with each member of staff
– A structured questionnaire on job satisfaction (top score = 50, lowest score = 0). Internal split-half reliability is measured at 0.86.
– A week of participant observation in each department (she does a small amount of teaching for each department, but members of staff know her true purpose).

The researcher finds that there is no significant difference in job satisfaction between departments shown by the questionnaire. However, among the more junior lecturers in the social work department she finds there is strong resentment over taking responsibility and she concludes that this is because they do not feel there is adequate reward or recognition for their participation.

## Questions

*Marks*

1 What advantages does the interview have over either of the other two methods?      2

2 What problems of biased responding might the questionnaire produce?      2

3 In what ways might the information from the participant observation method be unique and otherwise unavailable?      2

4 Can you give an alternative reason for the lecturers' resentment?      2

5 What level of measurement would the questionnaire scores best be taken as – nominal, ordinal or interval?      1

6 What is meant by 'internal reliability'?      2

7 Describe how the questionnaire has been tested for split-half internal reliability.      2

8  What sort of statistical test has produced the value of 0.86?                                              1

9  What does the value of 0.86 tell you about the reliability of this questionnaire?                          1

10 What other information would you need in order to decide whether this correlation value is significant?    1

11 What is the difference between the strength and significance of a correlation coefficient?                 2

12 How could the researcher's conclusions about the young lecturers be tested more objectively by further research?   2

13 Why might the questionnaires not have shown up the feelings of resentment?                                 2

14 What sort of ethical issues will the researcher face in publishing the results of her research?            3

# QUESTION 5

15 volunteer subjects are given Rorschach ink blot tests. These are abstract patterns which subjects are asked to look at. They are asked to report on what the shapes look like to them. Their responses are analysed for aggressive content by trained raters whose final rating score is on a scale from one to 25.

The subjects are then given tasks which are impossible to complete. This is intended to create frustration and increase aggression.

The Rorschach tests and ratings for aggression are then repeated and 'post-treatment' scores are obtained.

Differences between pre- and post-treatment scores are significant at the 5% level.

## Questions

*Marks*

1  In what way could this sample be biased?                                                                   1

2  (a) What are 'demand' characteristics?
   (b) Make a brief comment on ways in which demand characteristics might occur in this study                 3

3  One rater's scores for each subject are compared with another rater's. What sort of check is being carried out here?    2

4  What kind of statistical test would be used to compare the two raters' scores?                             1

5  A colleague of the researcher's argues that a confounding variable might be responsible for the change in aggression scores. It is argued that the scores might have risen even without the frustration.

(a) What exactly is a confounding variable?
(b) How could the researcher improve the design in order to deal
with the colleague's point?                                              3

6 The rating scale is not considered sensitive enough to count as interval
level data. What level would it be treated as?                           1

7 What statistical test would be performed to establish that the pre- and
post-treatment scores are significantly different?                       1

8 (a) State the hypothesis in this study.
(b) Is this hypothesis one- or two-tailed?                               2

9 What is the probability that this researcher has made a type one error? 1

10 Describe two main weaknesses of *unstructured* and *disguised* tests like
the Rorschach.                                                           4

11 Outline another method by which aggression could have been assessed.   3

12 (a) What is an 'operational definition'?
(b) What is the researcher's operational definition of 'aggression' in
this study?                                                              3

# QUESTION 6

One group of ten subjects is asked to solve two sets of six anagrams. One set is of
common words and the other set is of uncommon words. The sets of words for
the anagrams are selected at random from larger sets of frequently and
infrequently occurring words. The two conditions are counterbalanced. The time
taken to solve each anagram was measured by stopwatch and recorded. Results
appear in the table below.

*Table 60   Anagram results*

| Subject | Median solution time (in seconds) for six anagrams | |
|---|---|---|
| | Common words | Uncommon words |
| A | 14 | 27 |
| B | 23 | 85 |
| C | 35 | 32 |
| E | 27 | 130 |
| F | 5 | 13 |
| G | 25 | 60 |
| H | 32 | 125 |
| I | 17 | 33 |
| J | 21 | 28 |

The researcher argues that when people solve anagrams they actively generate words which might fit the letter combinations, rather than simply re-arranging letters in all possible ways. This research was intended to support this theory.

## Questions

Marks

1 What are the independent and dependent variables in this experiment?   2

2 What kind of experimental design is being employed?   1

3 (a) Why is counterbalancing carried out?   1
  (b) How exactly would the counterbalancing be carried out?   2
  (c) Without altering the design of the experiment, what other technique would have dealt with the problem which counterbalancing deals with?   1

4 If the researcher had used two different subject groups, one for each condition, why could this have been unsatisfactory?   1

5 Apart from changes in noise and lighting levels, suggest two random variables which might affect the subjects' performances.   2

6 The researcher asked experimenters to use a standardised procedure which included explaining the task in exactly the same words to each subject. Give two reasons for this approach.   2

7 The times for one of the subjects on each of the six anagrams of uncommon words are as follows:

85  97  119  131  156  287

  (a) When values are arranged like this, why is the median preferable to the mean?
  (b) Which subject do these times belong to?   2

8 At what level of measurement are the times shown in the table (nominal, ordinal, interval or ratio)?   1

9 (a) Does the level of measurement permit a parametric test?   1
  (b) State two conditions, other than level of measurement, which must be satisfied before carrying out a parametric test.   2

10 What are the advantages of using a parametric test?   2

11 What is meant by a 'level of significance'?   1

12 Do you think that the difference between the two sets of times in the table will be shown to be significant? Give reasons.   2

13 The researcher argues that people produce guesses at the word, from

among all the words they know, as they re-arrange the letters. They are
likely to produce less of the infrequent words as guesses. Can you think
of any other explanation for the slower times? 2

# QUESTION 7

A researcher predicts that younger teenage mothers will be more controlling with
their children. Three representative samples of mothers are asked to participate
in a cross-sectional study. The groups are 15, 17 and 19 years old. The
researcher's assistants record on videotape a thirty minute play session, once a
day, at exactly the same time, for a fortnight. The sessions are recorded in the
mother's own home. Several 'raters', who do not know the research hypothesis,
are given a rigorous coding system, and they analyse the videotape content in ten
second units.

The combined raters' scores for verbal control (items like 'Come here!' 'Leave
it alone!') are shown for the 15- and 19-year-old groups in table 61. The ratings
are out of a possible total of 100.

*Table 61   Verbal control ratings*

| 15-year-olds | 19-year-olds |
|:---:|:---:|
| 78 | 45 |
| 56 | 34 |
| 65 | 56 |
| 89 | 56 |
| 68 | 78 |

*Table 62   Rank chart*

| Rank | 1 | 2 | 3 | 4 | 5 | 6 | 7 | 8 | 9 | 10 |
|:---:|:---:|:---:|:---:|:---:|:---:|:---:|:---:|:---:|:---:|:---:|
| **Rating** | 34 | | | | | | | | | 89 |

## Questions

Marks

1 Is this an experiment? Give a reason for your answer. 2

2 What is meant by a 'cross-sectional' study? 1

3 Give one advantage and one disadvantage of cross-sectional studies. 2

4 What is one advantage and one disadvantage of carrying out a field study rather than a study in the laboratory?      2

5 What advantage does the use of videotape have over the method of coding behaviour on the spot, as it occurs?      1

6 (a) Why is it important to draw a representative sample?
  (b) What factors would be taken into account in trying to make these samples representative?      3

7 Why is it important that the recording sessions take place at the same time each day?      1

8 Why would the raters be kept unaware of the research hypothesis?      1

9 How could the reliability of two of the raters' judgements be tested?      2

10 It is decided not to treat the combined raters' scores as interval level data. Why might this be?      1

11 All ten scores in table 62 need to be ranked as one group. Put the ten scores into rank order using table 63. The highest and lowest have already been entered for you.      2

12 What test would be used to test for a significant difference between these two sets of ranks?      1

13 The result of this test shows the probability of the differences occurring was about 0.07. Does this mean the research idea should be abandoned? Give reasons for your answer.      2

14 How could interviews be used to strengthen the research findings?      2

15 Two of the mothers speak to the researcher at the end of the study. One wishes to know exactly what the whole project was about. The other wishes to remove her video recordings from the results since some of the events were extremely embarrassing. In each case, what should the researcher say or do?      2

# QUESTION 8

Eight babies between six and eight months old are brought to a laboratory as soon as they can crawl. They are placed on a safe shelf in the middle of a glass-topped table. On one side the chequered surface under the glass is lowered so there will *appear* to be a drop. On the other side the surface is just under the glass and looks safe.

    Each baby is placed on the central shelf and its mother stands on one side of the table and calls to it, encouraging it to cross to her. All the babies crossed the 'shallow' side.

The researchers predicted that the babies would fail to cross the 'deep' side. Results for the deep side are shown in table 63. A '+' means that the baby stayed on the central shelf.

*Table 63    'Deep' side results*

| Baby | Stayed on shelf |
|------|-----------------|
| A | + |
| B | + |
| C | + |
| D | − |
| E | + |
| F | + |
| G | + |
| H | + |

## Questions

|  | Marks |
|--|-------|
| 1 What kind of experimental design is used? | 1 |
| 2 Give one major advantage of this design. | 1 |

3 One major disadvantage is the presence of order effects.

| | |
|--|--|
| (a) Give two examples of order effects. | 2 |
| (b) Why might order effects be a problem in this experiment? | 1 |
| (c) How could the experimenter eliminate these order effects? | 1 |

| 4 Why is it necessary to check that babies do cross the shallow side? | 1 |
|--|--|

| 5 How could subject variables have a serious effect on the results of this experiment? | 2 |
|--|--|

6 This is a laboratory experiment.

| | |
|--|--|
| (a) Give two disadvantages of using the laboratory in psychology experiments. | 2 |
| (b) To what extent are these disadvantages important or not in this particular experiment? | 2 |

| 7 At what level of measurement are the data presented in the table? | 1 |
|--|--|

| 8 What test could be used to decide whether the number of babies refusing to cross was significant? | 1 |
|--|--|

| 9 Would you call this a very powerful test? Give your reasoning. | 2 |
|--|--|

| 10 Would a one- or two-tailed test be appropriate? | 1 |
|--|--|

11 The number of babies not crossing is found to be significant. Does this mean that the results cannot be a coincidence? Give your reasons.  2

12 How could the reliability of this experimental effect be demonstrated?  1

13 The researcher assumes that this result supports the view that infants have an innate ability to perceive depth. Are any other explanations possible?  2

14 One mother is upset that her baby seems to have 'failed' in the experiment by not crossing.

    (a) Why might the researcher have not informed her before the experiment that her child was not expected to cross?  1

    (b) What information should be given to all the mothers after the experiment is completed?  1

# QUESTION 9

Two groups of people were tested singly in a psychology laboratory. The people were asked to draw a number out of a bag to determine which group they were in. They were given a list of 15 words, presented by computer, one word at a time. One group were given instructions to repeat each word as many times as possible before they saw the next word. The other group were asked to form a vivid visual image of what the word represented and to link it dramatically to the next word. At the end of the list they were allowed to recall the words in any order. The researcher predicted that significantly more words would be recalled under imagery conditions than under rehearsal conditions. Results are shown in table 64.

*Table 64  No. of words recalled*

| Imagery | Rehearsal |
|---|---|
| 15 | 8 |
| 12 | 7 |
| 5 | 6 |
| 3 | 6 |
| 15 | 6 |
| 13 | |
| 10 | |
| 6 | |
| 14 | |
| Standard deviation = 4.32 | 1.17 |

**Questions**

*Marks*

1 Which experimental design is being used?  1

2 State one advantage and one disadvantage of the design used.　　　2

3 Explain *two* problems which would have to be dealt with if the same people took part in both conditions.　　　2

4 (a) What sort of method was used to divide people into groups?　　　1
　 (b) Why is this method employed?　　　1

5 Give one random variable which might affect results in this experiment, concerning either the equipment or the word list.　　　1

6 State the null hypothesis for this research.　　　1

7 The measure of central tendency gave a result of 10.33 for the imagery group and 7.2 for the rehearsal group. Are these means or medians?　　　1

8 What advantage has the mean over the median?　　　1

9 What is meant by the 'standard deviation'?　　　1

10 A statistical test which is very 'power efficient' is used on the data. What is meant by 'power efficient'?　　　1

11 State three conditions which must be satisfied before carrying out a parametric test.　　　3

12 Why might it be unwise to carry out a parametric test for differences between the two sets of scores shown in the table?　　　2

13 What test might be used instead?　　　1

14 If this research goes against traditional theory and research in this area, what significance level should the researcher aim at?　　　1

15 Why might the visual images *not* be responsible for the recall differences? Give two reasons and ways of testing these rival explanations　　　4

16 What would have been the value of a control group in this study?　　　1

# QUESTION 10

A group of 12 people with alcohol problems, attending a clinic, volunteer to take part in an experimental therapeutic programme. For each volunteer, a second alcoholic is selected who is like the volunteer on several important characteristics. After three months of the programme, both groups are assessed by two methods. One is a structured questionnaire, completed by participants. The other is a clinical interview, conducted by a therapist.

The treatment group show strong improvement, as measured by questionnaire, but this improvement is not so marked as measured by the therapists' interview rating. Correlation between the questionnaire score and interview ratings is 0.87.

## Questions

|  | Marks |
|---|---|
| 1 (a) What sort of design is being used here? | 1 |
| (b) State one advantage of the design. | 1 |

2 What is a major weakness of the clinical interview in psychological measurement?　　1

3 What problems might be encountered in constructing a questionnaire?　　2

4 Give two reasons why the questionnaire might have shown greater improvement than the interview?　　2

5 What is the purpose of measuring the correlation between the interview ratings and questionnaire scores?　　2

6 Why would it have been wise to use a placebo group in this research?　　2

7 What procedure might have been used with the placebo group?　　2

8 The data gathered are treated as ordinal data. Why have they not been treated as interval level?　　1

9 A non-parametric test is therefore used. What is one major disadvantage of using a non-parametric test?　　1

10 Which non-parametric test would be used?　　1

11 Would you say that the correlation of 0.87 is satisfactory? Please give your reasons.　　3

12 Under what circumstances would a correlation of 0.87 be non-significant?　　1

13 (a) What is a confounding variable?　　1
(b) Give two reasons why the treatment group may have improved *other than* because of the programme itself?　　2

14 After six months, the programme is obviously highly successful. Ethically, what should now happen to the control group and why?　　2

# Appendix 3 Statistical tables

## Table 1   Random numbers

| | | | | |
|---|---|---|---|---|
| 03 47 43 73 86 | 36 96 47 36 61 | 46 98 63 71 62 | 33 26 16 80 45 | 60 11 14 10 95 |
| 97 74 24 67 62 | 42 81 14 57 20 | 42 53 32 37 32 | 27 07 36 07 51 | 24 51 79 89 73 |
| 16 76 62 27 66 | 56 50 26 71 07 | 32 90 79 78 53 | 13 55 38 58 59 | 88 97 54 14 10 |
| 12 56 85 99 26 | 96 96 68 27 31 | 05 03 72 93 15 | 57 12 10 14 21 | 88 26 49 81 76 |
| 55 59 56 35 64 | 38 54 82 46 22 | 31 62 43 09 90 | 06 18 44 32 53 | 23 83 01 30 30 |
| 16 22 77 94 39 | 49 54 43 54 82 | 17 37 93 23 78 | 87 35 20 96 43 | 84 26 34 91 64 |
| 84 42 17 53 31 | 57 24 55 06 88 | 77 04 74 47 67 | 21 76 33 50 25 | 83 92 12 06 76 |
| 63 01 63 78 59 | 16 95 55 67 19 | 98 10 50 71 75 | 12 86 73 58 07 | 44 39 52 38 79 |
| 33 21 12 34 29 | 78 64 56 07 82 | 52 42 07 44 38 | 15 51 00 13 42 | 99 66 02 79 54 |
| 57 60 86 32 44 | 09 47 27 96 54 | 49 17 46 09 62 | 90 52 84 77 27 | 08 02 73 43 28 |
| 18 18 07 92 46 | 44 17 16 58 09 | 79 83 86 16 62 | 06 76 50 03 10 | 55 23 64 05 05 |
| 26 62 38 97 75 | 84 16 07 44 99 | 83 11 46 32 24 | 20 14 85 88 45 | 10 93 72 88 71 |
| 23 42 40 64 74 | 82 97 77 77 81 | 07 45 32 14 08 | 32 98 94 07 72 | 93 85 79 10 75 |
| 52 36 28 19 95 | 50 92 26 11 97 | 00 56 76 31 38 | 80 22 02 53 53 | 86 60 42 04 53 |
| 37 85 94 35 12 | 83 39 50 08 30 | 42 34 07 96 88 | 54 42 06 87 98 | 35 85 29 48 38 |
| 70 29 17 12 13 | 40 33 20 38 26 | 13 89 51 03 74 | 17 76 37 13 04 | 07 74 21 19 30 |
| 56 62 18 37 35 | 96 83 50 87 75 | 97 12 25 93 47 | 70 33 24 03 54 | 97 77 46 44 80 |
| 99 49 57 22 77 | 88 42 95 45 72 | 16 64 36 16 00 | 04 43 18 66 79 | 94 77 24 21 90 |
| 16 08 15 04 72 | 33 27 14 34 90 | 45 59 34 68 49 | 12 72 07 34 45 | 99 27 72 95 14 |
| 31 16 93 32 43 | 50 27 89 87 19 | 20 15 37 00 49 | 52 85 66 60 44 | 38 68 88 11 80 |
| 68 34 30 13 70 | 55 74 30 77 40 | 44 22 78 84 26 | 04 33 46 09 52 | 68 07 97 06 57 |
| 74 57 25 65 76 | 59 29 97 68 60 | 71 91 38 67 54 | 13 58 18 24 76 | 15 54 55 95 52 |
| 27 42 37 86 53 | 48 55 90 65 72 | 96 57 69 36 10 | 96 46 92 42 45 | 97 60 49 04 91 |
| 00 39 68 29 61 | 66 37 32 20 30 | 77 84 57 03 29 | 10 45 65 04 26 | 11 04 96 67 24 |
| 29 94 98 94 24 | 68 49 69 10 82 | 53 75 91 93 30 | 34 25 20 57 27 | 40 48 73 51 92 |
| 16 90 82 66 59 | 83 62 64 11 12 | 67 19 00 71 74 | 60 47 21 29 68 | 02 02 37 03 31 |
| 11 27 94 75 06 | 06 09 19 74 66 | 02 94 37 34 02 | 76 70 90 30 86 | 38 45 94 30 38 |
| 35 24 10 16 20 | 33 32 51 26 38 | 79 78 45 04 91 | 16 92 53 56 16 | 02 75 50 95 98 |
| 38 23 16 86 38 | 42 38 97 01 50 | 87 75 66 81 41 | 40 01 74 91 62 | 48 51 84 08 32 |
| 31 96 25 91 47 | 96 44 33 49 13 | 34 86 82 53 91 | 00 52 43 48 85 | 27 55 26 89 62 |
| 66 67 40 67 14 | 64 05 71 95 86 | 11 05 65 09 68 | 76 83 20 37 90 | 57 16 00 11 66 |
| 14 90 84 45 11 | 75 73 88 05 90 | 52 27 41 14 86 | 22 98 12 22 08 | 07 52 74 95 80 |
| 68 05 51 18 00 | 33 96 02 75 19 | 07 60 62 93 55 | 59 33 82 43 90 | 49 37 38 44 59 |
| 20 46 78 73 90 | 97 51 40 14 02 | 04 02 33 31 08 | 39 54 16 49 36 | 47 95 93 13 30 |
| 64 19 58 97 79 | 15 06 15 93 20 | 01 90 10 75 06 | 40 78 78 89 62 | 02 67 74 17 33 |
| 05 26 93 70 60 | 22 35 85 15 13 | 92 03 51 59 77 | 59 56 78 06 83 | 52 91 05 70 74 |
| 07 97 10 88 23 | 09 98 42 99 64 | 61 71 62 99 15 | 06 51 29 16 93 | 58 05 77 09 51 |
| 68 71 86 85 85 | 54 87 66 47 54 | 73 32 08 11 12 | 44 95 92 63 16 | 29 56 24 29 48 |
| 26 99 61 65 53 | 58 37 78 80 70 | 42 10 50 67 42 | 32 17 55 85 74 | 94 44 67 16 94 |
| 14 65 52 68 75 | 87 59 36 22 41 | 26 78 63 06 55 | 13 08 27 01 50 | 15 29 39 39 43 |

Abridged from R. A. Fisher and F. Yates, *Statistical Tables for Biological, Agricultural and Medical Research*, Oliver and Boyd Ltd, Edinburgh (1953), by permission of the authors and publishers (Longman Group UK Ltd.).

# Table 2 Areas under the normal distribution

| $z$ | 0 $z$ | 0 $z$ | $z$ | 0 $z$ | 0 $z$ | $z$ | 0 $z$ | 0 $z$ |
|------|--------|--------|------|--------|--------|------|--------|--------|
| 0.00 | 0.0000 | 0.5000 | 0.40 | 0.1554 | 0.3446 | 0.80 | 0.2881 | 0.2119 |
| 0.01 | 0.0040 | 0.4960 | 0.41 | 0.1591 | 0.3409 | 0.81 | 0.2910 | 0.2090 |
| 0.02 | 0.0080 | 0.4920 | 0.42 | 0.1628 | 0.3372 | 0.82 | 0.2939 | 0.2061 |
| 0.03 | 0.0120 | 0.4880 | 0.43 | 0.1664 | 0.3336 | 0.83 | 0.2967 | 0.2033 |
| 0.04 | 0.0160 | 0.4840 | 0.44 | 0.1700 | 0.3300 | 0.84 | 0.2995 | 0.2005 |
| 0.05 | 0.0199 | 0.4801 | 0.45 | 0.1736 | 0.3264 | 0.85 | 0.3023 | 0.1977 |
| 0.06 | 0.0239 | 0.4761 | 0.46 | 0.1772 | 0.3228 | 0.86 | 0.3051 | 0.1949 |
| 0.07 | 0.0279 | 0.4721 | 0.47 | 0.1808 | 0.3192 | 0.87 | 0.3078 | 0.1922 |
| 0.08 | 0.0319 | 0.4681 | 0.48 | 0.1844 | 0.3156 | 0.88 | 0.3106 | 0.1894 |
| 0.09 | 0.0359 | 0.4641 | 0.49 | 0.1879 | 0.3121 | 0.89 | 0.3133 | 0.1867 |
| 0.10 | 0.0398 | 0.4602 | 0.50 | 0.1915 | 0.3085 | 0.90 | 0.3159 | 0.1841 |
| 0.11 | 0.0438 | 0.4562 | 0.51 | 0.1950 | 0.3050 | 0.91 | 0.3186 | 0.1814 |
| 0.12 | 0.0478 | 0.4522 | 0.52 | 0.1985 | 0.3015 | 0.92 | 0.3212 | 0.1788 |
| 0.13 | 0.0517 | 0.4483 | 0.53 | 0.2019 | 0.2981 | 0.93 | 0.3238 | 0.1762 |
| 0.14 | 0.0557 | 0.4443 | 0.54 | 0.2054 | 0.2946 | 0.94 | 0.3264 | 0.1736 |
| 0.15 | 0.0596 | 0.4404 | 0.55 | 0.2088 | 0.2912 | 0.95 | 0.3289 | 0.1711 |
| 0.16 | 0.0636 | 0.4364 | 0.56 | 0.2123 | 0.2877 | 0.96 | 0.3315 | 0.1685 |
| 0.17 | 0.0675 | 0.4325 | 0.57 | 0.2157 | 0.2843 | 0.97 | 0.3340 | 0.1660 |
| 0.18 | 0.0714 | 0.4286 | 0.58 | 0.2190 | 0.2810 | 0.98 | 0.3365 | 0.1635 |
| 0.19 | 0.0753 | 0.4247 | 0.59 | 0.2224 | 0.2776 | 0.99 | 0.3389 | 0.1611 |
| 0.20 | 0.0793 | 0.4207 | 0.60 | 0.2257 | 0.2743 | 1.00 | 0.3413 | 0.1587 |
| 0.21 | 0.0832 | 0.4168 | 0.61 | 0.2291 | 0.2709 | 1.01 | 0.3438 | 0.1562 |
| 0.22 | 0.0871 | 0.4129 | 0.62 | 0.2324 | 0.2676 | 1.02 | 0.3461 | 0.1539 |
| 0.23 | 0.0910 | 0.4090 | 0.63 | 0.2357 | 0.2643 | 1.03 | 0.3485 | 0.1515 |
| 0.24 | 0.0948 | 0.4052 | 0.64 | 0.2389 | 0.2611 | 1.04 | 0.3508 | 0.1492 |
| 0.25 | 0.0987 | 0.4013 | 0.65 | 0.2422 | 0.2578 | 1.05 | 0.3531 | 0.1469 |
| 0.26 | 0.1026 | 0.3974 | 0.66 | 0.2454 | 0.2546 | 1.06 | 0.3554 | 0.1446 |
| 0.27 | 0.1064 | 0.3969 | 0.67 | 0.2486 | 0.2514 | 1.07 | 0.3577 | 0.1423 |
| 0.28 | 0.1103 | 0.3897 | 0.68 | 0.2517 | 0.2483 | 1.08 | 0.3599 | 0.1401 |
| 0.29 | 0.1141 | 0.3859 | 0.69 | 0.2549 | 0.2451 | 1.09 | 0.3621 | 0.1379 |
| 0.30 | 0.1179 | 0.3821 | 0.70 | 0.2580 | 0.2420 | 1.10 | 0.3643 | 0.1357 |
| 0.31 | 0.1217 | 0.3783 | 0.71 | 0.2611 | 0.2389 | 1.11 | 0.3665 | 0.1335 |
| 0.32 | 0.1255 | 0.3745 | 0.72 | 0.2642 | 0.2358 | 1.12 | 0.3686 | 0.1314 |
| 0.33 | 0.1293 | 0.3707 | 0.73 | 0.2673 | 0.2327 | 1.13 | 0.3708 | 0.1292 |
| 0.34 | 0.1331 | 0.3669 | 0.74 | 0.2704 | 0.2296 | 1.14 | 0.3729 | 0.1271 |
| 0.35 | 0.1368 | 0.3632 | 0.75 | 0.2734 | 0.2266 | 1.15 | 0.3749 | 0.1251 |
| 0.36 | 0.1406 | 0.3594 | 0.76 | 0.2764 | 0.2236 | 1.16 | 0.3770 | 0.1230 |
| 0.37 | 0.1443 | 0.3557 | 0.77 | 0.2794 | 0.2206 | 1.17 | 0.3790 | 0.1210 |
| 0.38 | 0.1480 | 0.3520 | 0.78 | 0.2823 | 0.2177 | 1.18 | 0.3810 | 0.1190 |
| 0.39 | 0.1517 | 0.3483 | 0.79 | 0.2852 | 0.2148 | 1.19 | 0.3830 | 0.1170 |

# Table 2  Continued

| z | 0 z | 0 z | z | 0 z | 0 z | z | 0 z | 0 z |
|---|-----|-----|---|-----|-----|---|-----|-----|
| 1.20 | 0.3849 | 0.1151 | 1.60 | 0.4452 | 0.0548 | 2.00 | 0.4772 | 0.0228 |
| 1.21 | 0.3869 | 0.1131 | 1.61 | 0.4463 | 0.0537 | 2.01 | 0.4778 | 0.0222 |
| 1.22 | 0.3888 | 0.1112 | 1.62 | 0.4474 | 0.0526 | 2.02 | 0.4783 | 0.0217 |
| 1.23 | 0.3907 | 0.1093 | 1.63 | 0.4484 | 0.0516 | 2.03 | 0.4788 | 0.0212 |
| 1.24 | 0.3925 | 0.1075 | 1.64 | 0.4495 | 0.0505 | 2.04 | 0.4793 | 0.0207 |
| 1.25 | 0.3944 | 0.1056 | 1.65 | 0.4505 | 0.0495 | 2.05 | 0.4798 | 0.0202 |
| 1.26 | 0.3962 | 0.1038 | 1.66 | 0.4515 | 0.0485 | 2.06 | 0.4803 | 0.0197 |
| 1.27 | 0.3980 | 0.1020 | 1.67 | 0.4525 | 0.0475 | 2.07 | 0.4808 | 0.0192 |
| 1.28 | 0.3997 | 0.1003 | 1.68 | 0.4535 | 0.0465 | 2.08 | 0.4812 | 0.0188 |
| 1.29 | 0.4015 | 0.0985 | 1.69 | 0.4545 | 0.0455 | 2.09 | 0.4817 | 0.0183 |
| 1.30 | 0.4032 | 0.0968 | 1.70 | 0.4554 | 0.0446 | 2.10 | 0.4821 | 0.0179 |
| 1.31 | 0.4049 | 0.0951 | 1.71 | 0.4564 | 0.0436 | 2.11 | 0.4826 | 0.0174 |
| 1.32 | 0.4066 | 0.0934 | 1.72 | 0.4573 | 0.0427 | 2.12 | 0.4830 | 0.0170 |
| 1.33 | 0.4082 | 0.0918 | 1.73 | 0.4582 | 0.0418 | 2.13 | 0.4834 | 0.0166 |
| 1.34 | 0.4099 | 0.0901 | 1.74 | 0.4591 | 0.0409 | 2.14 | 0.4838 | 0.0162 |
| 1.35 | 0.4115 | 0.0885 | 1.75 | 0.4599 | 0.0401 | 2.15 | 0.4842 | 0.0158 |
| 1.36 | 0.4131 | 0.0869 | 1.76 | 0.4608 | 0.0392 | 2.16 | 0.4846 | 0.0154 |
| 1.37 | 0.4147 | 0.0853 | 1.77 | 0.4616 | 0.0384 | 2.17 | 0.4850 | 0.0150 |
| 1.38 | 0.4162 | 0.0838 | 1.78 | 0.4625 | 0.0375 | 2.18 | 0.4854 | 0.0146 |
| 1.39 | 0.4177 | 0.0823 | 1.79 | 0.4633 | 0.0367 | 2.19 | 0.4857 | 0.0143 |
| 1.40 | 0.4192 | 0.0808 | 1.80 | 0.4641 | 0.0359 | 2.20 | 0.4861 | 0.0139 |
| 1.41 | 0.4207 | 0.0793 | 1.81 | 0.4649 | 0.0351 | 2.21 | 0.4864 | 0.0136 |
| 1.42 | 0.4222 | 0.0778 | 1.82 | 0.4656 | 0.0344 | 2.22 | 0.4868 | 0.0132 |
| 1.43 | 0.4236 | 0.0764 | 1.83 | 0.4664 | 0.0336 | 2.23 | 0.4871 | 0.0129 |
| 1.44 | 0.4251 | 0.0749 | 1.84 | 0.4671 | 0.0329 | 2.24 | 0.4875 | 0.0125 |
| 1.45 | 0.4265 | 0.0735 | 1.85 | 0.4678 | 0.0322 | 2.25 | 0.4878 | 0.0122 |
| 1.46 | 0.4279 | 0.0721 | 1.86 | 0.4686 | 0.0314 | 2.26 | 0.4881 | 0.0119 |
| 1.47 | 0.4292 | 0.0708 | 1.87 | 0.4693 | 0.0307 | 2.27 | 0.4884 | 0.0116 |
| 1.48 | 0.4306 | 0.0694 | 1.88 | 0.4699 | 0.0301 | 2.28 | 0.4887 | 0.0113 |
| 1.49 | 0.4319 | 0.0681 | 1.89 | 0.4706 | 0.0294 | 2.29 | 0.4890 | 0.0110 |
| 1.50 | 0.4332 | 0.0668 | 1.90 | 0.4713 | 0.0287 | 2.30 | 0.4893 | 0.0107 |
| 1.51 | 0.4345 | 0.0655 | 1.91 | 0.4719 | 0.0281 | 2.31 | 0.4896 | 0.0104 |
| 1.52 | 0.4357 | 0.0643 | 1.92 | 0.4726 | 0.0274 | 2.32 | 0.4898 | 0.0102 |
| 1.53 | 0.4370 | 0.0630 | 1.93 | 0.4732 | 0.0268 | 2.33 | 0.4901 | 0.0099 |
| 1.54 | 0.4382 | 0.0618 | 1.94 | 0.4738 | 0.0262 | 2.34 | 0.4904 | 0.0096 |
| 1.55 | 0.4394 | 0.0606 | 1.95 | 0.4744 | 0.0256 | 2.35 | 0.4906 | 0.0094 |
| 1.56 | 0.4406 | 0.0594 | 1.96 | 0.4750 | 0.0250 | 2.36 | 0.4909 | 0.0091 |
| 1.57 | 0.4418 | 0.0582 | 1.97 | 0.4756 | 0.0244 | 2.37 | 0.4911 | 0.0089 |
| 1.58 | 0.4429 | 0.0571 | 1.98 | 0.4761 | 0.0239 | 2.38 | 0.4913 | 0.0087 |
| 1.59 | 0.4441 | 0.0559 | 1.99 | 0.4767 | 0.0233 | 2.39 | 0.4916 | 0.0084 |

# Table 2   Continued

| z | 0 z | 0 z | z | 0 z | 0 z | z | 0 z | 0 z |
|---|---|---|---|---|---|---|---|---|
| 2.40 | 0.4918 | 0.0082 | 2.72 | 0.4967 | 0.0033 | 3.04 | 0.4988 | 0.0012 |
| 2.41 | 0.4920 | 0.0080 | 2.73 | 0.4968 | 0.0032 | 3.05 | 0.4989 | 0.0011 |
| 2.42 | 0.4922 | 0.0078 | 2.74 | 0.4969 | 0.0031 | 3.06 | 0.4989 | 0.0011 |
| 2.43 | 0.4925 | 0.0075 | 2.75 | 0.4970 | 0.0030 | 3.07 | 0.4989 | 0.0011 |
| 2.44 | 0.4927 | 0.0073 | 2.76 | 0.4971 | 0.0029 | 3.08 | 0.4990 | 0.0010 |
| 2.45 | 0.4929 | 0.0017 | 2.77 | 0.4972 | 0.0028 | 3.09 | 0.4990 | 0.0010 |
| 2.46 | 0.4931 | 0.0069 | 2.78 | 0.4973 | 0.0027 | 3.10 | 0.4990 | 0.0010 |
| 2.47 | 0.4932 | 0.0068 | 2.79 | 0.4974 | 0.0026 | 3.11 | 0.4991 | 0.0009 |
| 2.48 | 0.4934 | 0.0066 | 2.80 | 0.4974 | 0.0026 | 3.12 | 0.4991 | 0.0009 |
| 2.49 | 0.4936 | 0.0064 | 2.81 | 0.4975 | 0.0025 | 3.13 | 0.4991 | 0.0009 |
| 2.50 | 0.4938 | 0.0062 | 2.82 | 0.4976 | 0.0024 | 3.14 | 0.4992 | 0.0008 |
| 2.51 | 0.4940 | 0.0060 | 2.83 | 0.4977 | 0.0023 | 3.15 | 0.4992 | 0.0008 |
| 2.52 | 0.4941 | 0.0059 | 2.84 | 0.4977 | 0.0023 | 3.16 | 0.4992 | 0.0008 |
| 2.53 | 0.4943 | 0.0057 | 2.85 | 0.4978 | 0.0022 | 3.17 | 0.4992 | 0.0008 |
| 2.54 | 0.4945 | 0.0055 | 2.86 | 0.4979 | 0.0021 | 3.18 | 0.4993 | 0.0007 |
| 2.55 | 0.4946 | 0.0054 | 2.87 | 0.4979 | 0.0021 | 3.19 | 0.4993 | 0.0007 |
| 2.56 | 0.4948 | 0.0052 | 2.88 | 0.4980 | 0.0020 | 3.20 | 0.4993 | 0.0007 |
| 2.57 | 0.4949 | 0.0051 | 2.89 | 0.4981 | 0.0019 | 3.21 | 0.4993 | 0.0007 |
| 2.58 | 0.4951 | 0.0049 | 2.90 | 0.4981 | 0.0019 | 3.22 | 0.4994 | 0.0006 |
| 2.59 | 0.4952 | 0.0048 | 2.91 | 0.4982 | 0.0018 | 3.23 | 0.4994 | 0.0006 |
| 2.60 | 0.4953 | 0.0047 | 2.92 | 0.4982 | 0.0018 | 3.24 | 0.4994 | 0.0006 |
| 2.61 | 0.4955 | 0.0045 | 2.93 | 0.4983 | 0.0017 | 3.25 | 0.4994 | 0.0006 |
| 2.62 | 0.4956 | 0.0044 | 2.94 | 0.4984 | 0.0016 | 3.30 | 0.4995 | 0.0005 |
| 2.63 | 0.4957 | 0.0043 | 2.95 | 0.4984 | 0.0016 | 3.35 | 0.4996 | 0.0004 |
| 2.64 | 0.4959 | 0.0041 | 2.96 | 0.4985 | 0.0015 | 3.40 | 0.4997 | 0.0003 |
| 2.65 | 0.4960 | 0.0040 | 2.97 | 0.4985 | 0.0015 | 3.45 | 0.4997 | 0.0003 |
| 2.66 | 0.4961 | 0.0039 | 2.98 | 0.4986 | 0.0014 | 3.50 | 0.4998 | 0.0002 |
| 2.67 | 0.4962 | 0.0038 | 2.99 | 0.4986 | 0.0014 | 3.60 | 0.4998 | 0.0002 |
| 2.68 | 0.4963 | 0.0037 | 3.00 | 0.4987 | 0.0013 | 3.70 | 0.4999 | 0.0001 |
| 2.69 | 0.4964 | 0.0036 | 3.01 | 0.4987 | 0.0013 | 3.80 | 0.4999 | 0.0001 |
| 2.70 | 0.4965 | 0.0035 | 3.02 | 0.4987 | 0.0013 | 3.90 | 0.49995 | 0.00005 |
| 2.71 | 0.4966 | 0.0034 | 3.03 | 0.4988 | 0.0012 | 4.00 | 0.49997 | 0.00003 |

The left-hand column in each set of three shows the particular $z$-value. The centre column shows the area contained between the mean and this $z$-value. The right-hand column shows the area left in the whole distribution to the right of this $z$-value. The whole area is one unit and values shown are decimal portions of it. These are also the probabilities of finding a value within the area concerned. For percentages, multiply all area values by 100. For areas between $-z$ and $+z$, double the values shown.

SOURCE: R. P. Runyon and A. Haber, *Fundamentals of Behavioral Statistics*, Second Edition, Reading, Mass.: McGraw-Hill Publishing Co. (1971). Artwork from R. B. McCall. *Fundamental Statistics for Psychology*, Second Edition, New York: Harcourt Brace Jovanovich, Inc. (1975).

# Table 3   Critical values in the Binomial Sign Test

| N | Level of significance for one-tailed test | | | | |
|---|---|---|---|---|---|
| | 0.05 | 0.025 | 0.01 | 0.005 | 0.0005 |
| | Level of significance for two-tailed test | | | | |
| | 0.10 | 0.05 | 0.02 | 0.01 | 0.001 |
| 5 | 0 | — | — | — | — |
| 6 | 0 | 0 | — | — | — |
| 7 | 0 | 0 | 0 | — | — |
| 8 | 1 | 0 | 0 | 0 | — |
| 9 | 1 | 1 | 0 | 0 | — |
| 10 | 1 | 1 | 0 | 0 | — |
| 11 | 2 | 1 | 1 | 0 | 0 |
| 12 | 2 | 2 | 1 | 1 | 0 |
| 13 | 3 | 2 | 1 | 1 | 0 |
| 14 | 3 | 2 | 2 | 1 | 0 |
| 15 | 3 | 3 | 2 | 2 | 1 |
| 16 | 4 | 3 | 2 | 2 | 1 |
| 17 | 4 | 4 | 3 | 2 | 1 |
| 18 | 5 | 4 | 3 | 3 | 1 |
| 19 | 5 | 4 | 4 | 3 | 2 |
| 20 | 5 | 5 | 4 | 3 | 2 |
| 25 | 7 | 7 | 6 | 5 | 4 |
| 30 | 10 | 9 | 8 | 7 | 5 |
| 35 | 12 | 11 | 10 | 9 | 7 |

Calculated $S$ must be EQUAL TO or LESS THAN the table (critical) value for significance at the level shown.

SOURCE: F. Clegg, *Simple Statistics*, Cambridge Unversity Press, 1982.

# Table 4   Critical values of $\chi^2$

| | Level of significance for a one-tailed test | | | | | |
| | 0.10 | 0.05 | 0.025 | 0.01 | 0.005 | 0.0005 |
| | Level of significance for a two-tailed test | | | | | |
| $df$ | 0.20 | 0.10 | 0.05 | 0.02 | 0.01 | 0.001 |
|---|---|---|---|---|---|---|
| 1 | 1.64 | 2.71 | 3.84 | 5.41 | 6.64 | 10.83 |
| 2 | 3.22 | 4.60 | 5.99 | 7.82 | 9.21 | 13.82 |
| 3 | 4.64 | 6.25 | 7.82 | 9.84 | 11.34 | 16.27 |
| 4 | 5.99 | 7.78 | 9.49 | 11.67 | 13.28 | 18.46 |
| 5 | 7.29 | 9.24 | 11.07 | 13.39 | 15.09 | 20.52 |
| 6 | 8.56 | 10.64 | 12.59 | 15.03 | 16.81 | 22.46 |
| 7 | 9.80 | 12.02 | 14.07 | 16.62 | 18.48 | 24.32 |
| 8 | 11.03 | 13.36 | 15.51 | 18.17 | 20.09 | 26.12 |
| 9 | 12.24 | 14.68 | 16.92 | 19.68 | 21.67 | 27.88 |
| 10 | 13.44 | 15.99 | 18.31 | 21.16 | 23.21 | 29.59 |
| 11 | 14.63 | 17.28 | 19.68 | 22.62 | 24.72 | 31.26 |
| 12 | 15.81 | 18.55 | 21.03 | 24.05 | 26.22 | 32.91 |
| 13 | 16.98 | 19.81 | 22.36 | 25.47 | 27.69 | 34.53 |
| 14 | 18.15 | 21.06 | 23.68 | 26.87 | 29.14 | 36.12 |
| 15 | 19.31 | 22.31 | 25.00 | 28.26 | 30.58 | 37.70 |
| 16 | 20.46 | 23.54 | 26.30 | 29.63 | 32.00 | 39.29 |
| 17 | 21.62 | 24.77 | 27.59 | 31.00 | 33.41 | 40.75 |
| 18 | 22.76 | 25.99 | 28.87 | 32.35 | 34.80 | 42.31 |
| 19 | 23.90 | 27.20 | 30.14 | 33.69 | 36.19 | 43.82 |
| 20 | 25.04 | 28.41 | 31.41 | 35.02 | 37.57 | 45.32 |
| 21 | 26.17 | 29.62 | 32.67 | 36.34 | 38.93 | 46.80 |
| 22 | 27.30 | 30.81 | 33.92 | 37.66 | 40.29 | 48.27 |
| 23 | 28.43 | 32.01 | 35.17 | 38.97 | 41.64 | 49.73 |
| 24 | 29.55 | 33.20 | 36.42 | 40.27 | 42.98 | 51.18 |
| 25 | 30.68 | 34.38 | 37.65 | 41.57 | 44.31 | 52.62 |
| 26 | 31.80 | 35.56 | 38.88 | 42.86 | 45.64 | 54.05 |
| 27 | 32.91 | 36.74 | 40.11 | 44.14 | 46.96 | 55.48 |
| 28 | 34.03 | 37.92 | 41.34 | 45.42 | 48.28 | 56.89 |
| 29 | 35.14 | 39.09 | 42.69 | 49.69 | 49.59 | 58.30 |
| 30 | 36.25 | 40.26 | 43.77 | 47.96 | 50.89 | 59.70 |
| 32 | 38.47 | 42.59 | 46.19 | 50.49 | 53.49 | 62.49 |
| 34 | 40.68 | 44.90 | 48.60 | 53.00 | 56.06 | 65.25 |
| 36 | 42.88 | 47.21 | 51.00 | 55.49 | 58.62 | 67.99 |
| 38 | 45.08 | 49.51 | 53.38 | 57.97 | 61.16 | 70.70 |
| 40 | 47.27 | 51.81 | 55.76 | 60.44 | 63.69 | 73.40 |
| 44 | 51.64 | 56.37 | 60.48 | 65.34 | 68.71 | 78.75 |
| 48 | 55.99 | 60.91 | 65.17 | 70.20 | 73.68 | 84.04 |
| 52 | 60.33 | 65.42 | 69.83 | 75.02 | 78.62 | 89.27 |
| 56 | 64.66 | 69.92 | 74.47 | 79.82 | 83.51 | 94.46 |
| 60 | 68.97 | 74.40 | 79.08 | 84.58 | 88.38 | 99.61 |

Calculated value of $\chi^2$ must EQUAL or EXCEED the table (critical) value for significance at the level shown.

Abridged from Fisher and Yates, *Statistical Tables for Biological, Agricultural and Medical Research*, Oliver and Boyd Ltd., Edinburgh (1963) (Longman Group UK Ltd.).

# Table 5  Critical values in the Mann–Witney U Test (two-tailed test)

$n_L$ = larger sample size
$n_S$ = smaller sample size

The upper-right portion of the grid (including the diagonal) gives the critical values for the **0.05** level; the lower-left portion gives the critical values for the **0.01** level. For the 0.05 values the row index is $n_S$ and the column index is $n_L$; for the 0.01 values the row index is $n_L$ and the column index is $n_S$.

| | 2 | 3 | 4 | 5 | 6 | 7 | 8 | 9 | 10 | 11 | 12 | 13 | 14 | 15 | 16 | 17 | 18 | 19 | 20 | 21 | 22 | 23 | 24 | 25 |
|---|---|---|---|---|---|---|---|---|---|---|---|---|---|---|---|---|---|---|---|---|---|---|---|---|
| **2** | — | — | — | — | — | — | 0 | 0 | 0 | 0 | 1 | 1 | 1 | 1 | 1 | 2 | 2 | 2 | 2 | 3 | 3 | 3 | 3 | 3 |
| **3** | — | — | — | 0 | 1 | 1 | 2 | 2 | 3 | 3 | 4 | 4 | 5 | 5 | 6 | 6 | 7 | 7 | 8 | 8 | 9 | 9 | 10 | 10 |
| **4** | — | — | 0 | 1 | 2 | 3 | 4 | 4 | 5 | 6 | 7 | 8 | 9 | 10 | 11 | 11 | 12 | 13 | 14 | 15 | 16 | 17 | 17 | 18 |
| **5** | — | — | — | 2 | 3 | 5 | 6 | 7 | 8 | 9 | 11 | 12 | 13 | 14 | 15 | 17 | 18 | 19 | 20 | 22 | 23 | 24 | 25 | 27 |
| **6** | — | — | 0 | 1 | 5 | 6 | 8 | 10 | 11 | 13 | 14 | 16 | 17 | 19 | 21 | 22 | 24 | 25 | 27 | 29 | 30 | 32 | 33 | 35 |
| **7** | — | — | 0 | 1 | 3 | 8 | 10 | 12 | 14 | 16 | 18 | 20 | 22 | 24 | 26 | 28 | 30 | 32 | 34 | 36 | 38 | 40 | 42 | 44 |
| **8** | — | — | 1 | 2 | 4 | 6 | 13 | 15 | 17 | 19 | 22 | 24 | 26 | 29 | 31 | 34 | 36 | 38 | 41 | 43 | 45 | 48 | 50 | 53 |
| **9** | — | 0 | 1 | 3 | 5 | 7 | 9 | 17 | 20 | 23 | 26 | 28 | 31 | 34 | 37 | 39 | 42 | 45 | 48 | 50 | 53 | 56 | 59 | 62 |
| **10** | — | 0 | 2 | 4 | 6 | 9 | 11 | 13 | 23 | 26 | 29 | 33 | 36 | 39 | 42 | 45 | 48 | 52 | 55 | 58 | 61 | 64 | 67 | 71 |
| **11** | — | 0 | 2 | 5 | 7 | 10 | 13 | 16 | 18 | 30 | 33 | 37 | 40 | 44 | 47 | 51 | 55 | 58 | 62 | 65 | 69 | 73 | 76 | 80 |
| **12** | — | 1 | 3 | 6 | 9 | 12 | 15 | 18 | 21 | 24 | 37 | 41 | 45 | 49 | 53 | 57 | 61 | 65 | 69 | 73 | 77 | 81 | 85 | 89 |
| **13** | — | 1 | 3 | 7 | 10 | 13 | 17 | 20 | 24 | 27 | 31 | 45 | 50 | 54 | 59 | 63 | 67 | 72 | 76 | 80 | 85 | 89 | 94 | 98 |
| **14** | — | 1 | 4 | 7 | 11 | 15 | 18 | 22 | 26 | 30 | 34 | 38 | 55 | 59 | 64 | 69 | 74 | 78 | 83 | 88 | 93 | 98 | 102 | 107 |
| **15** | — | 2 | 5 | 8 | 12 | 16 | 20 | 24 | 29 | 33 | 37 | 42 | 46 | 64 | 70 | 75 | 80 | 85 | 90 | 96 | 101 | 106 | 111 | 117 |
| **16** | — | 2 | 5 | 9 | 13 | 18 | 22 | 27 | 31 | 36 | 41 | 45 | 50 | 55 | 75 | 81 | 86 | 92 | 98 | 103 | 109 | 115 | 120 | 126 |
| **17** | — | 2 | 6 | 10 | 15 | 19 | 24 | 29 | 34 | 39 | 44 | 49 | 54 | 60 | 65 | 87 | 93 | 99 | 105 | 111 | 117 | 123 | 129 | 135 |
| **18** | — | 2 | 6 | 11 | 16 | 21 | 26 | 31 | 37 | 42 | 47 | 53 | 58 | 64 | 70 | 75 | 99 | 106 | 112 | 119 | 125 | 132 | 138 | 145 |
| **19** | 0 | 3 | 7 | 12 | 17 | 22 | 28 | 33 | 39 | 45 | 51 | 57 | 63 | 69 | 74 | 81 | 87 | 113 | 119 | 126 | 133 | 140 | 147 | 154 |
| **20** | 0 | 3 | 8 | 13 | 18 | 24 | 30 | 36 | 42 | 48 | 54 | 60 | 67 | 73 | 79 | 86 | 92 | 99 | 127 | 134 | 141 | 149 | 156 | 163 |
| **21** | 0 | 3 | 8 | 14 | 19 | 25 | 32 | 38 | 44 | 51 | 58 | 64 | 71 | 78 | 84 | 91 | 98 | 105 | 112 | 142 | 150 | 157 | 165 | 173 |
| **22** | 0 | 4 | 9 | 14 | 21 | 27 | 34 | 40 | 47 | 54 | 61 | 68 | 75 | 82 | 89 | 96 | 104 | 111 | 118 | 125 | 158 | 166 | 174 | 182 |
| **23** | 0 | 4 | 9 | 15 | 22 | 28 | 35 | 43 | 50 | 57 | 64 | 72 | 79 | 87 | 94 | 102 | 109 | 117 | 125 | 132 | 139 | 175 | 183 | 192 |
| **24** | 0 | 4 | 10 | 16 | 23 | 30 | 37 | 45 | 52 | 60 | 68 | 75 | 83 | 91 | 99 | 107 | 115 | 123 | 131 | 139 | 147 | 154 | 192 | 201 |
| **25** | 0 | 5 | 10 | 17 | 24 | 32 | 39 | 47 | 55 | 63 | 71 | 79 | 87 | 96 | 104 | 112 | 121 | 129 | 138 | 146 | 155 | 163 | 172 | |

# Table 5 continued

**Equal sample sizes**

| n | 1 | 2 | 3 | 4 | 5 | 6 | 7 | 8 | 9 | 10 | 11 | 12 | 13 | 14 | 15 | 16 | 17 | 18 | 19 | 20 | 21 | 22 | 23 | 24 | 25 |
|---|---|---|---|---|---|---|---|---|---|----|----|----|----|----|----|----|----|----|----|----|----|----|----|----|----|
| 0.05 | – | – | – | 0 | 2 | 5 | 8 | 13 | 17 | 23 | 30 | 37 | 45 | 55 | 64 | 75 | 87 | 99 | 113 | 127 | 142 | 158 | 175 | 192 | 211 |
| 0.01 | – | – | – | – | 0 | 2 | 4 | 7 | 11 | 16 | 21 | 27 | 34 | 42 | 51 | 60 | 70 | 81 | 93 | 105 | 118 | 133 | 148 | 164 | 180 |

| n | 26 | 27 | 28 | 29 | 30 | 31 | 32 | 33 | 34 | 35 | 36 | 37 | 38 | 39 | 40 | 41 | 42 | 43 | 44 | 45 | 46 | 47 | 48 | 49 | 50 |
|---|----|----|----|----|----|----|----|----|----|----|----|----|----|----|----|----|----|----|----|----|----|----|----|----|----|
| 0.05 | 230 | 250 | 272 | 294 | 317 | 341 | 365 | 391 | 418 | 445 | 473 | 503 | 533 | 564 | 596 | 628 | 662 | 697 | 732 | 769 | 806 | 845 | 884 | 924 | 965 |
| 0.01 | 198 | 216 | 235 | 255 | 276 | 298 | 321 | 344 | 369 | 394 | 420 | 447 | 475 | 504 | 533 | 564 | 595 | 627 | 660 | 694 | 729 | 765 | 802 | 839 | 877 |

Calculated $U$ must be EQUAL TO or LESS THAN the table (critical) value for significance at the level shown.
For a one-tailed test, probabilities shown are halved.

SOURCE: H. R. Neave, *Statistical Tables*, George Allen and Unwin, London (1978) with the kind permission of the author and publisher (Harper and Row, Publisher, Inc.).

# Table 6   Critical values of *T* in the Wilcoxon Rank Sum test

| | Level of significance | | Number of scores in the smaller sample ($n_2$) | | | | | | | | | | | | | | | | | | |
|---|---|---|---|---|---|---|---|---|---|---|---|---|---|---|---|---|---|---|---|---|---|---|
| | One-tailed | Two-tailed | 1 | 2 | 3 | 4 | 5 | 6 | 7 | 8 | 9 | 10 | 11 | 12 | 13 | 14 | 15 | 16 | 17 | 18 | 19 | 20 |
| **3** | 0.10 | 0.20 | 3 | 7 | | | | | | | | | | | | | | | | | | |
| | 0.05 | 0.10 | | 6 | | | | | | | | | | | | | | | | | | |
| | 0.025 | 0.05 | | | | | | | | | | | | | | | | | | | | |
| | 0.005 | 0.01 | | | (4) | | | | | | | | | | | | | | | | | |
| **4** | 0.10 | 0.20 | 3 | 7 | 13 | | | | | | | | | | | | | | | | | |
| | 0.05 | 0.10 | | 6 | 11 | | | | | | | | | | | | | | | | | |
| | 0.025 | 0.05 | | | 10 | | | | | | | | | | | | | | | | | |
| | 0.005 | 0.01 | | | | (5) | | | | | | | | | | | | | | | | |
| **5** | 0.10 | 0.20 | 4 | 8 | 14 | 20 | | | | | | | | | | | | | | | | |
| | 0.05 | 0.10 | 3 | 7 | 12 | 19 | | | | | | | | | | | | | | | | |
| | 0.025 | 0.05 | | 6 | 11 | 17 | | | | | | | | | | | | | | | | |
| | 0.005 | 0.01 | | | | 15 | (6) | | | | | | | | | | | | | | | | |
| **6** | 0.10 | 0.20 | 4 | 9 | 15 | 22 | 30 | | | | | | | | | | | | | | | |
| | 0.05 | 0.10 | 3 | 8 | 13 | 20 | 28 | | | | | | | | | | | | | | | |
| | 0.025 | 0.05 | | 7 | 12 | 18 | 26 | | | | | | | | | | | | | | | |
| | 0.005 | 0.01 | | | 10 | 16 | 23 | (7) | | | | | | | | | | | | | | | |
| **7** | 0.10 | 0.20 | 4 | 10 | 16 | 23 | 32 | 41 | | | | | | | | | | | | | | |
| | 0.05 | 0.10 | 3 | 8 | 14 | 21 | 29 | 39 | | | | | | | | | | | | | | |
| | 0.025 | 0.05 | | 7 | 13 | 20 | 27 | 36 | | | | | | | | | | | | | | |
| | 0.005 | 0.01 | | | 10 | 16 | 24 | 32 | (8) | | | | | | | | | | | | | | |
| **8** | 0.10 | 0.20 | 5 | 11 | 17 | 25 | 34 | 44 | 55 | | | | | | | | | | | | | |
| | 0.05 | 0.10 | 4 | 9 | 15 | 23 | 31 | 41 | 51 | | | | | | | | | | | | | |
| | 0.025 | 0.05 | 3 | 8 | 14 | 21 | 29 | 38 | 49 | | | | | | | | | | | | | |
| | 0.005 | 0.01 | | | 11 | 17 | 25 | 34 | 43 | (9) | | | | | | | | | | | | |
| **9** | 0.10 | 0.20 | 1 | 5 | 11 | 19 | 27 | 36 | 46 | 58 | 70 | | | | | | | | | | | |
| | 0.05 | 0.10 | | 4 | 9 | 16 | 24 | 33 | 43 | 54 | 66 | | | | | | | | | | | |
| | 0.025 | 0.05 | | 3 | 8 | 14 | 22 | 31 | 40 | 51 | 62 | | | | | | | | | | | |
| | 0.005 | 0.01 | | | 6 | 11 | 18 | 26 | 35 | 45 | 56 | (10) | | | | | | | | | | |
| **10** | 0.10 | 0.20 | 1 | 6 | 12 | 20 | 28 | 38 | 49 | 60 | 73 | 87 | | | | | | | | | | |
| | 0.05 | 0.10 | | 4 | 10 | 17 | 26 | 35 | 45 | 56 | 69 | 82 | | | | | | | | | | |
| | 0.025 | 0.05 | | 3 | 9 | 15 | 23 | 32 | 42 | 53 | 65 | 78 | | | | | | | | | | |
| | 0.005 | 0.01 | | | 6 | 12 | 19 | 27 | 37 | 47 | 58 | 71 | (11) | | | | | | | | | |
| **11** | 0.10 | 0.20 | 1 | 6 | 13 | 21 | 30 | 40 | 51 | 63 | 76 | 91 | 106 | | | | | | | | | |
| | 0.05 | 0.10 | | 4 | 11 | 18 | 27 | 37 | 47 | 59 | 72 | 86 | 100 | | | | | | | | | |
| | 0.025 | 0.05 | | 3 | 9 | 16 | 24 | 34 | 44 | 55 | 68 | 81 | 96 | | | | | | | | | |
| | 0.005 | 0.01 | | | 6 | 12 | 20 | 28 | 38 | 49 | 61 | 73 | 87 | (12) | | | | | | | | |
| **12** | 0.10 | 0.20 | 1 | 7 | 14 | 22 | 32 | 42 | 54 | 66 | 80 | 94 | 110 | 127 | | | | | | | | |
| | 0.05 | 0.10 | | 5 | 11 | 19 | 28 | 38 | 49 | 62 | 75 | 89 | 104 | 120 | | | | | | | | |
| | 0.025 | 0.05 | | 4 | 10 | 17 | 26 | 35 | 46 | 58 | 71 | 84 | 99 | 115 | | | | | | | | |
| | 0.005 | 0.01 | | | 7 | 13 | 21 | 30 | 40 | 51 | 63 | 76 | 90 | 105 | | | | | | | | |

# Table 6   Continued

|  | Level of significance | | Number of scores in the smaller sample ($n_2$) | | | | | | | | | | | | | | | | | | | |
|---|---|---|---|---|---|---|---|---|---|---|---|---|---|---|---|---|---|---|---|---|---|---|
| $n_1$ | One-tailed | Two-tailed | 1 | 2 | 3 | 4 | 5 | 6 | 7 | 8 | 9 | 10 | 11 | 12 | 13 | 14 | 15 | 16 | 17 | 18 | 19 | 20 |
| **13** | 0.10 | 0.20 | 1 | 7 | 15 | 23 | 33 | 44 | 56 | 69 | 83 | 98 | 114 | 131 | 149 | | | | | | | |
| | 0.05 | 0.10 | | 5 | 12 | 20 | 30 | 40 | 52 | 64 | 78 | 92 | 108 | 125 | 142 | | | | | | | |
| | 0.025 | 0.05 | | 4 | 10 | 18 | 27 | 37 | 48 | 60 | 73 | 88 | 103 | 119 | 136 | | | | | | | |
| | 0.005 | 0.01 | | | 7 | 14 | 22 | 31 | 41 | 53 | 65 | 79 | 93 | 109 | 125 | (14) | | | | | | |
| **14** | 0.10 | 0.20 | 1 | 7 | 16 | 25 | 35 | 46 | 59 | 72 | 86 | 102 | 118 | 136 | 154 | 174 | | | | | | |
| | 0.05 | 0.10 | | 5 | 13 | 21 | 31 | 42 | 54 | 67 | 81 | 96 | 112 | 129 | 147 | 166 | | | | | | |
| | 0.025 | 0.05 | | 4 | 11 | 19 | 28 | 38 | 50 | 62 | 76 | 91 | 106 | 123 | 141 | 160 | | | | | | |
| | 0.005 | 0.01 | | | 7 | 14 | 22 | 32 | 43 | 54 | 67 | 81 | 96 | 112 | 129 | 147 | (15) | | | | | |
| **15** | 0.10 | 0.20 | 1 | 8 | 16 | 26 | 37 | 48 | 61 | 75 | 90 | 106 | 123 | 141 | 159 | 179 | 200 | | | | | |
| | 0.05 | 0.10 | | 6 | 13 | 22 | 33 | 44 | 56 | 69 | 84 | 99 | 116 | 133 | 152 | 171 | 192 | | | | | |
| | 0.025 | 0.05 | | 4 | 11 | 20 | 29 | 40 | 52 | 65 | 79 | 94 | 110 | 127 | 145 | 164 | 184 | | | | | |
| | 0.005 | 0.01 | | | 8 | 15 | 23 | 33 | 44 | 56 | 69 | 84 | 99 | 115 | 131 | 151 | 171 | (16) | | | | |
| **16** | 0.10 | 0.20 | 1 | 8 | 17 | 27 | 38 | 50 | 64 | 78 | 93 | 109 | 127 | 145 | 165 | 185 | 206 | 229 | | | | |
| | 0.05 | 0.10 | | 6 | 14 | 24 | 34 | 46 | 58 | 72 | 87 | 103 | 120 | 138 | 156 | 176 | 197 | 219 | | | | |
| | 0.025 | 0.05 | | 4 | 12 | 21 | 30 | 42 | 54 | 67 | 82 | 97 | 113 | 131 | 150 | 169 | 190 | 211 | | | | |
| | 0.005 | 0.01 | | | 8 | 15 | 24 | 34 | 46 | 58 | 72 | 86 | 102 | 119 | 136 | 155 | 175 | 196 | (17) | | | |
| **17** | 0.10 | 0.20 | 1 | 9 | 18 | 28 | 40 | 52 | 66 | 81 | 97 | 113 | 131 | 150 | 170 | 190 | 212 | 235 | 259 | | | |
| | 0.05 | 0.10 | | 6 | 15 | 25 | 35 | 47 | 61 | 75 | 90 | 106 | 123 | 142 | 161 | 182 | 203 | 225 | 249 | | | |
| | 0.025 | 0.05 | | 5 | 12 | 21 | 32 | 43 | 56 | 70 | 84 | 100 | 117 | 135 | 154 | 174 | 195 | 217 | 240 | | | |
| | 0.005 | 0.01 | | | 8 | 16 | 25 | 36 | 47 | 60 | 74 | 89 | 105 | 122 | 140 | 159 | 180 | 201 | 223 | (18) | | |
| **18** | 0.10 | 0.20 | 1 | 9 | 19 | 30 | 42 | 55 | 69 | 84 | 100 | 117 | 135 | 155 | 175 | 196 | 218 | 242 | 266 | 291 | | |
| | 0.05 | 0.10 | | 7 | 15 | 26 | 37 | 49 | 63 | 77 | 93 | 110 | 127 | 146 | 166 | 187 | 208 | 231 | 255 | 280 | | |
| | 0.025 | 0.05 | | 5 | 13 | 22 | 33 | 45 | 58 | 72 | 87 | 103 | 121 | 139 | 158 | 179 | 200 | 222 | 246 | 270 | | |
| | 0.005 | 0.01 | | | 8 | 16 | 26 | 37 | 49 | 62 | 76 | 92 | 108 | 125 | 144 | 163 | 184 | 206 | 228 | 252 | (19) | |
| **19** | 0.10 | 0.20 | 2 | 10 | 20 | 31 | 43 | 57 | 71 | 87 | 103 | 121 | 139 | 159 | 180 | 202 | 224 | 248 | 273 | 299 | 325 | |
| | 0.05 | 0.10 | 1 | 7 | 16 | 27 | 38 | 51 | 65 | 80 | 96 | 113 | 131 | 150 | 171 | 192 | 214 | 237 | 262 | 287 | 313 | |
| | 0.025 | 0.05 | | 5 | 13 | 23 | 34 | 46 | 60 | 74 | 90 | 107 | 124 | 143 | 163 | 182 | 205 | 228 | 252 | 277 | 303 | |
| | 0.005 | 0.01 | | 3 | 9 | 17 | 27 | 38 | 50 | 64 | 78 | 94 | 111 | 129 | 147 | 168 | 189 | 210 | 234 | 258 | 283 | (20) |
| **20** | 0.10 | 0.20 | 2 | 10 | 21 | 32 | 45 | 59 | 74 | 90 | 107 | 125 | 144 | 164 | 185 | 207 | 230 | 255 | 280 | 306 | 333 | 361 |
| | 0.05 | 0.10 | 1 | 7 | 17 | 28 | 40 | 53 | 67 | 83 | 99 | 117 | 135 | 155 | 175 | 197 | 220 | 243 | 268 | 294 | 320 | 348 |
| | 0.025 | 0.05 | | 5 | 14 | 24 | 35 | 48 | 62 | 77 | 93 | 110 | 128 | 147 | 167 | 188 | 210 | 234 | 258 | 283 | 309 | 337 |
| | 0.005 | 0.01 | | 3 | 9 | 18 | 28 | 39 | 52 | 66 | 81 | 97 | 114 | 132 | 151 | 172 | 193 | 215 | 239 | 263 | 289 | 315 |

*(Left side vertical label: Number of scores in the larger sample ($n_1$))*

Calculated $T$ must be EQUAL TO or LESS THAN the table (critical) value for significance at the level shown.

SOURCE: Tate and Clelland, *Non-parametric and short-cut statistics*, Interstate Printers and Publishers Inc., Eanville, Illinois (1957) by kind permission of the authors and publishers.

# Table 7 Critical values of *T* in the Wilcoxon Signed Ranks test

| | Levels of significance | | | |
|---|---|---|---|---|
| | One-tailed test | | | |
| | 0.05 | 0.025 | 0.01 | 0.001 |
| | Two-tailed test | | | |
| Sample size | 0.1 | 0.05 | 0.02 | 0.002 |
| N = 5 | T ≤ 0 | | | |
| 6 | 2 | 0 | | |
| 7 | 3 | 2 | 0 | |
| 8 | 5 | 3 | 1 | |
| 9 | 8 | 5 | 3 | |
| 10 | 10 | 8 | 5 | 0 |
| 11 | 13 | 10 | 7 | 1 |
| 12 | 17 | 13 | 9 | 2 |
| 13 | 21 | 17 | 12 | 4 |
| 14 | 25 | 21 | 15 | 6 |
| 15 | 30 | 25 | 19 | 8 |
| 16 | 35 | 29 | 23 | 11 |
| 17 | 41 | 34 | 27 | 14 |
| 18 | 47 | 40 | 32 | 18 |
| 19 | 53 | 46 | 37 | 21 |
| 20 | 60 | 52 | 43 | 26 |
| 21 | 67 | 58 | 49 | 30 |
| 22 | 75 | 65 | 55 | 35 |
| 23 | 83 | 73 | 62 | 40 |
| 24 | 91 | 81 | 69 | 45 |
| 25 | 100 | 89 | 76 | 51 |
| 26 | 110 | 98 | 84 | 58 |
| 27 | 119 | 107 | 92 | 64 |
| 28 | 130 | 116 | 101 | 71 |
| 30 | 151 | 137 | 120 | 86 |
| 31 | 163 | 147 | 130 | 94 |
| 32 | 175 | 159 | 140 | 103 |
| 33 | 187 | 170 | 151 | 112 |

Calculated *T* must be EQUAL TO or LESS THAN the table (critical) value for significance at the level shown.

SOURCE: Adapted from R. Meddis, *Statistical Handbook for Non-Statisticians*, McGraw-Hill, London (1975), with the kind permission of the author.

# Table 8   Critical values of *t*

| Degrees of freedom | Level of significance for a one-tailed test | | | |
| | 0.05 | 0.025 | 0.01 | 0.005 |
| | Level of significance for a two-tailed test | | | |
| | 0.10 | 0.05 | 0.02 | 0.01 |
|---|---|---|---|---|
| 1 | 6.314 | 12.706 | 31.821 | 63.657 |
| 2 | 2.920 | 4.303 | 6.965 | 9.925 |
| 3 | 2.353 | 3.182 | 4.541 | 5.841 |
| 4 | 2.132 | 2.776 | 3.747 | 4.604 |
| 5 | 2.015 | 2.571 | 3.365 | 4.032 |
| 6 | 1.943 | 2.447 | 3.143 | 3.707 |
| 7 | 1.895 | 2.365 | 2.998 | 3.499 |
| 8 | 1.860 | 2.306 | 2.896 | 3.355 |
| 9 | 1.833 | 2.262 | 2.821 | 3.250 |
| 10 | 1.812 | 2.228 | 2.764 | 3.169 |
| 11 | 1.796 | 2.201 | 2.718 | 3.106 |
| 12 | 1.782 | 2.179 | 2.681 | 3.055 |
| 13 | 1.771 | 2.160 | 2.650 | 3.012 |
| 14 | 1.761 | 3.145 | 2.624 | 2.977 |
| 15 | 1.753 | 2.131 | 2.602 | 2.947 |
| 16 | 1.746 | 2.120 | 2.583 | 2.921 |
| 17 | 1.740 | 2.110 | 2.567 | 2.898 |
| 18 | 1.734 | 2.101 | 2.552 | 2.878 |
| 19 | 1.729 | 2.093 | 2.539 | 2.861 |
| 20 | 1.725 | 2.086 | 2.528 | 2.845 |
| 21 | 1.721 | 2.080 | 2.518 | 2.831 |
| 22 | 1.717 | 2.074 | 2.508 | 2.819 |
| 23 | 1.714 | 2.069 | 2.500 | 2.807 |
| 24 | 1.711 | 2.064 | 2.492 | 2.797 |
| 25 | 1.708 | 2.060 | 2.485 | 2.787 |
| 26 | 1.706 | 2.056 | 2.479 | 2.779 |
| 27 | 1.703 | 2.052 | 2.473 | 2.771 |
| 28 | 1.701 | 2.048 | 2.467 | 2.763 |
| 29 | 1.699 | 2.045 | 2.462 | 2.756 |
| 30 | 1.697 | 2.042 | 2.457 | 2.750 |
| 40 | 1.684 | 2.021 | 2.423 | 2.704 |
| 60 | 1.671 | 2.000 | 2.390 | 2.660 |
| 120 | 1.658 | 1.980 | 2.358 | 2.617 |
| ∞ | 1.645 | 1.960 | 2.326 | 2.576 |

Calculated *t* must EQUAL or EXCEED the table (critical) value for significance at the evel shown.

SOURCE: Fisher and Yates, *Statistical Tables for Biological, Agricultural and Medical Research*, Oliver and Boyd, Edinburgh (1953) (Longman Group UK Ltd.).

# Table 9　Critical values of Spearman's $r_s$

| | Level of significance for a two-tailed test | | | |
|---|---|---|---|---|
| | 0.10 | 0.05 | 0.02 | 0.01 |
| | Level of significance for a one tailed text | | | |
| | 0.05 | 0.025 | 0.01 | 0.005 |
| $n=4$ | 1.000 | | | |
| 5 | 0.900 | 1.000 | 1.000 | |
| 6 | 0.829 | 0.886 | 0.943 | 1.000 |
| 7 | 0.714 | 0.786 | 0.893 | 0.929 |
| 8 | 0.643 | 0.738 | 0.833 | 0.881 |
| 9 | 0.600 | 0.700 | 0.783 | 0.833 |
| 10 | 0.564 | 0.648 | 0.745 | 0.794 |
| 11 | 0.536 | 0.618 | 0.709 | 0.755 |
| 12 | 0.503 | 0.587 | 0.671 | 0.727 |
| 13 | 0.484 | 0.560 | 0.648 | 0.703 |
| 14 | 0.464 | 0.538 | 0.622 | 0.675 |
| 15 | 0.443 | 0.521 | 0.604 | 0.654 |
| 16 | 0.429 | 0.503 | 0.582 | 0.635 |
| 17 | 0.414 | 0.485 | 0.566 | 0.615 |
| 18 | 0.401 | 0.472 | 0.550 | 0.600 |
| 19 | 0.391 | 0.460 | 0.535 | 0.584 |
| 20 | 0.380 | 0.447 | 0.520 | 0.570 |
| 21 | 0.370 | 0.435 | 0.508 | 0.556 |
| 22 | 0.361 | 0.425 | 0.496 | 0.544 |
| 23 | 0.353 | 0.415 | 0.486 | 0.532 |
| 24 | 0.344 | 0.406 | 0.476 | 0.521 |
| 25 | 0.337 | 0.398 | 0.466 | 0.511 |
| 26 | 0.331 | 0.390 | 0.457 | 0.501 |
| 27 | 0.324 | 0.382 | 0.448 | 0.491 |
| 28 | 0.317 | 0.375 | 0.440 | 0.483 |
| 29 | 0.312 | 0.368 | 0.433 | 0.475 |
| 30 | 0.306 | 0.362 | 0.425 | 0.467 |

For $n > 30$, the significance of $r_s$ can be tested by using the formula:

$$t = r_s \sqrt{\frac{n-2}{1-r_s^2}} \qquad df = n-2$$

and checking the value of $t$ in table 8.

Calculated $r_s$ must EQUAL or EXCEED the table (critical) value for significance at the level shown.

SOURCE: J. H. Zar, Significance testing of the Spearman Rank Correlation Coefficient, *Journal of the American Statistical Association*, 67, 578–80.

## Table 10   Critical values of Pearson's *r*

| | Level of significance for a one-tailed test | | | |
| --- | --- | --- | --- | --- |
| | 0.05 | 0.025 | 0.005 | 0.0005 |
| | Level of significance for two-tailed test | | | |
| *df* (N − 2) | 0.10 | 0.05 | 0.01 | 0.001 |
| 2 | 0.9000 | 0.9500 | 0.9900 | 0.9999 |
| 3 | 0.805 | 0.878 | 0.9587 | 0.9911 |
| 4 | 0.729 | 0.811 | 0.9172 | 0.9741 |
| 5 | 0.669 | 0.754 | 0.875 | 0.9509 |
| 6 | 0.621 | 0.707 | 0.834 | 0.9241 |
| 7 | 0.582 | 0.666 | 0.798 | 0.898 |
| 8 | 0.549 | 0.632 | 0.765 | 0.872 |
| 9 | 0.521 | 0.602 | 0.735 | 0.847 |
| 10 | 0.497 | 0.576 | 0.708 | 0.823 |
| 11 | 0.476 | 0.553 | 0.684 | 0.801 |
| 12 | 0.475 | 0.532 | 0.661 | 0.780 |
| 13 | 0.441 | 0.514 | 0.641 | 0.760 |
| 14 | 0.426 | 0.497 | 0.623 | 0.742 |
| 15 | 0.412 | 0.482 | 0.606 | 0.725 |
| 16 | 0.400 | 0.468 | 0.590 | 0.708 |
| 17 | 0.389 | 0.456 | 0.575 | 0.693 |
| 18 | 0.378 | 0.444 | 0.561 | 0.679 |
| 19 | 0.369 | 0.433 | 0.549 | 0.665 |
| 20 | 0.360 | 0.423 | 0.537 | 0.652 |
| 25 | 0.323 | 0.381 | 0.487 | 0.597 |
| 30 | 0.296 | 0.349 | 0.449 | 0.554 |
| 35 | 0.275 | 0.325 | 0.418 | 0.519 |
| 40 | 0.257 | 0.304 | 0.393 | 0.490 |
| 45 | 0.243 | 0.288 | 0.372 | 0.465 |
| 50 | 0.231 | 0.273 | 0.354 | 0.443 |
| 60 | 0.211 | 0.250 | 0.325 | 0.408 |
| 70 | 0.195 | 0.232 | 0.302 | 0.380 |
| 80 | 0.183 | 0.217 | 0.283 | 0.357 |
| 90 | 0.173 | 0.205 | 0.267 | 0.338 |
| 100 | 0.164 | 0.195 | 0.254 | 0.321 |

Calculated *r* must EQUAL or EXCEED the table (critical) value for significance at the level shown.

SOURCE: F. C. Powell, *Cambridge Mathematical and Statistical Tables*, Cambridge University Press (1976).

# Appendix 4 Answers to exercises

For the end-of-chapter questions only direct and specific answers are given. They are not included where the reader is asked to conduct an exercise or give an open-ended description.

**Chapter 2**

1  IV                           DV

| | IV | DV |
|---|---|---|
| (a) | Type of propaganda | Strength of attitude |
| (b) | Noise level | Work efficiency |
| (c) | Time of day | Attention span |
| (d) | Amount of practice | Level of performance |
| (e) | Smile given or not | Smile received or not |
| (f) | Level of frustration | Level of aggression |
| (g) | Order of birth | Personality and intellectual level |
| (h) | Presence or absence of crowd | People's behaviour |

2  Examples:
*Noise*: Use specific audio recording of mechanical noise. IV in terms of measured decibel levels.
*Attention span*: Measured by number of 'blips' noticed on a radar-like screen.
*Smile*: As recognised by rater who doesn't know research aim and lasting longer than one second.

3  (a) IV: pre-school education or not
       DV: cognitive skills and sociability
   (b) e.g.: pre-school children's parents more educationally concerned?
   (c) match parents (on educational concern) in both groups

**Chapter 3**

1 Test participants (or equivalent control group) *without* the confederates

2 e.g. area, number of children, age, etc.

3 Only volunteers; must read bulletin; no teetotallers

4 Only *c*

5 Placebo group; no special programme but with some attention, and where parents expect child to improve

6 e.g. left side contained a 'clever' clique

## Chapter 4
1 (b) in normal circumstances is most genuine
2 (a) measures well but *what?*
(b) gets at genuine information but results hard to generalise to other situations/ can't compare with other measures

## Chapter 5
1 (a) Field investigation – *ex post facto* because IV is sex
(b) Laboratory investigation; *ex post facto*
(c) Field experiment
(d) Laboratory experiment
(e) Laboratory quasi-experiment
(f) Laboratory investigation; *ex post facto*
(g) Field investigation
(h) Natural experiment

2 (a) a and c
(b) g and h
(c) all
(d) all

## Chapter 6
1 IV – complexity of pattern. DV – time spent gazing. Design – repeated measures (with randomisation and simultaneous presentation of IV

2 Add condition with same babies enticed over the shallow side – this gives repeated measures; *or*, have control group enticed over shallow side – independent samples

3 Repeated measures. Randomisation of IV stimuli. Avoid order effects

4 Repeated measures. Counterbalancing

5 Single subject

6 Matched pairs. Also a natural experiment

## Chapter 7
4 The raters vary very much from each other. Correlation is used and gives 0.24. Reliability is far too low

## Chapter 8
1 See page 92

3 (a) Non-random. Start of snowball sample.
  (b) Initial interviewee unwilling to admit problem; initial interviewee gives fewer further contacts; interviewer doesn't see some incidents as 'serious';

interviewer doesn't want to record the incidents for personal political reasons; interviewer is a poor questioner, is aggressive, shows prejudice etc.
(c) Structured questionnaire more reliable and objective; larger sample more representative.

5 The sixth formers are volunteers. Only schools which agreed to the study can be sampled from. Those without telephones cannot be included. Those who use the youth club are more likely to be selected.

## Chapter 9
1 (a) It has been found reliable, hence should be all right to use
  (b) Recent nuclear accident?

2 (a) Compare results with interview data?
  (b) Can't test the students again under similar circumstances so reliability will have to be checked only internally

3 Reliable, not necessarily valid

4 (a) Question invites agreement
  (b) Assumes children *should* be punished
  (c) Is this easy to answer?
  (d) Double barrelled – 'people *aren't* the same, but should be treated with respect' is a possible response
  (e) Double negative
  (f) Ambiguous responding. Extreme sexist and feminist might well agree
  (g) Technical jargon

5 Use blind assessment

## Chapter 12
2 Ordinal
3 Nominal
4 (a) Ordinal
  (b) Ratio
  (c) Interval-like but treat as ordinal
  (d) Nominal
5 Box b
6 'Top' is a measure on an ordinal scale. We don't know how far ahead of the others she was
7 Nominal – did/didn't hit kerb; Ordinal – rate smoothness on one to ten scale; Interval/ratio – measure speed in race

8

| Consistent | Inconsistent | | Consistent | Inconsistent |
|---|---|---|---|---|
| 4 | 7 | | | |
| 6 | 5 | Above Mean | 2 | 3 |
| 1 | 8 | | | |
| 9 | 10 | Below Mean | 3 | 2 |
| 2 | 3 | | | |

## Chapter 13

1 Males: mean = 171.6; median = 132. Females: mean = 367; median = 345

2 Data is skewed, therefore use median. Median = 79.25

3 Mean = 19.43

5 Since there is absolutely no variation, all scores must be the same; all scores are therefore 0.8 and the mean is 0.8

6 (a) 75.3  (b) 25.14%  (c) 1.33

7 Negative skew

## Chapter 14

1 (a) 1.32 and −0.78 are not significant. 1.75 and −1.9 are
  (b) 1.89 and −1.6 are not significant. −2.05 and 1.98 are

2 (a) 1%  (b) More likely

3 (b) true  (c) true  (d) true  (e) true  (f) false

4 (a) Type one  (b) accepting

## Chapter 15

1 Yes. None of the expected frequencies is less than five

2 (a) 'Goodness of fit' Chi-square, one variable, two categories
  (b) one-tailed, if direction predicted
  (c) No. $\chi^2$ cannot be performed on percentages. We require actual frequencies.

3 (a) 4 *df*  (b) No. More than 20% of expected frequencies are below five

4 (a) *U*: 0.025 (one-tail), 0.05 (two-tail); *T*(WRS): 0.025 (one-tail), 0.05 (two-tail)
  (b) *U*: 0.005 (one-tail), 0.01 (two-tail), *T*(WRS): Not sig. (one- or two-tail)
  (c) *T*(WSR): 0.025 (one-tail), 0.05 (two-tail)
  (d) 0.001 (one-tail), 0.002 (two-tail)

5 $N = 8, S = 1$. Result is significant at 5%, one-tailed only. We assume a nega ve evaluation wasn't predicted. Hence not significant (two-tail)

## Chapter 16

1 (a) No homogeneity of variance, unrelated design and very different subject numbers. Therefore very unwise. Mann–Whitney/Wilcoxon Rank Sum
  (b) Lack of homogeneity of variance but related design. Therefore, safe to carry on with *t*

2 No. *df* = 10. *cv* (two-tailed) at $p < 0.01 = 3.169$

3 (a) *NS*, keep NH
  (b) 0.01, 1%, reject NH
  (c) NS, keep NH
  (d) 0.005, 0.5%, reject NH
  (e) NS, keep NH
  (f) 0.01, 1%, reject NH

4 Distributions are skewed, contrary to normal distribution assumption. Since samples are large, assume this mirrors the whole population.

## Chapter 17

1 (c) negative
  (d) strong/very strong
  (e) $p < 0.0005$

2 (a) accept  (b) accept  (c) reject  (d) accept  (e) reject  (f) accept
(g) accept

3 No. For Pearson, data must meet parametric requirements

4 Spearman. Data should be treated as ordinal because human judgement

5 Check her calculations – highest possible is 1

6 Sex is a nominal variable only

## Chapter 18

1 Unrelated $t$; simpler alternative – Mann–Whitney or Wilcoxon Rank Sum

2 Mann–Whitney or Wilcoxon Rank Sum

3 Chi-square

4 Chi-square

5 Sign test

6 (a) Related $t$; simpler alternative – Wilcoxon Signed Ranks
  (b) Pearson's correlation; simpler alternative – Spearman

7 Pearson; simpler alternative – Spearman; Validity test – unrelated $t$

8 Spearman correlation

9 Chi-square – 'goodness of fit'

10 Chi-square

11 Related $t$; simpler alternative – Wilcoxon Signed Ranks

12 Wilcoxon Signed Ranks

## ANSWERS TO STRUCTURED QUESTIONS

## STRUCTURED QUESTION 1

1 Attendance at the project or not
2 Provides baseline comparison so we can rule out the possiblity that any changes or IQ values gained would have occurred irrespective of the project.
3 No. This is systematic sampling – every child does *not* have an equal chance of being selected.
4 Other parents probably didn't volunteer. Project parents may be particularly interested in their children's education and therefore might stimulate their children more *outside* the project.
5 Nominal.
6 Chi-squared. Data are nominal, in frequency form. The test is of difference (or association). Design is unrelated.
7 If more than 20% of expected frequency cell values are less than 5 – in this case if *any* expected cell is less than 5. Also, if frequencies in any cell are linked to frequencies in any other cell. Also, if cell values are proportions.
8 Mann–Whitney, Wilcoxon Rank Sum or unrelated *t* test. Safer to use rank tests because IQ scores not true interval scale data. Tests are preferable because they make use of more information about the data. Therefore more sensitive.
9 Groups' scores are significantly different. Reject idea that they vary at chance level only.
10 They had rejected the null hypothesis when true.
11 (a) It produces similar results on similar occasions.
    (b) Tested on large sample of target population. Unreliable items rejected. Norms for population established.
12 Reasons given in answer to question 4. Children might be aware of 'special' nature of study and try harder (or parents may push them). Children enjoy special attention given.
13 If project works well, are all the other children disadvantaged by not participating? Families shown information which might identify them, asked for permission to publish, asked to comment on report.

## STRUCTURED QUESTION 2

1 Longitudinal; correlational; *ex post facto*.
2 Longitudinal – subjects drop out; correlational and *ex post facto* – no control over extraneous variables.
3 Children not attending playgroup could not be selected. Only those staying a long time were selected.
4 So that children experience some similarity in environment over the period of the study and do not suffer school disruption (for instance).
5 Researcher bias. She knows their last result and may expect certain performances. Could use tester 'blind' to the previous scores of each child.

6

IQ
15 years

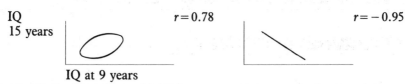

$r = 0.78$  $r = -0.95$

IQ at 9 years

7 (a) 122.5  (b) 16% (or 15.87%)
8 Have to treat IQ scores as interval. Some would argue they're really ordinal. However, if standardisation is good can assume interval level.
9 One-tailed (expect positive correlation).
10 (a) no  (b) $p < 0.01$ or 1%
11 As one increased the other decreased.
12 (a) IQ scores of the children at ages nine and 15 will not correlate significantly (or, will correlate at a chance level only).
   (b) rejected
13 New researcher has fewer subjects
14 The non-significant result fails to support; the significant result supports.
15 Cultural bias. Only useful with population on whom test was standardised. Tests narrow range of intellectual skill – not creative problem solving, for instance.

## STRUCTURED QUESTION 3

1 *Advantages*: no between-subject variables; subject is own control; quicker; cheaper. *Disadvantages*: generalising to larger group is hazardous; subject becomes specialised – not representative behaviour.
2 IV – left- or right-side presentation. DV – speed of word recognition.
3 Words are comparatively similar (in size, length, frequency etc).
4 Subject may be trying to be fast by guessing.
5 (a) So subject cannot predict nature or position of next item.  (b) tables, computer, selection from jumbled item numbers.
6 Ratio.
7 Data do not come from a normal distribution. Also data are unrelated. Perhaps variances were very different.
8 Mann–Whitney or Wilcoxon Rank Sum.
9 See figure 28, page 160.
10 (a) Perhaps subject, contrary to instruction, always looks to the left of the screen. Perhaps subject does not have language centres mostly left hemisphere located (perhaps a left hander)  (b) It should be retained; although difference was significant, researcher made a one-tailed prediction in the opposite direction.
11 $p$ at least less than 0.01
12 (a) Independent samples  (b) *Advantage*: no order effects. *Disadvantage*: subject variables  (c) Random allocation to conditions.

## STRUCTURED QUESTION 4

1 Unstructured, therefore richer, perhaps more genuine information. Quicker than observation and less likely to cause bias through researcher's deeper personal involvement.

2 Response set; social desirability.

3 Participants may not offer information under questioning of either form. Researcher has longer to gain trust and assure confidentiality.

4 Lecturers may have a lot more work in their department; head may be harder to work for.

5 Ordinal.

6 Test is consistent within itself. Participants do not score high on some items but low on items with similar sense and direction.

7 Items randomly split into two equal sets and participants results on the two sets correlated.

8 (Spearman's) correlation.

9 It is high.

10 Number in sample; significance level set.

11 Strength relates to the actual correlation value. Significance relates to the improbability of obtaining that value, given the number of participants.

12 More specific questionnaire. Look for similar effects in similar departments elsewhere.

13 Questionnaires more impersonal; participants may not have trusted assurances of confidentiality.

14 Disclosure, perhaps indirectly, of participants' views and consequences for them. Effect on morale of departments. Checking report with participants first.

## STRUCTURED QUESTION 5

1 They are volunteers.

2 (a) Cues to subject about research aim  (b) The impossibility of the tasks, if extreme, may alert subjects to experimenter's aim.

3 Inter-rater reliability.

4 Correlation.

5 (a) Variable, other than the IV, responsible for changes observed  (b) Compare with control group.

6 Ordinal.

7 Wilcoxon Signed Ranks.

8 (a) Post-treatment scores will be significantly higher than pre-treatment scores  (b) One-tailed.

9 Less than 0.05.

10 Subjective assessment/interpretation of rating scale; generally low reliability. reliability.

11 Open questionnaire; reactions to violent film; physiological measures.

12 (a) Steps taken to measure phenomenon  (b) Rorschach rating scale.

## STRUCTURED QUESTION 6

1 IV: common or uncommon words. DV: time taken to solve each anagram.

2 Repeated measures.

3 (a) To avoid order effects  (b) Half the subjects do common words first. The other half do uncommon words first.  (c) Randomising the anagrams into one list (or leaving a long time between testing each condition).

4 Presence of subject variables.

5 Subjects' unfamiliarity with certain words; timing errors, if unsystematic.
6 Variations in wording and approach cannot be said to be responsible for any changes observed. Sticking to this procedure, experimenters cannot be tempted to give help or clues to the design.
7 (a) Mean would be distorted in value by the last, very high value.
  (b) $H$ (because median is 125).
8 Ratio/Interval.
9 (a) Yes  (b) Values must come from normally distributed population. Variances should not be too dissimilar.
10 More sensitive, power efficient, generalisable.
11 Level at which null hypothesis rejected. Results too unlikely to be chance fluctuation.
12 Yes. Nine out of ten uncommon times are longer than common. Differences are mostly quite large.
13 Uncommon words formed by unusual letter combinations (e.g. '*psychology*').

# STRUCTURED QUESTION 7

1 No. Independent variable not controlled.
2 Subjects drawn at same time from several groups, in this case age groups of mothers.
3 *Advantage*: don't lose subjects, as happens in longitudinal studies; immediate results. *Disadvantages*: subject variables; one group may have experienced public changes which other group haven't.
4 *Advantage*: more natural behaviour. *Disadvantage*: less control.
5 Can code all behaviour in detail after data collection at appropriate speed.
6 (a) So results can be generalised, and effects noted aren't linked to particular features of this sample  (b) Class, area, schooling etc.
7 Variables (such as arrival of milkman) might otherwise affect any consistency in behaviour observed.
8 So they don't slant their ratings towards or away from it.
9 Use correlation of their two sets of results.
10 Human judgements like these can't be said to have equal intervals between the whole number units.
11 34  45  56  56  56  65  68  78  78  89
12 Mann–Whitney or Wilcoxon Rank Sum.
13 No. Although we can't reject the null hypothesis, a result with probability less than 0.07 is so close to significance that we may well be making a type-two error. It is worth replicating.
14 Ask mothers about discipline and why it is necessary. Look for categories of response, including those stressing need to control.
15 All participants should be given a complete report. Researcher should anyway sit and explain the project in non-specialist language. The mother has the right to remove her material, though researcher might try to assuage her doubts about confidentiality and the security of the raw video data.

# STRUCTURED QUESTION 8

1 Repeated measures.
2 Each baby is its own control for comparison.

3 (a) Practice, fatigue  (b) Babies may well get tired or get used to the supportive feel of the glass as compared to its appearance on the deep side  (c) Counterbalance conditions.

4 To provide baseline comparison with the deep-side behaviour.

5 Older babies may have crawled on 'risky' surfaces already.

6 (a) Artificial environment may produce unrepresentative behaviour: Can only test narrow range of behaviour over short period  (b) Cliff is artificial and novel anyway so perhaps laboratory location less of a problem; Cliff *does* only test narrow range of child's possible reactions to visual depth environments.

7 Nominal.

8 Binomial sign test.

9 No. It uses the lowest, least sensitive level of measurement.

10 One-tailed.

11 They *could* still be a coincidence. The significance level of 5% just tells us that if it *is* a coincidence, it is one which would occur less times than five in a hundred on average.

12 By replication.

13 Yes. Babies could have learned to respond to depth cues over the period up until they were able to crawl and hence, to be tested.

14 (a) If she knew she might somehow help the child to conform to the researcher's expectations (or not)  (b) A full report, outlining the relevance of the research and the usual response of babies, should be given to each participant.

# STRUCTURED QUESTION 9

1 Independent samples/groups/subjects.

2 *Advantage*: Eliminates order effects. *Disadvantage*: Introduces subject variables as possibly responsible for differences between conditions.

3 Order effects dealt with by counterbalancing. Two equivalent lists of words would be needed.

4 (a) Random allocation  (b) So there is no bias in the selection of subjects for each group.

5 Computer might blink erratically. For some subjects certain words might be unfamiliar.

6 Differences in number of words recalled in the two conditions (imagery and recall) will not be higher than would be expected if scores in the two conditions differ at a chance level only.

7 Means.

8 More sensitive. Useful for parametric tests.

9 Measure of dispersion used on interval level data. Measure of how widely or not scores are distributed around the mean.

10 Better able to detect real differences if there.

11 Interval level data or above; values from normally distributed population; variances not too dissimilar.

12 Unrelated data for which variances are quite different as are numbers of subjects in the two groups.

13 Mann–Whitney or Wilcoxon Rank Sum.

14 1% (or $p < 0.01$).
15 Could be just the 'story' created by the links – test on people with poor visual imagery. Could be that subjects just found the imagery condition very interesting; could try to make rehearsal condition interesting too.
16 To show how people perform with no explicit instruction. Serves as comparative baseline.

## STRUCTURED QUESTION 10

1 (a) Matched pairs design  (b) Reduces likelihood of subject variables being responsible for differences observed.
2 Interpersonal factors can influence participants' responses.
3 Various question weaknesses, see page (000). Making questionnaire reliable.
4 Participants might try to 'look good' on the questionnaire. Therapist can perhaps get closer to the truth.
5 Test of concurrent validity.
6 Because participants in the experimental programme might improve solely because they know they're expected to or are getting special attention.
7 They would be given an arbitrary treatment, say simple discussion of irrelevant issues.
8 Scores on a questionnaire, or human estimates on a numerical scale, cannot be said to have equal intervals between each value. They only have sense as comparisons with other scores or ratings.
9 Less sensitive since less subtle information is used in the test compared with a parametric test.
10 Wilcoxon $T$ (note: matched pairs produce related data).
11 Yes. 0.87 is fairly high. 1.0 is the highest value achievable.
12 When there are few subjects/pairs of scores.
13 (a) Variable other than the independent variable which is responsible for all or part of changes observed  (b) The treatment group volunteered – may have had higher motivation to improve; participants may improve because their expectancy of improvement provides motivation.
14 The controls should also join the programme if they wish to.

# References

Ainsworth, M. D. S. (1967) *Infancy in Uganda*. Baltimore: John Hopkins University Press.

Ainsworth, M. D. S., Bell, S. M. & Stayton, D. J. (1971) Individual differences in strange situation behaviour of one-year-olds. In Schaffer, H. R. (ed.) (1971) *The Origins of Human Social Relations*. London: Academic Press.

Allport, G. W. (1947) *The Use of Personal Documents in Psychological Science*. London: Holt, Rinehart and Winston.

American Psychological Association (1987) *Casebook on Ethical Principles of Psychologists*. Washington: American Psychological Association.

Aronson, E. & Carlsmith, J. M. (1968) Experimentation in social psychology. In Lindzey, G. & Aronson, E. (eds.) (1968) *Handbook of Social Psychology*, 2: Reading, Mass.: Addison–Wesley.

Asch, S. E. (1956) Studies of independence and submission to group pressure. 1. A minority of one against a unanimous majority. In *Psychological Monographs*, 70 (9) (Whole No. 416).

Bandura, A. (1965) Influence of models' reinforcement contingencies on the acquisition of imitative responses. *Journal of Personality and Social Psychology*, 1, 589–95.

Bandura, A. (1977) *Social Learning Theory*. Englewood Cliffs, NJ: Prentice–Hall.

Barber, T. X. (1976) *Pitfalls in Human Research*. Oxford: Pergamon.

Becker, H. S. (1958) Inference and proof in participant observation. *American Sociological Review*, 23, 652–60.

Benedict, R. (1934) *Patterns of Culture*. Boston: Houghton Mifflin.

Block, N. J. & Dworkin, G. (1974) IQ – heritability and inequality. *Philosophy and Public Affairs*, 3, 331–407.

Bogardus, E. S. (1925) Measuring social distance. *Journal of Applied Sociology*, 9, 299–308.

Bowlby, J. (1951) *Maternal Care and Mental Health*. Geneva: World Health Organisation.

Bowlby, J. (1953) *Child Care and the Growth of Love*. Harmondsworth: Penguin.

Bramel, D. A. (1962) A dissonance theory approach to defensive projection. *Journal of Abnormal and Social Psychology*, 64, 121–9.

British Psychological Society (1978) Ethical Principles for Research with Human Subjects. Statement at Annual General Meeting. April, 1978.

British Psychological Society (1985) A code of conduct for psychologists. *Bulletin of the British Psychology Society*, 38, 41–3.

Bromley, D. B. (1986) *The Case Study Method in Psychology and Related Disciplines*. Chichester: Wiley.

Brown, R. (1965) *Social Psychology*. New York: Free Press.

Brown, R. Fraser, C. & Bellugi, U. (1964) *The Acquisition of Language*. Monographs of the Society for Research in Child Development 29. 92.

Bruner, E. M. & Kelso, J. P. (1980) Gender differences in graffiti: a semiotic perspective. In *Women's Studies International Quarterly*, 3, 239–52.

Bryant, B. Harris, M. & Newton, D. (1980) *Children and Minders*. London: Grant McIntyre.

Burgess, R. G. (1984) *In the Field: an Introduction to Field Research*. Allen & Unwin: Hemel Hempstead.

Caldwell, B. M. & Bradley, R. H. (1978) Manual for the home observation of the environment, Unpublished manuscript. Little Rock, Ark.: University of Arkansas.

Charlesworth, R. & Hartup, W. W. (1967) Positive social reinforcement in the nursery school peer group. *Child Development*, 38, 993–1002.

Cohen, L. & Holliday, M. (1982) *Statistics for Social Scientists*. London: Harper & Row.

Crano, W. D. & Brewer, M. B. (1973) *Principles of Research in Social Psychology*. New York: McGraw-Hill.

Cronbach, L. J. (1960) *Essentials of Psychological Testing*. New York: Harper & Row.

Darwin, C. (1877) A biographical sketch of an infant. *Mind*, 2, 285–94.

Davie, R., Butler, N. & Goldstein, H. (1972) From Birth to Seven. London: Longman.

Davis, J. H., Kerr, H. L., Atkin, R. H. & Meek, D. (1975) The decision processes of 6 and 12 person mock juries assigned unanimous and two thirds majority rules. *Journal of Personality and Social Psychology*, 32, 1–14.

De Waele, J.–P. and Harré, R. (1979) Autobiography as a psychological method. In Ginsburg, G. P. (1979) (ed.) *Emerging Strategies in Social Psychological Research*. Chichester: Wiley.

Diesing, P. (1972) *Patterns of Discovery in the Social Sciences*. London: Routledge and Kegan Paul.

Doob, A. N. & Gross, A. E. (1968) Status of frustration as an inhibitor of horn-honking response. *Journal of Social Psychology*, 76, 213–8.

Douglas, J. D. (1972) *Research on Deviance*. New York: Random House.

Elton, B. (1989) *Stark*. London: Sphere Books.

Eron, L. D., Huesmann, L. R., Lefkowitz, M. M. & Walder, L. D. (1972) Does television violence cause aggression? *American Psychologist*, 27, 253–63.

Eysenck, H. J. (1970) *The Structure of Human Personality*. London: Methuen.

Eysenck, H. J. & Eysenck, S. B. G. (1975) *Manual of the Eysenck Personality Questionnaire*. London: Hodder and Stoughton.

Festinger, L., Riecken, H. W. & Schachter, S. (1956) *When Prophecy Fails*. Minneapolis: University of Minnesota Press.

Finch, J. (1984) 'It's great to have someone to talk to': the ethics and politics of interviewing women. In Bell, C. & Roberts, H. (eds.) (1984) *Social Researching: Policies, Problems and Practice*. London: Routledge and Kegan Paul.

Frankenburg, R. (1957) *Village on the border*. London: Cohen and West.

Friedman, N. (1967) *The Social Nature of Psychological Research*. New York: Basic Books.

Friedrich, L. K. & Stein, A. H. (1973) Aggressive and prosocial television programs and the natural behaviour of pre-school children. *Monographs of the Society for Research in Child Development*. 38(4, serial No. 51).

Gerbner, G., Gross, L., Signorielli, N., Morgan, M. & Jacksonbeeck, M. (1979) Violence profile No. 10: trends in network television drama and view conceptions of reality. Annenberg School of Communications, University of Pennsylvania (mimeo).

Glaser, B. G. & Strauss, A. L. (1967) *The Discovery of Grounded Theory: Strategies for Qualitative Research*. Chicago: Aldine.

Gregory, R. L. & Wallace, J. G. (1963) *Recovery from Early Blindness*. Cambridge: Heffer.

Gross, R. D. (1987) *Psychology: The Science of Mind and Behaviour*. London: Hodder and Stoughton.

Guttman, L. (1950) The third component of scalable attitudes. *International Journal of Opinion and Attitude Research*, 4, 285–7.

Hall, B. L. (1975) Participatory research: an approach for change. *Convergence, an International Journal of Adult Education*, 8(2), 24–32.

Hammond, K. R. (1948) Measuring attitudes by error-choice: an indirect method. *Journal of Abnormal Social Psychology*, 43, 38–48.

Hampden-Turner, C. (1971) *Radical Man*. London: Duckworth.

Harré, R. (1981) The positivist–empiricist approach and its alternative. In Reason, R. & Rowan, J. (1981) *Human Inquiry: A Sourcebook of New Paradigm Research*. Chichester: Wiley.

Hatfield, E. & Walster, G. W. (1981) *A New Look at Love*. Reading, Mass.: Addison–Wesley.

Heather, N. (1976) *Radical Perspectives in Psychology*. London: Methuen.

Hinckley, E. D. (1932) The influence of individual opinion on construction of an attitude scale. *Journal of Social Psychology*, 3, 283–96.

Hofling, K. C., Brotzman, E., Dalrymple, S., Graves, N. & Pierce, C. M. (1966) An experimental study in the nurse–physician relationship. *Journal of Nervous and Mental Disorders*, 143, 171–80.

Horowitz, I. A. & Rothschild, B. H. (1970) Conformity as a function of deception and role-playing. *Journal of Personality and Social Psychology*, 14, 224–6.

Humphreys, L. (1970) *Tearoom Trade*. Chicago: Aldine.

Jahoda-Lazarsfeld, M. & Zeisl, H. (1932) *Die Arbeitslosen von Marienthal*. Leipzig: Hirzel.

Jowell, R. & Topf, R. (1988) *British Social Attitudes*. London: Gower.

Joynson, R. B. (1989) *The Burt Affair*. London: Routledge.

Kagan, J., Kearsley, R. B. & Zelazo, P. R. (1980) *Infancy – Its Place in Human Development*. Cambridge, Mass.: Harvard University Press.

Kamin, L. J. (1977) *The Science and Politics of IQ*. Harmondsworth: Penguin.

Kerlinger, F. N. (1969) *Foundations of Behavioural Research*. London: Holt, Rinehart and Winston.

Kidder, L. H. (1981) *Selltiz Wrightsman and Cook's Research Methods in Social Relations*, 4th ed. New York: Holt, Rinehart and Winston.

Kinsey, A. C., Pomeroy, W. B., Martin, C. E. & Gebhard, P. H. (1953) *Sexual Behaviour in the Human Female*. Philadelphia: Saunders.

Kinsey, A. C., Pomeroy, W. B. & Martin, C. E. (1948) *Sexual Behaviour in the Human Male*. Philadelphia: Saunders.

Kohlberg, L. (1981) *Essays on Moral Development*. New York: Harper and Row.

Kohler, W. (1925) *The Mentality of Apes*. New York: Harcourt Brace Jovanovich.

Kounin, J. & Gump, P. (1961) The comparative influence of punitive and non-punitive teachers upon children's concepts of school misconduct. *Journal of Educational Psychology*, 52, 44–9.

Kuhn, T. (1962) *The Structure of Scientific Revolutions*. Chicago, Ill.: University of Chicago.

Latané, B. & Darley, J. M. (1976) *Help in a Crisis: Bystander Response to an Emergency*. Morristown, NJ: General Learning Press.

Leeper, R. (1935) A study of a neglected portion of the field of learning – the development of sensory organisation. *Journal of Genetic Psychology*, 46, 41–74.

Levin, R. B. (1978) An empirical test of the female castration complex. In Fisher, S. & Greenberg, R. P. (1978) *The Scientific Evaluation of Freud's Theories and Therapy*. New York: Basic Books.

Leyens, J., Camino, L., Parke, R. D. & Berkowitz, L. (1975) Effects of movie violence on aggression in a field setting as a function of group dominance and cohesion. *Journal of Personality and Social Psychology*, 32, 346–60.

Likert, R. A. (1932) A technique for the measurement of attitudes, *Archives of Psychology*, 140, 55.

Luria, A. R. (1969) *The Mind of a Mnemonist*. London: Jonathan Cape.

Madge, J. (1953) *The Tools of Social Science*. London: Longman.

Marsh, P. (1978) *The Rules of Disorder*. London: Routledge.

Masling, J. (1966) Role-related behaviour of the subject and psychologist and its effect upon psychological data. In Levine, D. (ed.) (1966) Nebraska Symposium on Motivation. Lincoln, Neb.: University of Nebraska Press.

Medawar, P. B. (1963) Is the scientific paper a fraud? *The Listener*, 10, 377–8.

Menges, R. J. (1973) Openess and honesty versus coercion and deception in psychological research. *American Psychologist*, 28, 1030–34.

Milgram, S. (1974) *Obedience to Authority*. New York: Harper and Row.

Milgram, S. (1963) Behavioural study of obedience. *Journal of Abnormal and Social Psychology*, 67, 371–8.

Mitroff, I. I. (1974) Studying the lunar rock scientist. *Saturday Review World*, 2 Nov. 64–5.

Mixon, D. (1974) If you won't deceive what can you do? In Armistead, N. (ed.) (1974) *Reconstructing Social Psychology*. London: Penguin Education.

Mixon, D. (1979) Understanding shocking and puzzling conduct. In Ginsburg, G. P. (ed.) (1979) *Emerging Strategies in Social Psychological Research*. Chichester: Wiley.

Ogilvie, D. M., Stone, D. J. & Shniedman, E. S. (1966) Some characteristics of genuine versus simulated suicide notes. In Stone, P. J., Dunphy, C. Smith, M. S. & Ogilvie, D. M. (eds.) (1966) *The General Enquirer: A Computer Approach to Content Analysis in the Behavioral Sciences*. Cambridge: MIT Press.

Ora, J. P. (1965) Characteristics of the volunteer for psychological investigations. Office of Naval Research Contract 2149(03), Technical Report 27.

Orne, M. T. (1962) On the social psychology of the psychological experiment: with particular reference to demand characteristics and their implications. *American Psychologist*, 17, 776–83.

Osgood, C. E., Luria, Z., Jeans, R. F. & Smith, S. W. (1976) The three faces of Evelyn: a case report. *Journal of Abnormal Psychology*, 85, 247–86.

Osgood, C. E., Suci, G. J. & Tannenbaum, P. H. (1957) *The Measurement of Meaning*. Urbana: University of Illinois.

Patton, M. Q. (1980) *Qualitative Evaluation Methods*. London: Sage.

Peronne, V., Patton, M. Q. & French, B. (1976) *Does Accountability Count without Teacher Support?* Minneapolis: Centre for Social Research, University of Minnesota.

Piliavin, I. M., Rodin, J. & Piliavin, J. A. (1969) Good samaritanism: an underground phenomenon? *Journal of Personality and Social Psychology*, 13, 289–99.

Potter, J. & Wetherell, M. (1987) *Discourse and Social Psychology: Beyond Attitudes and Behaviour*. London: Sage.

Raffetto, A. M. (1967) Experimenter effect on subjects' reported hallucinatory experiences under visual and auditory deprivation. Master's thesis, San Francisco State College.

Reason, P. & Rowan, J. (1981) (eds.) *Human Enquiry: A Sourcebook in New Paradigm Research*. Chichester: Wiley.

Ring, K., Wallston, K. & Corey, M. (1970) Mode of debriefing as a factor affecting subjective reaction to a Milgram-type obedience experiment: an ethical inquiry. *Representative Research in Social Psychology*, 1, 67–88.

Roethlisberger, F. J. & Dickson, W. J. (1939) *Management and the Worker*. Cambridge, Mass.: Harvard University Press.

Rogers, C. R. (1961) *On Becoming a Person: a Therapist's View of Psychotherapy*. London: Constable.

Rokeach, M. (1960) *The Open and Closed Mind*. New York: Basic Books.

Rosenhahn, D. L. (1973) On being sane in insane places. *Science*, 179, 250–8.

Rosenthal, R. (1966) *Experimenter Effects in Behavioural Research*. New York: Appleton-Century-Crofts.

Rutter, M. (1971) Parent–child separation: psychological effects on the children. *Journal of Child Psychology and Psychiatry*. 12, 233–60.

Sears, R. R., Maccoby, E. & Levin, H. (1957) *Patterns of Child Rearing*. Evanston, Ill.: Row, Petersen & Co.

Seligman, M. (1972) *Biological Boundaries of Learning*. New York: Appleton-Century-Crofts.

Shaffer, D. R. (1985) *Developmental Psychology: Theory, Research and Applications*. Pacific Grove, Ca.: Brooks/Cole.

Shneidman, E. S. (1963) Plan 11. The logic of politics. In Arons, L. & May, M. A. (eds.) (1963) *Television and Human Behaviour*. New York: Appleton-Century-Crofts.

Sims, D. (1981) From ethogeny to endogeny: how participants in research projects can end up doing action research on their own awareness. In Reason, P. and Rowan, J. (1981) (eds.) *Human Enquiry: A Sourcebook in New Paradigm Research*. Chichester: Wiley.

Storms, M. D. (1973) Videotape and the attribution process: reversing actors' and observers' points of view. *Journal of Personality and Social Psychology*, 27, 165–75.

Tandon, R. (1981) Dialogue as inquiry and intervention. In Reason, P. & Rowan, J. (1981) *Human Inquiry: A Sourcebook in New Paradigm Research*. Chichester: Wiley.

Thurstone, L. L. (1931) The measurement of social attitudes. *Journal of Abnormal and Social Psychology*, 26, 249–69.

Torbert, W. R. (1981) Why educational research has been so uneducational: the case for a new model of social science based on collaborative enquiry. In Reason, P. & Rowan, J. (1981) *Human Inquiry*. Chichester: Wiley.

Valentine, E. R. (1982) *Conceptual Issues in Psychology*. London: Allen and Unwin.

Vidich, A. J. & Bensman, J. (1958) *Small Town in Mass Society*. Princeton, NJ: Princeton University Press.

Watson, J. B. & Rayner, R. (1920) Conditioned emotional reactions. *Journal of Experimental Psychology*, 3, 1–14.

Weber, S. J. & Cook, T. D. (1972) Subject effects in laboratory research: an examination of subject roles, demand characteristics and valid inference. *Psychological Bulletin*, 77, 273–95.

Whorf, B. L. (1957) *Language, Thought and Reality*. Cambridge, Mass.: MIT Press.

Whyte, W. F. (1943) *Street Corner Society: the Social Structure of an Italian Slum*. Chicago: The University of Chicago Press.

Wilkinson, S. (1986) *Feminist Social Psychology*. Milton Keynes: Open University Press.

Williams, J. E., Bennett, S. M. & Best, D. L. (1975) Awareness and expression of sex stereotypes in young children. *Developmental Psychology*, 11, 635–42.

Word, C. H., Zanna, M. P. & Cooper, J. (1974) The non-verbal mediation of self-fulfilling prophecies in interracial interaction. *Journal of Experimental Social Psychology*, 10, 109–20.

Zimbardo, P. G. (1972) Pathology of imprisonment. *Society*, April 1972.

# Index